WITHDRAWN

MONTGOMERY COLLEGE LIBRARY
GERMANTOWN CAMPUS

THE WORLD'S
GREAT RELIGIOUS POETRY

THE WORLD'S
GREAT RELIGIOUS POETRY

EDITED BY
CAROLINE MILES HILL, Ph.D.

GREENWOOD PRESS, PUBLISHERS
WESTPORT, CONNECTICUT

Library of Congress Cataloging in Publication Data

Hill, Caroline (Miles) 1866-1951, ed.
The world's great religious poetry.

Reprint of the 1938 ed. published by Macmillan,
New York.
1. Religious poetry. I. Title.
PN6110.R4H5   1973   808.81'5   70-137058
ISBN 0-8371-5521-5

COPYRIGHTED

All rights reserved—no part of this book may
be reproduced in any form without permission
in writing from the publisher, except by re-
viewers who wish to quote brief passages in con-
nection with a review written for inclusion in
magazines or newspapers.

Originally published in 1938 by the Macmillan Company,
New York

Reprinted in 1973 by Greenwood Press, Inc.,
51 Riverside Avenue, Westport, CT 06880

Library of Congress catalog card number 70-137058
ISBN 0-8371-5521-5

Printed in the United States of America

10 9 8 7 6 5 4 3 2

ACKNOWLEDGMENTS

Thanks are due to the following publishers for permission to include selections from the volumes enumerated below:

The Macmillan Company for
  Selections from the collected poems of:

Ananda Acharya
Matthew Arnold
Alice Brown
Dinah Muloch Craik
Mary Carolyn Davies
Edward Dowden
Mrs. Edward Dowden
Norman Gale
Hamlin Garland
Wilfrid W. Gibson
Wm. Ernest Henley
Ralph Hodgson
William Noel Hodgson
Horace Holley
Kabir (E. Indian, trans. by Tagore)

Vachel Lindsay
Percy Mackaye
John Masefield
Frederick Wm. H. Myers
John G. Neihardt
Edwin Arlington Robinson
George Wm. Russell (*A. E.*)
James Stephens
Rabindranath Tagore
Sara Teasdale
Edith M. Thomas
Alfred Tennyson
William Watson
William B. Yeats
Israel Zangwill

D. Appleton and Company for
  William Cullen Bryant—From Thanatopsis.
  William Cullen Bryant—To a Waterfowl.
  William Cullen Bryant—The Poet.
  Wm. E. H. Lecky—Of an Old Song.
  Richard Henry Dana—Immortality.

Allen and Unwin for
  Edward Carpenter—Five selections from "Towards Democracy."

Basil Blackwell for
  Gerald Gould—The Happy Tree (from "Collected Poems").

Bobbs-Merrill Company for
  James W. Riley—Away! (from "Collected Poems").

Boni and Liveright for
  Two selections from "The Modern Book of French Verse."
  One selection from "The Path of the Rainbow" (Cronyn).

Brentano's for
  Harry Kemp—He Did Not Know (from "Chanteys and Ballads").
  Harry Kemp—God the Architect and Prayer (from "The Cry of Youth").

A. C. Fifield for
  Wm. H. Davies—Christ the Man (from "Songs of Joy").

Century Company for
  Wm. C. Gannett—The Highway.
  Wm. C. Gannett—The Stream of Faith.
  Wm. C. Gannett—Consider the Lilies (from "Collected Poems").

vi ACKNOWLEDGMENTS

Helen Keller—The Garden of the Lord (from "The World I Live In").
S. Weir Mitchell—Vespers (from "Complete Poems").
James Oppenheim—The New God (from "War and Laughter").
Cale Young Rice—The Mystic (from "Collected Poems and Plays").
Cale Young Rice—Providence (from "Wraiths and Realities").
Cale Young Rice—Litany for Latter Day Mystics (from "Earth and New Earth").
Richard Wightman—The Pilgrim, and The Servants (from "Ashes and Sparks").

Cambridge University Press for
Chas. Hamilton Sorley—Selections from "Marlborough and other Poems."

W. B. Conkey Company for
Selections from the collected poems of Ella Wheeler Wilcox.

T. Y. Crowell Company for
Selections from collected poems of George Eliot, Sarah K. Bolton, Alice Cary, Phœbe Cary.

George H. Doran Company for
Wilton Agnew Barrett—A New England Church (from "Songs of the Journey").
Joyce Kilmer—Trees, and Poets (from "Collected Poems").
Charles Hanson Towne—Silence.
Charles Hanson Towne—Of One Self-Slain (from "A World of Windows").
John Oxenham—Some Blesseds (from "The Vision Splendid").

E. P. Dutton and Company for
Katharine Lee Bates—America the Beautiful
Katharine Lee Bates—The Kings of the East (from "The Return").
Mrs. Edward Dowden—Adrift.
Frances Ridley Havergal—Reality.
Frances Ridley Havergal—Thou Art Coming!
Winifred M. Letts—The Spires of Oxford.
Sir Alfred C. Lyall—Meditations of a Hindu Prince.
George MacDonald—Prayer.
George MacDonald—Lost and Found.
George MacDonald—That Holy Thing.
St. Patrick—The Deer's Cry (from "Ancient Irish Poetry").
Sir Lewis Morris—Beginnings of Faith.
May Riley Smith—The Uninvited Guest.

Doubleday, Page and Company for
Rudyard Kipling—The Sons of Martha.
Rudyard Kipling—L'Envoi.
Edwin Markham—Poesy (from "Gates of Paradise and other Poems").
Edwin Markham—Prayer, and The Man with the Hoe (from "The Man with the Hoe and Other Poems").
Edwin Markham—Revelation (from "The Shoes of Happiness and other Poems").
Edwin Markham—A Guard of the Sepulcher (from "Lincoln and other Poems").
Seumas MacManus—In Dark Hour.
Walt Whitman—Five selections from collected works.

Duffield and Company for
Richard Hovey—Immanence.
Richard Hovey—Transcendence.
Richard Hovey—Unmanifest Destiny.
D. H. Lawrence—Dreams Old and Nascent.
George Santayana—Two sonnets.
William Sharp (*Fiona Macleod*)—Five selections from "Collected Poems."

ACKNOWLEDGMENTS

Four Seas Company for
  Richard Aldington—Vicarious Atonement.

Funk and Wagnalls Company for
  Richard Realf—The Word.
  Israel Zangwill—Selections from "Blind Children."

Harcourt, Brace and Company for
  Louis Untermeyer—Prayer (from "Challenge").
  Carl Sandburg—Manufactured Gods (from "Smoke and Steel").

Harr Wagner Company (San Francisco) for
  Joaquin Miller—The Fortunate Isles (from "Complete Poetical Works").

Harper and Brothers for
  Don Marquis—The God-Maker, Man (from "Dreams and Dust").
  Algernon C. Swinburne—The Hymn of Man.
  Albert Bigelow Paine—The Hills of Rest.

Henry Holt and Company for
  Arthur Colton—Harps Hung Up in Babylon.
  Carl Sandburg—To a Contemporary Bunkshooter (from "Chicago Poems").
  Herbert Trench—I Seek Thee in the Heart Alone.
  Margaret Widdemer—Barter.
  Margaret Widdemer—The New Victory.
  Margaret Widdemer—The Awakened War God.

Houghton, Mifflin Company for
  Selections from collected works of:
  Joel Benton
  Anna H. Branch
  John Burroughs
  Christopher Pearse Cranch
  Sir Aubrey deVere
  Hilda Doolittle
  Ralph Waldo Emerson
  Oliver W. Holmes
  Julia Ward Howe
  Richard Watson Gilder
  John Hay
  Emma Lazarus
  Henry W. Longfellow
  Samuel Longfellow
  Amy Lowell
  James Russell Lowell
  Edward Rowland Sill
  Wm. Wetmore Story
  Edmund C. Stedman
  Harriet Beecher Stowe
  Henry D. Thoreau
  Edith M. Thomas
  John Drinkwater
  Margaret Deland
  Wm. Dean Howells
  Wm. Vaughn Moody
  John G. Whittier
  Josephine P. Peabody
  Jones Very

B. W. Huebsch for
  D. H. Lawrence—Dreams Old and Nascent (from "Amores").
  Irene Rutherford Macleod—The Rebel.

Mitchell Kennerly for
  Florence Kiper Frank—The Jew to Jesus.
  Yone Noguchi—The Poet.
  Shaemas O'Sheel—"They Went Forth to Battle. but They Always Fell."
  Shaemas O'Sheel—"He Whom a Dream Hath Possessed."

Alfred A. Knopf for
  Eunice Tietjens—The Great Man.
  Osbert Sitwell—How Shall We Rise to Greet the Dawn? (from "Argonaut
    and Juggernaut").

John Lane Company for
  Lascelles Abercrombie—Selection from "The Seeker."
  Rupert Brooke—Three Sonnets.
  Ethel Clifford—The Harp of Sorrow (from "Songs and Dreams").
  William J. Dawson—Inspirations (from "America and Other Poems").
  Ernest Dowson—Vitæ Summæ Brevis (from "Collected Poems").

ACKNOWLEDGMENTS

G. K. Chesterton—Five selections from "Collected Poems."
Angela Morgan—Hail Man! and God Prays! (from "Forward March").
Sir Henry Newbolt—The Final Mystery.
Stephen Philipps—Grief and God, and The Poet's Prayer (from "New Poems").
Francis Thompson—Three selections from "Collected Works."
Richard Le Gallienne—The Second Crucifixion.

Little, Brown and Company for

Selections from collected works of:
Edwin Arnold
Francis W. Bourdillon
John White Chadwick
Emily Dickinson
Helen Hunt Jackson
Jean Ingelow
Edward Everett Hale

Longmans, Green and Company for

Eva Gore Booth—Harvest.
Eva Gore Booth—Crucifixion.
William Morris—The Day is Coming.

Lothrop, Lee and Shepard Company for

Richard Burton—God's Garden and The Song of the Unsuccessful (from "Message and Melody").
Alfred Domett—A Christmas Hymn.
Sam Walter Foss—The Higher Catechism, and The House by the Side of the Road (from "Dreams in Homespun").
Ednah D. Cheney—The Larger Prayer.

Thomas Bird Mosher for

Thomas S. Jones, jr.—The Path of the Stars (from "A Voice in the Silence").
Lizette Woodworth Reese—A Little Song of Life (from "A Wayside Lute").
John Addington Symonds—Invocation, and The Human Outlook (from "Collected Poems").
Arthur W. Upson—Failures (from "Collected Poems").
John Vance Cheney—The Happiest Heart.

Newbegin for

Thomas Edward Brown.—Disguises, and My Garden.

The Oxford University Press for

Rhys Carpenter—The Master Singers.
Rhys Carpenter—Who Bids Us Sing? (from "The Sun-Thief and Other Poems").
John Clare—The Peasant Poet.

William Rider and Son for

Arthur Edward Waite—Selections from "Collected Poems."

G. P. Putnam's Sons for

Wm. H. Carruth—Each in His Own Tongue and other Poems.
Jeannette Gilder—My Creed (*Putnam's Magazine*).
Ella Heath—Poetry.
Charles Hamilton Sorley—The Seekers, Expectans Expectavi, and another selection from "Marlborough."

A. M. Robertson (San Francisco) for

George Sterling—Omnia Exeunt in Mysterium (from "The Breakers").

Sidgwick and Jackson for

Lawrence Housman—The Continuing City (from "Selected Poems").
Katherine Tynan Hinkson—Three selected poems.

ACKNOWLEDGMENTS

Elliott Stock (London) for
  H. C. Leonard—Selections from "Sacred Songs of the World."

Charles Scribner's Sons for
  Selections from collected poems of:
    Maltbie Babcock.
    Mary Mapes Dodge.
    Josiah Gilbert Holland.
    Sidney Lanier.
    Alan Seeger.
    Robert Louis Stevenson.
    Henry van Dyke.
    John Hall Wheelock.

Skeffington & Sons (London) for
  John S. Arkwright—The Supreme Sacrifice.

F. A. Stokes Company for
  Stephen Crane—The Peaks (from "War is Kind").

Talbot Press (Dublin, Ireland) for
  Joseph Mary Plunkett—I See His Blood upon the Rose.

James T. White and Company for
  Thomas Curtis Clark—Selections from "Love Off to the War."

MAGAZINES

Asia Magazine for
  Rabindranath Tagore—Autumn.

The Chap-Book (London) for
  Shane Leslie—Priest or Poet.

The Detroit Free Press for
  Elizabeth York Case—There Is No Unbelief.

The Masses for
  Max Eastman—Invocation.
  Max Eastman—At the Aquarium.
  Sarah N. Cleghorn—Comrade Jesus.

New York Sun for
  Charles Wharton Stork—God, You Have Been too Good to Me.

The Outlook for
  Hamlin Garland—The Cry of the Age.

The Poetry Review (London) for
  Ivan Adair—Real Presence.

Saturday Review (London) for
  Louis Golding—Second Seeing.

Scribner's Magazine for
  Theodosia Garrison—Stains.

Yale University Press for
  Karle Wilson Baker—Creeds, Good Company, the Ploughman (from "Blue
    Smoke").
  William Rose Benét—The Falconer of God (from "The Falconer of God
    and Other Poems").
  Gamaliel Bradford—God (from "Shadow Verses").
  William A. Percy—Farmers (from "In April Once").

And to the following authors:

James Vila Blake—In Him.
Witter Bynner—Ecce Homo.
Witter Bynner—The New God.
John Vance Cheney—The Happiest Heart.
Rhys Carpenter—The Master Singers.
Rhys Carpenter—Who Bids Us Sing?
Alice Corbin Henderson—Nodes.
Dudley Foulke—The City's Crown.
Arthur Guiterman—In the Hospital.
Fanny Heaslip Lea—The Dead Faith.
Shane Leslie—Priest or Poet.
Harold Monro—God (from "Dawn").
Angela Morgan—Reality, the Poet, Hail Man! and God Prays.
James Oppenheim—The New God.
James Oppenheim—Death.
Edwin Ford Piper—The Church.
Mrs. William Sharp—Selections from W. Sharp (*Fiona Macleod*).
Victor Starbuck—The Seekers.
Arthur Edward Waite—At the End of Things.
Seumas MacManus—In Dark Hour.
John Oxenham—Seeds.
Kenneth Saunders—Translation of Proofs of Buddha's Existence.

The generous coöperation of poets and publishers has made possible the inclusion of many poems which are still in copyright. We wish to express our grateful obligation to those poets who have added their permission to that of their publishers.

EDITOR'S PREFACE

The most obvious facts about this collection of poetry are that it is not all great and that it makes strange combinations and sequences. It ranges from the Psalms of David and the Hymn of Cleanthes to the latest free verse. The great hymns that are translated from the Latin and the most radical of the twentieth century verse are alike only in that they show human feeling about the concept that is the foundation of all religion. Many poems that are far from being great belong here because they are significant.

There are some persons who say that our age has no religion; others say it is more sincerely religious than any of the great ages of faith that are gone. The most intelligent thought of the present bases the authority of religion, not upon revelation, but upon the nature of man. Man's hunger for God is as fundamental and legitimate as his hunger for food and love. Our age may be lost as to what it should believe, but we were never so sure that we must and do believe. The good swimmer knows best how to trust the water; the best life is most reliant upon what some call the Integrity of the Universe and one of the greatest poets called the Everlasting Arms.

The great poets have always spoken with authority. In them has the Word been made flesh. Now a war-weary world in search of faith turns to them.

The Bible is an anthology of Hebrew literature—the Great Anthology. If no future poets ever rise to so great a height of constructive imagination as those of the classic Hebrew period it will always remain the Bible of the race. A cursory view of other religious poetry shows little that is not based upon the biblical poetry, but the spiritual assets of mankind have never been gathered together that we may see what they are. This book is a step in that direction.

Its purpose is to furnish delightful reading, to give comfort

and consolation, to "restore the soul" as well as to supply ma-
terial for the study of the history and psychology of religion—
the last subject to be approached by scientific methods.

The poems have been arranged in twelve divisions under the
twelve religious concepts, a few of which have been arranged
chronologically. The Idea of God is the core of the collection
and furnishes the clue for the study of the thought moulds of
different periods of thought. The longing for companionship
with God has the highest emotional coloring of any of the
approaches to Reality. The Faith section contains many poems
of doubt which represent the work of the groping intellect.
Merely sentimental poetry has been avoided.

The poems of Nature and of the Search after God will be
perhaps the most interesting to the twentieth century. Nature
makes mystics of us all. The section on Immortality will be
eagerly sought by those who are already sending their souls
through the invisible, "some letter of that after life to spell."

The cumulative effect of reading so many religious poems, of
seeing so many glimpses of the invisible through so many eyes
and during so many centuries is both elevating and sobering.
To know only hymns is to be carried away against one's will,
but to read the world poetry of religion is to be convinced by
a cloud of witnesses. There must be a spiritual world. The
telescope and the microscope and the X-ray have opened new
worlds to us. What is there that will open the spiritual world?

A common language might be a great step to knowledge of
spiritual things. The oriental religions, Christianity and the
modern cults all use different terms, but seek the same realities.
There was a prophet-poet who lived in Galilee who said "I am
the Way." The path He took, with all the greatest saints of
all religions is the only path we know to the Other World. His
language regarding the eternal verities has been the greatest
unifying force ever projected into the world of human rela-
tions. The language of poetry is universal and may lead to
the outer gate.

CAROLINE MILES HILL, PH.D.

INTRODUCTION

THE RELIGIOUS SPIRIT IN THE WORLD'S POETRY

HERBERT L. WILLETT, PH.D.

It is significant that the narrative of world beginnings with which the Bible opens has been called the Poem of Creation. For though it purports to describe the origin of the heavens and the earth in accordance with the inherited tradition of the Semitic peoples, it handles the materials of that tradition with the masterful genius of the poet, the true creator of fresh and inspiring ideals. It is the type and symbol of all real poetry. It is rhythmical, artistic, imaginative, and marked by the creative passion that reforms and vitalizes the common materials and conceptions of a time, and brings into being a majestic, beautiful and inspiring work of art.

All poetry that is worthy of the name is essentially creative. There may be verses that conform in all the outward marks of rhyme and metre to poetic canons, and yet are only the assembling of words in description or argument. Poetry moves on the higher levels of power and emotion. It is the product of a maker of ideas, not a finder and collector of phrases. In all poetic writing that has possessed the power of survival, something of this high and impressive quality resides. Only the creative artist is gifted with the ability to take the common facts and experiences of human life and invest them with the character of epic and enduring realities. As Ruskin has insisted, he is not a mere troubadour or finder; he is a poet, a creator.

Poetry is the natural language of youth, freedom, joyousness and love of beauty. It is therefore the language of childhood, and of the youth of the race. The great poetry that has survived the centuries is rarely the result of formal compliance with rule and convention. It is the bold, free, spontaneous

xiii

utterance of the youthful spirit of romance, adventure, admiration, the quest of the wonder and mystery of the world. Whatever touches the soul of man with the sense of marvel, of yearning and hope, kindles the flame of poetic passion and speech.

Of all the interests which have engaged the attention of humanity, religion has proved the most powerful and the most inspiring. It is only one among many such objects of attention, but it appears the most pervasive and unescapable. Men have concerned themselves with a great variety of affairs, such as food, clothing, shelter, mating, family life, industry, war, government, institutions, customs and traditions. But above all there has been the brooding and persistent sense of relationship with higher powers. Inspired by that sense the innumerable expressions of the religious life have taken form in doctrine and ritual. Hardly a community in all the world is without them. Individuals there are who appear to be religionless, but no race or nation or tribe. It would seem to be the most essential characteristic of the intellectual and emotional life of mankind.

If this is true, it is not strange that the poetry of religion should be the most natural and universal sort of composition. The spirit of man seeks expression for its most elemental feelings in the elevated phrases of rhythmic speech. Other forms of verse have occupied the attention of the bards and singers of all the ages, but religion has had the primal place. This is true in a double sense. The themes deliberately chosen by the great poets, as by the supreme artists in other areas of human interest, have been those related to the moral and spiritual life. It is largely true that the masterpieces of painting, sculpture, architecture and music, as well as poetry, have had a religious theme or purpose. In a very real sense they were works of devotion, the effort to give artistic utterance to the mood of worship. But it is also true that the best product of the artistic mind is essentially religious. The purpose to put into an epic, a statue, a landscape, an edifice or a symphony the supreme effort of which the artist is capable, with the resolution to make it an instrument of education, happiness, and inspiration to noble ideals and worthful living, is truly religious. Indeed it is doubtful if any genuinely great work of the sort can be successfully performed without the religious motive.

One of the sure tests of great poetry is its power of survival. The race preserves what it prizes. To be sure there are trage- dies that destroy some of the past's incalculable hoard of liter- ary treasures. Many of the Greek dramas were swept away in the fire that destroyed the Alexandrian library when Omar, the Moslem, burned that priceless collection of documents. But in most instances the books and other writings that have won their way to the souls of men have been preserved and handed on. Probably this is the reason why so much of the poetry that has come down from the distant past is of the religious character. But the same sifting process will decide between the best and the second best in this and all later days. The larger number of the poems that endure will continue to deal with religion.

From all the centuries and from all the nations, these poems of the faith have come. The life of God is limited to no nation or age. He has never left Himself without witness among any people. The Babylonian records of the beginnings of time were hymns in celebration of Marduk and the other gods of the pantheon. The Assyrians treasured the temple psalms in honor of Asshur and Ishtar. The Egyptians paid the tribute of prayers and honorific inscriptions to Ammon, Mut and Khonsu. The ancient Aryans of India composed their Vedic hymns to the glory of Brahma, Vishnu and Siva. The Greeks immortalized their religious conceptions in their epics and tragedies, and made the names of Zeus, Artemis and Apollo familiar to the whole of the Mediterranean world. In all the other regions of the east and west the worship of the Eternal has provided the central theme of poetic inspiration, though the names by which He has been known have been as varied as the hundred divine titles graven on Akbar's tomb.

The literature of religion is as farflung as humanity. Every people has had its bible. Much of this holy writing was in the form of poetry. Nothing less artistic and elevated was deemed worthy of the faith. It was natural, therefore, that the Hebrew writings that have survived to us should deal with the central theme of religion. They are a curious illustration of the fact that religious material tended always to take precedence of other writings in their survival value. The Hebrews must have had a considerable body of writings of various sorts during the classic period while Hebrew was a living speech. Yet, all that has survived to us is the collection we know as the Old Testament, and this deals almost wholly with the religious life of the nation. Furthermore, a large portion of this surviving group of documents is poetic in form. The Book of Job is the unapproached masterpiece of the ages. The Psalms are the most beautiful of lyrics dealing with the life of trust. The Proverbs are a marvellous anthology of wit and wisdom based upon the moral ideals of the sages. Much of the preaching of the prophets is in the form of poetic oracles, and even the prose narratives of national life are made vivid by the use of such ancient poems as the Song by the Sea, the Song of Deborah, and the Song of the Bow.

The New Testament, the source-book for a study of the origins of Christianity, is less moved by the poetic motive than the older collection. Its writers were the friends of Jesus, who went forth in a sort of breathless haste to tell the story of his life and work. The Gospels are brief and simple narratives of the Master's ministry. The Book of Acts is a short and vivid record of the beginnings of the new society. The Epistles are direct and searching messages to churches and individuals who needed instruction. And the Apocalypse is a fierce and forceful denunciation of the imperial power of Rome, and a triumphant announcement of its speedy overthrow. Here is little opportunity for the poetic spirit to utter itself. And yet from the pages of the New Testament have come such great hymns as the Gloria in Excelsis, the Ave Maria, the Nunc Dimittis, the Benedictus, Paul's Psalm of Love, and the comforting and exultant songs of the Revelation.

Such a group of writings as the Bible contains, selected from a vastly larger literature, and made the canon of religious instruction and the manual of devotion for the whole of Christendom, could hardly fail to stimulate the production of a vast body of writings through all the centuries since the days of Jesus. It is of every sort, historical, sermonic, doctrinal, apologetic, expository and devotional. But perhaps no order of literature dealing with the Christian religion has equalled in volume the poetry which it has inspired. Men and women who have had no zest for formal treatises regarding the faith have poured out their souls in poems which have become immortal. Movements and crises come and go in the history of religion; controversies break out and die away; sects, parties and denominations rise and decline; but the stream of poetic reflection upon the supreme facts of life and death is constant and refreshing. It is little concerned with the disputes of theologians or the researches of critics. It is above the sky-line of creedal animosities. It is the utterance of those who are seeking the inner way which the pilgrims of all the ages have trodden toward the city of God.

The poetry of religion is as varied as are the experiences of humanity in its experiments with the great mystery of the soul's relationship to God. In the anthology of the singers of the faith there are all sorts of voices, and all moods of the spirit. As in the Bible itself, so in this larger bible of the ages, all notes are struck from those of rapturous confidence to those of darkest doubt and uttermost despair. The vast problems of sorrow, sin, temptation, failure, scepticism, cynicism, inquiry, hope, confidence, attainment, and rapturous fulfilment are all included in the many-sided complex of expression which is taking form in the ever-changing multitude of human strivings for life. Seekers after God are all the sons of men. He is the soul's companion and necessity. But who of all the race have found and fully known Him? Only those choice spirits whom history has enshrined as the prophets of the faith. Them, and One who passed this way, not so long ago, and not so far from where we dwell; One whose words hang in the air like banners, and whose sentences walk through all the earth like spirits. These have known, and they have stretched the terms of human speech to their utmost tension to give us some adequate conception of the great reality.

Next after the prophets, in whose ranks the Master finds his appointed place, come the poets, whose eyes have seen something of the vision, whose hearts have been stirred by the divine emotion, and out of these rich experiences they have given us their interpretations of the mystery. They do not deal in argument. They have little formal logic or careful science to bring to our aid. But they provide us with a knowledge that comes only from the depths of emotion and the wells of experience. And so they have made us their continual debtors, for we have little to draw with, and the wells are deep

'Though the poets speak in all tones of confidence or doubt, their best messages are those of assurance, and they leave us with the conviction that it is faith and not denial that has the last word.

Such an anthology of religious poetry as has been attempted in this volume must, in the nature of the case, be limited to a small portion of the great total of such materials lying at hand in the storehouse of the years. To make selection where the store is so rich and so abundant is an act of courage. Along the fringes of the collection there will be room for much variation of judgment. Some things will be missed that one would have included; some are given place that one would have passed by. This would be true of any such amalgam of religious poetry. But the heart and core of the best works of the spirit of reverence and devotion which the years have produced will be found here. And that is much; perhaps it is enough. To wander through the aisles of this great cathedral of music and song; to thread these forest paths where the saints have walked; to drink of these streams in which the generations of suffering and rejoicing pilgrims of the holy life have quenched their thirst—this is itself a joy and an enrichment, a renewal of fellowship with the best who have gone this way, a fresh discovery of the eternal secret of friendship with God.

TABLE OF CONTENTS

xix

IV. FAITH

a. The Old Faith

b. Modern Faith

xxvi   TABLE OF CONTENTS

TABLE OF CONTENTS xxix

TABLE OF CONTENTS

THE WORLD'S GREAT
RELIGIOUS POETRY

I. INSPIRATION
    a. HOW TO THE SINGER COMES THE SONG?
    b. WHENCE TO THE SINGER COMES THE SONG?

THE POET

JOEL BENTON

The poet's words are winged with fire,
Forever young is his desire,—
Touched by some charm the gods impart,
Time writes no wrinkles on his heart.

The messenger and priest of truth,
His thought breathes of immortal youth;
Though summer hours are far away,
Midsummer haunts him day by day.

The harsh fates do not chill his soul,—
For him all streams of splendor roll;
Sweet hints come to him from the sky,—
Birds teach him wisdom as they fly.

He gathers good in all he meets,
The fields pour out for him their sweets;
Life is excess; one sunset's glow
Gives him a bliss no others know.

Beauty to him is Paradise—
He never tires-of lustrous eyes;
Quaffing his joy, the world apart,
Love lives a summer in his heart.

His lands are never bought nor sold—
His wealth is more to him than gold;
On the green hills, when life is done,
He sleeps like fair Endymion.

THE BARD

WILLIAM BLAKE

Hear the voice of the Bard,
Who present, past and future sees;
Whose ears have heard
The Holy Word
That walked among the ancient trees.

From A LOST GOD

FRANCIS W. BOURDILLON

Ah, happy who have seen Him, whom the world
Calls madmen! These alone are poets—not
The apt mellifluous metrist,—not the deft
Industrious rhymer,—needs the fire of heaven,
The earthquake, the long lonely hour with God,
Before our flower-edged lyric rivulets
Flood over with the impetuous dithyramb.

What is it makes a poet's utterance strong
Except the striving to make wings of words,
And mount from apprehended thought to thought
Unapprehended? And what impulse moves
To such ill-guerdoned labor but the sense
Of things insensuous, the glint of rays

Nebulous, indistinguished, which the eyes
Must gaze and gaze at till they fix the star,—
Visions of water in the vacant sand,—
Elysian stands in the waste of sea?
Such have I seen, such phantasms all my life
Have followed, knowing somewhere they must lie
Discoverable—in our eyes unreal,
Yet real somewhere.

THE POET

ELIZABETH BARRETT BROWNING

The poet hath the child's sight in his breast,
And sees all *new*. What oftenest he has viewed,
He views with the first glory. Fair and good
Pall never on him, at the fairest, best,
But stand before him holy and undressed
In week-day false conventions, such as would
Drag other men down from the altitude
Of primal types, too early dispossessed.
Why, God would tire of all his heavens, as soon
As thou, O godlike, childlike poet, didst,
Of daily and nightly sights of sun and moon!
And therefore hath he set thee in the midst,
Where men may hear thy wonder's ceaseless tune,
And praise his world forever, as thou bidst.

THE PEASANT POET

JOHN CLARE

He loved the brook's soft sound,
  The swallow swimming by,
He loved the daisy-covered ground,
  The cloud-bedappled sky.
To him the dismal storm appeared
  The very voice of God:

And where the evening rock was reared
Stood Moses with his rod.
And everything his eyes surveyed,
The insects in the brake,
Were creatures God Almighty made,
He loved them for His sake—
A silent man in life's affairs,
A thinker from a boy,
A peasant in his daily cares,
A poet in his joy.

THE POET'S CALL

Thomas Curtis Clarke

By day the fields and meadows cry;
By night the bright stars plead;
He hears the message from on high,
And to the call gives heed.

The roses tremble as he nears,
And cry, "Rejoice, rejoice!"
The rocks break forth as he appears,
"God sends a Voice, a Voice!"

FRAGMENT

William Cowper

Pity, Religion has so seldom found
A skilful guide into poetic ground!
The flowers would spring where'er she deigned to stray
And every muse attend her on her way.

THOUGHT

CHRISTOPHER PEARSE CRANCH

Thought is deeper than all speech,
 Feeling deeper than all thought,
Souls to souls can never teach
 What unto themselves was taught.

We are spirits clad in veils;
 Man by man was never seen;
All our deep communing fails
 To remove the shadowy screen.

Heart to heart was never known;
 Mind with mind did never meet;
We are columns left alone
 Of a temple once complete.

Like the stars that gem the sky,
 Far apart, though seeming near,
In our light we scattered lie;
 All is thus but starlight here

What is social company
 But a babbling summer stream?
What our wise philosophy
 But the glancing of a dream?

Only when the sun of love
 Melts the scattered stars of thought,
Only when we live above
 What the dim-eyed world hath taught,

Only when our souls are fed
 By the fount which gave them birth,
And by inspiration led
 Which they never drew from earth,

We, like parted drops of rain,
    Swelling till they meet and run,
Shall be all absorbed again,
    Melting, flowing into one.

INSPIRATIONS

William James Dawson

Sometimes, I know not why, nor how, nor whence
    A change comes over me, and then the task
    Of common life slips from me. Would you ask
What power is this which bids the world go hence?
    Who knows? I only feel a faint perfume
Steal through the rooms of life; a saddened sense
Of something lost; a music as of brooks
That babble to the sea; pathetic looks
    Of closing eyes that in a darkened room
    Once dwelt on mine: I feel the general doom
Creep nearer, and with God I stand alone.
    O mystic sense of sudden quickening!
Hope's lark-song rings, or life's deep undertone
    Wails through my heart—and then I needs must sing.

THE DREAM OF DAKIKI
Firdausi (From the Persian)

Translated by A. V. Williams Jackson

I a.

My heart was fired, as from his sight it turned
Toward the world's Sovereign Throne, and inly yearned,
    'May I lay hand upon that book some day
    And tell, in my own words, that ancient lay!'

Countless the persons whom I sought for aid,
As I of fleeting time was sore afraid
    Lest I in turn not long enough should live,
    But to another's hand the task must give.

Nay, more—lest that my means should ne'er suffice,—
For such a work there was no buyer's price;
The age forsooth was filled with wars of greed,
A straitened world it was for those in need.

Some time in that condition did I live,
Yet of my secret not a word did give,
Finding no person who my aims would share,
Nor act for me with friendly patron care . . .

By hap, a friend beloved at Tus I had;
Thou would'st have said 'Two souls in one skin clad!'
To me he spake, 'Good is thy whole project,
Thy foot toward fortune now is turned direct;
That book, which written is in Pahlavi,
I'll get for thee; but slack thou must not be;
Thine is the gift of speech; and youth is thine
To tell the tale of champions' deeds—in fine,
Do thou the Kingly Book anew relate
And seek through it renown among the great.'

When he at last that book before me laid
He made ablaze with light my soul of shade!

INSPIRATION

Wilfrid Wilson Gibson

On the outermost far-flung ridge of ice and snow
That over pits of sunset fire hangs sheer
My naked spirit poises, then hangs clear
From the cold crystal into the furnace glow
Of ruby and amber lucencies, and dives,
In the brief moment of ten thousand lives
Through fathomless infinities of light,
Then cleansed by lustral flame and frost returns;
And for an instant through my body burns;
The immortal fires of cold-white ecstasy
As down the darkening valley of the night
I keep the old track of mortality.

HOW TO THE SINGER COMES THE SONG?

RICHARD WATSON GILDER

I

How to the singer comes the song?
At times a joy, 'alone;
A wordless tone
Caught from the crystal gleam of ice-bound trees;
Or from the violet-perfumed breeze;
Or the sharp smell of the seas
In sunlight glittering many an emerald mile;
Or the keen memory of a love-lit smile.

II

Thus to the singer comes the song:
Gazing at crimson skies
Where burns and dies
On day's wide hearth the calm celestial fire,
The poet with a wild desire
Strikes the impassioned lyre,
Takes into tunèd sound the flaming sight
And ushers with new song the ancient night.

III

How to the singer comes the song?
Bowed down by ill and sorrow
On every morrow—
The unworded pain breaks forth in heavenly singing;
Not all too late dear solace bringing
To broken spirits winging
Through mortal anguish to the unknown rest—
A lyric balm for every wounded breast.

IV

How to the singer comes the song?
How to the summer fields

Come flowers? How yields
Darkness to happy dawn? How doth the nigh.
Bring stars? O, how do love and light
Leap at the sound and sight
Of her who makes this dark world seem less wrong—
Life of his life, and soul of all his song!

POETRY

Ella Heath

I am the reality of things that seem:
The great transmuter, melting loss to gain,
Languor to love, and fining joy from pain;
I am the waking, who am called the dream;
I am the sun, all light reflects my gleam;
I am the altar fire within the fane;
I am the force of the refreshing rain;
I am the sea which flows to every stream;
I am the utmost height there is to climb;
I am the truth mirrored in fancy's glass;
I am stability, all else will pass;
I am eternity, encircling time;
Kill me, none may; conquer me, nothing can,—
I am God's soul, fused in the soul of man.

POETS

Joyce Kilmer

Vain is the chiming of forgotten bells
That the wind sways above a ruined shrine.
Vainer his voice in whom no longer dwells
Hunger that craves immortal Bread and Wine.

Light songs we breathe that perish with our breath
Out of our lips that have not kissed the rod.
They shall not live who have not tasted death.
They only sing who are struck dumb by God.

OF AN OLD SONG

WM. E. H. LECKY

Little snatch of an ancient song,
What has made thee live so long?
Flying on thy wings of rhyme
Lightly down the depths of time,
Telling nothing strange or rare,
Scarce a thought or image there,
Nothing but the old, old tale
Of a hapless lover's wail;
Offspring of an idle hour,
Whence has come thy lasting power?
By what turn of rhythm or phrase,
By what subtle careless grace,
Can thy music charm our ears,
After full three hundred years?
Landmarks of the human mind
One by one are left behind,
And a subtle change is wrought
In the mould and cast of thought:
Modes of reasoning pass away,
Types of beauty lose their sway;
Creeds and Causes that have made
Many noble lives must fade,
And the words that thrilled of old
Now seem hueless, dead and cold;
Fancy's rainbow tints are flying,
Thoughts, like men, are slowly dying:
All things perish and the strongest
Often do not last the longest;
The stately ship is seen no more,
The fragile skiff attains the shore;
And while the great and wise decay,
And all their trophies pass away,
Some sudden thought, some careless rhyme
Still floats above the wrecks of Time.

THE FATE OF THE PROPHETS

HENRY WADSWORTH LONGFELLOW

From *The Divine Tragedy*

Alas! how full of fear
Is the fate of the Prophet and Seer!
For evermore, for evermore,
It shall be as it hath been heretofore;
The age in which they live will not forgive
The splendor of the everlasting light,
That makes their foreheads bright,
Nor the sublime
Fore-running of their time!

THE POET

AMY LOWELL

What instinct forces man to journey on,
  Urged by a longing blind but dominant!
  Nothing he sees can hold him, nothing daunt
His never-failing eagerness. The sun
Setting in splendor every night has won
  His vassalage; those towers flamboyant
  Of airy cloudland palaces now haunt
His daylight wanderings. Forever done
With simple joys and quiet happiness
  He guards the vision of the sunset sky;
Though faint with weariness he must possess
  Some fragments of the sunset's majesty;
He spurns life's human friendships to profess
Life's loneliness of dreaming ecstasy.

THE POET

EDWIN MARKHAM

His home is on the heights; to him
Men wage a battle weird and dim,
Life is a mission stern as fate,
And Song a dread apostolate.
The toils of prophecy are his,
To hail the coming centuries—
To ease the steps and lift the load
Of souls that falter on the road.
The perilous music that he hears
Falls from the vortice of the spheres.

He presses on before the race
And sings out of a silent place.
Like faint notes of a forest bird
On heights afar that voice is heard;
And the dim path he breaks today
Will sometime be the trodden way.
But when the race comes toiling on
That voice of wonder will be gone—
But heard on higher peaks afar,
Moved upward with the morning star.

O men of earth, that wandering voice
Still goes the upward way: rejoice!

SOVEREIGN POETS

LLOYD MIFFLIN

They who create rob death of half its stings;
They, from the dim inane and vague opaque
Of nothingness, build with their thought, and make
Enduring entities and beauteous things;
They are the Poets—they give airy wings

To shapes marmorean; or they overtake
The Ideal with the brush, or, soaring, wake
Far in the rolling clouds their glorious strings.
The Poet is the only potentate;
His sceptre reaches o'er remotest zones;
His thought remembered and his golden tones
Shall, in the ears of nations uncreate,
Roll on for ages and reverberate
When kings are dust beside forgotten thrones.

THE POET

YONE NOGUCHI

Out of the deep and the dark,
A sparkling mystery, a shape,
Something perfect,
Comes like the stir of the day:
One whose breath is an odor,
Whose eyes show the road to stars,
The breeze in his face,
The glory of Heaven on his back,
He steps like vision hung in air,
Diffusing the passion of Eternity;
His abode is the sunlight of morn,
The music of eve his speech:
In his sight
One shall turn from the dust of the grave,
And move upward to the woodland.

THE PROPHET

ALEXANDER PUSHKIN

Translated by Babette Deutsch

I dragged my feet through desert gloom,
Tormented by the spirit's yearning,
And saw a six-winged Seraph bloom
Upon the footpath's barren turning.

And as a dream in slumber lies
So light his finger on my eyes,—
My wizard eyes grew wide and wary:
An eagle's, started from her eyrie.

He touched my ears. And lo! a sea
Of storming voices burst on me,
I heard the whirling heaven's tremor,
The angel's flight and soaring sweep,
The sea-snakes coiling in the deep,
And sap the vine's green tendrils carry.

And to my lips the Seraph clung—
And tore from me my sinful tongue,
My cunning tongue and idle-worded;
The subtle serpent's sting he set
Between my lips—his hand was wet,
His bloody hand my mouth begirded.

And with a sword he cleft my breast
And took the heart with terror turning,
And in my gaping bosom pressed
A coal that throbbed there, black and burning.

Upon the wastes, a lifeless clod,
I lay, I heard the voice of God;
"Arise, oh prophet, watch and hearken,
And with my Will thy soul engird
Through lands that din and seas that darken,
Burn thou men's hearts with this, my Word."

INSPIRATION

John B. Tabb

No hint upon the hill top shows
    The flush of climbing feet;
But where the heaven above it glows
    Triumphal glances meet,

Anon to vanish in the plain,
And leave the hill its heaven again.

No sign celestial hath the soul
    Its coming dreams to tell,
Unheralded the tidal roll
    Returns—a rhythmic swell,
Anon with silence, as with sand,
To strew the surf-forsaken strand.

SONG MAKING

Sara Teasdale

My heart cried like a beaten child
    Ceaselessly the whole night long;
I had to take my own cries
    And thread them into a song.

One was a cry at black midnight
    And one when the first cock crew—
My heart was like a beaten child,
    But no one ever knew.

Life, you have put me in your debt
    And I must serve you long—
But oh, the debt is terrible
    That must be paid in song.

THE SOVEREIGN POET

William Watson

He sits above the clang and dust of Time,
With the world's secret trembling in his lip
He asks not converse nor companionship
In the cold starlight where thou canst not climb.

The undelivered tidings in his breast
Suffer him not to rest.
He sees afar the immemorable throng,
And binds the scattered ages with a song.

The glorious riddle of his rhythmic breath,
His might, his spell, we know not what they be:
We only feel, whate'er he uttereth,
This savours not of death,
This hath a relish of eternity.

b. WHENCE TO THE SINGER COMES THE SONG?

WHO BIDS US SING?

RHYS CARPENTER

Who bids us sing? What need has the world for song,
What need of the spring when autumn is harsh and strong?
The winter comes, the winter drear,
The year is dead, the marvellous fruitful year;
Who bids us sing? What need has the world for song?

What need? Under the earth the blossoms hide
Through all the cold of the winter tide;
Who shall waken them, who shall call
When the first sweet days of the springtime fall?
Who else? Under the earth the blossoms hide.

THE MASTER SINGERS

RHYS CARPENTER

They move on tracks of never-ending light;
They pierce the darkness with the burning thorn
Of star-point and of sun; with shadows torn
From wind and rain, with storm clouds in their flight,

They glut the whirlpools of abysmal night;
They gather up the flaming shreds of morn;
With streams and forests of a world unborn
They set the hills of Eden in her sight.

True poet-soul, is ought beyond your power?
The very sea in all her caves is still
When you, prophetic, from life's utmost hill,
With song's unearthly vision in your eyes,
Stretch forth your hands,—a watcher on his tower,
God in his heaven bidding light arise.

THE PROBLEM

RALPH WALDO EMERSON

I like a church; I like a cowl;
I love a prophet of the soul;
And on my heart monastic aisles
Fall like sweet strains or pensive smiles:
Yet not for all his faith can see,
Would I that cowled churchman be.
Why should the vest on him allure,
Which I could not on me endure?

Not from a vain or shallow thought
His awful Jove young Phidias brought;
Never from the lips of cunning fell
The thrilling Delphic oracle;
Out of the heart of Nature rolled
The burdens of the Bible old;
The litanies of nations came,
Like the volcano's tongue of flame,
Up from the burning core below,—
The canticles of love and woe:
The hand that rounded Peter's dome,
And groined the aisles of Christian Rome,
Wrought in a sad sincerity;
Himself from God he could not free;

He builded better than he knew;—
The conscious stone to beauty grew.

Know'st thou what wove yon woodbird's nest
Of leaves, and feathers from her breast?
Or how the fish outbuilt her shell,
Painting with morn each annual cell?
Or how the sacred pine-tree adds
To her old leaves new myriads?
Such and so grew these holy piles,
Whilst love and terror laid the tiles.
Earth proudly wears the Parthenon,
As the best gem upon her zone,
And Morning opes with haste her lids,
To gaze upon the Pyramids;
O'er England's abbeys bends the sky,
As on its friends, with kindred eye;
For, out of Thought's interior sphere,
These wonders rose to upper air;
And Nature gladly gave them place,
Adopted them into her race,
And granted them an equal date
With Andes and with Ararat.

These temples grew as grows the grass;
Art might obey but not surpass.
The passive master lent his hand,
To the vast soul that o'er him planned;
And the same power that reared the shrine
Bestrode the tribes that knelt within.
Ever the fiery Pentecost
Girds with one flame the countless host,
Trances the heart through chanting choirs,
And through the priest the mind inspires.
The word unto the prophet spoken
Was writ on tables yet unbroken;
The word by seer or sibyls told,
In groves of oak, or fanes of gold,
Still floats upon the morning wind,

Still whispers to the willing mind.
One accent of the Holy Ghost
The heedless world hath never lost.
I know what say the fathers wise,—
The Book itself before me lies,—
Old Chrysostom, best Augustine,
And he who blent both in his line,
The younger Golden Lips or mines,
Taylor, the Shakespeare of divines.
His words are music in my ear,
I see his cowlèd portrait dear;
And yet, for all his faith could see,
I would not the good bishop be.

MILTON'S PRAYER FOR PATIENCE

Elizabeth Lloyd Howell

I am old and blind!
Men point at me as smitten by God's frown:
Afflicted and deserted of my kind,
Yet am I not cast down.

I am weak, yet strong;
I murmur not that I no longer see;
Poor, old, and helpless, I the more belong,
Father supreme, to thee!

All-merciful One!
When men are furthest, then art Thou most near;
When friends pass by, my weaknesses to shun,
Thy chariot I hear.

Thy glorious face
Is leaning toward me; and its holy light
Shines in upon my lonely dwelling place,—
And there is no more night.

On my bended knee
I recognize thy purpose clearly shown:
My vision thou hast dimmed, that I may see
Thyself, thyself alone.

I have naught to fear;
This darkness is the shadow of thy wing;
Beneath it I am almost sacred; here
Can come no evil thing.

Oh, I seem to stand
Trembling, where foot of mortal ne'er hath ocen,
Wrapt in that radiance from the sinless land,
Which eye hath never seen!

Visions come and go:
Shapes of resplendent beauty around me.throng;
From angel lips I seem to hear the flow
Of soft and holy song.

It is nothing now,
When heaven is opening on my sightless eyes,
When airs from Paradise refresh my brow,
That earth in darkness lies.

In a purer clime
My being fills with rapture,—waves of thought
Roll in upon my spirit,—strains sublime
Break over me unsought.

Give me now my lyre!
I feel the stirrings of a gift divine:
Within my bosom glows unearthly fire,
Lit by no skill of mine.

INSPIRATION

Samuel Johnson

Life of Ages, richly poured,
    Love of God unspent and free,
Flowing in the Prophet's word
And the People's liberty.

Never was to chosen race
  That unstinted tide confined;
Thine is every time and place,
  Fountain sweet of heart and mind!

Secret of the morning stars,
  Motion of the oldest hours,
Pledge through elemental wars
  Of the coming spirits powers!

Rolling planet, flaming sun,
  Stand in nobler man complete;
Prescient laws thine errands run,
  Frame the shrine for Godhead meet.

Homeward led, the wandering eye
  Upward yearned in joy or awe,
Found the love that waited nigh,
  Guidance of thy guardian Law.

In the touch of earth it thrilled;
  Down from mystic skies it burned;
Right obeyed and passion stilled
  It eternal gladness earned.

Breathing in the thinker's creed,
  Pulsing in the hero's blood,
Nerving simplest thought and deed,
  Freshening time with truth and good.

Consecrating art and song,
  Holy book and pilgrim track,
Hurling floods of tyrant wrong
  From the sacred limits back.

Life of Ages, richly poured,
  Love of God, unspent and free,
Flow still in the Prophet's word,
  And the People's Liberty!

FRAGMENT

AMY LOWELL

What is poetry? Is it a mosaic
  Of colored stones which curiously are wrought
  Into a pattern? Rather glass that's taught
By patient labor any hue to take
And glowing with a sumptuous splendor, make
  Beauty a thing of awe; where sunbeams caught,
  Transmuted fall in sheafs of rainbows fraught
With storied meaning for religion's sake.

GOD IS NOT DUMB

JAMES RUSSELL LOWELL

From *Bibliolaters*

God is not dumb, that He should speak no more;
  If thou hast wanderings in the wilderness
And findest not Sinai, 'tis thy soul is poor;
  There towers the Mountain of the Voice no less,
Which whoso seeks shall find; but he who bends,
Intent on manna still and mortal ends,
  Sees it not, neither hears its thundered lore.

Slowly the Bible of the race is writ,
  And not on paper leaves nor leaves of stone;
Each age, each kindred, adds a verse to it,
  Texts of despair and hope, of joy or moan.
While swings the sea, while mists the mountains shroud,
  While thunders' surges burst on cliff of cloud,
Still at the prophets' feet the nations sit.

THE POET

Angela Morgan

Why hast thou breathed, O God, upon my thoughts
And tuned my pulse to thy high melodies,
Lighting my soul with love, my heart with flame,
Thrilling my ear with songs I cannot keep—
Only to set me in the market place
Amid the clamor of the bartering throng,
Whose ears are deaf to my impassioned plea,
Whose hearts are heedless of the word I bring?

And yet—dear God, forgive! I will sing on.
I will sing until that shining day
When one, perchance, one only may it be—
Shall turn aside from out the sordid way,
List'ning with eager ears that understand
Until that day—thy day—help me to bear
The hurt of cold indifference and the pain
Of seeing all the multitude rush by,
Drowning thy music with their cry for gold!

HE WHOM A DREAM HATH POSSESSED

Shaemus O Sheel

He whom a dream hath possessed knoweth no more of doubting,
For mist and the blowing of winds and the mouthing of words
    he scorns;
Not the sinuous speech of schools he hears, but a knightly
    shouting,
And never comes darkness down, yet he greeteth a million
    morns.

He whom a dream hath possessed knoweth no more of roaming;
All roads and the flowing of waves and the speediest flight
    he knows,

But wherever his feet are set, his soul is forever homing,
And going, he comes, and coming he heareth a call and goes.

He whom a dream hath possessed knoweth no more of sorrow,
At death and the dropping of leaves and the fading of suns
    he smiles,
For a dream remembers no past, and scorns the desire of a
    morrow,
And a dream in a sea of doom sets surely the ultimate isles.

He whom a dream hath possessed treads the impalpable
    marches,
From the dust of the day's long road he leaps to a laughing star,
And the ruin of worlds that fall he views from eternal arches,
And rides God's battlefield in a flashing and golden car.

THE FOUNTS OF SONG

WILLIAM SHARP (*Fiona Macleod*)

"What is the song I am singing?"
Said the pine tree to the wave:
"Do you not know the song
You have sung so long
Down in the dim green alleys of the sea,
And where the great blind tides go swinging
Mysteriously,
And where the countless herds of the billows are hurl'd
On all the wild and lonely beaches of the world?"

"Ah, pine tree," sighed the wave,
"I have no song but what I catch from thee:
Far off I hear thy strain
Of infinite sweet pain
That floats along the lovely phantom land.
I sigh, and murmur it o'er and o'er and o'er,
When 'neath the slow compelling hand
That guides me back and far from the loved shore,

I wander long
Where never falls the breath of any song,
But only the loud, empty, crashing roar
Of seas swung this way and that for evermore."

"What is the song I am singing?"
Said the poet to the pine:
"Do you not know the song
You have sung so long
Here in the dim green alleys of the woods,
Where the wild winds go wandering in all moods,
And whisper often o'er and o'er
Or in tempestuous clamours roar
Their dark eternal secret evermore?"

"Oh, Poet," said the pine,
"Thine
Is that song!
Not mine!
I have known it, loved it, long!
Nothing I know of what the wild winds cry
Through dusk and storm and night,
Or prophesy
When tempests whirl us with their awful might.
Only, I know that when
The poet's voice is heard
Among the woods
The infinite pain from out the hearts of men
Is sweeter than the voice of wave or branch or bird
In these dumb solitudes."

From INSPIRATION

HENRY DAVID THOREAU

If with light head erect I sing,
Though all the Muses lend their force,
From my poor love of anything,
The verse is weak and shallow as its source.

But if with bended neck I grope,
Listening behind me for my wit,
With faith superior to hope, ·
More anxious to keep back than forward it,—

Making my soul accomplice there
Unto the flame my heart hath lit,
Then will the verse forever wear,—
Time cannot bend the line that God hath writ.

I hearing get, who had but ears,
And sight, who had but eyes before;
I moments live, who lived but years,
And truth discern, who knew but learning's lore.

GENIUS

Edward Lucas White

He cried aloud to God: "The men below
Are happy, for I see them come and go,
Parents and mates and friends, paired,
       clothed with love;
They heed not, see not, need me not above,—
I am alone here. Grant me love and peace,
Or if not them, grant me at least release."

God answered him: "I set you here on high
Upon my beacon tower, you know not why,
Your soul-torch by the cruel gale is blown,
As desperate as our aching heart is lone.
You may not guess but that it shines in vain,
Yet, till it is burned out, you must remain."

II. The Search after God

a. THE SUCCESSFUL SEARCHERS

From PAULINE

Robert Browning

O God, where do they tend—these struggling aims?
What would I have? What is this 'sleep' which seems
To bound all? Can there be a 'waking' point
Of crowning life? The soul would never rule;
It would be first in all things, it would have
Its utmost pleasure filled,—but, that complete,
Commanding for commanding sickens it.
The last point I can trace is, rest beneath
Some better essence than itself—in weakness;
This is 'myself'—not what I think should be,
And what is that I hunger for but God?
My God, my God, let me for once look on thee
As though naught else existed, we alone!
And as creation crumbles, my soul's spark
Expands till I can say, 'Even from myself
I need thee, and I feel thee, and I love thee;
I do not plead my rapture in thy works
For love of thee, nor that I feel as one
Who cannot die: but there is that in me
Which turns to thee, which loves, or which should love.'

Why have I girt myself with this hell-dress?
Why have I laboured to put out my life?
Is it not in my nature to adore,
And e'en for all my reason do I not
Feel him, and thank him, and pray to him—*now?*

Can I forgo the trust that he loves me?
Do I not feel a love which only ONE . . .
O thou pale form, so dimly seen, deep-eyed!
I have denied thee calmly—do I not
Pant when I read of thy consummate power,
And burn to see thy calm pure truths out-flash
The brightest gleams of earth's philosophy?
Do I not shake to hear aught question thee?
If I am erring save me, madden me,
Take from me powers and pleasures,—let me die
Ages, so I see thee! I am knit round
As with a charm, by sin and lust and pride,
Yet though my wandering dreams have seen all shapes
Of strange delight, oft have I stood by thee—
Have I been keeping lonely watch with thee
In the damp night by weeping Olivet,
Or leaning on thy bosom, proudly less,
Or dying with thee on the lonely cross,
Or witnessing thine outburst from the tomb!

THE AWAKENING OF MAN

Robert Browning

From *Paracelsus,* Pt. V

Progress is
The law of life, man is not Man as yet.
Nor shall I deem his object served, his end
Attained, his genuine strength put fairly forth,
While only here and there a star dispels
The darkness, here and there a towering mind
O'erlooks its prostrate fellows: when the host
Is out at once to the despair of night,
When all mankind alike is perfected,
Equal in full-blown powers—then, not till then,
I say, begins man's general infancy.
For wherefore make account of feverish starts
Of restless members of a dormant whole,

Impatient nerves which quiver while the body
Slumbers as in a grave? Oh, long ago
The brow was twitched, the tremulous lids astir,
The peaceful mouth disturbed; half uttered speech
Ruffled the lip, and then the teeth were set,
The breath drawn sharp, the strong right hand clenched
      stronger,
As it would pluck a lion by the jaw;
The glorious creature laughed out, even in sleep!
But when full roused, each giant-limb awake,
Each sinew strung, the great heart pulsing fast,
He shall start up and stand on his own earth,
Then shall his long triumphant march begin,
Thence shall his being date—thus wholly roused,
What he achieves shall be set down to him.
When all the race is perfected alike
As man, that is; all tended to mankind,
And, man produced, all has its end thus far;
But in completed man begins anew
A tendency to God. Prognostics told
Man's near approach; so in man's self arise
August anticipations, symbols, types
Of a dim splendor ever on before
In that eternal circle life pursues.
For men begin to pass their nature's bound,
And find new hopes and cares which fast supplant
Their proper joys and griefs; they grow too great
For narrow creeds of right and wrong, which fade
Before the unmeasured thirst for good; while peace
Rises within them ever more and more.
Such men are even now upon the earth,
Serene amid the half-formed creatures round
Who should be saved by them and joined with them.

A PSALM OF THE EARLY BUDDHIST SISTERS

Now here, now there, lightheaded, crazed with grief,
Mourning my child, I wandered up and down,
Naked, unheeding, streaming hair unkempt,

Lodging in scourings of the streets, and where
The dead lay still, and by the chariot-roads—
So three years long I fared, starving, athirst.

And then at last I saw Him, as He went
Within that blessed city Mithila:
Great Tamer of untamed hearts, yea, Him,
The Very Buddha, Banisher of fear.
Came back my heart to me, my errant mind;
Forthwith to Him I went low worshipping,
And there, e'en at His feet I heard the Norm.
For of His great compassion on us all,
'Twas He who taught me, even GOTAMA.

I heeded all He said and left the world
And all its cares behind, and gave myself
To follow where He taught, and realize
Life in the Path to great good fortune bound.
Now all my sorrows are hewn down, cast out,
Uprooted, brought to utter end,
In that I now can grasp and understand
The base on which my miseries were built.

VESTIGIA

BLISS CARMAN

I took a day to search for God,
And found Him not. But as I trod
   By rocky ledge, through woods untamed,
   Just where one scarlet lily flamed,
I saw His footprint in the sod.

Then suddenly, all unaware,
Far off in the deep shadows, where
   A solitary hermit thrush
   Sang through the holy twilight hush—
I heard His voice upon the air.

And even as I marveled how
God gives us Heaven here and now,
  In a stir of wind that hardly shook
  The poplar leaves beside the brook—
His hand was light upon my brow.

At last with evening as I turned
Homeward, and thought what I had learned
  And all that there was still to probe—
  I caught the glory of His robe
Where the last fires of sunset burned.

Back to the world with quickening start
I looked and longed for any part
  In making saving Beauty be . . .
  And from that kindling ecstasy
I knew God dwelt within my heart.

THE SEARCH

Thomas Curtis Clarke

  I sought his love in sun and stars,
    And where the wild seas roll,
  And found it not. As mute I stood,
    Fear overwhelmed my soul;
  But when I gave to one in need,
  I found the Lord of Love indeed.

  I sought his love in lore of books,
    In charts of science' skill;
  They left me orphaned as before—
    His love eluded still;
  Then in despair I breathed a prayer;
  The Lord of Love was standing there!

FEET

Mary Carolyn Davies

Where the sun shines in the street
There are very many feet
Seeking God, all unaware
That their hastening is a prayer.
Perhaps these feet would deem it odd
(Who think they are on business bent)
If some one went,
And told them, "You are seeking God."

SEEKING GOD

Edward Dowden

I said, "I will find God," and forth I went
To seek him in the clearness of the sky,
But he over me, stood unendurably
Only a pitiless sapphire firmament
Ringing the world,—blank splendor; yet intent
Still to find God, "I will go seek," said I,
"His way upon the waters," and drew nigh
An ocean marge weed-strewn and foam-besprent;
And the waves dashed on idle sand and stone,
And very vacant was the long, blue sea;
But in the evening as I sat alone,
My window open to the vanishing day,
Dear God! I could not choose but kneel and pray,
And it sufficed that I was found of Thee.

CHILD OF LONELINESS

Norman Gale

.   .   .   .

The pith of faith is gone. And as there lie
Along the desert shanks of lions slain,
So in this world whose needs are grown so high,
Half hid, half seen, Faith moulders in the plain!

Tenderly take the priceless wondrous bones,
And wend away from all that plucks thy dress,
And with a few chance boughs or scattered stones
Build up thine altar, Child of loneliness.

The Master is not only in the court
Where doves are sold and money-changers cry:
Nor will He leave the country-side untaught
If ears be open as He passes by:
In secret paths that thread the forest land
He waits to heal thee and divinely bless;
While from the hill with voice and waving hand
The shepherd calls thee, Child of loneliness.

 .   .   .   .   ꞓ

But be thou faithful to thine altar set
Within the temple of the stilly glade,
For Christ is there, nor will His heart forget
The striving of thy soul. Be not afraid!
O priest and people mingled into and one,
Within thy green cathedral aisles no less
He stands above thee when, the prayer begun,
Thou callest Him, O Child of loneliness.

'Tis sweet where every downy throat's a well
Of song itself—to worship in the grass,
Thine altar's base fast-founded on a swell
Near a glade where elms and beeches pass:
There is space for breath, and there, content,
If aught should be forgiven, kneel, confess;
Over thy head the boundless firmament,
God's love, God's wisdom, Child of loneliness.

 .   .   .   .

From the HIERARCHIE OF THE BLESSED ANGELS

Thomas Heywood

I sought thee round about, O thou my God!
        In thine abode.
I said unto the earth, "Speak, art thou he?"
        She answered me,

"I am not." I inquired of creatures all,
   In general,
Contained therein. They with one voice proclaim
That none amongst them challenged such a name.

I asked the seas and all the deeps below,
   My God to know;
I asked the reptiles and whatever is
   In the abyss,—
Even from the shrimp to the leviathan
   Inquiry ran;
But in those deserts which no line can sound,
The God I sought for was not to be found.

I asked the air if that were he! but lo!
   It told me "No."
I from the towering eagle to the wren
   Demanded then
If any feathered fowl 'mongst them were such;
   But they all, much
Offended with my question, in full choir,
Answered, "To find thy God thou must look higher."

I asked the heavens, sun, moon, and stars; but they
   Said, "We obey
The God thou seekest." I asked what eye or ear
   Could see or hear,—
What in the world I might descry or know
   Above, below;
With an unanimous voice, all these things said,
"We are not God, but we by him were made."

I asked the world's great universal mass
   If that God was;
Which with a mighty and strong voice replied,
   As stupefied,—
"I am not he, O man! for know that I
   By him on high
Was fashioned first of nothing; thus instated
And swayed by him by whom I was created."

I sought the court; but smooth-tongued flattery there
    Deceived each ear;
I' the thronged city there was selling, buying,
    Swearing, and lying;
I' the country, craft in simpleness arrayed,
    And then I said,—
"Vain is my search, although my pains be great;
Where my God is there can be no deceit."

A scrutiny within myself I then
    Even thus began:
"O man, what art thou?" What more could I say
    Than dust and clay,—
Frail, mortal, fading, a mere puff, a blast,
    That cannot last;
Enthroned today, tomorrow in an urn,
Formed from that earth to which I must return?

I asked myself what this great God might be
    That fashioned me.
I answered: The all-potent, sole, immense,
    Surpassing sense;
Unspeakable, inscrutable, eternal,
    Lord over all;
The only terrible, strong, just, and true,
Who hath no end, and no beginning knew.

He is the well of life, for he doth give
    To all that live
Both breath and being; he is the Creator
    Both of the water,
Earth, air, and fire. Of all things that subsist
    He hath the list,—
Of all the heavenly host, or what earth claims,
He keeps the scroll, and calls them by their names.

And now, my God, by thine illumining grace,
    Thy glorious face
(So far forth as it may discovered be)
    Methinks I see;

And though invisible and infinite,
    To human sight
Thou, in thy mercy, justice, truth, appearest,
In which, to our frail senses thou comst nearest.

O, make us apt to seek and quick to find,
    Thou, God, most kind!
Give us love, hope, and faith, in thee to trust,
    Thou, God, most just!
Remit all our offences, we entreat,
    Most good! most great!
Grant that our willing, though unworthy quest
May, through thy grace, admit us 'mongst the blest.

THE HILL

Horace Holley

Be not too certain, life!
(Or is that power of death, that tedious power
Which with insistent sneer
Shatters continually and steeps in slime
The difficult house I raise
The house of consciousness?)—
Be not too certain of me;
Deem me not wholly tamed,
Content with labour ineffectual
Upon this ruined house of thought;
Or, turning to things outside,
Content to hurry a life-time through these streets
Darkened with vaster ineffectiveness
Even this sea-flung, sea-swift fog
Makes so pathetic romance of!
    Count not too long upon my slavehood!
For as I have often dreamed,
There is a hill
Sloping against the dizzy, mystic sky
Whither, in a moment, I can go.
    There is a hill

And, pausing for courageous breath
Pace after pace I'll climb
Fleeing from thee, O insufficient life!
A weak, yet conscious Christ
Bearing his cross of aspiration,
O, bleeding and gasping on that hill
To me the vision of things
Already perfect, consummated present
Sudden will rise, and I shall thrill
With powers you know not of,
Old tedious world of streets,—
Inevitable failure, self-deception
Death-in-life;
For, writhing as I might be
In supreme pain, and broken
Upon the wheel of dissolution,
Never was so great aspiration void;
And I shall wholly triumph
Convinced at last of my own perfect soul,
And God, the soul's desire.

LOST AND FOUND

George MacDonald

I missed him when the sun began to bend;
I found him not when I had lost his rim;
With many tears I went in search of him,
Climbing high mountains which did still ascend,
And gave me echoes when I called my friend;
Through cities vast and charnel-houses grim,
And high cathedrals where the light was dim,
Through books and arts and works without an end,
But found him not—the friend whom I had lost.
And yet I found him—as I found the lark,
A sound in fields I heard but could not mark;
I found him nearest when I missed him most;
I found him in my heart, a life in frost,
A light I knew not till my soul was dark.

REVELATION

Edwin Markham

I made a pilgrimage to find the God:
I listened for His voice at holy tombs,
Searched for the print of His immortal feet
In dust of broken altars: yet turned back
With empty heart. But on the homeward road,
A great light came upon me, and I heard
The God's voice singing in a nestling lark;
Felt his sweet wonder in a swaying rose;
Received his blessing from a wayside well;
Looked on his beauty in a lover's face;
Saw his bright hand send signals from the suns.

CREDO

Edwin Arlington Robinson

I cannot find my way: there is no star
In all the shrouded heavens anywhere;
And there is not a whisper in the air
Of any living voice but one so far
That I can hear it only as a bar
Of lost, imperial music, played when fair
And angel fingers wove, and unaware,
Dead leaves to garlands where no roses are.

No, there is not a glimmer, nor a call,
For one that welcomes, welcomes when he fears,
The black and awful chaos of the night;
For through it all,—above, beyond it all,—
I know the far-sent message of the years,
I feel the coming glory of the Light!

THE UNKNOWN GOD

GEORGE WILLIAM RUSSELL (*A. E.*)

Far up the dim twilight fluttered
  Moth wings of vapour and flame:
The lights danced over the mountains,
  Star after star they came.

The lights grew thicker unheeded,
  For silent and still were we;
Our hearts were drunk with a beauty
  Our eyes could never see.

WHO BY SEARCHING CAN FIND OUT GOD?

ELIZA SCUDDER

I cannot find Thee! Still on restless pinion
My spirit beats the void where Thou dost dwell;
I wander lost through all Thy vast dominion,
And shrink beneath Thy light ineffable.

I cannot find Thee! Even when most adoring
Before Thy shrine I bend in lowliest prayer,
Beyond these bounds of thought, my thought upsoaring,
From farthest quest comes back: Thou art not there.

Yet high above the limits of my seeing,
And folded far within the inmost heart,
And deep below the deeps of conscious being,
Thy splendor shineth; there, O God, Thou art.

I cannot lose Thee! Still in Thee abiding
The end is clear, how wide so e'er I roam;
The Law that holds the worlds my steps is guiding,
And I must rest at last in Thee, my home.

MASTERY

Sara Teasdale

I would not have a god come in
To shield me suddenly from sin,
And set my house of life to rights;
Nor angels with bright burning wings
Ordering my earthly thoughts and things;
Rather my own frail guttering lights
Windblown and nearly beaten out,
Rather the terror of the nights
And long sick groping after doubt.
Rather be lost than let my soul
Slip vaguely from my own control—
Of my own spirit let me be
In sole, though feeble, mastery.

DOUBT

Alfred Tennyson

From *In Memoriam*, XCVI

You say, but with no touch of scorn,
　Sweet-hearted, you, whose light-blue eyes
　Are tender over drowning flies,
You tell me, doubt is Devil-born.

I know not: one indeed I knew
　In many a subtle question versed,
　Who touched a jarring lyre at first,
But ever strove to make it true;

Perplexed in faith, but pure in deeds,
　At last he beat his music out.
　There lives more faith in honest doubt,
Believe me, than in half the creeds.

He fought his doubts and gather'd strength,
  He would not make his judgment blind,
  He faced the spectres of the mind
And laid them: Thus he came at length

To find a stronger faith his own,
  And Power was with him in the night,
  Which makes the darkness and the light,
And dwells not in the light alone,

But in the darkness and the cloud,
  As over Sinai's peaks of old,
  While Israel made their gods of gold,
Although the trumpet blew so loud.

THE LARGER HOPE

ALFRED TENNYSON

From *In Memoriam*, LIV

O, yet we trust that somehow good
  Will be the final goal of ill,
  To pangs of nature, sins of will,
Defects of doubt and taints of blood;

That nothing walks with aimless feet;
  That not one life shall be destroyed,
  Or cast as rubbish to the void,
When God hath made the pile complete;

That not a worm is cloven in vain;
  That not a moth with vain desire
  Is shrivelled in a fruitless fire,
Or but subserves another's gain.

Behold, we know not anything;
  I can but trust that good shall fall
  At last—far off—at last, to all,
And every winter change to spring.

So runs my dream; but what am I?
An infant crying in the night;
An infant crying for the light,
And with no language but a cry.

IN NO STRANGE LAND

FRANCIS THOMPSON

O world invisible, we view thee,
O world intangible, we touch thee,
O world unknowable, we know thee,
Inapprehensible, we clutch thee!

Does the fish soar to find the ocean,
The eagle plunge to find the air
That we ask of the stars in motion
If they have rumor of thee there?

Not where the wheeling systems darken,
And our benumbed conceiving soars!
The drift of pinions, would we harken,
Beats at our own clay-shuttered doors.

The angels keep their ancient places;—
Turn but a stone and start a wing!
'Tis ye, 'tis your estranged faces,
That miss the many-splendored thing.

But (when so sad thou canst not sadder)
Cry; and upon thy so sore loss
Shall shine the traffic of Jacob's ladder
Pitched between Heaven and Charing Cross.

Yea, in the night, my Soul, my daughter,
Cry, clinging heaven by the hems:
And lo, Christ walking on the water,
Not of Gennesaret, but Thames!

THE HOUND OF HEAVEN

FRANCIS THOMPSON

I fled Him, down the nights and down the days;
I fled Him down the arches of the years;
I fled Him down the labyrinthine ways
  Of my own mind; and in the midst of tears
I hid from Him and under running laughter.
      Up vistaed hopes I sped;
      And shot, precipitated
   Adown titanic glooms of chasmèd fears,
From those strong Feet that followed, followed after.
     But with unhurrying chase
     And unperturbèd pace,
  Deliberate speed, majestic instancy
    They beat—and a Voice beat
    More instant than the Feet—
"All things betray thee, who betrayest Me."

I pleaded, outlaw-wise,
By many a hearted casement, curtained red,
  Trellised with intertwining charities;
(For, though I knew His love Who followèd,
    Yet I was sore adread
Lest having Him I must have naught beside;)
But, if one little casement parted wide,
  The gust of His approach would clash it to.
Fear wist not to evade as Love wist to pursue.
Across the margent of the world I fled,
  And troubled the gold gateways of the stars,
  Smiting for shelter on their clangèd bars;
    Fretted to dulcet jars
And silvern chatter the pale ports o' the moon.
I said to dawn, Be sudden; to eve, Be soon;
  With thy young skyey blossoms heap me over
    From this tremendous Lover!
Float thy vague veil about me, lest He see!
  I tempted all His servitors. but to find

My own betrayal in their constancy,
In faith to Him their fickleness to me,
　　Their traitorous trueness, and their loyal deceit.
To all swift things for swiftness did I sue;
　　Clung to the whistling mane of every wind.
But whether they swept, smoothly fleet,
The long savannahs of the blue;
　　Or, whether, thunder-driven,
They clanged His chariot 'thwart a heaven
Plashy with flying lightnings round the spurn o'
　　their feet;—
Fear wist not to evade as Love wist to pursue.
Still with unhurrying chase
And unperturbèd pace,
Deliberate speed, majestic instancy,
　　Came on the following Feet,
　　And a Voice above their beat—
"Naught shelters thee, who wilt not shelter Me."

I sought no more that after which I strayed,
　　In face of man or maid;
But still within the little children's eyes
　　Seems something, something that replies;
They are at least for me, surely for me!
I turned me to them very wistfully;
But just as their young eyes grew sudden fair
　　With dawning answers there,
Their angel plucked them from me by the hair.
"Come, then, ye other children—Nature's—share
With me" (said I) "your delicate fellowship;
　　Let me greet you, lip to lip,
　　Let me twine you with caresses,
　　　　Wantoning
With our Lady Mother's vagrant tresses,
　　　　Banqueting
With her in her wind-walled palace,
Underneath her azure dais.
Quaffing, as your taintless way is,
　　From a chalice
Lucent-weeping out of the dayspring."
　　So it was done:

I in their delicate fellowship was one—
Drew the bolt of nature's secrecies.
I knew all the swift importings
   Of the wilful face of the skies,
   I knew how the clouds arise
    Spumèd of the wild sea snortings;
       All that's born or dies
   Rose and drooped with—made them shapers
Of mine own moods, or wailful or Divine—
   With them joyed or was bereaven.
   I was heavy with the even
   When she lit her glimmering tapers
   Round the day's dead sanctities.
   I laughed in the morning's eyes.
I triumphed and I saddened with all weather,
      Heaven and I wept together,
And its sweet tears were salt with mortal mine;
Against the red throb of its sunset-heart
    I laid my own to beat,
    And share commingling heat;
But not by that, by that, was eased my human smart.
In vain my tears were wet on Heaven's grey cheek.
For ah! we know not what each other says,
   These things and I; in sound *I* speak—
Their sound is but their stir, they speak by silences.
Nature, poor stepdame, cannot slake my drouth;
   Let her, if she would owe me,
Drop yon blue bosom-veil of sky, and show me
   The breasts o' her tenderness:
Never did any milk of hers once bless
     My thirsting mouth.
     Nigh and nigh draws the chase
     With unperturbèd pace,
  Deliberate speed, majestic instancy;
     And past those noisèd Feet
     A voice comes yet more fleet—
"Lo, naught contents thee, who content'st not Me."

Naked I wait thy love's uplifted stroke.
My harness, piece by piece, thou hast hewn from me,

And smitten me to my knee;
I am defenseless utterly.
I slept, methinks, and woke
And slowly gazing, find me stripped in sleep.
In the rash lustihood of my young powers,
I stood the pillaring hours
And pulled my life upon me; grimed with smears
I stand amid the dust o' the mounded years—
My mangled youth lies dead beneath the heap.
My days have crackled and gone up in smoke,
Have puffed and burst as sun-starts on a stream.
Yea, faileth now even dream
The dreamer, and the lute the lutanist;
Even the linked fantasies in whose blossomy twist
I swung the earth, a trinket at my wrist,
Are yielding; cords of all too weak account
For earth with heavy griefs so overplussed.
Ah! is Thy love indeed
A weed, albeit an amaranthine weed,
Suffering no flowers except its own to mount?
Ah! must—
Designer Infinite!—
Ah, must Thou char the wood ere Thou canst limn
with it?
My freshness spent its wavering shower i' the dust:
And now my heart is as a broken fount,
Wherein tear-drippings stagnate, spilt down ever
From the dank thoughts that shiver
Upon the sighful branches of my mind.
Such is; what is to be?
The pulp so bitter, how shall taste the rind?
I dimly guess what Time in mists confounds:
Yet ever and anon a trumpet sounds
From the hid battlements of Eternity;
Those shaken mists a space unsettle, then
Round the half-glimpsèd turrets slowly wash again.
But not ere him who summoneth
I first have seen, enwound
With glooming robes purpureal, cypress-crowned;

His name I know and what his trumpet saith.
Whether man's heart or life it be which yields
   Thee harvest, must Thy harvest fields
   Be dunged with rotten death?

      Now of that long pursuit
      Comes on at hand the bruit;
   That Voice is round me like a bursting sea:
      "And is thy earth so marred,
      Shattered in shard on shard?
   Lo, all things fly thee, for thou flyest Me!
   Strange, piteous, futile thing,
Wherefore should any set thee love apart?
Seeing none but I makes much of naught" (He said),
"And human love needs human meriting:
   How hast thou merited--
Of all man's clotted clay the dingiest clot?
   Alack, thou knowest not
How little worthy of any love thou art!
Whom wilt thou find to love ignoble thee
   Save Me, save only Me?
All which I took from thee, I did but take
   Not for thy harms,
But just that thou mightst seek it in My arms.
   All which thy child's mistake
Fancies as lost, I have stored for thee at home:
   Rise, clasp My hand and come!"

   Halts by me that footfall:
   Is my gloom, after all,
Shade of His hand, outstretched caressingly?
      "Ah, fondest, blindest, weakest,
      I am He Whom thou seekest!
Thou dravest love from thee, who dravest Me."

THE SEARCH

Psalms XLII and XLIII

From Moulton's *Modern Readers' Bible*

As the hart panteth after the water brooks,
  So panteth my soul after thee, O God.
My soul thirsteth for God, for the living God:
  When shall I come and appear before God:
My tears have been my meat day and night,
  While they continually say unto me, Where is thy God?
These things I remember,
  And pour out my soul within me,
How I went with the throng, and led them to the house of God,
  With the voice of joy and praise, a multitude keeping holyday.

Refrain:

    Why art thou cast down, O my soul?
    And why art thou disquieted within me?
    Hope thou in God
    For I shall yet praise Him,
    Who is the health of my countenance,
    And my God.

My soul is cast down within me:
  Therefore do I remember thee from the land of Jordan,
  And the Hermons, from the hill Mizar.
Deep calleth unto deep at the noise of thy water-spouts:
  All thy waves and thy billows are gone over me.
Yet the Lord will command his loving kindness in the daytime,
  And in the night his song shall be with me,
  Even as a prayer unto the God of my life.
I will say unto God my rock, Why hast thou forgotten me?
  Why go I mourning because of the oppression of mine enemy?
As with a sword in my bones, mine adversaries reproach me;
  While they continually say unto me, Where is thy God?

REFRAIN:

> *Why art thou cast down, O my soul?*
> *And why art thou disquieted within me?*
> *Hope thou in God*
> *For I shall yet praise Him,*
> *Who is the health of my countenance,*
> *And my God.*

Judge me, O God, and plead my cause against an ungodly
     nation:
  O deliver me from the deceitful and unjust man.
For thou art the God of my strength, why hast thou cast me off?
  Why go I mourning because of the oppression of mine enemy?
O send out thy light and thy truth;
  Let them lead me:
Let them bring me unto the holy hill,
  And to thy tabernacles.
Then will I go unto the altar of God,
Unto God my exceeding joy:
  And upon the harp will I praise thee, O God, my God.

REFRAIN:

> *Why art thou cast down, O my soul?*
> *And why art thou disquieted within me?*
> *Hope thou in God*
> *For I shall yet praise Him,*
> *Who is the health of my countenance,*
> *And my God.*

AT THE END OF THINGS

ARTHUR EDWARD WAITE

The world uprose as a man to find Him—
  Ten thousand methods, ten thousand ends—
Some bent on treasure; the more on pleasure;
  And some on the chaplet which fame attends:
But the great deep's voice in the distance dim
Said: Peace, it is well; they are seeking Him.

When I heard that all the world was questing,
    I look'd for a palmer's staff and found,
By a reed-fringed pond, a fork'd hazel wand
    On a twisted tree, in a bann'd waste-ground;
But I knew not then what the sounding strings
Of the sea harps say at the end of things.

They told me, world, you were keen on seeking;
    I cast around for a scrip to hold
Such meagre needs as the roots of weeds—
    All weeds, but one with a root of gold;
Yet I knew not then how the clangs ascend
When the sea horns peal and the searchings end.

An old worn wallet was that they gave me,
    With twelve old signs on its seven old skins;
And a star I stole for the good of my soul,
    Lest the darkness come down on my sins;
For I knew not who in their life had heard
Of the sea pipes shrilling a secret word.

I join'd the quest that the world was making,
    Which follow'd the false ways far and wide,
While a thousand cheats in the lanes and streets
    Offer'd that wavering crowd to guide;
But what did they know of the sea reed's speech
When the peace-words breathe at the end for each?

The fools fell down in the swamps and marshes;
    The fools died hard on the crags and hills;
The lies which cheated, so long repeated,
    Deceived, in spite of their evil wills,
Some knaves themselves at the end of all—
Though how should they hearken when sea flutes call?

But me the scrip and the staff had strengthen'd;
    I carried the star; that star led me:
The paths I've taken, of most forsaken,
    Do surely lead to an open sea:
As a clamour of voices heard in sleep,
Come shouts through the dark on the shrouded deep.

Now it is noon; in the hush prevailing
  Pipes, harps and horns into flute-notes fall;
The sea, conceding my star's true leading,
  In tongues sublime at the end of all
Gives resonant utterance far and near:—

> "Cast away fear;
> Be of good cheer;
> He is here,
>   Is here!"

And now I know that I sought Him only
  Even as child, when for flowers I sought;
In the sins of youth, as in search for truth,
  To find Him, hold Him alone I wrought.
The knaves too seek Him, and fools beguiled—
So speak to them also, sea voices mild!

Which then was wisdom and which was folly?
  Did my star more than the cozening guide?
The fool, as I think, at the chasm's brink,
  Prone by the swamp or the marsh's side,
Did, even as I, in the end rejoice,
Since the voice of death must be His true voice.

GOD-SEEKING

William Watson

God-seeking thou hast journeyed far and nigh.
  On dawn-lit mountain top thy soul did yearn
To hear His trailing garments wander by:
  And where, 'mid thunderous glooms great sunsets
    burn,
Vainly thou soughtest His shadow on sea and sky:
  Or, gazing up, at noon tide, couldst discern
Only a neutral heaven's indifferent eye
  And countenance austerely taciturn.

Yet whom thou soughtest I have found at last,
  Neither where tempest dims the world below,
Nor where the westering daylight reels aghast
  In conflagrations of red overthrow;
But where this virgin brooklet silvers past
  And yellowing either bank the king-cups blow.

REFRACTED LIGHTS

CELIA PARKER WOOLEY

The evening star that softly sheds
  Its tender light on me,
Hath other place in the heavenly blue,
  Than that I seem to see.
Too faint and slender is that beam
  To keep its pathway true
In the vast space of cloud and mist
  It seeks an exit through.

Nor light of star nor truth of God
  To earth-born clouds and doubts
Can straightway pierce the hearts of men
  And drive the darkness out.
On bent, misshapen lines of faith
  We backward strive to trace
The love and glory that we ne'er
  Could look on face to face.

Each fails thru dim and wandering sight
  The vision whole to see;
But none are there so poor and blind
  But catch some glimpse of Thee—
Some knowledge of the better way
  And of that life divine
Of which our yearning hope is both
  The prophecy and sign.

ZOROASTER DEVOUTLY QUESTIONS ORMAZD

Translated by A. V. Williams Jackson

This I ask Thee—tell it to me truly, Lord!
Who the Sire was, Father first of Holiness?
Who the pathway for the sun and stars ordained?
Who, through whom its moon doth wax and wane again?
This and much else do I long, O God, to know.

This I ask Thee—tell it to me truly, Lord!
Who set firmly earth below, and kept the sky
Sure from falling? Who the streams and trees did make?
Who their swiftness to the winds and clouds hath yoked?
Who, O Mazda, was the Founder of Good Thought?

This I ask Thee—tell it to me truly, Lord!
Who, benignant, made the darkness and the light?
Who, benignant, sleep and waking did create?
Who the morning, noon, and evening did decree
As reminders to the wise, of duty's call?

b. THE UNSUCCESSFUL SEARCHERS

THE FALCONER OF GOD

WILLIAM ROSE BENÉT

I flung my soul to the air like a falcon flying.
I said, "Wait on! wait on! while I ride below!
    I shall start a heron soon
    In the marsh beneath the moon—
A strange white heron, rising with silver on its wings,
        Rising and crying
    Wordless, wondrous things;

The secret of the stars, of the world's heart-strings,
    The answer to their woe.
Then stoop thou upon him, and grip and hold him so!"

My soul waited on as falcons hover.
I beat the reedy fens as I trampled past.
    I heard the mournful loon
    In the marsh beneath the moon.
And then, with feathery thunder, the bird of my desire
        Broke from the cover
        Flashing silver fire.
    High up among the stars I saw his pinions spire.
        The pale clouds gazed aghast
As my falcon stooped upon him, and gript and held him fast.

My soul dropped through the air—with heavenly plunder?—
Gripping the dazzling bird my dreaming knew?
    Nay! but a piteous freight,
    A dark and heavy weight
Despoiled of silver plumage, its voice forever stilled—
        All of the wonder
        Gone that ever filled
    Its guise with glory. O bird that I have killed,
        How brilliantly you flew
Across my rapturous vision when first I dreamed of you!

Yet I fling my soul on high with new endeavor,
As I ride the world below with a joyful mind.
    I shall start a heron soon
    In the marsh below the moon—
A wondrous silver heron its inner darkness fledges!
        I beat forever
        The fens and the sedges.
    The pledge is still the same—for all disastrous pledges,
        All hopes resigned!
My soul still flies above me for the quarry it shall find!

GOD

Gamaliel Bradford

Day and night I wander widely through the wilderness of
    thought,
Catching dainty things of fancy most reluctant to be caught,
Shining tangles leading nowhere persistently unravel,
Tread strange paths of meditation very intricate to travel.

Gleaming bits of quaint desire tempt my steps beyond the decent,
I confound old solid glory with publicity too recent.
But my one unchanged obsession, wheresoe'er my feet have trod,
Is a keen, enormous, haunting, never-sated thirst for God.

AN UNBELIEVER

Anna Hempstead Branch

All these on whom the sacred seal was set,
They could forsake thee while *thine* eyes were wet.
Brother, not once have I believed in thee,
Yet, having seen, I cannot once forget.

I have looked long into those friendly eyes,
And found thee dreaming, fragile and unwise.
Brother, not once have I believed in thee,
Yet have I loved thee for thy gracious lies.

One broke with thee a kiss at eventide,
And he that loved thee well has thrice denied.
Brother, I have no faith in thee at all,
Yet must I seek thy hands, thy feet, thy side.

Behold that John that leaned upon thy breast;
His eyes grew heavy and he needs must rest.
I watched unseen through dark Gethsemane
And might not slumber, for I loved thee best.

Peace thou wilt give to them of troubled mind,
Bread to the hungry, spittle to the blind.
My heart is broken for my unbelief,
But that thou canst not heal, though thou art kind.

They asked one day to sit beside thy throne;
I made one prayer, in silence and alone.
Brother, thou knowest my unbelief in thee.
Bear not my sins, for thou must bear thine own.

Even he that grieves thee most, "Lord, Lord," he saith,
So will I call on thee with my last breath!
Brother, not once have I believed in thee.
Yet I am wounded for thee unto death.

THE WILD KNIGHT

Gilbert K. Chesterton

Prologue

The wasting thistle whitens on my crest,
The barren grasses blow upon my spear,
A green pale pennon: blazon of my faith
And love of fruitless things: yea, of my love,
Among the golden loves of all the knights
Alone: most hopeless, sweet and blasphemous,
The love of God:

    I hear the crumbling creeds
Like cliffs, washed down by water, change and pass;
I hear a noise of words, age after age,
A new cold wind that blows across the plains,
And all the shrines stand empty; and to me
All these things are nothing: priests and schools may doubt
Who never have believed: but I have loved.
Ah, friends, I know it passing well, the love
Wherewith I love: it shall not bring to me
Return or hire or any pleasant thing—

Ay, I have tried it: Ay, I know its roots.
Earthquake and plague have burst on it in vain,
And rolled back shattered—

      Babbling neo-phytes!
Blind, startled fools—think you I know it not?
Think you to teach me? Know I not His ways?
Strange-visaged blunders—mystic cruelties;
All! all! I know Him for I love Him. Go!

So, with the wan waste grasses in my spear,
I ride forever, seeking after God.
My hair grows whiter than my thistle-plume,
And all my bones are loose; but in my eyes
The star of an unconquerable praise:
For in my soul one hope forever sings,
That at the next white corner of a road
My eyes may look on Him. . . .
      Hush—I shall know
The place where it is found: a twisted path
Under a twisted pear-tree—this I saw
In the first dream I had e'er I was born,
Wherein He spoke. . . .
      But the grey clouds come down
In hail upon the icy plains: I ride
Burning forever in consuming fire.

AT THE AQUARIUM

Max Eastman

Serene the silver fishes glide
Stern-lipped, and pale, and wonder-eyed!
As through the aged deeps of ocean,
They glide with wan and wavy motion!
They have no pathway where they go,
They flow like water to and fro.
They watch with never winking eyes,
They watch with staring, cold surprise,

The level people in the air,
The people peering, peering there;
They also wander to and fro,
And know not why or where they go,
Yet have a wonder in their eyes,
Sometimes a pale and cold surprise.

From THE RUBAIYAT

Omar Khayyam

Translated by Edward Fitzgerald

Myself when young did eagerly frequent
Doctor and Saint, and heard great argument
    About it and about: but evermore
Came out by the same door where in I went.

With them the seed of Wisdom did I sow,
And with mine own hand wrought to make it grow;
    And this was all the Harvest that I reaped—
"I came like Water, and like Wind I go."

Into this Universe and Why not Knowing
Nor Whence, like Water willy-nilly flowing;
    And out of it, as Wind along the Waste,
I know not Whither, willy-nilly blowing.

What, without asking, hither hurried Whence?
And, without asking, Whither hurried hence?
    Oh, many a Cup of this forbidden Wine
Must drown the memory of that insolence!

Up from Earth's Center, through the Seventh Gate
I rose, and on the Throne of Saturn sate,
    And many a Knot unravelled by the Road;
But not the Master Knot of Human Fate.

There was the Door to which I found no Key;
There was the Veil through which I might not see;
    Some little talk awhile of *Me* and *Thee*
There was—and then no more of *Thee* and *Me*.

Earth could not answer, nor the Seas that mourn
In flowing purple, of their lord forlorn;
    Nor rolling Heaven, with all his signs revealed
And hidden by the sleeve of Night and Morn.

Then of the *Thee in Me* who works behind
The Veil, I lifted up my hands to find
    A lamp amid the darkness; and I heard,
As from without—*"The Me within Thee blind."*

Then to the Lip of this poor earthen Urn
I leaned, the Secret of my Life to learn:
    And, Lip to Lip, it murmured—"While you live,
Drink!—for, once dead, you never shall return."

  .   .   .   .
I sent my soul through the Invisible
Some letter of that After-life to spell:
    And by and by my soul returned to me,
And answered, *"I Myself am Heaven and Hell."*

Heaven but the Vision of fulfilled Desire
And Hell the shadow of a Soul on fire
    Cast on the Darkness into which Ourselves
So late emerged from, shall so soon expire.

TO FINDE GOD

ROBERT HERRICK

Weigh me the fire; or canst thou find
A way to measure out the wind;
Distinguish all those floods that are
Mixt in that watrie theater;
And taste thou them as saltless there,
As in their channel first they were.

Tell me the peoples that do keep
Within the kingdomes of the deep;
Or fetch me back that cloud againe,
Beshivered into seeds of raine;
Tell me the motes, dust, sand and speares
Of corn, when summer shakes his eares;
Show me that world of stars, and whence
They noiseless spill their influence:
This if thou canst; then shew me Him
That rides the glorious *Cherubim!*

JOB'S COMFORTERS

Job XI, 7-8

From Moulton's *Modern Readers' Bible*

Canst thou by searching find out God?
Canst thou find out the Almighty unto perfection?
    It is as high as heaven;
    What canst thou do?
    Deeper than Sheol;
    What canst thou know?
    The measure thereof is longer than the earth,
    And broader than the sea.
    If he pass through, and shut up,
    And call unto judgment, then who can hinder him?

I WENT DOWN INTO THE DESERT
TO MEET ELIJAH

Vachel Lindsay

I went down into the desert
To meet Elijah
Arisen from the dead.
I thought to find him in an echoing cave,
For so my dream had said.

I went down into the desert
To meet John the Baptist,
I walked with feet that bled,
Seeking that prophet lean and brown and bold,
I spied the foul fiends instead.

I went down into the desert
To meet my God
By Him be comforted.
I went down into the desert
To meet my God
And I met the devil in red.

I went down into the desert
To meet my God
Oh, Lord, my God, awaken from the dead!
I see you there, your thorn crown on the ground,
I see you there half-buried in the sand;
I see you there, your white bones, glistening, bare,
The carrion-birds a-wheeling round your head.

MEDITATIONS OF A HINDU PRINCE

Sir Alfred Comyns Lyall

All over the world, I wonder, in lands that I never have trod,
Are the people eternally seeking for the signs and steps of a
      God?
Westward across the ocean, and northward ayont the snow,
Do they all stand gazing, as ever, and what do the wisest know?

Here in this mystical India, the deities hover and swarm,
Like wild bees heard in the tree tops, or the gusts of a gath-
      ering storm;
In the air men hear their voices, their feet on the rocks are
      seen
Yet we all say, "whence is the message, and what may the
      wonders mean?"

A million shrines stand open, and ever the censer swings,
As they bow to a mystic symbol or the figures of ancient kings,
And the incense rises ever, and rises the endless cry
Of those who are heavy laden, and of cowards loath to die.

For Destiny drives us together like deer in the pass of the hills;
Above is the sky, and around us the sound and shot that kills;
Pushed by a power we see not, and struck by a hand unknown,
We pray to the trees for shelter and press our lips to a stone.

The trees wave a shadowy answer and the rocks frown hollow
        and grim,
And the form and nod of a demon are caught in the twilight
        dim;
And we look at the sunlight falling afar on the mountain
        crest:—
Is there never a path runs upward to a refuge there and a rest?

The path, ah! who has shown it, and who is the faithful guide?
The haven, ah! who has known it? for steep is the mountain
        side,
Forever the shot strikes surely, and ever the wasted breath
Of the praying multitude rises, whose answer only is death.

Here are the tombs of my kinsfolk, the first of an ancient name,
Chiefs who were slain on the war-field, and women who died in
        flame;
They are gods, these kings of the foretime, they are spirits who
        guard our race;
Forever I watch and worship; they sit with a marble face.

And the myriad idols around me, and the legion of muttering
        priests,
The revels and rites unholy, the dark, unspeakable feasts!
What have they wrung from the Silence? Hath ever a whisper
        come
Of the secret? Whence and whither? Alas! for the gods are
        dumb.

Shall I list to the word of the English who come from the
    uttermost sea?
"The secret! Hath it been told you, and what is your message
    to me?"
It is naught but the world-wide story, how the heavens and
    earth began,
How the gods are glad and angry, and the Deity once was
    man.

I had thought "Perchance in the cities, where the rulers of
    India dwell,
Whose orders flash from the far land, who girdle the earth
    with a spell,
They have fathomed the depths we float on, they have meas·
    ur'd the unknown main."
Sadly they turn from the venture, and say that the quest is
    vain.

Is life, then, a dream and delusion, and where shall the dreamer
    awake?
Is the world seen like shadows on water? And what if the
    mirror break?
Shall it pass as a camp that is struck, as a tent that is gathered
    and gone?
From the sands that were lamp-lit at eve, and at morning are
    level and lone?

Is there naught in the heavens above, whence the rain and
    leaven are hurled
But the wind that is swept around us by the rush of the rolling
    world?
The wind that shall scatter my ashes, and bear me to silence
    and sleep
With the dirge, and the sound of lamenting and voices of
    women who weep?

THE SEEKERS

JOHN MASEFIELD

Friends and loves we have none, nor wealth nor blest abode,
But the hope of the City of God at the other end of the road.

Not for us are content, and quiet, and peace of mind,
For we go seeking a city that we shall never find.

There is no solace on earth for us—for such as we—
Who search for a hidden city that we shall never see.

Only the road and the dawn, the sun, the wind, and the rain,
And the watch fire under stars, and sleep, and the road again.

We seek the City of God, and the haunt where beauty dwells,
And we find the noisy mart and the sound of burial bells.

Never the golden city, where the radiant people meet,
But the dolorous town where mourners are ,going about the
     street.

We travel the dusty road till the light of the day is dim,
And sunset shows us spires away on the world's rim.

We travel from dawn to dusk, till the day is past and by,
Seeking the Holy City beyond the rim of the sky.

Friends and loves we have none, nor wealth nor blest abode,
But the hope of the City of God at the other end of the road.

THE MYSTIC

CALE YOUNG RICE

There is a quest that calls me
     In nights when I am lone,
The need to ride where the ways divide

The unknown from the known.
I mount what thought is near me
    And soon I reach the place,
The tenuous rim where the Seen grows dim
    And the Sightless hides its face.

> *I have ridden the wind,*
> *I have ridden the sea,*
> *I have ridden the moon and stars,*
> *I have set my feet in the stirrup seat*
> *Of a comet coursing Mars.*
> *And everywhere,*
> *Thro' earth and air*
> *My thought speeds, lightning-shod,*
> *It comes to a place where checking pace*
> *It cries, "Beyond lies God."*

It calls me out of the darkness,
    It calls me out of sleep,
"Ride, ride! for you must, to the end of Dust!"
    It bids—and on I sweep
To the wide outposts of Being
    Where there is Gulf alone—
And thro' a vast that was never passed
    I listen for Life's tone.

> *I have ridden the wind*
> *I have ridden the night,*
> *I have ridden the ghosts that flee*
> *From the vaults of death like a chilling breath*
> *Over eternity.*
> *And everywhere*
> *Is the world laid bare—*
> *Ether and star and clod—*
> *Until I wind to its brink and find*
> *But the cry, "Beyond lies God!"*

It calls me and ever calls me!
    And vainly I reply,
"Fools only ride where the ways divide
    What Is from the Whence and Why!"

I'm lifted into the saddle
  Of thoughts too strong to tame
And down the deeps and over the steeps
  I find—ever the same.

> *I have ridden the wind,*
> *I have ridden the stars*
> *I have ridden the force that flies*
> *With far intent through the firmament*
> *And each to each allies.*
> *And everywhere*
> *That a thought may dare*
> *To gallop, mine has trod—*
> *Only to stand at last on the strand*
> *Where just beyond lies God.*

THE SEEKERS

Victor Starbuck

One asked a sign from God; and day by day
The sun arose in pearl, in scarlet set,
Each night the stars appeared in bright array,
Each morn the thirsting grass with dew was wet.
The corn failed not its harvest, nor the vine.
And yet he saw no sign.

One longed to hear a prophet; and he strayed
Through crowded streets, and by the open sea.
He saw men send their ships for distant trade,
And build for generations yet to be.
He saw the farmer sow his acres wide,
But went unsatisfied.

One prayed a sight of heaven; and erewhile
He saw a workman at his noontime rest.
He saw one dare for honor, and the smile
Of one who held a babe upon her breast;
At dusk two lovers walking hand in hand;
But did not understand.

THE CATTLE OF HIS HAND

WILBUR UNDERWOOD

All night long, through the starlit air and the stillness,
Through the wanness of dawn and the burning of noontide,
Onward we strain with a mighty resounding of hoof-beats.

Heaven and earth are ashake with the terrible trampling;
Wild straying of feet of a vast and hastening army;
Wistful eyes that helplessly seek one another.

Hushed is the dark to hear the plaint of our lowing,
Mournful cry of the dumb-tired hearts within us,
Faint to death with thirst and the gnawing of hunger.

Day by day through the dust and the heat have we thirsted;
Day by day through stony ways have we hungered;
Naught but a few bitter herbs that grew by the wayside.

What we flee that is far behind in the darkness,
Where the place of abiding for us, we know not;
Only we hark for the voice of the Master Herdsman.

Many a weary day must pass ere we hear it,
Blown on the winds, now close, now far in the distance,
Deep as the void above us and sweet as the dawn-star.

He it is who drives us and urges us always,
Faint with a need that is ever present within us,
Struggling onward and toiling one by the other.

Ever we long and cry for rest, but it comes not;
Broke are our feet and sore and bruised by the climbing;
Sharp is his goad in our quivering flanks when we falter.

And some fall down with a plaintive moaning and perish;
But upward we strain nor stop, for the Voice comes to us,
Driving us on once more to the press and the struggle.

Then when we know His Presence the hard way lightens;
Turn we our piteous eyes to the far-stretching highway;
Struggle ahead in the dark as trusting as children.

What we flee that is far behind in the darkness,
Where the place of abiding for us, we know not;
Only we hark for the Voice—till hope fades from us.

Heaven and earth are ashake with the terrible trampling,
Wild straying feet of a vast and hastening army,
Wistful hearts that helplessly seek one another.

All night long through the star-lit air and the stillness,
Through the cool wanness of dawn and the burning of noontide,
Onward we strain with mighty resounding of hoof-beats.

c. THE SEARCH IS ITS OWN REWARD

A GRAMMARIAN'S FUNERAL

SHORTLY AFTER THE REVIVAL OF LEARNING IN EUROPE

ROBERT BROWNING

Let us begin and carry up this corpse,
　　Singing together.
Leave we the common crofts, the vulgar thorpes,
　　Each in its tether
Sleeping safe on the bosom of the plain,
　　Cared-for till cock-crow:
Look out if yonder be not day again
　　Rimming the rock-row!
That's the appropriate country; there, man's thought,
　　Rarer, intenser,
Self-gathered for an outbreak, as it ought,
　　Chafes in the censer.

.　　.　　.　　.　　.　　.　　.　　.　　.

Till lo, the little touch, and youth was gone!
　　Cramped and diminished,

Moaned he, "New measures, other feet anon!
    My dance is finished"?
No, that's the world's way: (keep the mountainside,
    Make for the city!)
He knew the signal, and stepped on with pride
    Over men's pity;
Left play for work, and grappled with the world
    Bent on escaping:
"What's in the scroll," quoth he, "thou keepest furled?
    Show me their shaping,
Theirs who most studied man, the bard and sage,—
    Give!"—So, he gowned him,
Straight got by heart that book to its last page:
    Learned, we found him.
Yea, but we found him bald too, eyes like lead,
    Accents uncertain:
"Time to taste life," another would have said,
    "Up with the curtain!"
This man said rather, "Actual life comes next?
    Patience a moment!
Grant I have mastered learning's crabbed text,
    Still there's the comment.
Let me know all! Prate not of most or least,
    Painful or easy!
Even to the crumbs I'd fain eat up the feast,
    Ay, nor feel queasy."
Oh, such a life as he resolved to live,
    When he had learned it,
When he had gathered all books had to give!
    Sooner, he spurned it.
Image the whole, then execute the parts—
    Fancy the fabric
Quite, ere you build, ere steel strike fire from quartz,
    Ere mortar dab brick!

(Here's the town-gate reached; there's the market-place
    Gaping before us.)
Yea, this in him was the peculiar grace
    (Hearten our chorus!)

That before living he'd learn how to live—
    No end to learning:
Earn the means first—God surely will contrive
    Use for our earning.
Others mistrust and say, "But time escapes!
    Live now or never!"
He said, "What's time? Leave Now for dogs and apes!
    Man has Forever."
Back to his book then: deeper drooped his head:
    Calculus racked him:
Leaden before, his eyes grew dross of lead:
    Tussis attacked him.
"Now, master, take a little rest!"—not he!
    (Caution redoubled,
Step two abreast, the way winds narrowly!)
    Not a whit troubled,
Back to his studies, fresher than at first,
    Fierce as a dragon
He (soul-hydroptic with a sacred thirst)
    Sucked at the flagon.
Oh, if we draw a circle premature,
    Heedless of far gain,
Greedy for quick returns of profit, sure
    Bad is our bargain!
Was it not great? did not he throw on God,
    (He loves the burthen)—
God's task to make the heavenly period
    Perfect the earthen?
Did not he magnify the mind, show clear
    Just what it all meant?
He would not discount life, as fools do here,
    Paid by instalment.
He ventured neck or nothing—heaven's success
    Found, or earth's failure:
"Wilt thou trust death or not?" He answered "Yes!
    Hence with life's pale lure!"
That low man seeks a little thing to do,
    Sees it and does it:
This high man, with a great thing to pursue,
    Dies ere he knows it.

That low man goes on adding one to one,
     His hundred's soon hit:
This high man, aiming at a million,
     Misses an unit.
That, has the world here—should he need the next,
     Let the world mind him!
This, throws himself on God, and unperplexed
     Seeking shall find Him.
So, with the throttling hands of death at strife,
     Ground he at grammar;
Still, thro' the rattle, parts of speech were rife:
     While he could stammer
He settled *Hoti's* business—let it be!—
     Properly based *Oun*—
Gave us the doctrine of the enclitic *De*,
     Dead from the waist down.
Well, here's the platform, here's the proper place:
     Hail to your purlieus,
All ye highfliers of the feathered race,
     Swallows and curlews:
Here's the top-peak; the multitude below
     Live, for they can, there:
This man decided not to Live but Know—
     Bury this man there?
Here—here's his place, where meteors shoot, clouds form,
     Lightnings are loosened,
Stars come and go! Let joy break with the storm,
     Peace let the dew send!
Lofty designs must close in like effects:
     Loftily lying,
Leave him—still loftier than the world suspects,
     Living and dying.

THE HIGHER CATECHISM

Sam Walter Foss

Let us ask ourselves some questions; for that man is truly wise
Who can make a catechism that will really catechise.
All can make a catechism,—none can keep it in repair.

Where's the workman can construct one that he'll guarantee
  will wear?
We are confronted from our birthday onward to the day we die
With a maximum of questions and a minimum reply.
So we make our catechism; but our work is never done—
For a father's catechism never fits a father's son.

What are we here for? That's the first one; that's the first
  we want to know.
We are here and all born little, just because we're here to
  grow.
What is sin? Why sin's not growing; all that stops the growth
  within,
Plagues the eternal upward impulse, stunts the spirit—that is
  sin.
Who are sinners? All are sinners; but this is no hopeless
  plaint,
For there never was a sinner who was not likewise a saint
What's the devil? A convenient but imagined elf
Each man builds to throw his sins on when he won't "own up"
  himself.

And where is hell? And where is heaven? In some vague
  distance dim?
No, they are here and now in you—in me, in her, in him.
When is the Judgment Day to dawn? Its true date who can
  say?
Look in your calendar and see what day it is today!
Today is always Judgment Day; and Conscience throned within
Brings up before its judgment seat each soul to face his sin.
We march to judgment, each along an uncompanioned way—
Stand up, man, and accuse yourself and meet your Judgment
  Day.

Where shall we get religion? Beneath the open sky,
The sphere of crystal silence surcharged with deity.
The winds blow from a thousand ways and waft their balms
  abroad,
The winds blow toward a million goals—but all winds blow
  from God.

The stars the old Chaldeans saw still weave their maze on
    high
And write a thousand thousand years their bible in the sky.
The midnight earth sends incense up sweet with the breath of
    prayer—
Go out beneath the naked night and get religion there.

Where shall we get religion? Beneath the blooming tree,
Beside the hill-encircling brooks that loiter to the sea,
Beside all twilight waters, beneath the noonday shades,
Beneath the dark cathedral pines and through the tangled
    glades;
Wherever the old urge of life provokes the dumb dead sod
To tell its thought in violets, the soul takes hold on God.
Go smell the growing clover, and scent the blooming pear,
Go forth to seek religion—and find it anywhere.

What is the church? The church is man when his awed soul
    goes out,
In reverence to a mystery that swathes him all about.
When any living man in awe gropes godward in his search;
Then in that hour, that living man becomes the living church,
Then, though in wilderness or in waste, his soul is swept along
Down naves of prayer, through aisles of praise, up altar-stairs
    of song.
And where man fronts the Mystery with spirit bowed in prayer,
There is the universal church—the church of God is there.

Where are the prophets of the soul? Where dwells the sacred
    clan?
Ah, they live in fields and cities, yea, wherever dwells a man,
Whether he prays in cloistered cell or delves the hillside
    clod,
Wherever beats the heart of man, there dwells a priest of
    God.
Who are the apostolic line? The men who hear a voice
Well from the soul within the soul that cries aloud, "Rejoice!"
Who listen to themselves and hear this world-old voice divine—
These are the lineage of seers, the apostolic line.

And what is faith? The anchored trust that at the core of
 things
Health, goodness, animating strength flow from exhaustless
 springs;
That no star rolls unguided down the rings of endless maze,
That no feet tread an aimless path through wastes of empty
 days;
That trusts the everlasting voice, the glad, calm voice that
 saith
That Order grows from Chaos, and that life is born from
 death;
That from the wreck of rendering stars behind the storm and
 scathe,
There dwells a heart of central calm;—and this, and this is
 faith.

What is the world's true Bible—'tis the highest thought of man,
The thought distilled through ages since the dawn of thought
 began.
And each age adds a word thereto, some psalm or promise
 sweet—
And the canon is unfinished and forever incomplete.
O'er the chapters that are written long and lovingly we pore—
But the best is yet unwritten, for we grow from more to more.

Let us heed the voice within us and its messages rehearse;
Let us build the growing Bible—for we too must write a verse.
What is the purport of the scheme toward which all time is
 gone?
What is the great æonian goal? The joy of going on.
And are there any souls so strong, such feet with swiftness
 shod,
That they shall reach it, reach some bourne, the ultimate of
 God?
There is no bourne, no ultimate. The very farthest star
But rims a sea of other stars that stretches just as far.
There's no beginning and no end. As in the ages gone,
The greatest joy of joys shall be the joy of going on.

THE MYSTERY

RALPH HODGSON

He came and took me by the hand
  Up to a red rose tree,
He kept His meaning to Himself,
  But gave a rose to me.

I did not pray Him to lay bare
  The mystery to me;
Enough the rose was heaven to smell,
  And His own face to see.

GRADATIM

JOSIAH GILBERT HOLLAND

Heaven is not reached by a single bound;
  But we build the ladder by which we rise
  From the lowly earth to the vaulted skies,
And we mount to its summit round by round.

I count this thing to be grandly true:
  That a noble deed is a step toward God,
  Lifting the soul from the common clod
To a purer air and a broader view.

We rise by the things that are under feet;
  By what we have mastered of good and gain;
  By the pride deposed and the passion slain,
And the vanquished ills that we hourly meet.

We hope, we aspire, we resolve, we trust,
  When the morning calls us to life and light,
  But our hearts grow weary, and, ere the night,
Our lives are trailing the sordid dust.

We hope, we resolve, we aspire, we pray,
  And we think that we mount the air on wings

Beyond the recall of sensual things,
While our feet still cling to the heavy clay.

Wings for angels but feet for men!
    We may borrow the wings to find the way—
    We may hope and resolve, and aspire, and pray;
But our feet must rise or we fall again.

Only in dreams is a ladder thrown
    From the weary earth to the sapphire walls;
    But the dreams depart, and the vision falls,
And the sleeper wakes on his pillow of stone

Heaven is not reached by a single bound;
    But we build the ladder by which we rise
    From the lowly earth to the vaulted skies,
And we mount to its summit, round by round.

VIA, VERITAS, ET VITA

Alice Meynell

"You never attained to Him."   "If to attain
Be to abide, then that may be."
"Endless the way, followed with how much pain."
"The way was *He*."

BEFORE DAY

Siegfried Sassoon

Come in this hour to set my spirit free
When earth is no more mine though night goes out
And stretching forth these arms I cannot be
Lord of winged sunrise and dim Arcady:
When fieldward boys far off with clack and shout
From orchards scare the birds in sudden rout,
Come, ere my heart grows cold and full of doubt
In the still summer dawns that waken me.

When the first lark goes up to look for day,
And morning glimmers out of dreams, come then,
Out of the songless valleys, over gray
Wide misty lands to bring me on my way:
For I am lone, a dweller among men,
Hungered for what my heart shall never say.

THE SEEKERS

CHARLES HAMILTON SORLEY

The gates are open on the road
That leads to beauty and to God.

Perhaps the gates are not so fair,
Nor quite so bright as once they were,
When God Himself on earth did stand
And gave to Abraham His hand
And led him to a better land.

For lo! the unclean walk therein,
And those that have been soiled with sin.
The publican and harlot pass
Along: they do not stain its grass.
In it the needy has his share,
In it the foolish do not err.
Yes, spurned and fool and sinner stray
Along the highway and the way.

And what if all its ways are trod
By those whom sin brings near to God?
This journey soon will make them clean:
Their faith is greater than their sin.

For still they travel slowly by
Beneath the promise of the sky,
Scorned and rejected utterly;
Unhonoured; things of little worth
Upon the highroads of this earth;

Afflicted, destitute and weak:
Nor find the beauty that they seek,
The God they set their trust upon:
—Yet still they march rejoicing on.

From MARLBOROUGH

CHARLES HAMILTON SORLEY

So, there, when sunset made the downs look new
    And earth gave up her colours to the sky,
And far away the little city grew
    Half into sight, new-visioned was my eye.

I, who have lived, and trod her lovely earth,
    Raced with her winds and listened to her birds,
Have cared but little for their worldy worth
    Nor sought to put my passion into words.

But now it's different; and I have no rest
    Because my hand must search, dissect and spell
The beauty that is better not expressed,
    The thing that all can feel, but none can tell.

EPIGRAM

WILLIAM WATSON

When whelmed are altar, priest and creed;
    When all the faiths are passed;
Perhaps from darkening incense freed,
    God may emerge at last.

III. THE EXISTENCE AND IDEA OF GOD

BRAHMA, THE WORLD IDEA

Rig-Veda, X, 129 (East Indian), 1500 B. C.

Not-Being was not, Being was not then,
  Air was not, nor sky beyond.
What was the covering—where, in whose ward?
  Was there water, deep, profound?

Death was not, nor deathlessness then,
  No token was there of night or day.
The One breathed windless, of its own power;
  Beyond this there was naught whatsoever.

Darkness there was, hidden in darkness, at first;
  This universe was a tokenless flood.
When the living was covered by the void,
  By the power of Heat was born the One.

Desire in the beginning came upon it,
  Which was the first seed of Thought.
The root of Being in Not-Being was found
  By sages tracing it with understanding in their hearts.

Was their line stretched out across,
  Or was it below, or was it above?
Sowers of seed there were, Powers there were,
  Potency beneath, Energy beyond.

Who knows in sooth, who may declare here,
  Whence this creation was born, whence it was?

The gods were later in the creating thereof;
　　So who knows whence it arose?

Whence this creation arose,
　　Whether He made it or not,
He who watches over it in the highest heaven
　　Knows indeed—or haply knows not.

PROOFS OF BUDDHA'S EXISTENCE

ANONYMOUS, Fourth Century B. C.

As men who see a city fitly planned
Infer the greatness of its architect,
So when the 'City of Good Law' is scanned
Work of the Blessed One can those who will detect.

As men who see the ocean rollers break
Infer the greatness of th' encompassing sea,
So may they judge of him whose teachings take
Throughout the listening world their course of victory.

Of him, the Victor who allays all grief
Who purged his heart of Tanha, seed of woe,
Well may the men to whom he brings relief
Cry, 'Great our Master, far his goodly precepts flow!'

As men who see far-off Himalaya's snows
Can judge the mountain-barrier's soaring height:
So they on whom the Teacher peace bestows
Behold the 'Mount of Dharma' gleaming clear and white,

Steadfast, unshaken, towering on high,
Unmoved by all the passion-blasts of lust,
In air serene, where ill and Karma die,
Infer 'How great the Hero in whose word we trust!'

As those who find some track of elephant
Infer the vastness of his kingly form,
So when they see the work of Bhagavant,
'How mighty,' cry they, 'was the Teacher of the Norm!'

As men behold the jungle-folk afraid
And know 'The King of beasts is surely near,'
So when false teachers fly, and are dismayed,
We judge ' 'Tis wisdom of the royal Sage they fear!'

And when the earth rejoices fresh and green,
'The gracious rain,' we say, 'hath come at last,'
So judge we, when the hearts of weary men
Rejoice, 'His gracious words into their lives have passed.'

Seeing the wide fields turned into a flood,
'Some mighty stream hath poured its waters here,'
Men cry: so judge they of the Law how good
It is, because they see men here and everywhere.

In the wide ocean of its waters pure,
Cleansed from the mud of sin and suffering.
As men who scent the fragrant air are sure
That the great forest trees hard-by are blossoming;

So, finding righteous actions wafting round
All sweet fragrance of their loveliness,
Men gladly sniff the air, and cries resound,
'Here surely lived a Buddha, Lord of Righteousness!'

*For Egyptian and Babylonian and Greek see Section VIIIa.
See also Sections II, III, V, VI, VIII, IX, XI, XII for Psalms.*

b. EARLY CHRISTIAN AND MEDIÆVAL

THE END OF BEING

SENECA, Fourth Century B. C.

Translated by H. C. Leonard.

The end of being is to find out God!
And what is God? A vast almighty Power
Great and unlimited, whose potent will
Brings to achievement whatsoe'er He please.

He is all mind. His being infinite—
All that we see and all that we do not see.
The Lord of heaven and earth, the God of Gods.
Without Him nothing is. Yet what He is
We know not! When we strive to comprehend
Our feeble guesses leave the most concealed.
To Him we owe all good we call our own.
To Him we live, to Him ourselves approve.
He is a friend forever at our side.
What cares He for the bleeding sacrifice?
O purge your hearts and lead the life of good!
Not in the pride of temples made with stone
His pleasure lies, but in the piety
Of consecrated hearts and lives devout.

THE LOVE OF GOD

BERNARD RASCAS

From the Provencal

Translated by William Cullen Bryant

All things that are on earth shall wholly pass away,
Except the love of God, which shall live and last for aye.
The forms of men shall be as they had never been;
The blasted groves shall lose their fresh and tender green;
The birds of the thicket shall end their pleasant song,
And the nightingale shall cease to chant the evening long.
The kine of the pasture shall feel the dart that kills,
And all the fair white flocks shall perish from the hills.
The goat and antlered stag, the wolf and the fox,
The wild boar of the wood, and the chamois of the rocks,
And the strong and fearless bear, in the trodden dust shall lie;
And the dolphin of the sea, and the mighty whale, shall die.
And realms shall be dissolved, and empires be no more,
And they shall bow to death, who ruled from shore to shore;
And the great globe itself, so the Holy Writings tell,

With the rolling firmament, where the starry armies dwell,
Shall melt with fervent heat,—they shall all pass away,
Except the love of God, which shall live and last for aye!

NOTE: Bernard Rascas was a Limousin poet who died in 1353.
He is said to have been kinsman of the popes Clement VI and
Innocent VI. He endowed the Hospital of St. Bernard, at Avignon.

THE UNITY OF GOD

PANATATTU, E. Indian, 10th Century A. D.

Into the bosom of the one great sea
Flow streams that come from hills on every side.
Their names are various as their springs.
And thus in every land do men bow down
To one great God, though known by many names.
This mighty Being we would worship now.

What though the six religions loudly shout
That each alone is true, all else are false?
Yet when in each the wise man worships God,
The great almighty *One* receives the prayer.

Oh Lord, when may I hope
To find the clue that leads
From out the labyrinth
Of brawling erring sects?

Six blind men once described an elephant
That stood before them all. One felt the back.
The second noticed pendent ears. The third
Could only find the tail. The beauteous tusks
Absorbed the admiration of the fourth.
While of the other two, one grasped the trunk.
The last sought for small things and found
Four thick and clumsy feet. From what each learned,
He drew the beast. Six monsters stood revealed.

Just so the six religions learned of God,
And tell their wondrous tales. Our God is one.

Men talk of penance, fastings, sacred streams—
Make pilgrimage to temples, offer gifts;
Performing to the letter all the rules
Of senseless complicated ritual.
Yet are they doomed to sorrow's deepest pain.
Oh, fling such things away and fix thy heart
On rest and peace to come. Seek that alone.

To them that fully know the heavenly truth,
There is no good or ill; nor anything
To be desired, unclean or purely clean.
To them there is no good can come from fast
Or penance pains. To them the earth has naught
For hope or fear, in thought or word or deed.

They hear the four great Vedas shout aloud
That he who has true wisdom in his heart
Can have no thought for fleeting worldly things.
Where God is seen, there can be naught but God.
His heart can have no place for fear or shame,
For caste, uncleanness, hate or wandering thought.
Impure and pure are all alike to him.

TRUE KNOWLEDGE

PANATATTU, E. Indian, 10th Century A. D.

My God is not a chiselled stone,
Or lime-block, so clear and bright:
Nor is he cleaned with tamarind,
Like images of bronze.

I cannot worship such as these,
But loudly make my boast
That in my heart I place the feet,
The golden feet of God.

If He be mine what can I need?
My God is everywhere!
Within, beyond man's highest word,
My God existeth still.

In sacred books, in darkest night,
In deepest, bluest sky,
In those who know the truth, and in
The faithful few on earth;—

My God is found in all of these,
But can the Deity
Descend to images of stone
Or copper dark or red?

Whene'er wind blows or compass points,
God's light doth stream and shine,
Yet see yon fool—beneath his arm
He bears the sacred roll.

How carefully he folds the page
And draws the closing string!
See how he binds the living book
That not a leaf escape!

Ah! Yes; the truth should fill his heart,
But 'tis beneath his arm.
To him who "knows," the sun is high;
To this, 'tis starless night.

If still, oh sinful man, with ash
Thou dost besmear thy face,
Or bathest oft, that thus thy soul
May cast away its load,

Thou knowest naught of God, nor of
Regeneration's work.
Your mantras, what are they? The Veds
Are burdened with their weight.

If knowledge be not thine, thou art
As one in deep mid-stream,
A stream so wide that both the banks
Are hidden from thine eyes.

Alas! How long did I adore
The chiselled stone, and serve
An image made of lime or brass
That's cleaned with tamarind.

See also the Hymns in Section VIII.

C. SIXTEENTH AND SEVENTEENTH CENTURIES

THE IMAGE OF GOD

FRANCESCO DE ALDANA (From the Spanish)
Translated by Henry W. Longfellow

O Lord! who seest from yon starry height,
Centred in one the future and the past,
Fashioned in thine own image, see how fast
The world obscures in me what once was bright!
Eternal sun! the warmth which thou hast given,
To cheer life's flowery April, fast decays;
Yet in the hoary winter of my days,
Forever green shall be my trust in heaven.
Celestial King! oh, let thy presence pass
Before my spirit, and an image fair
Shall meet that look of mercy from on high,
As the reflected image in a glass
Doth meet the look of him who seeks it there,
And owes its being to the gazer's eye.

THE PROTECTION OF JEHOVAH

PSALM XXIII

From Moulton's *Modern Readers' Bible*

The Lord is my shepherd;
I shall not want.

> He maketh me to lie down in green pastures:
> He leadeth me beside still waters.
> He restoreth my soul:
> He guideth me in paths of righteousness for his name's
> sake.

> Yea, though I walk through the valley of the shadow of
> death
> I will fear no evil;
> For thou art with me:
> Thy rod and thy staff, they comfort me.

> Thou preparest a table before me
> In the presence of mine enemies:
> Thou anointest my head with oil:
> My cup runneth over.

Surely goodness and mercy shall follow me all the days of my
life:
And I will dwell in the house of the Lord forever.

THE DELIVERANCE OF JEHOVAH

PSALM XXVII

From Moulton's *Modern Readers' Bible*

The Lord is my light and my salvation;
    Whom shall I fear?
The Lord is the strength of my life;
    Of whom shall I be afraid?

When evil-doers came upon me
   To eat up my flesh,
Even mine adversaries and my foes,
   They stumbled and fell.
Though an host should encamp against me,
   My heart shall not fear:
Though war should rise against me,
   Even then will I be confident.

One thing have I asked of the Lord,
   That will I seek after;
That I may dwell in the house of the Lord
   All the days of my life,
To behold the beauty of the Lord,
   And to inquire in his temple.
For in the day of trouble he shall keep me secretly in his
     pavilion,
   In the covert of his tabernacle shall he hide me;
He shall lift me up upon a rock.
   And now shall mine head be lifted up above mine
     enemies round about me;
I will offer in his tabernacle sacrifices of joy;
   I will sing, yea, I will sing praises unto the Lord.

   "Hear, O Lord, when I cry with my voice:
   Have mercy also upon me and answer me.
   "Seek ye my face"—
"My heart said unto thee, Thy face, Lord, will I seek.
Hide not thy face from me;
Put not thy servant away in anger.

"Thou hast been my help, cast me not off:
Neither forsake me, O God of my salvation.
When my father and my mother forsake me,
The Lord will take me up.

"Teach me thy way, O Lord,
And lead me in a plain path because of mine enemies;
Deliver me not over to the will of mine adversaries:
For false witnesses are risen up against me, and such as
   breathe out cruelty."

I had fainted, unless I had believed to see the goodness of the
     Lord
   In the land of the living.
Wait on the Lord: be strong and let thine heart take courage;
   Yea, wait thou on the Lord.

JEHOVAH'S IMMOVABLE THRONE

PSALM XCIII

The Lord reigneth; he is apparelled with majesty;
The Lord is apparelled, he hath girded himself with strength.
The world also is stablished, that it cannot be moved:
Thy throne is established of old: thou art from everlasting.

   The floods have lifted up, O LORD,
   The floods have lifted up their voice;
   The floods lift up their waves.

   Above the voices of many waters,
   The mighty breakers of the sea,
   The LORD on high is mighty.

Thy testimonies are very sure:
Holiness becometh thine house, O LORD, forevermore.

THE PLAN OF SALVATION

JOHN MILTON

From *Paradise Lost*, Bk. III
(Speech of the Almighty)

O thou in heaven and earth the only peace
Found out for mankind under wrath, O thou
My sole complacence! well thou know'st how dear
To me are all my works, nor man the least,
Though last created, that for him I spare

Thee from my bosom and right hand, to save,
By losing thee awhile, the whole race lost.
Thou therefore whom thou only can'st redeem
Their nature also to thy nature join;
And be thyself Man among men on earth,
Made flesh, when time shall be, of virgin seed,
By wondrous birth: be thou in Adam's room
The head of all mankind, though Adam's son.
As in him perish all men, so in thee,
As from a second root, shall be restored,
As many as are restored, without thee none.
His crime makes guilty all his sons; thy merit
Imputed shall absolve them who renounce
Their own both righteous and unrighteous deeds,
And live in thee transplanted, and from thee
Receive new life. So man, as is most just,
Shall satisfy for man, be judged and die;
And dying rise, and rising with him raise
His brethren, ransomed with his own dear life.
So heavenly love shall outdo hellish hate,
Giving to death, and dying to redeem,
So dearly to redeem what hellish hate
So easily destroyed, and still destroys
In those who, when they may, accept not grace.
Nor shalt thou by descending to assume
Man's nature lessen or degrade thine own.
Because thou hast, though throned in highest bliss
Equal to God, and equally enjoying
God-like fruition, quitted all to save
A world from utter loss, and hast been found
By merit more than birthright, Son of God,
Found worthiest to be so by being good,
Far more than great or high; because in thee
Love hath abounded more than glory abounds;
Therefore thy humiliation shall exalt
With thee thy manhood also to this throne;
Here shalt thou sit incarnate, here shalt reign
Both God and Man, Son both of God and Man,
Anointed universal king; all power
I give thee, reign for ever, and assume

Thy merits; under thee as head supreme
Thrones, Princedoms, Powers, Dominions, I reduce:
All knees to thee shall bow, of them that bide
In heaven, or earth, or under earth in hell.
When thou, attended gloriously from heaven,
Shalt in the sky appear, and from thee send
The summoning archangels to proclaim
Thy dread tribunal, forthwith from all winds
The living, and forthwith the cited dead
Of all past ages, to the general doom
Shall hasten, such a peal shall rouse their sleep.
Then, all thy saints assembled, thou shalt judge
Bad men and angels; they arraigned shall sink
Beneath thy sentence; hell, her numbers full,
Thenceforth shall be forever shut.   Meanwhile
The world shall burn, and from her ashes spring
New heaven and earth, wherein the just shall dwell,
And after all their tribulations long
See golden days, fruitful of golden deeds,
With joy and love triumphing, and fair truth:
Then thou thy regal sceptre shalt lay by,
For regal sceptre then no more shall need,
God shall be All in All. But all ye Gods
Adore Him, who to compass all this dies,
Adore the Son, and honour him as me.

From SONG TO DAVID

Christopher Smart

Tell them, I am, Jehovah said
To Moses; while earth heard in dread,
   And, smitten to the heart,
At once above, beneath, around,
All Nature, without voice or sound,
   Replied, O Lord, Thou art.

Thou art—to give and to confirm
For each his talent and his term;

All flesh thy bounties share:
Thou shalt not call thy brother fool;
The porches of the Christian school
    Are meekness, peace, and pray'r.

.   .   .   .

Sweet is the dew that falls betimes,
And drops upon the leafy limes;
    Sweet Hermon's fragrant air:
Sweet is the lily's silver bell,
And sweet the wakeful tapers' smell,
    That watch for early pray'r.

Sweet the young nurse with love intense,
Which smiles o'er sleeping innocence;
    Sweet when the lost arrive:
Sweet the musician's ardour beats,
While his vague mind's in quest of sweets
    The choicest flow'rs to hive.

Sweeter in all the strains of love,
The language of thy turtle dove,
    Pair'd to thy swelling chord;
Sweeter with ev'ry grace endued,
The glory of thy gratitude,
    Respir'd unto the Lord.

Strong is the lion—like a coal
His eye-ball—like a bastion's mole
    His chest against the foes:
Strong the gier-eagle on his sail,
Strong against tide, th' enormous whale
    Emerges, as he goes.

But stronger still, in earth and air,
And in the sea, the man of pray'r;
    And far beneath the tide;
And in the seat to faith assign'd,
Where ask is have, where seek is find,
    Where knock is open side.

Beauteous the fleet before the gale;
Beauteous the multitudes in mail,
    Rank'd arms and crested heads:
Beauteous the garden's umbrage mild—
Walk, water, meditated wild,
    And all the bloomy beds.

Beauteous the moon full on the lawn;
And beauteous, when the veil's withdrawn,
    The virgin to her spouse:
Beauteous the temple deck'd and fill'd,
When to the heav'n of heav'ns they build
    Their heart-directed vows.

Precious the penitential tear;
And precious is the sigh sincere,
    Acceptable to God:
And precious are the winning flow'rs,
In gladsome Israel's feast of bow'rs
    Bound on the hallow'd sod.

More precious that diviner part
Of David, ev'n the Lord's own heart,
    Great, beautiful, and new:
In all things where it was intent,
In all estreams, in each event,
    Proof—answ'ring true to true.

Glorious the sun in mid career,
Glorious th' assembled fires appear,
    Glorious the comet's train:
Glorious the trumpet and alarm,
Glorious th' Almighty's stretch'd-out arm,
    Glorious th' enraptur'd main:

Glorious the northern lights astream,
Glorious the song, when God's the theme,
    Glorious the thunder's roar:
Glorious hosanna from the den,
Glorious the Catholic amen,
    Glorious the martyr's gore:

Glorious—more glorious—is the crown
Of Him, that brought salvation down
 By meekness, call'd Thy Son;
Thou that stupendous truth believ'd;—
And now the matchless deed's achiev'd,
 Determin'd, dar'd, and done!

From AN HYMN OF HEAVENLY BEAUTY

Edmund Spenser

But whoso may, thrice happy man him hold
Of all on earth whom God so much doth grace
And lets his own Beloved to behold;
For in the view of her celestial face
All joy, all bliss, all happiness have place;
Ne ought on earth can want unto the wight
Who of herself can win the wishful sight.

For she out of her secret treasury,
Plenty of riches forth on him will pour,
Even heavenly riches, which there hidden lie
Within the closet of her chastest bower,
The eternal portion of her precious dower,
Which mighty God hath given to her free,
And to all those which thereof worthy be.

None thereof worthy be but those whom she
Vouchsafeth to her presence to receive,
And letteth them her lovely face to see,
Whereof such wondrous pleasure they conceive,
And sweet contentment, that it doth bereave
Their soul of sense, through infinite delight,
And them transport from flesh into the spright.

In which they see such admirable things
As carries them into ecstasy,
And hear such heavenly notes and carollings
Of God's high praise, that fills the brazen sky;

And feel such joy and pleasure inwardly
That maketh them all worldly cares forget,
And only think on that before them set.

. . . .

Ah, then, my hungry soul! which long hast fed
On idle fancies of thy foolish thought,
And, with false beauties' flattering bait misled,
Hast after vain deceitful shadows sought,
Which all are fled, and now have left thee nought
But late repentance through thy folly's prief;
Ah! cease to gaze on matter of thy grief.

And look at last up to that sovereign Light,
From whose pure beams all perfect beauty springs,
That kindleth love in every godly spright,
Even the Love of God; which loathing brings
Of this vile world and these gay-seeming things;
With whose sweet pleasures being so possessed,
Thy straying thoughts henceforth forever rest.

THE MAJESTY OF GOD

Thomas Sternhold

The Lord descended from above,
    And bowed the heavens most high,
And underneath his feet he cast
    The darkness of the sky.

On Cherubim and Seraphim
    Full royally he rode,
On the wings of mighty winds
    Came flying all abroad.

He sat serene upon the floods,
    Their fury to restrain;
And he, as sovereign Lord and King
    Forevermore shall reign.

RELIGIOUS MUSINGS

SAMUEL TAYLOR COLERIDGE

I

There is one Mind, one omnipresent Mind,
Omnific. His most holy name is Love.
Truth of subliming import! With the which
Who feeds and saturates his constant soul,
He from his small particular orbit flies,
With blest outstarting! from Himself he flies,
Stands in the Sun, and with no partial gaze
Views all creation; and he loves it all,
And blesses it, and calls it very good!
This is indeed to dwell with the Most High!
Cherubs and rapture—trembling Seraphim
Can press no nearer to the Almighty's throne.
But that we roam unconscious, or with hearts
Unfeeling of our universal Sire,
And that in His vast family no Cain
Injures uninjured (in her best-aimed blow
Victorious Murder a blind Suicide)
Haply for this some younger Angel now
Looks down on Human Nature: and behold!
A sea of blood bestrewed with wrecks, where mad
Embattling Interests on each other rush
With unhelmed Rage!
        'Tis the sublime of man
Our noontide majesty, to know ourselves
Parts and proportions of one wondrous whole!
This fraternizes man, this constitutes
Our charities and bearings. But 'tis God
Diffused through all that doth make all one whole;
Aught to desire, Supreme Reality!
The plentitude and permanence of bliss!

II

Toy-bewitched,
Made blind by lusts, disinherited of soul,
No common center Man, no common sire
Knoweth! A sordid solitary thing,
Mid countless brethren, with a lonely heart
Through courts and cities the smooth savage roams
Feeling himself, his own low self, the whole;
When by sacred sympathy might make
The whole one Self! Self, that no alien knows!
Self, far-diffused as fancy's wing can travel!
Self, spreading still! Oblivious of its own,
Yet all of all possessing! That is Faith!
'Tis the Messiah's destined victory.

From RELIGIO LAICI

John Dryden

. . . .

Thus man by his own strength to Heaven would soar
And would not be obliged to God for more.
Vain, wretched creature, how thou art misled,
To think thy wit these God-like notions bred!
These truths are not the product of thy mind,
But dropp'd from heaven, and of a nobler kind.
Revealed religion first informed thy sight,
And reason saw not till faith sprung the light.
Hence all thy natural worship takes the source:
'Tis Revelation what thou think't Discourse.
Else how com'st thou to see these truths so clear,
Which so, obscure to heathens did appear?
Not Plato these, nor Aristotle found:
Not he whose wisdom oracles renowned.
Hast thou a wit so deep, or so sublime,
Or canst thou lower dive, or higher climb?
Canst thou by reason more of Godhead know
Than Plutarch, Seneca or Cicero?

Those giant wits in happier ages born,
When arms and arts did Greece and Rome adorn,
Knew no such system; no such piles could raise
Of natural worship, built on prayer and praise.
To one sole GOD:
Nor did remorse to expiate sin prescribe,
But slew their fellow-creatures for a bribe:
The guiltless victim groaned for their offence,
And cruelty and blood was penitence.
If sheep and oxen could atone for men,
Ah! at how cheap a rate the rich might sin!
And great oppressors might heaven's wrath beguile
By offering his own creatures for a spoil!
    Darest thou, poor worm, offend Infinity?
And must the terms of peace be given by Thee?
Then thou art Justice in the last appeal;
Thy easy God instructs thee to rebel:
And, like a king remote, and weak, must take
What satisfaction thou art pleased to make.
    But if there be a Power too just and strong
To wink at crimes and hear unpunished wrong,
Look humbly upward, see his will disclose
The forfeit first and then the fine impose:
A mulct thy poverty could never pay,
Had not Eternal Wisdom found the way:
And with celestial wealth supplied thy store:
His justice makes the fine, His mercy quits the score.
See God descending in thy human frame;
The Offended suffering in the offender's name:
All thy deeds to Him imputed see,
And all His righteousness devolved on Thee.

    .   .   .   .   ·   ·   ·   s

Proof needs not here; for whether we compare
The impious, idle, superstitious ware
Of rites, lustrations, offerings, which before,
In various ages, various countries bore,
With Christian Faith and Virtues, we shall find
None answering the great needs of human kind,
But his one rule of life; that shows us best
How God may be appeased and mortals blest.

Whether from length of time its worth we draw,
The world is scarce more ancient than the law:
Heaven's early care prescribed for every age;
First, in the soul, and after, in the page,
Or, whether more abstractedly we look,
Or in the writers, or in the written book,
Whence, but from heaven could men, unskilled in arts,
In several ages born, in several parts,
Weave such agreeing truths? or how, or why
Should all conspire to cheat us with a lie?
Unasked their pains, ungrateful their advice,
Starving their gain, and martyrdom their price.
       If on the Book itself we cast our view,
Concurrent, heathens prove the story true:
The doctrine, miracles; which must convince,
For Heaven in them appeals to human sense;
And though they prove not, they confirm the cause,
When what is taught agrees with Nature's laws.
       Then for the style, majestic and divine,
It speaks no less than God in every line:
Commanding words; whose force is still the same
As the first fiat that produced our frame.
All faiths aside or did by arms ascend,
Or, sense indulged, has made mankind their friend:
This only doctrine does our lusts oppose—
Unfed by nature's soil, in which it grows;
Cross to our interests, curbing sense and sin;
Oppressed without, and undermined within,
It thrives through pain; its own tormentors tires;
And with a stubborn patience still aspires,
To what can Reason such affects assign,
Transcending Nature, but to laws divine?
Which in that sacred volume are contained;
Sufficient, clear, and for that use ordained.

THE MAJESTY AND MERCY OF GOD

Sir Robert Grant

Oh, worship the King all glorious above;
Oh, gratefully sing his power and his love;
Our shield and defender, the Ancient of Days
Pavilioned in splendor and girded with praise.

Oh, tell of his might, Oh, sing of his grace,
Whose robe is the light, whose canopy space;
His chariots of wrath the deep thunder clouds form,
And dark is his path on the wings of the storm.

The earth, with its store of wonders untold,
Almighty, thy power hath founded of old,
Hath stablished it fast by a changeless decree,
And round it hath cast, like a mantle, the sea.

Thy bountiful care what tongue can recite?
It breathes in the air, it shines in the light,
It streams from the hills, it descends to the plain,
And sweetly distills in the dew and the rain.

Frail children of dust and feeble as frail
In thee do we trust, nor find thee to fail.
Thy mercies how tender, how firm to the end,
Our Maker, Defender, Redeemer and Friend.

Oh, measureless Might, ineffable Love,
While angels delight to hymn thee above,
The humbler creation, though feeble their lays,
With true adoration shall lisp to thy praise.

From THE ESSAY ON MAN

ALEXANDER POPE

All are but parts of one stupendous whole,
Whose body Nature is, and God the soul;
That, changed through all, and yet in all the same,
Great in the earth, as in th'ethereal frame,
Warms in the sun, refreshes in the breeze,
Glows in the stars and blossoms in the trees,
Lives through life, extends through all extent,
Spreads undivided, operates unspent:
Breathes in our soul, informs our mortal part;
As full, as perfect, in a hair as heart;
As full, as perfect, in vile man that mourns
As the rapt Seraphim, that adores and burns:
To him, no high, no low, no great, no small—
He fills, he bounds, connects and equals all . . .
All nature is but art, unknown to thee:
All chance, direction, which thou canst not see:
All discord, harmony not understood;
All partial evil, universal good.

e. NINETEENTH CENTURY

From AURORA LEIGH

ELIZABETH BARRETT BROWNING

Truth, so far, in my book;—the truth which draws
Through all things upwards,—that a twofold world
Must go to a perfect cosmos. Natural things
And spiritual,—who separates those two
In art, in morals, or the social drift,
Tears up the bond of nature and brings death,
Paints futile pictures, writes unreal verse,

Leads vulgar days, deals ignorantly with men,
Is wrong, in short, at all points. We divide
This apple of life, and cut it through the pips:—
The perfect round which fitted Venus' hand
Has perished as utterly as if we ate
Both halves. Without the spiritual, observe,
The natural's impossible,—no form,
No motion: without sensuous, spiritual
Is inappreciable,—no beauty or power:
And in this twofold sphere the twofold man
(For still the artist is intensely a man)
Holds firmly by the natural, to reach
The spiritual beyond it,—fixes still
The type with mortal vision, to pierce through,
With eyes immortal, to the antetype
Some call the ideal,—better called the real.
And certain to be called so presently,
When things shall have their names. Look long enough
On any peasant's face here, coarse and lined,
You'll catch Antinous somewhere in that clay,
As perfect-featured as he yearns at Rome
From marble pale with beauty; then persist,
And, if your apprehension's competent,
You'll find some fairer angel at his back,
As much exceeding him as he the boor,
And pushing him with empyreal disdain
For ever out of sight. Aye, Carrington
Is glad of such a creed: an artist must,
Who paints a tree, a leaf, a common stone
With just his hand, and finds it suddenly
A-piece with and conterminous to his soul.
Why else do these things move him,—leaf or stone?
The bird's not moved, that pecks at a spring shoot:
Nor yet the horse, before a quarry a-graze:
But man, the twofold creature, apprehends
The twofold manner, in and outwardly,
And nothing in the world comes single to him,
A mere itself,—cup, column or candlestick,
All patterns of what shall be in the Mount;
The whole temporal show related royally,

And built up to eterne significance
Through the open arms of God. "There's nothing great
Nor small," has said a poet of our day,
Whose voice will ring beyond the curfew of eve
And not be thrown out by the matin's bell;
And truly, I reiterate, nothing's small!
No lily-muffled hum of a summer bee,
But finds some coupling with the spinning stars;
No pebble at your foot, but proves a sphere;
No chaffinch, but implies the cherubim;
And (glancing on my own thin, veinèd wrist)
In such a little tremor of the blood
The whole strong clamor of a vehement soul
Doth utter itself distinct. Earth's crammed with heaven
And every common bush afire with God;
But only he who sees takes off his shoes,
The rest sit round it and pluck blackberries,
And daub their natural faces unaware
More and more from the first similitude.

ABT VOGLER

Robert Browning

Would that the structure brave, the manifold music I build,
  Bidding my organ obey, calling its keys to their work,
Claiming each slave of the sound, at a touch, as when Solomon
    willed
  Armies of angels that soar, legions of demons that lurk,
Man, brute, reptile, fly,—alien of end and of aim,
  Adverse, each from the other heaven-high, heel-deep
      removed—
Should rush into sight at once as he named the ineffable Name,
And pile him a palace straight, to pleasure the princess he loved.

Would it might tarry like his, the beautiful building of mine,
  This which my keys in a crowd pressed and importuned to
      raise!
Ah, one and all, how they helped, would dispart now and now
    combine,

Zealous to hasten the work, heighten their master his praise!
And one would bury his brow with a blind plunge down to hell,
Burrow awhile and build, broad on the roots of things,
Then up again swim into sight, having based me my palace well,
Founded it, fearless of flame, flat on the nether springs.

And another would mount and march, like the excellent minion
he was,
Ay, another and yet another, one crowd but with many a
crest,
Raising my rampired walls of gold as transparent as glass,
Eager to do and die, yield each his place to the rest:
For higher still and higher (as a runner tips with fire,
When a great illumination surprises a festal night—
Outlined round and round Rome's dome from space to spire)
Up, the pinnacled glory reached, and the pride of my soul
was in sight.

In sight? Not half! for it seemed, it was certain, to match
man's birth,
Nature in turn conceived, obeying an impulse as I;
And the emulous heaven yearned down, made effort to reach
the earth,
As the earth had done her best, in my passion, to scale the
sky:
Novel splendors burst forth, grew familiar and dwelt with mine,
Not a point nor peak but found and fixed its wandering star;
Meteor-moons, balls of blaze: and they did not pale nor pine,
For earth had attained to heaven, there was no more near
nor far.

Nay more; for there wanted not who walked in the glare and
glow,
Presences plain in the place; or, fresh from the Protoplast,
Furnished for ages to come, when a kindlier wind should blow,
Lured now, to begin and live, in a house to their liking at
last;
Or else the wonderful Dead who have passed through the body
and gone,
But were back once more to breathe in an old world worth
their new:

What never had been, was now; what was, as it shall be anon;
  And what is,—shall I say, matched both? for I was made
    perfect too.

All thro' my keys that gave their sounds to a wish of my soul,
  All thro' my soul that praised as its wish flowed visibly forth,
All thro' music and me! For think, had I painted the whole,
  Why, there it had stood, to see, nor the process so wonder-
    worth:
Had I written the same, made verse—still, effect proceeds from
  cause,
  Ye know why the forms are fair, ye hear how the tale is
    told:
It is all triumphant art, but art in obedience to laws,
  Painter and poet are proud, in the artist-list enrolled:—

But here is the finger of God, a flash of the will that can,
  Existent behind all laws, that made them, and lo, they are!
And I know not if, save in this, such gift be allowed to man,
  That out of three sounds he frame, not a fourth sound, but
    a star.
Consider it well: each tone of our scale in itself is naught:
  It is everywhere in the world—loud, soft, and all is said:
Give it to me to use! I mix it with two in my thought:
  And, there! Ye have heard and seen: consider and bow
    the head!

Well, it is gone at last, the palace of music I reared;
  Gone! and the good tears start, the praises that come too
    slow;
For one is assured at first, one scarce can say that he feared,
  That he even gave it a thought, the gone thing was to go.
Never to be again! But many more of the kind
  As good, nay, better perchance: is this your comfort to me?
To me, who must be saved because I cling with my mind
  To the same, same self, same love, same God: ay, what was
    shall be.

Therefore to whom turn I but to thee, the ineffable Name?
  Builder and maker, Thou, of houses not made with hands!

What, have fear of change from Thee who art ever the same?
　Doubt that Thy power can fill the heart that Thy power
　　expands?
There shall never be one lost good! What was, shall live as
　before;
　The evil is null, is naught, is silence implying sound;
What was good shall be good, with, for evil, so much good
　more;
　On the earth the broken arcs; in the heaven a perfect
　round.

All we have willed or hoped or dreamed of good shall exist;
　Not its semblance but itself; no beauty, nor good nor power
Whose voice has gone forth, but each survives for the melodist
　When eternity affirms the conception of an hour.
The high that proved too high, the heroic for earth too hard,
　The passion that left the ground to lose itself in the sky,
Are music sent up to God by the lover and the bard;
　Enough that he heard it once; we shall hear it by and by.

And what is our failure here but a triumph's evidence
　For the fulness of the days? Have we withered or agonized?
Why else was the pause prolonged but that singing might issue
　thence?
　Why rushed the discords in but that harmony should be
　prized?
Sorrow is hard to bear, and doubt is slow to clear,
　Each sufferer says his say, his scheme of the weal and woe:
But God has a few of us whom he whispers in the ear;
　The rest may reason and welcome; 'tis we musicians know.

Well, it is earth with me; silence resumes her reign:
　I will be patient and proud, and soberly acquiesce.
Give me the keys. I feel for the common chord again,
　Sliding by semi-tones till I sink to a minor,—yes,
And I blunt it into a ninth, and I stand on alien ground,
　Surveying a while the heights I rolled from into the deep;
Which, hark, I have dared and done, for my resting-place is
　found,
　The C Major of this life: so, now I will try to sleep.

CALIBAN UPON SETEBOS

or

NATURAL THEOLOGY IN THE ISLAND

ROBERT BROWNING

"Thou thoughtest that I was altogether such an one as thyself."

['Will sprawl, now that the heat of day is best,
Flat on his belly in the pit's much mire,
With elbows wide, fists clenched to prop his chin.
And, while he kicks both feet in the cool slush,
And feels about his spine small eft-things course,
Run in and out each arm, and make him laugh:
And while above his head a pompion-plant,
Coating the cave-top as a brow its eye,
Creeps down to touch and tickle hair and beard,
And now a flower drops with a bee inside,
And now a fruit to snap at, catch and crunch,—
He looks out o'er yon sea which sunbeams cross
And recross till they weave a spider web,
(Meshes of fire, some great fish breaks at times)
And talks to his own self, howe'er he please,
Touching that other, whom his dam called God.
Because to talk about Him, vexes—ha,
Could He but know! and time to vex is now,
When talk is safer than in winter-time.
Moreover Prosper and Miranda sleep
In confidence he drudges at their task,
And it is good to cheat the pair, and gibe,
Letting the rank tongue blossom into speech.]

    Setebos, Setebos, and Setebos!
'Thinketh, He dwelleth i' the cold o' the moon.

    'Thinketh He made it, with the sun to match,
But not the stars; the stars came otherwise;
Only made clouds, winds, meteors, such as that:

Also this isle, what lives and grows thereon,
And snaky sea which rounds and ends the same.
'Thinketh, it came of being ill at ease:
He hated that He cannot change His cold,
Nor cure its ache. 'Hath spied an icy fish
That longed to 'scape the rock-stream where she lived,
And thaw herself within the lukewarm brine
O' the lazy sea her stream thrusts far amid,
A crystal spike 'twixt two warm walls of wave;
Only, she ever sickened, found repulse
At the other kind of water, not her life,
(Green-dense and dim-delicious, bred o' the sun)
Flounced back from bliss she was not born to breathe,
And in her old bounds buried her despair,
Hating and loving warmth alike: so He.

'Thinketh, He made thereat the sun, this isle,
Trees and the fowls here, beast and creeping thing.
Yon otter, sleek-wet, black, lithe as a leech;
Yon auk, one fire-eye in a ball of foam,
That floats and feeds; a certain badger brown,
He hath watched hunt with that slant white-wedge eye
By moonlight; and the pie with the long tongue
That pricks deep into oakwarts for a worm,
And says a plain word when she finds her prize,
But will not eat the ants; the ants themselves
That build a wall of seeds and settled stalks
About their hole—He made all these and more,
Made all we see, and us, in spite: how else?
He could not, Himself, make a second self
To be His mate: as well have made Himself:
He would not make what He mislikes or slights,
An eyesore to Him, or not worth His pains;
But did, in envy, listlessness, or sport,
Make what Himself would fain, in a manner, be—
Weaker in most points, stronger in a few,
Worthy, and yet mere playthings all the while,
Things He admires and mocks too,—that is it!
Because, so brave, so better tho' they be,
It nothing skills if He begin to plague.

Look now, I melt a gourd-fruit into mash,
Add honeycomb and pods, I have perceived,
Which bite like finches when they bill and kiss,—
Then, when froth rises bladdery, drink up all,
Quick, quick, till maggots scamper thro' my brain;
Last, throw me on my back i' the seeded thyme,
And wanton, wishing I were born a bird.
Put case, unable to be what I wish,
I yet could make a live bird out of clay:
Would not I take clay, pinch my Caliban
Able to fly?—for there, see, he hath wings,
And great comb like the hoopoe's to admire,
And there, a sting to do his foes offence,
There, and I will that he begin to live,
Fly to yon rock-top, nip me off the horns
Of grigs high up that make the merry din,
Saucy thro' their veined wings, and mind me not.
In which feat, if his leg snapped, brittle clay,
And he lay stupid-like,—why, I should laugh;
And if he, spying me, should fall to weep,
Beseech me to be good, repair his wrong,
Bid his poor leg smart less or grow again,—
Well, as the chance were, this might take or else
Not take my fancy: I might hear his cry,
And give the mankin three sound legs for one,
Or pluck the other off, leave him like an egg,
And lessoned he was mine and merely clay.
Were this no pleasure, lying in the thyme,
Drinking the mash, with brain become alive,
Making and marring clay at will? So He.

'Thinketh such shows nor right nor wrong in Him,
Nor kind, nor cruel: He is strong and Lord.
'Am strong myself compared to yonder crabs
That march now from the mountain to the sea;
'Let twenty pass, and stone the twenty-first,
Loving not, hating not, just choosing so.
'Say, the first straggler that boasts purple spots
Shall join the file, one pincer twisted off;
'Say, this bruised fellow shall receive a worm.

And two worms he whose nippers end in red:
As it likes me each time, I do: so He.

Well then, 'supposeth He is good i' the main,
Placable if His mind and ways were guessed,
But rougher than His handiwork, be sure!
Oh, He hath made things worthier than Himself,
And envieth that, so helped, such things do more
Than He who made them! What consoles but this?
That they, unless thro' Him, do naught at all,
And must submit: what other use in things?
'Hath cut a pipe of pithless elder-joint
That, blown through, gives exact the scream o' the jay
When from her wing you twitch the feathers blue:
Sound this, and little birds that hate the jay
Flock within stone's throw, glad their foe is hurt:
Put case such pipe could prattle and boast forsooth
"I catch the birds, I am the crafty thing,
I make the cry my maker cannot make
With his great round mouth; he must blow thro' mine!"
Would not I smash it with my foot? So He.

But wherefore rough, why cold and ill at ease?
Aha, that is a question! Ask, for that,
What knows,—the something over Setebos
That made Him, or He, may be, found and fought,
Worsted, drove off and did to nothing, perchance.
There may be something quiet o'er His head,
Out of His reach, that feels nor joy nor grief,
Since both derive from weakness in some way.
I joy because the quails come; would not joy
Could I bring quails here when I have a mind:
This Quiet, all it hath a mind to, doth.
'Esteemeth stars the outposts of its couch,
But never spends much thought nor care that way.
It may look up, work up,—the worse for those
It works on! 'Careth but for Setebos
The many-handed as a cuttle-fish,
Who, making Himself feared thro' what He does,
Looks up, first, and perceives he cannot soar

To what is quiet and hath happy life;
Next looks down here, and out of very spite
Makes this a bauble-world to ape yon real,
These good things to match those as hips do grapes.
'Tis solace making baubles, ay, and sport.
Himself peeped late, eyed Prosper at his books
Careless and lofty, lord now of the isle:
Vexed, 'stitched a book of broad leaves, arrow-shaped
Wrote thereon, he knows what, prodigious words;
Has peeled a wand and called it by a name;
Weareth at whiles for an enchanter's robe
The eyed skin of a supple oncelot;
And hath an ounce sleeker than youngling mole,
A four-legged serpent he makes cower and couch,
Now snarl, now hold its breath and mind his eye,
And saith she is Miranda and my wife:
'Keeps for his Ariel a tall pouch-bill crane
He bids go wade for fish and straight disgorge;
Also a sea-beast, lumpish, which he snared,
Blinded the eyes of, and brought somewhat tame,
And split its toe-webs, and now pens the drudge
In a hole o' the rock, and calls him Caliban;
A bitter heart that bides its time and bites.
'Plays thus at being Prosper in a way,
Taketh his mirth with make-believes: so He.

His dam held that the Quiet made all things
Which Setebos vexed only: 'holds not so.
Who made them weak, meant weakness He might vex.
Had He meant other, while His hand was in,
Why not make horny eyes no thorn could prick,
Or plate my scalp with bone against the snow,
Or overscale my flesh 'neath joint and joint,
Like an orc's armour? Ay,—so spoil His sport!
He is the One now: only He doth all.

'Saith, He may like, perchance, what profits Him.
Ay, himself loves what does him good; but why?
'Gets good no otherwise. This blinded beast
Loves whoso places flesh-meat on his nose.

But, had he eyes, would want no help, but hate
Or love, just as it liked him: He hath eyes.
Also it pleaseth Setebos to work,
Use all His hands, and exercise much craft,
By no means for the love of what is worked.
'Tasteth, himself, no finer good i' the world
When all goes right, in this safe summer-time,
And he wants little, hungers, aches not much,
Than trying what to do with wit and strength.
'Falls to make something; 'piled yon pile of turfs,
And squared and stuck there squares of soft white chalk.
And, with a fish-tooth, scratched a moon on each,
And set up endwise certain spikes of tree,
And crowned the whole with a sloth's skull a-top,
Found dead i' the woods, too hard for one to kill.
No use at all i' the work, for work's sole sake;
'Shall some day knock it down again: so He.

'Saith He is terrible: watch His feats in proof!
One hurricane will spoil six good months' hope.
He hath a spite against me, that I know.
Just as He favours Prosper, who knows why?
So it is, all the same, as well I find.
'Wove wattles half the winter, fenced them firm
With stone and stake to stop she-tortoises
Crawling to lay their eggs here: well, one wave,
Feeling the foot of Him upon its neck,
Gaped as a snake does, lolled out its large tongue,
And licked the whole labour flat; so much for spite!
'Saw a ball flame down late (yonder it lies)
Where, half an hour before, I slept i' the shade:
Often they scatter sparkles: there is force!
'Dug up a newt He may have envied once
And turned to stone, shut up inside a stone.
Please Him and hinder this?—What Prosper does?
Aha, if he would tell me how. Not he!
There is the sport: discover how or die!
All need not die, for of the things o' the isle
Some flee afar, some dive, some run up trees;
Those at His mercy,—why, they please Him most

When . . . when . . . well, never try the same way twice!
Repeat what act has pleased, He may grow wroth.
You must not know His ways, and play Him off,
Sure of the issue. 'Doth the like himself:
'Spareth a squirrel that it nothing fears
But steals the nut from underneath my thumb,
And when I threat, bites stoutly in defence:
'Spareth an urchin that contrariwise,
Curls up into a ball, pretending death
For fright at my approach: the two ways please.
But what would move my choler more than this,
That either creature counted on its life
Tomorrow, next day and all days to come,
Saying forsooth in the inmost of its heart,
"Because he did so yesterday with me,
And otherwise with such another brute,
So must he do henceforth and always." Ay?
'Would teach the reasoning couple what "must" means!
'Doth as he likes, or wherefore Lord? So He.

'Conceiveth all things will continue thus,
And we shall have to live in fear of Him
So long as He lives, keeps His strength: no change,
If He have done His best, make no new world
To please Him more, so leave off watching this,—
If He surprise not even the Quiet's self
Some strange day,—or, suppose, grow into it
As grubs grow butterflies: else, here are we,
And there is He, and nowhere help at all.

'Believeth with the life the pain shall stop.
His dam held different, that after death
He both plagued enemies and feasted friends:
Idly! He doth His worst in this our life,
Giving just respite lest we die thro' pain,
Saving last pain for worst,—with which, an end.
Meanwhile, the best way to escape His ire
Is, not to seem too happy. 'Sees, himself,
Yonder two flies, with purple films and pink,
Bask on the pompion-bell above: kills both.

'Sees two black painful beetles roll their ball
On head and tail as if to save their lives:
'Moves them the stick away they strive to clear.

Even so, 'would have him misconceive, suppose
This Caliban strives hard and ails no less,
And always, above all else, envies Him;
Wherefore he mainly dances on dark nights,
Moans in the sun, gets under holes to laugh,
And never speaks his mind save housed as now:
Outside, 'groans, curses. If He caught me here,
O'erheard this speech, and asked "What chucklest at?"
'Would to appease Him, cut a finger off,
Or of my three kid yearlings burn the best,
Or let the toothsome apples rot on tree,
Or push my tame beast for the orc to taste:
While myself lit a fire, and made a song
And sung it, *"What I hate, be consecrate
To celebrate Thee and Thy state, no mate
For Thee; what see for envy in poor me?"*
Hoping the while, since evils sometimes mend,
Warts rub away and sores are cured with slime,
That some strange day, will either the Quiet catch
And conquer Setebos, or likelier He
Decrepit may doze, doze, as good as die.

[What, what? A curtain o'er the world at once!
Crickets stop hissing; not a bird—or, yes,
There scuds His raven, that hath told Him all!
It was fool's play, this prattling! Ha! The wind
Shoulders the pillared dust, death's house o' the move,
And fast invading fires begin! White blaze—
A tree's head snaps—and there, there, there, there, there,
His thunder follows! Fool to gibe at Him!
So! 'Lieth flat and loveth Setebos!
'Maketh his teeth meet thro' his upper lip,
Will let those quails fly, will not eat this month
One little mess of whelks, so he may 'scape!]

SAUL

Robert Browning

XIII

"Yea, my King,"

I began—"thou dost well in rejecting mere comforts that spring
From the mere mortal life held in common by man and by brute:
In our flesh grows the branch of this life, in our soul it bears fruit.
Thou hast marked the slow rise of the tree,—how its stem trembled first
Till it passed the kid's lip, the stag's antler; then safely outburst
The fan-branches all round; and thou mindest when these too, in turn
Broke a-bloom and the palm tree seemed perfect: yet more was to learn,
E'en the good that comes in with the palm-fruit. Our dates shall we slight,
When their juice brings a cure for all sorrow? or care for the plight
Of the palm's self whose slow growth produced them? Not so! stem and branch
Shall decay, nor be known in their place, while the palm-wine shall staunch
Every wound of man's spirit in winter. I pour thee such wine.
Leave the flesh to the fate it was fit for! the spirit be thine!
By the spirit, when age shall o'ercome thee, thou still shalt enjoy
More indeed, than at first when, inconscious, the life of a boy.
Crush that life, and behold its wine running! Each deed thou hast done
Dies, revives, goes to work in the world; until e'en as the sun

Looking down on the earth, tho' clouds spoil him, tho' tempests efface,

Can find nothing his own deed produced not, must everywhere trace

The results of his past summer-prime,—so, each ray of thy will.

Every flash of thy passion and prowess, long over, shall thrill

Thy whole people, the countless, with ardour, till they too give forth

A like cheer to their sons: who in turn, fill the South and the North

With the radiance thy deed was the germ of. Carouse in the past!

But the license of age has its limit; thou diest at last.

As the lion when age dims his eyeball, the rose at her height,

So with man—so his power and his beauty forever take flight.

No! Again a long draught of my soul-wine! Look forth o'er the years!

Thou hast done now with eyes for the actual; begin with the seer's!

Is Saul dead? In the depth of the vale make his tomb—bid arise

A gray mountain of marble heaped four-square, till, built to the skies,

Let it mark where the great First King slumbers: whose fame would ye know?

Up above see the rock's naked face, where the record shall go

In great characters cut by the scribe,—Such was Saul, so he did;

With the sages directing the work, by the populace chid,—

For not half, they'll affirm, is comprised there! Which fault to amend,

In the grove with his kind grows the cedar, whereon they shall spend

(See, in tablets 'tis level before them) their praise, and record

With the gold of the graver, Saul's story,—the statesman's great word

Side by side with the poet's sweet comment. The river's a-wave

With smooth paper-reeds grazing each other when prophet-winds rave:

So the pen gives unborn generations their due and their part
In thy being! Then, first of the mighty, thank God that thou
    art!"

XIV

And behold while I sang . . . but O Thou who didst **grant**
    me that day,
And before it not seldom hast granted Thy help to essay,
Carry on and complete an adventure,—my shield and my sword
In that act where my soul was Thy servant, Thy word was
    my word,—
Still be with me, who then at the summit of human endeavour
And scaling the highest, man's thought could, gazed hopeless
    as ever
On the new stretch of heaven above me—till, mighty to save,
Just one lift of Thy hand cleared that distance—God's throne
    from man's grave!
Let me tell out my tale to its ending—my voice to my heart
Which can scarce dare believe in what marvels last night I took
    part,
As this morning I gather the fragments, alone with my sheep,
And still fear lest the terrible glory evanish like sleep!
For I wake in the gray dewy covert, while Hebron upheaves
The dawn struggling with night on his shoulder, and Kidron
    retrieves
Slow the damage of yesterday's sunshine.

XV

                  I say then,—my song
While I sang thus, assuring the monarch, and, ever more strong,
Made a proffer of good to console him—he slowly resumed
His old motions and habitudes kingly. · The right hand replumed
His black locks to their wonted composure, adjusted the swathes
Of his turban, and see—the huge sweat that his countenance
    bathes,
He wipes off with the robe; and he girds now his loins as of
    yore,
And feels slow for the armlets of price, with the clasp set before.
He is Saul, ye remember in glory,—ere error had bent

The broad brow from the daily communion; and still, tho'
   much spent
Be the life and bearing that front you, the same, God did choose,
To receive what a man may waste, desecrate, never quite lose.
So sank he along by the tent-prop, till, stayed by the pile
Of his armour and war-cloak and garments, he leaned there
   awhile,
And sat out my singing,—one arm round the tent-prop, to raise
His bent head, and the other hung slack—till I touched on the
   praise
I foresaw from all men in all time, to the man patient there;
And thus ended, the harp falling forward.   Then first I was
   'ware
That he sat, as I say, with my head just above his vast knees
Which were thrust out each side around me, like oak roots
   which please
To encircle a lamb when it slumbers.   I looked up to know
If the best I could do had brought solace: he spoke not, but
   slow
Lifted up the hand slack at his side, till he laid it with care
Soft and grave, but in mild settled will, on my brow: thro' my
   hair
The large fingers were pushed, and he bent back my head, with
   kind power—
All my face back, intent to peruse it, as men do a flower.
Thus held he me there with his great eyes that scrutinized
   mine—
And oh, all my heart how it loved him! but where was the
   sign?
I yearned—"Could I help thee, my father, inventing a bliss,
I would add, to that life of the past, both the future and
   this;
I would give thee new life altogether, as good, ages hence,
As this moment,—had love but the warrant, love's heart to
   dispense!"

XVI

Then the truth came upon me.   No harp more—no song more!
   outbroke—

XVII

"I have gone the whole round of creation: I saw and I spoke;
I, a work of God's hand for that purpose, received in my brain
And pronounced on the rest of his handwork—returned him
   again
His creation's approval or censure: I spoke as I saw,
Reported, as man may of God's work—all's love, yet all's law.
Now I lay down the judgeship he lent me. Each faculty tasked
To perceive him has gained an abyss, where a dewdrop was
   asked.
Have I knowledge? confounded it shrivels at Wisdom laid
   bare.
Have I forethought? how purblind, how blank, to the Infinite
   Care!
Do I task any faculty highest, to image success?
I but open my eyes,—and perfection, no more and no less,
In the kind I imagined, full-fronts me, and God is seen God
In the star, in the stone, in the flesh, in the soul and the clod.
And thus looking within and around me, I ever renew
(With that stoop of the soul which in bending upraises it too)
The submission of man's nothing-perfect to God's all complete,
As by each new obeisance in spirit, I climb to His feet.
Yet with all this abounding experience, this deity known,
I shall dare to discover some province, some gift of my own.
There's a faculty pleasant to exercise, hard to hoodwink,
I am fain to keep still in abeyance (I laugh as I think),
Lest, insisting to claim and parade in it, wot ye, I worst
E'en the Giver in one gift.—Behold, I could love if I durst!
But I sink the pretension as fearing a man may o'ertake
God's own speed in the one way of love; I abstain for love's
   sake.
—What, my soul? see thus far and no farther? when doors
   great and small,
Nine-and-ninety flew ope at our touch, should the hundredth
   appal?
In the least things have faith, yet distrust in the greatest of all?
Do I find love so full in my nature, God's ultimate gift,
That I doubt His own love can compete with it? Here, the
   parts shift?

Here, the creature surpass the creator,—the end, what began?
Would I fain in my impotent yearning do all for this man,
And dare doubt He alone shall not help him, who yet alone can?
Would it ever have entered my mind, the bare will, much less
  power,
To bestow on this Saul what I sang of, the marvellous dower
Of the life he was gifted and filled with? to make such a soul,
Such a body, and then such an earth for insphering the whole?
And doth it not enter my mind (as my warm tears attest),
These good things being given, to go on, and give one more,
  the best?
Ay, to save and redeem and restore him, maintain at the height
This perfection,—succeed with life's dayspring, death's minute
  of night?
Interpose at the difficult minute, snatch Saul the mistake,
Saul the failure, the ruin he seems now,—and bid him awake
From the dream, the probation, the prelude, to find himself set
Clear and safe in new light and new life,—a new harmony yet
To be run and continued, and ended—who knows?—or endure!
The man taught enough by life's dream, of the rest to make
  sure;
By the pain-throb, triumphantly winning intensified bliss,
And the next world's reward and repose, by the struggles in
  this.

XVIII

"I believe it! 'Tis Thou, God, that givest, 'tis I who receive:
In the first is the last, in Thy will is my power to believe.
All's one gift: Thou canst grant it, moreover, as prompt to
  my prayer,
As I breathe out this breath, as I open these arms to the air.
From Thy will stream the worlds, life and nature, Thy dread
  Sabaoth:
I will?—the mere atoms despise me! Why am I not loath
To look that, even that in the face too? Why is it I dare
Think but lightly of such impuissance? What stops my despair?
This;—'tis not what man Does which exalts him, but what man
  Would do!
See the King—I would help him, but cannot, the wishes fall
  through.

Could I wrestle to raise him from sorrow, grow poor to enrich,
To fill up his life, starve my own out, I would—knowing which,
I know that my service is perfect. Oh, speak thro' me now!
Would I suffer for him that I love? So wouldst Thou—so wilt
    Thou!
So shall crown Thee the topmost, ineffablest. uttermost crown—
And Thy love fill infinitude wholly, nor leave up nor down
One spot for the creature to stand in! It is by no breath,
Turn of eye, wave of hand, that salvation joins issue with
    death!
As thy love is discovered almighty, almighty be proved
Thy power, that exists with and for it, of being Beloved!
He who did most, shall bear most; the strongest shall stand
    the most weak.
'Tis the weakness in strength, that I cry for! my flesh, that I
    seek
In the Godhead! I seek and I find it. O Saul, it shall be
A Face like my face that receives thee; a Man like to me,
Thou shalt love and be loved by, forever: a Hand like this
    hand
Shall throw open the gates of new life to thee! See the Christ
    stand!"

XIX

I know not too well how I found my way home in the night.
There were witnesses, cohorts about me, to left and to right,
Angels, powers, the unuttered, unseen, the alive, the aware:
I repressed, I got thro' them as hardly, as strugglingly there,
As a runner beset by the populace famished for news—
Life or death. The whole earth was awakened, hell loosed with
    her crews;
And the stars of night beat with emotion, and tingled and shot
Out in fire the strong pain of pent knowledge: but I fainted not,
For the Hand still impelled me at once and supported, suppressed
All the tumult, and quenched it with quiet, and holy behest,
Till the rapture was shut in itself, and the earth sank to rest.

REALITY

SIR AUBREY DE VERE

Love thy God and love Him only:
And thy breast will ne'er be lonely.
In that one great Spirit meet
All things mighty, grave and sweet.
Vainly strives the soul to mingle
With a being of our kind:
Vainly heart with our hearts are twined:
For the deepest still is single.
An impalpable resistance
Holds like nature's still at distance.
Mortal! Love that Holy One!
Or dwell for aye alone.

From WOODNOTES

RALPH WALDO EMERSON

'All the forms are fugitive,
But the substances survive.
Ever fresh the broad creation,
A divine improvisation,
From the heart of God proceeds,
A single will, a million deeds.
Once slept the world an egg of stone,
And pulse, and sound, and light was none;
And God said, "Throb!" and there was motion
And the vast mass became vast ocean.
Onward and on, the eternal Pan,
Who layeth the world's incessant plan,
Halteth never in one shape,
But forever doth escape,
Like wave or flame, into new forms
Of gem, and air, of plants, and worms.
I, that today am a pine,

Yesterday was a bundle of grass.
He is free and libertine,
Pouring of his power the wine
To every age, to every race;
Unto every race and age
He emptieth the beverage;
Unto each and unto all,
Maker and original.
The world is the ring of his spells,
And the plan of his miracles.
As he giveth to all to drink,
Thus or thus they are and think.
With one drop sheds form and feature;
With the next a special nature;
The third adds heat's indulgent spark;
The fourth gives light which eats the dark;
Into the fifth himself he flings,
And conscious Law is King of kings.
As the bee through the garden ranges,
From world to world the godhead changes;
As the sheep go feeding in the waste,
From form to form He maketh haste;
This vault which glows immense with light
Is the inn where he lodges for a night.
What recks such Traveller if the bowers
Which bloom and fade like meadow flowers
A bunch of fragrant lilies be,
Or the stars of eternity?
Alike to him the better, the worse,—
The glowing angel, the outcast corse.
Thou metest him by centuries,
And lo! he passes like the breeze;
Thou seek'st in glade and galaxy,
He hides in pure transparency;
Thou askest in fountains and in fires,
He is the essence that inquires.
He is the axis of the star;
He is the sparkle of the spar;
He is the heart of every creature;
He is the meaning of each feature;

And his mind is the sky,
Than all it holds more deep, more high.'

THE BOHEMIAN HYMN

Ralph Waldo Emerson

In many forms we try
To utter God's infinity,
But the boundless hath no form,
And the Universal Friend
Doth as far transcend
An angel as a worm.

The great Idea baffles wit,
Language falters under it,
It leaves the learned in the lurch;
No art, nor power, nor toil can find
The measure of the eternal Mind,
Nor hymn, nor prayer, nor church.

THE LIVING GOD

Charlotte Perkins Gilman

The Living God. The God that made the world
Made it and stood aside to watch and wait.
Arranging a predestined plan
To save the erring soul of man—
Undying destiny—unswerving fate.
I see His hand in the path of life,
His law to doom and save,
His love divine in the hopes that shine
Beyond the sinner's grave,
His care that sendeth sun and rain,
His wisdom giving rest,
His price of sin that we may not win
The heaven of the blest.

> Not near enough! Not clear enough!
>   O God, come nearer still!
> I long for thee! Be strong for me!
>   Teach me to know Thy will!

The Living God. The God that makes the world,
Makes it—is making it in all its worth;
His spirit speaking sure and slow
In the real universe we know,—
God living in the earth.
I feel His breath in the blowing wind,
His pulse in the swinging sea,
And the sunlit sod is the breast of God
Whose strength we feel and see.
His tenderness in the springing grass,
His beauty in the flowers,
His living love in the sun above,—
All here, and near, and ours!

> Not near enough! Not clear enough!
>   O God, come nearer still!
> I long for Thee! Be strong for me!
>   Teach me to know thy will!

The Living God. The God that is the world.
The world? The world is man—the work of man.
Then—dare I follow what I see?—
Then—By Thy Glory—it must be
That we are in thy plan!
That strength divine in the work we do?
That love in our mothers' eyes?
That wisdom clear in our thinking here?
That power to help us rise?
God in the daily work we've done,
In the daily path we've trod?
Stand still, my heart, for I am a part—
I too—of the Living God!

> Ah, clear as light! As near! As bright!
>   O God! My God! My own!
> Command thou me! I stand for thee!
>   And I do not stand alone!

BRAND SPEAKS

Hendrik Ibsen

Translated by C. H. Herford

As Catholics make of the Redeemer
A baby at the breast, so ye
Make God a dotard and a dreamer,
Verging on second infancy.
And as the Pope on Peter's throne
Calls little but his keys his own,
So to the Church ye would confine
The world-wide realm of the Divine;
Twixt Life and Doctrine set a sea,
Nowise concern yourselves to BE.
Bliss for your souls ye would receive
Not utterly and wholly LIVE.
Ye need such feebleness to brook,
A God who'll through his fingers look,
Who like yourselves, is hoary grown,
And keeps a cap for his bald crown.
Mine is another kind of God!
Mine is a storm, where thine's a lull;
Implacable where thine's a clod,
All-loving there, where thine is dull;
And He is young like Hercules,
No hoary sipper of life's lees!
His voice rang through the dazzled night
When He, within the burning wood
By Moses upon Horeb's height
As by a pygmy's pygmy stood.
In Gibeon's vale He stay'd the sun,
And wonders without end would do,
Were not the age grown sick—like you.
Nothing that's new do I demand;
For Everlasting Right I stand.
It is not for a church I cry,
It is not dogmas I defend;

Day dawn'd on both, and possibly,
Day may on both of them descend.
What's made has "finis" for its brand;
Of moth and worm it feels the flaw,
And then, by nature and by law,
Is for an embyro thrust aside.
But there is One that shall abide;—
The Spirit, that was never born,
That in the world's fresh gladsome Morn
Was rescued when it seemed forlorn,
That built with valiant faith a road
Whereby from Flesh it climbed to God.
Now but in shreds and scraps is dealt
The Spirit we have faintly felt;
But from these scraps and from these shreds,
These headless hands and handless heads,
These torso-stumps of soul and thought,
A Man complete and whole shall grow,
And God, His glorious child shall know,
His heir, the Adam that he wrought!

From THE TEST OF MANHOOD

George Meredith

In fellowship Religion has its founts;
The solitary his own God reveres:
Ascend no sacred Mounts
Our hungers or our fears.
As only for the numbers Nature's care
Is shown, and she the personal nothing heeds,
So to Divinity the spring of prayer
From brotherhood the one way upward leads.
Like the sustaining air
Are both for flowers and weeds:
But he who claims in spirit to be flower
Will find them both an air that doth devour.

THE INNER LIGHT

Frederick William Henry Myers

Lo, if some pen should write upon your rafter
　MENE and MENE in the folds of flame,
Think you could any memories thereafter
　Wholly retrace the couplet as it came?

Lo, if some strange, intelligible thunder
　Sang to the earth the secret of a star
Scarce could ye catch, for terror and for wonder,
　Shreds of the story that was pealed so far.

Scarcely I catch the words of his revealing,
　Hardly I hear Him, dimly understand,
Only the Power that is within me pealing
　Lives on my lips and beckons to my hand.

Whoso has felt the Spirit of the Highest
　Cannot confound nor doubt Him nor deny:
Yea, with one voice, O, world, though thou deniest,
　Stand thou on that side, for on this am I.

Rather the earth shall doubt when her retrieving
　Pours in the rain and rushes from the sod.
Rather than he for whom the great conceiving
　Stirs in his soul to quicken into God.

Ay, though thou then shouldst strike from him his glory,
　Blind and tormented, maddened and alone,
Even on the cross would he maintain his story,
　Yes, and in hell would whisper, I have known.

THE REDEEMER

WILLIAM SHARP (*Fiona Macleod*)

I know that my Redeemer liveth—but out of the depths of time
He hath not called to me yet.   But from th' immeasurable tracts
That widen unending to where beginneth eternity
Falleth at times a voice, heart-thrilling, soul-piercing, life-giving,
High sometimes and clear, as a lark singing in a holy dawn,
Hushed and far off again as a dreaming wave upon seas
Lit by a low vast moon, and windlessly sleeping, but ever
Sweet with a human love, and full of ineffable yearning,
And crying of soul unto soul from infinite deep unto deep.
And sometimes I look and gaze out upon uttermost darkness
And hear the wail of desolate winds moaning around the
    world—
Till darkness shivers to light, and clashing through earth and
    heaven
I hear great wings make music, and marvellous thunderous
    songs
Shout "Thy Redeemer liveth, and calleth for thee!"

AN INVOCATION

JOHN ADDINGTON SYMONDS

To God, the everlasting, who abides,
One Life within things infinite that die:
To Him whose purity no thought divides:
Whose breath is breathed through immensity.

Him neither eye hath seen, nor ear hath heard;
Yet reason, seated in the souls of men,
Though, pondering oft on the mysterious word,
Hath e'er revealed His Being to mortal ken.

Earth changes, and the starry wheels roll round;
The seasons come and go, moons wax and wane;
The nations rise and fall, and fill the ground,
Storing the sure results of joy and pain:

Slow knowledge widens toward a perfect whole,
From that first man who named the heaven,
To him who weighs the planets as they roll,
And knows what laws to every life are given.

Yet He appears not. Round the extreme sphere
Of science still thin ether floats unseen:
Darkness still wraps Him round; and ignorant fear
Remains of what we are, and what have been.

Only we feel Him; in aching dreams,
Swift intuitions, pangs of keen delight,
The sudden vision of His glory seems
To sear our souls, dividing the dull night:

And we yearn toward Him. Beauty, Goodness, Truth;
These three are one; one life, one thought, one being;
One source of still rejuvenescent youth;
One light for endless and unclouded seeing.

Mere symbols we perceive—the dying beauty,
The partial truth that few can comprehend,
The vacillating faith, the painful duty,
The virtue laboring to a dubious end.

O God, unknown, invisible, secure,
Whose being by dim resemblances we guess,
Who in man's fear and love abidest sure,
Whose power we feel in darkness and confess!

Without Thee nothing is, and Thou art nought
When on Thy substance we gaze curiously:
By Thee impalpable, named Force and Thought,
The solid world ceases not to be.

Lead Thou me, God, Law, Reason, Duty, Life!
All names for Thee alike are vain and hollow—
Lead me, for I will follow without strife;
Or, if I strive, still must I blindly follow.

COMMUNION

John B. Tabb

Once when my heart was passion free
    To learn of things divine,
The soul of nature suddenly
    Outpoured itself in mine.

I held the secrets of the deep
    And of the heavens above;
I knew the harmonies of sleep,
    The mysteries of love.

And for a moment's interval
    The earth, the sky, the sea—
My soul encompassed each and all,
    As now they encompass me.

To one in all, to all in one—
    Since love the work began
Life's everwidening circles run
    Revealing God to man.

GOD

James Cowden Wallace

There is an Eye that never sleeps
    Beneath the wing of night;
There is an ear that never shuts
    When sink the beams of light.

There is an arm that never tires
  When human strength gives way;
There is a love that never fails
  When earthly loves decay.

That Eye unseen o'erwatcheth all;
  That Arm upholds the sky;
That Ear doth hear the sparrows call;
  That Love is ever nigh.

From THE PASSAGE TO INDIA

WALT WHITMAN

Ah, more than any priest, O soul, we too believe in God,
But with the mystery of God we dare not dally.

O soul thou pleasest me, I thee
Sailing these seas or on the hills, or waking in the night,
Thoughts, silent thoughts, of Time and Space and Death, like
    waters flowing,
Bear me indeed as through the regions infinite,
Whose air I breathe, whose ripples hear, lave me all over,
Bathe me, O God, in thee, mounting to thee,
I and my soul to range in range of thee.

O Thou transcendent,
Nameless, the fibre and the breath,
Light of the light, shedding forth universes, thou center of them,
Thou mightier center of the true, the good, the loving,
Thou moral spiritual fountain—affection's source—thou reservoir
(O pensive soul of me—O thirst unsatisfied—waitest not there?
Waitest not haply for us, somewhere there, the Comrade per-
    fect?)
Thou pulse, thou motive of the stars, suns, systems,
That circling, move in order, safe, harmonious,
Athwart the shapeless vastnesses of Space!
How should I think, how breathe a single breath, how speak,
If, out of myself I could not launch, to those superior universes?

Swiftly I shrivel at the thought of God,
At Nature and its wonders, Time and Space and Death,
But that I, turning, call to thee, O soul, thou actual Me,
And lo, thou gently masterest the orbs,
Thou matest Time, smilest content at Death,
And fillest, swellest full, the vastnesses of Space.

Greater than stars or suns,
Bounding, O soul, thou journeyest forth;
What love than thine and ours could wider amplify?
What aspirations, wishes, outvie thine and ours, O soul?
What dreams of the ideal? What plan of purity, perfection,
     strength?
What cheerful willingness for others' sake to give up all?
For others' sake to suffer all?

Reckoning ahead, O soul, when thou, the time achieved,
The seas all crossed, weather'd the capes, the voyage done,
Surrounded, copest, frontest God, yieldest, the aim attained,
As, filled with friendship, love complete, the Elder Brother found,
The Younger melts in fondness in his arms.

Passage to more than India!
Are thy wings plumed indeed for such far flights?
O soul, voyagest thou indeed on voyages like these?
Disportest thou on waters such as these?
Soundest below the Sanscrit and the Vedas?
Then have thy bent unleashed.

Passage to you, your shores, ye aged fierce enigmas!
Passage to you, to mastership of you, ye strangling problems!
You, strewed with the wrecks of skeletons that, living, never
     reached you.

Passage to more than India!
O secret of the earth and sky!
Of you, O waters of the sea! O winding creeks and rivers!
Of you, O woods and fields! Of you, strong mountains of
     my land!
Of you, O prairies! Of you, grey rocks!
O morning red! O clouds! O rain and snows!
O day and night, passage to you!

O sun and moon and all you stars! Sirius and Jupiter!
Passage to you!

Passage, immediate Passage! the blood burns in my veins!
Away, O soul, hoist instantly the anchor!
Cut the hawsers—haul out—shake out every sail!
Have we not stood here like trees in the ground long enough?
Have we not grovel'd here long enough, eating and drinking like
    mere brutes?
Have we not darken'd and dazed ourselves with books long
    enough?

Sail forth—steer for the deep waters only,
Reckless, O soul, exploring, I with thee and thou with me,
For we are bound where mariner has not yet dared to go,
And we will risk the ship, ourselves and all.

O my brave soul!
O farther, farther sail!
O daring joy, but safe! Are they not all the seas of God?
O farther, farther, farther sail!

THE OVER-HEART

JOHN GREENLEAF WHITTIER

Above, below, in sky and sod
    In leaf and spar, in star and man,
    Well might the wise Athenian scan
The geometric signs of God,
    The measured order of his plan.

And India's mystics sang aright
    Of the One Life pervading all,—
    One Being's tidal rise and fall
In soul and form, in sound and sight,—
    Eternal outflow and recall.

God is: and man in guilt and fear
    This central fact of Nature owns;—

Kneels, trembling, by his altar-stones,
And darkly dreams the ghastly smear
    Of blood appeases and atones.

Guilt shapes by Terror: deep within
    The human heart the secret lies
    Of all the hideous deities;
And, painted on a ground of sin,
    The fabled gods of torment rise!

And what is He?—The ripe grain nods,
    The sweet dews fall, the flowers blow;
    But darker signs his presence show:
The earthquake and the storm are God's
    And good and evil interflow.

O hearts of love! O souls that turn
    Like sunflowers to the pure and best!
    To you the truth is manifest:
For they the mind of Christ discern
    Who lean like John upon his breast!

In him of whom the Sybil told
    For whom the prophet's heart was toned,
    Whose need the sage and magian owned,
The loving heart of God behold,
    The hope for which the ages groaned!

Fade, pomp of dreadful imagery
    Wherewith mankind have deified
    Their hate, and selfishness, and pride!
Let the scared dreamer wake to see
    The Christ of Nazareth at his side!

What doth that holy Guide require?—
    No rite of pain, nor gift of blood,
    But man a kindly brotherhood,
Looking, where duty is desire,
    To him, the beautiful and good.

Gone be the faithlessness of fear,
  And let the pitying heaven's sweet rain
  Wash out the altar's bloody stain;
The law of Hatred disappear,
  The law of Love alone remain.

How fall the idols false and grim!—
  And, Lo! the hideous wreck above
  The emblems of the Lamb and Dove!
Man turns from God, not God from him;
  And guilt, in suffering, whispers Love!

The world sits at the feet of Christ,
  Unknowing, blind and unconsoled;
  It yet shall touch his garment's fold,
And feel the heavenly Alchemist
  Transform its very dust to gold.

The theme befitting angel tongues
  Beyond a mortal's scope has grown.
  O heart of mine, with reverence own
The fulness which to it belongs,
  And trust the unknown for the known.

ILLUSION

ELLA WHEELER WILCOX

God and I in space alone
  And nobody else in view.
"And where are the people, O Lord!" I said.
"The earth below and the sky o'erhead
  And the dead whom once I knew?"

"That was a dream," God smiled and said,
  "A dream that seemed to be true,
There were no people, living or dead,
There was no earth and no sky o'erhead
  There was only myself—and you."

"Why do I feel no fear," I asked,
   "Meeting you here in this way,
For I have sinned I know full well,
And there is heaven and there is hell,
   And is this the judgment day?"

"Nay, those were dreams," the great God said,
   "Dreams that have ceased to be.
There are no such things as fear or sin,
There is no you—you have never been—
   There is nothing at all but Me."

From THE EXCURSION

WILLIAM WORDSWORTH

A curious child, who dwelt upon a tract
Of inland ground, applying to his ear
The convolutions of a smooth-lipped shell;
To which, in silence hushed, his very soul
Listened intensely; and his countenance soon
Brightened with joy; for murmurings from within
Were heard, sonorous cadences! whereby
To his belief, the monitor expressed
Mysterious union with his native sea.
Even in such a shell the Universe itself
Is to the ear of Faith: and there are times,
I doubt not, when to you it doth impart
Authentic tidings of invisible things;
Of ebb and flow and ever-during power;
And central peace, subsisting at the heart
Of endless agitation.

THE SEEKER

From *The Fools' Adventure*

LASCELLES ABERCROMBIE

I have achieved. That which the lonely man
Spoke of, core of the world, that Self, I know.
Like one small pool to the reach of Heaven, I
Am open to a vastness. Hearken, thou,
Do I not know thee right? Thou art the deep
Whereunto all things yearn unwearyingly,
Some unaware, some hating that they yearn,
But all into a stillness, into Thee,
Falling at length, and their unrest is done,
Until again thou blurt them out of thee,
Out of the middle to the rind. And yet
Not them, but piecemeal what they were.
New-fangled into other companies.
It is as if, not only once, far off,
Aloof from place and being I had watched
The spell betwixt two happenings end again;—
The dark's distress, slow qualms mastering it,
Blind thrills, and last, the sudden pang of light.
Methinks, plainly as I've felt earth's swoon
Wince at the touch of spring, awakening her,
The peace, thy region, shudder I have felt
When with it meddles thy new imagining;
And in the smooth element, ruffling, grows a throb,
Marring with its strong rhythm the prone calm,
Beat of the fresh beginning of an order;
One settled eddy at last, whose scouring kirtles
Gather to substance and perplexèd shape
To thickening spots of coarse, and curds of fire.
Again within the unform'd principle

Stress, that it have a grain; and yet more stress,
Till the unbounded shiver of light shatter
Innumerously, and into the clear inane
Come like a ghost another swarm of motes
Shepherded by thy thought into new flocks,
Away from thee, outward, circling, numberless kinds;
Yet the same partner, the old lust, is with them,
Unrest, severance from thy quietude.
Nor first, nor last of them, this swirl of stars
Unlike the others, but in this thing alike.
I from the place in Being called Mankind
Am come, seeking thee, and look, I know thee.
Not with my sense and reason only; these
Man fashioned for near needs of common life:
Good tools, but to find thee of no more use
Than ladders to thatch houses reach the sun.
Not Reason finds thee, though he walk with gait
Taking gulfs in his stride as far across
As in his yearly bout the throw of Saturn.
My wisdom was to practice with the power
Emotion, since I knew it was, though stall'd
In Somewhere, yet a piece of the Everywhere.

ECCE HOMO

WITTER BYNNER

Behold the man alive in me,
  Behold the man in you!
If there is a God—am I not he?
  Shall I myself undo?

I have been waiting long enough. . . .
  Impossible gods, goodby!
I wait no more: the way is rough—
  But the god who climbs, is I.

THE NEW GOD

WITTER BYNNER

From *The New World*

In temporary pain
The age is bearing a new breed
Of men and women, patriots of the world
And one another. Boundaries in vain,
Birthrights and countries, would constrain
The old diversity of seed
To be diversity of soul.
   O mighty patriots maintain
Your loyalty!—till flags unfurled
For battle shall arraign
The traitors who unfurled them, shall remain
And shine over an army with no slain,
And men from every nation shall enroll,
And women—in the hardihood of peace!
   What can my anger do but cease?
Whom shall I fight and who shall be my enemy
When he is I and I am he?

   Let me have done with that old God outside
Who watched with preference and answered prayer,
The Godhead that replied
Now here, now there,
Where heavy cannon were
Or coins of gold!
Let me receive communion with all men
Acknowledging our one and only soul!
   For not till then
Can God be God till we ourselves are whole!

RENUNCIATION

Mark Wilks Call

Wakeful all night I lay and thought of God,
Of heaven, and of crowns pale martyrs gain,
Of souls in high and purgatorial pain,
And the red path which murdered seers have trod:
I heard the trumpets which the angels blow
I saw the cleaving sword, the measuring rod,
I watched the stream of sound continuous flow
Past the gold towers where seraphs make abode.

But now I let that aching splendor go,
I dare not call the crownèd angels peers
Henceforth.   I am content to dwell below
Mid common joys, with humble smiles and tears
Delighted in the sun and breeze to grow,
A child of human hopes and human fears.

EACH IN HIS OWN TONGUE

William Herbert Carruth

A fire-mist and a planet,—
  A crystal and a cell,—
A jellyfish and a saurian,
  And caves where the cavemen dwell;
Then a sense of law and beauty,
  And a face turned from the clod,—
Some call it Evolution,
  And others call it God.

A haze on the far horizon,
  The infinite tender sky,
The rich ripe tint of the corn-fields,
  And the wild geese sailing high,—

And all over the upland and lowland
  The charm of the golden rod,—
Some of us call it autumn,
  And others call it God.

Like tides on the crescent seabeach,
  When the moon is new and thin,
Into our hearts high yearnings,
  Come welling and surging in,—
Come from the mystic ocean
  Whose rim no foot has trod,—
Some of us call it Longing,
  And others call it God.

A picket frozen on duty,—
  A mother starved for her brood,—
Socrates drinking the hemlock,
  And Jesus on the rood;
And millions who humble and nameless,
  The straight hard pathway plod,—
Some call it Consecration,
  And others call it God.

PYGMALION

In part

HILDA DOOLITTLE (*Mrs. Richard Aldington*)

. . . .

I made god upon god
Step from the cold rock,
I made the gods less than men,
For I was a man and they my work.
. . . .

And now what is it that has come to pass?
. . . .

Each of the gods, perfect
Cries out from a perfect throat:

You are useless,
No marble can bind me
No stone suggest.
They have melted into the light
And I am desolate.
They have melted
Each from his plinth,
Each one departs.

They have gone:
What agony can express my grief?
Each from his marble base
Has stepped into the light
And my work is for naught?

A COMMON INFERENCE

Charlotte Perkins Gilman

A NIGHT: mysterious, tender, quiet, deep,
Heavy with flowers; full of life asleep;
Thrilling with insect voices; thick with stars;
No cloud between the dew drops and red Mars;
The small earth whirling softly on her way,
The moonbeams and the waterfalls at play;
A million worlds that move in peace,
A million mighty laws that never cease;
And one small ant-heap, hidden by small weeds,
Rich with eggs, slaves, and store of millet seeds.
    They sleep beneath the sod
        And trust in God.

A DAY: all glorious, royal, blazing bright;
Heavy with flowers, full of life and light;
Great fields of corn and sunshine; courteous trees;
Snow-sainted mountains; earth-embracing seas;
Wide golden deserts; slender silver streams;
Clear rainbows where the tossing fountain gleams;
And everywhere, in happiness and peace,

A million forms of life that never cease;
And one small ant-heap, crushed by passing tread,
Hath scarce enough alive to mourn the dead!
   They shriek beneath the sod,
     "There is no God!"

GIVE WAY!

Charlotte Perkins Gilman

Shall we not open the human heart
Swing the doors till the hinges start;
   Stop our worrying, doubt, and din,
   Hunting heaven and dodging sin?
There is no need to search so wide,
Open the door and stand aside—
    Let God in!

Shall we not open the human heart
To loving labor in field and mart;
   Working together for all about
   The good, large labor that knows not doubt?
Can He be held in our narrow rim?
Do the work that is work for Him—
    Let God out!

Shall we not open the human heart,
Never to close and stand apart?
   God is a force to give way to!
   God is a thing you have to do!
God can never be caught by prayer,
Hid in your heart and fastened there—
    Let God through!

AGNOSTO THEO

Thomas Hardy

Long have I framed weak phantasies of Thee,
  O Willer masked and dumb!
  Who makest Life become,—
As though by laboring all-unknowingly,
  Like one whom reveries numb.

How much of consciousness informs Thy will,
  Thy biddings, as if blind,
  Of death-inducing kind,
Nought shows to us ephemeral ones who fill
  But moments in Thy mind.

Perhaps Thy ancient rote-restricted ways
  Thy ripening rule transcends;
  That listless effort tends
To grow percipient with advance of days,
  And with percipience mends.

For, in unwonted purlieus, far and nigh,
  At whiles or short or long,
  May be discerned a wrong
Dying as of self-slaughter; whereat I
  Would raise my voice in song.

GOD'S FUNERAL

Thomas Hardy

I

I saw a slowly stepping train—
Lined on the brows, scoop-eyed, and bent and hoar—
Following in files across a twilit plain
A strange and mystic form the foremost bore.

II

And by contagious throbs of thought
Or latent knowledge that within me lay
And had already stirred me, I was wrought
To consciousness of sorrow even as they.

III

The forborne shape, to my blurred eyes,
At first seemed man-like, and anon to change
To an amorphous cloud of marvellous size,
At times endowed with wings of glorious range.

IV

And this phantasmal variousness
Ever possessed it as they drew along:
Yet throughout all it symboled none the less
Potency vast and loving-kindness strong.

V

Almost before I knew I bent
Towards the moving columns without a word;
They growing in bulk and numbers as they went,
Struck out sick thoughts that could be overheard:—

VI

"O man-projected Figure, of late
Imaged as we, thy knell who shall survive?
Whence came it we were tempted to create
One whom we can no longer keep alive?

VII

"Framing him jealous, fierce at first,
We gave him justice as the ages rolled,
Will to bless those by circumstance accursed,
And long-suffering, and mercies manifold.

VIII

"And, tricked by our own early dream
And need of solace we grew self-deceived,
Our making soon our maker we did deem,
And what we had imagined we believed.

IX

"Till, in Time's stayless stealthy swing,
Uncompromising rude reality
Mangled the monarch of our fashioning,
Who quavered, sank; and now has ceased to be.

X

"So, toward our myth's oblivion,
Darkling and languid-lipped, we creep and grope
Sadlier than those who wept in Babylon,
Whose Zion was a still abiding hope.

XI

"How sweet it was in years far hied
To start the wheels of day with trustful prayer
To lie down liegely at the eventide
And feel a blessed assurance He was there!

XII

"And who or what shall fill his place?
Whither will wanderers turn distracted eyes
For some fixed star to stimulate their pace
Towards the goal of their enterprise?"

XIII

Some in the background then I saw,
Sweet women, youths, men, all incredulous
Who chimed: "This is a counterfeit of straw,
This requiem mockery! Still he lives to us!"

XIV

I could not buoy their faith: and yet
Many I had known; with all I sympathized,
And though struck speechless, I did not forget
That what was mourned for, I, too, long had prized.

XV

Still, how to bear such loss I deemed
The insistent question for each animate mind,
And gazing, to my growing sight there seemed
A pale yet positive gleam low down behind,

XVI

Whereof, to lift the general night,
A certain few who stood aloof had said
"See you upon the horizon that small light—
Swelling somewhat?" Each mourner shook his head.

XVII

And they composed a crowd of whom
Some were right good, and many nigh the best . . .
Thus dazed and puzzled 'twixt the gleam and gloom
Mechanically, I followed with the rest.

DREAMS OLD AND NASCENT

D. H. LAWRENCE

My world is a painted fresco, where coloured shapes
Of old, ineffectual lives linger blurred and warm;
An endless tapestry the past has woven drapes
The halls of my life, compelling my soul to conform.

The surface of dreams is broken,
The picture of the past is shaken and scattered.
Fluent, active figures of men pass along the railway, and I am
woken
From the dreams that the distance flattered.

Along the railway, active figures of men.
They have a secret that stirs in their limbs as they move
Out of the distance, nearer, commanding my dreamy world.

Here in the subtle, rounded flesh
Beats the active ecstasy.
In the sudden lifting my eyes, it is clearer,
The fascination of the quick, restless Creator moving through
     the mesh
Of men, vibrating in ecstasy through the rounded flesh.

Oh my boys, bending over your books,
In you is trembling and fusing
The creation of a new-patterned dream, dream of a generation:
And I watch to see the Creator, the power that patterns the
     dream.

The old dreams are beautiful, beloved, soft-toned, and sure,
But the dream-stuff is molten and moving mysteriously,
Alluring my eyes; for I, am I not also dream-stuff,
Am I not quickening, diffusing myself in the pattern, shaping
     and shapen?

Here in my class is the answer for the great yearning:
Eyes where I can watch the swim of old dreams reflected on
     the molten metal of dreams,
Watch the stir which is rhythmic and moves them all as a
     heart-beat moves the blood,
Here in the swelling flesh the great activity working,
Visible there in the change of eyes and the mobile features.

Oh the great mystery and fascination of the unseen Shaper,
The power of the melting, fusing Force—heat, light, all in one,
Everything great and mysterious in one, swelling and shaping
     the dream in the flesh,
As it swells and shapes a bud into blossom.

Oh the terrible ecstasy of the consciousness that I am life!
Oh the miracle of the whole, the widespread, labouring con-
     centration

Swelling mankind like one bud to bring forth the fruit of a
    dream,
Oh the terror of lifting the innermost I out of the sweep of
    the impulse of life,
And watching the Great Thing labouring through the whole
    round flesh of the world;
And striving to catch a glimpse of the shape of the coming
    dream,
As it quickens within the labouring, white-hot metal,
Catch the scent and the colour of the coming dream,
Then to fall back exhausted into the unconscious, molten life!

THE GOD-MAKER, MAN

Don Marquis

Nevermore
Shall the shepherds of Arcady follow
    Pan's moods as he lolls by the shore
Of the mere, or lies hid in the hollow;
    Nevermore
Shall they start at the sound of his reed-fashioned flute;

    Fallen mute
Are the strings of Apollo
    His lyre and his lute;
And the lips of the Memnons are mute
    Evermore;
And the Gods of the North,—are they dead or forgetful
    Our Odin and Baldur and Thor?
Are they drunk or grown weary of worship and fretful,
    Our Odin and Baldur and Thor?

And into what night have the Orient deities strayed?
Swart gods of the Nile, in dark splendors arrayed,
    Brooding Isis and somber Osiris,
    You were gone ere the fragile papyrus
That bragged you eternal decayed.

The avatars
But illumine their limited evens
    And vanish like plunging stars;
They are fixed in the whirling heavens
    No firmer than falling stars;
Brief lords of the changing soul, they pass
Like a breath from the face of a glass,
Or a blossom of summer blown, shallop-like, over the clover
And tossed tides of grass.

Sink to silence the psalms and the pæans
    The Shibboleths shift, and the faiths,
And the temples that challenged the æons
    Are tenanted only by wraiths;
Swoon to silence the cymbals and psalters,
The worship grows senseless and strange
And the mockers ask, *"Where be thy altars?"*
Crying *"Nothing is changeless, but Change!"*

Yes, nothing seems changeless, but Change.
And yet, through the creed-wrecking years
One story forever appears;
The tale of a City Supernal
The whisper of Something eternal—
A passion, a hope and a vision
    That peoples the silence with Powers;
A fable of meadows Elysian
    Where Time enters not, with his Hours;—
Manifold are the tale's variations,
    Race and clime ever tinting the dreams,
Yet its essence through endless mutations,
    Immutable gleams.

Deathless, though godheads be dying,
    Surviving the creeds that expire;
Illogical, reason-defying,
    Lives that passionate, primal desire;
Insistent, persistent, forever,
Man cries to the silences, *"Never*
    Shall death reign the lord of my soul,
    Shall dust be the ultimate goal—

I will storm the black bastions of Night!
  I will tread where my vision has trod,
I will set in the darkness, a light,
  In the vastness, a god!"

As the forehead of Man grows broader,
  So do his creeds;
And his gods they are shaped in his image,
  And mirror his needs;
And he clothes them with thunders and beauty,
  He clothes them with music and fire,
Seeing not, as he bows by their altars,
  That he worships his own desire;
And, mixed with his trust there is terror,
  And, mixed with his madness is ruth,
And every man grovels in error,
  Yet every man glimpses a truth.

For all of the creeds are false, and all of the creeds are true;
And low at the shrines where my brothers bow, there will I
    bow too;
For no form of a god, and no fashion
Man has made in his desperate passion
But is worthy some worship of mine;—
Not too hot with a gross belief,
Nor yet too cold with pride,
I will bow down where my brothers bow,
    Humble, but open-eyed!

GOD

Harold Monro

From *Dawn*

(The Speech of Geoffrey, the poet)

To church! I heard a sermon once in spring,
When last I went to church five years ago—
Such a dry, withered, cracked and crabbèd thing
As might have made the flowers forget to grow.

To church! God is a spirit, not a creed;
He is an inner outward-moving power:
Go to the heart of all, and watch the seed
Strive godward and at last become the flower.

. . . .

Once, long before the birth of time, a storm
Of white Desire, took form,
Strove, won, survived; and God became the world.

Next, some internal force began to move
Within the bosom of that latest earth:
The spirit of an elemental love
Stirred outward from itself, and God was birth.

Then outward, upward, with heroic thew,
Savage from young and bursting blood of life,
Desire took form, and conquered, and anew
Strove, conquered and took form; and God was strife.

Thus, like a comet, fiery flight on flight;
Flash upon flash, and purple dawn on dawn:
But always out of agony—delight;
And out of death—God evermore reborn.

Till, waxing fast and subtle and supreme,
Desiring his own spirit to possess,
Man of the bright eyes and the ardent dream
Saw paradise, and God was consciousness.

He is that one Desire, that life, that breath,
That Soul which, with infinity of pain,
Passes through revelation and through death
Onward and upward to itself again.

Out of the lives of heroes and their deeds,
Out of the miracle of human thought,
Out of the songs of singers, God proceeds;
And of the souls of them his soul is wrought.

Nothing is lost: all that is dreamed or done
Passes unaltered the eternal way,
Immerging in the everlasting One,
Who was the dayspring and who is the day.

. . . .

I sing forever though I sing in vain.

REALITY

Angela Morgan

I dreamed a dream last night, when all was still,
When earth in sleep forgot her murmurings;
I saw the soul, the spirit,—what you will—
Of this vast world; I saw the heart of things.

We call it real, this world of shapes and sounds,
These objects we can see and touch and hear,
Nor know we of the wonder-world that bounds
And thrills beneath, behind, the human ear.

I looked beneath, nor was I aught afraid,
And saw the living centre, fine as flame,
I sensed the substance whereof man is made—
That which defies analysis or name.

I saw that back of everything there lies
This wondrous, shining essence, finer far
Than all the gathered gold of western skies,
More lasting still than suns or planets are.

This, this is real, for this it is that gives
Life, color, motion, form, to what we see.
This hidden something that forever lives,
Sustaining all with subtle certainty.

And have you not, at some portentous time—
Some crisis in your life, some pregnant hour—

Felt a swift breath from out this realm sublime,
Thrilled to the core of being by its power?

That night of fierce soul struggle, when you knelt
And cried aloud that Death unlock the bars;
Then looked above in sudden awe and felt
The mute compassion of a million stars?

That time you listened to some magic strain
Of master music, shaken by its might,
And, all a-quiver with its joy and pain
Your soul swept on into some sphere of light?

In vain do men of science seek to prove
The hidden world that throbs behind the seen;
The ever-present cause of things that move
Eludes their searching sight, however keen.

As well might sunbeams seek to prove the sun
And rivulets the ocean, as that man—
A living flame from out the Central One—
Should seek to prove the Source where life began.

Within that unseen realm, all thought is born;
Each inspiration and each lofty theme
Is mothered there, and like a ray of morn
Comes shining down into the poet's dream.

We have an outlook on this world of forms,
While deeply rooted in the hidden sphere;
Impregnable to terrors and to storms,
The self-invisible knows naught of fear.

Would man but grasp, with focused powers of mind
The subtle laws that rule the finer realm,
Abandoning the lesser aims that blind,
The grosser joys that dull and overwhelm,

This dawning century would bring to light
The deepest truths for which we vainly grope;

Would open up new worlds to human sight,
In large fulfillment of our biggest hope!

THE NEW GOD

James Oppenheim

Ye morning glories, ring in the gale your bells,
And with dew water the walk's dust for the burden-bearing
　　ants;
Ye swinging spears of the larkspur, open your wells of gold
And pay your honey-tax to the humming-bird. . . .

O now I see by the opening of blossoms,
And of bills of hungry fledglings,
And the bright travel of the sun-drunk insects,
Morning's business is afoot: Earth is busied with a million
　　mouths.

Where goes eaten grass and thrush-snapped dragon-fly?
Creation eats itself, to spawn in swarming sun rays. . . .
Bull and cricket go to it: life lives on life . . .
But, O, ye flame-daubed irises, and ye hosts of gnats,
Like a well of light moving in the morning's light,
What is this garmented animal that comes eating and drinking
　　among you?
What is this upright one, with spade and shears?

He is the visible and the invisible,
Behind his mouth and eyes are other mouth and eyes. . . .
Thirster after visions
He sees the flowers to their roots and the Earth back through
　　its silent ages:
He parts the sky with his gaze:
He flings a magic on the hills, clothing them with Upanishad
　　music,
Peopling the valley with dreamed images that vanished in
　　Greece millenniums back;
And in the actual morning, out of longing, shapes on the hills
Tomorrow's golden grandeur. . . .

O ye million hungerers and ye sun rays
Ye are the many mothers of this invisible god,
This Earth's star and the sun that rise singing and toiling
    among you,
This that is I, in joy, in the garden,
Singing to you, ye morning glories.
Calling to you, ye swinging spears of the larkspur.

MANUFACTURED GODS

Carl Sandburg

They put up big wooden gods.
Then they burned the big wooden gods
And put up brass gods and
Changing their minds suddenly
Knocked down the brass gods and put up
A dough-face god with gold ear-rings.
The poor mutts, the pathetic slant heads,
They didn't know a little tin god
Is as good as anything in the line of gods,
Nor how a little tin god answers prayer
And makes rain and brings luck
The same as a big wooden god or a brass
Or dough-face god with golden ear-rings.

A MYSTIC AS SOLDIER

Siegfried Sassoon

I lived my days apart,
Dreaming fair songs for God,
By the glory of my heart
Covered and crowned and shod.

Now God is in the strife,
And I must seek Him there,
Where death outnumbers life,
And fury smites the air.

I walk the secret way
With anger in my brain.
O music through my clay,
When will you sound again?

THE HIDDEN WEAVER

ODELL SHEPARD

There where he sits, in the cold, in the gloom,
Of his far-away place by his thundering loom,
He weaves on the shuttles of day and of night
The shades of our sorrow and shapes of delight.
He has wrought him a glimmering garment to fling
Over the sweet swift limbs of the Spring,
He has woven a fabric of wonder to be
For a blue and a billowy robe to the sea,
He has fashioned in somber, funereal dyes
A tissue of gold for the midnight skies.

But sudden the woof all turns to red.
Has he lost his craft? Has he snapped his thread?
Sudden the web all sanguine runs.
Does he hear the yell of the thirsting guns?
While the scarlet crimes and the crimson sins
Grow from the dizzying outs and ins
Of the shuttle that spins, does he see it and feel?
Or is he the slave of a tyrannous wheel?

Inscrutable faces, mysterious eyes,
Are watching him out of the drifting skies;
Exiles of chaos crowd through the gloom
Of the uttermost cold to that thundering room
And whisper and peer through the dusk to the mark
What thing he is weaving there in the dark.
Will he leave the loom that he won from them
And rend his fabric from hem to hem?
Is he weaving with daring and skill sublime
A wonderful winding-sheet for time?

Ah, but he sits in a darkling place,
Hiding his hands, hiding his face,
Hiding his art behind the shine
Of the web that he weaves so long and fine.
Loudly the great wheel hums and rings
And we hear not even the song that he sings.
Over the whirr of the shuttles and all
The roar and the rush, does he hear when we call?

Only the colors that grow and glow
Swift as the hurrying shuttles go,
Only the figures vivid or dim
That flow from the hastening hands of him,
Only the fugitive shapes are we,
Wrought in the web of eternity.

HOW SHALL WE RISE TO GREET THE DAWN?

OSBERT SITWELL

How shall we rise to greet the dawn?
Not timidly
With a hand above our eyes,
But greet the strong light
Joyfully:
Nor will we mistake the dawn
For the mid-day.

We must create and fashion a new God—
A God of power, of beauty and of strength—
Created painfully, cruelly,
Labouring from the revulsion of men's minds.

It is not that the money changers
Ply their trade
Within the sacred places;
But that the old God
Has made the Stock Exchange his Temple.
We must drive him from it.

Why should we tinker with clay feet?
We will fashion
A perfect unity
Of precious metals.

.   .   .   .

Let us dig up the dragon's teeth
From this fertile soil;
Swiftly,
Before they fructify;
Let us give them as medicine
To the writhing monster itself.

We must create and fashion a new God—
A God of power, of beauty and of strength;
Created painfully, cruelly,
Labouring from the revulsion of men's minds.
Cast down the idols of a thousand years,
Crush them to the dust
Beneath the dancing rhythm of our feet.
Oh! Let us dance upon the weak and cruel:
We must create and fashion a new God.

WHAT TOMAS AN BUILE SAID IN A PUB

James Stephens

I saw God. Do you doubt it?
Do you dare to doubt it?
I saw the Almighty Man. His hand
Was resting on a mountain, and
He looked upon the World and all about it:
I saw Him plainer than you see me now,
You mustn't doubt it.

He was not satisfied;
His look was all dissatisfied.
His beard swung on a wind far out of sight
Behind the world's curve, and there was light

Most fearful from His forehead, and He sighed,
"That star went always wrong, and from the start
I was dissatisfied."
He lifted up His hand—
I say He heaved a dreadful hand
Over the spinning Earth, then I said: "Stay—
You must not strike it, God; I'm in the way;
And I will never move from where I stand."
He said, "Dear child, I feared that you were dead,"
And stayed His hand.

From GITANJALI

RABINDRANATH TAGORE

45

Have you not heard his silent steps?
He comes, comes, ever comes.
Every moment and every age, every day and every night he
    comes, comes, ever comes.
Many a song have I sung in many a mood of mind, but their
    notes have always proclaimed, "He comes, comes, ever
    comes."
In the fragrant days of sunny April through the forest path
    he comes, comes, ever comes.
In the rainy gloom of July nights, on the thundering chariot
    of clouds he comes, comes, ever comes.
In sorrow after sorrow it is his steps that press upon my heart,
    and it is the golden touch of his feet that makes my joy
    to shine.

46

I know not from what distant time thou art ever coming nearer
    to meet me.
Thy sun and thy stars can never keep thee hidden from me
    for aye.
 In many a morning and eve thy footsteps have been heard
    and thy messenger has come within my heart and called
    me in secret.

I know not why today my life is all astir, and a feeling of
    tremulous joy is passing through my heart.
It is as if my time were come to wind up my work, and I feel
    in the air a faint sweet smell of thy presence.

72

He it is, the innermost one, who awakens my being with his
    deep hidden touches.
He it is who puts his enchantment upon these eyes and joy-
    fully plays on the chords of my heart in varied cadence
    of pleasure and pain.
He it is who weaves the web of this *maya* in evanescent
    hues of gold and silver, blue and green, and lets peep
    out from the folds his feet, at whose touch I forget
    myself.
Days come and ages pass, and it is ever he who moves my
    heart in many a name, in many a guise, in many a rapture
    of joy and sorrow.

73

Deliverance is not for me in renunciation. I feel the embrace
    of freedom in a thousand bonds of delight.
Thou ever pourest for me the fresh draught of thy wine of
    various colors and fragrance, filling this earthen vessel
    to the brim.
My world will light its hundred different lamps with thy
    flame and place them before the altar of thy temple.
No, I will never shut the doors of my senses. The delights
    of touch and hearing will bear thy delight.
Yes, all my illusions will burn into illumination of joy, and
    all my desires ripen into fruits of love.

THE HOPE OF THE WORLD

WILLIAM WATSON

I

Higher than heaven they sit,
   Life and her consort Law;
And One · whose countenance lit
   In mine more perfect awe,
Fain had I deemed their peer,
   Beside them throned above:
Ev'n him who casts out fear,
   Unconquerable Love.
Ah, 'twas on earth alone that I his beauty saw.

II

On earth, in homes of men,
   In hearts that crave and die.
Dwells he not also, then,
   With Godhead, throned on high?
This and but this I know:
   His face I see not there:
Here find I him below,
   Nor find him otherwhere;
Born of an aching world, Pain's bridegroom, Death's ally.

III

Did Heaven vouchsafe some sign
   That through all Nature's frame
Boundless ascent benign
   Is everywhere her aim,
Such as man hopes it here,
   Where he from beasts hath risen,—
Then might I read full clear,
   Ev'n in my sensual prison,
That Life and Law and Love are one symphonious name.

IV

Such sign hath Heaven yet lent?
   Nay, on this earth, are we
So sure 'tis real ascent
   And very gain we see?
'Gainst Evil striving still,
   Some spoils of war we wrest:
Not to discover Ill
   Were haply state as blest.
We vaunt, o'er doubtful foes, a dubious victory.

V

In cave and bosky dene
   Of old there crept and ran
The gibbering form obscene
   That was and was not man.
The desert beasts went by
   In fairer covering clad;
More speculative eye
   The couchant lion had,
The goodlier speech the birds, than we when we began.

VI

Was it some random throw
   Of heedless Nature's die,
That from estate so low
   Uplifted man so high?
Through untold æons vast
   She let him lurk and cower:
'Twould seem he climbed at last
   In mere fortuitous hour,
Child of a thousand chances 'neath the indifferent sky.

VII

A soul so long deferred
   In his blind brain he bore,
It might have slept unstirred
   Ten million noontides more.

Yea, round him Darkness might
   Till now her folds have drawn,
O'er that enormous night
   So casual came the dawn,
Such hues of hap and hazard Man's Emergence wore!

VIII

If, then, our rise from gloom
   Hath this capricious air,
What ground is mine to assúme
   An upward process *there,*
In yonder worlds that shine
   From alien tracts of sky?
Nor ground to assume is mine
   Nor warrant to deny.
Equal, my source of hope, my reason for despair.

IX

And though within me here
   Hope lingers unsubdued,
'Tis because airiest cheer
   Suffices for her food!
As some adventurous flower,
   On savage crag-side grown,
Seems nourished hour by hour
   From its wild self alone,
So lives inveterate Hope, on her own hardihood.

X

She tells me, whispering low:
   'Wherefore and whence thou wast,
Thou shalt behold and know
   When the great bridge is crossed.
For not in mockery He
   Thy gift of wondering gave,
Nor bade thine answer be
   The blank stare of the grave.
Thou shalt behold and know; and find again thy lost.

XI

With rapt eyes fixed afar,
  She tells me: 'Throughout Space,
Godward each peopled star
  Runs with thy Earth a race.
Wouldst have the goal so nigh,
  The course so smooth a field,
That Triumph should thereby
  One half its glory yield?
And can Life's pyramid soar all apex and no base?'

XII

She saith: 'Old dragons lie
  In bowers of pleasance curled;
And dost thou ask me why?
  It is a Wizard's world!
Enchanted princes these,
  Who yet their scales shall cast,
And through his sorceries
  Die into kings at last.
Ambushed in Winter's heart the rose of June is furled.'

XIII

Such are the tales she tells:
  Who trusts, the happier he:
But nought of *virtue* dwells
  In that felicity!
I think the harder feat
  Were his who should *withstand*
A voice so passing sweet,
  And so profuse a hand,—
Hope, I forego the wealth thou fling'st abroad so free!

XIV

Carry thy largess hence,
  Light Giver! Let me learn
To abjure the opulence
  I have done nought to earn;

And on this world no more
  To cast ignoble slight,
Counting it but the door
  Of other worlds more bright.
Here, where I fail or conquer, here is my concern:

xv

Here, where perhaps alone
  I conquer or I fail.
Here, o'er the dark Deep blown,
  I ask no perfumed gale;
I ask the unpampering breath
  That fits me to endure
Chance, and victorious Death,
  Life, and my doom obscure,
Who know not whence I am sped, nor to what port I sail.

THE UNKNOWN GOD

William Watson

When, over-arched by gorgeous night,
  I wave my trivial self away;
When all I was to all men's sight
  Shares the erasure of the day;
Then do I cast my cumbering load,
Then do I gain a sense of God.

Not him that with fantastic boasts
  A sombre people dreamed they knew;
The mere barbaric God of Hosts
  That edged their sword and braced their thew:
A God they pitted 'gainst a swarm
Of neighbor Gods less vast of arm;

A God like some imperious king,
  Wroth were his realm not duly awed;
A God forever hearkening
  Unto his self-commanded laud;

A God forever jealous grown
Of carven wood and graven stone;

A God whose ghost, in arch and aisle,
  Yet haunts his temple and his tomb;
But follows in a little while
  Odin and Zeus to equal doom;
A God of kindred seed and line;
Man's giant shadow, hailed divine.

O streaming worlds, O crowded sky,
  O Life, and mine own soul's abyss,
Myself am scarce so small that I
  Should bow to Deity like this!
This my Begetter? This was what
Man in his violent youth begot.

The God I know of, I shall ne'er
  Know, though he dwells exceeding high.
Raise thou the stone and find me there,
  Cleave thou the wood and there am I.
Yea, in my flesh his spirit doth flow,
Too near, too far, for me to know.

Whate'er my deeds, I am not sure
  That I can pleasure him or vex:
I that must use a speech so poor
  It narrows the supreme with sex.
Notes he the good or ill in man?
To hope he cares is all I can.

I hope, with fear. For did I trust
  The vision granted me at birth,
The sire of heaven would seem less just
  Than many a faulty son of earth.
And so he seems indeed! But then!
  I trust it not, this bounded ken.

And dreaming much, I never dare
  To dream that in my prisoned soul

The flutter of a trembling prayer
  Can move the Mind that is the Whole.
Though kneeling nations watch and yearn,
Does the primordial purpose turn?

Best by remembering God, say some,
  We keep our high imperial lot.
Fortune, I fear, hath oftenest come
  When we forgot—when we forgot!
A lovelier faith their happier crown,
But history laughs and weeps it down!

Know they not well, how seven times seven,
  Wronging our mighty arms with rust,
We dared not do the work of heaven!
  Lest heaven should hurl us in the dust?
The work of heaven! 'Tis waiting still
The sanction of the heavenly will.

Unmeet to be profaned by praise
  Is he whose coils the world unfold;
The God on whom I never gaze,
  The God I never once behold:
Above the cloud, beneath the clod:
  The Unknown God, The Unknown God.

THE AWAKENED WAR GOD

Margaret Widdemer

The War God wakened drowsily;
  There were gold chains about his hands.
  He said: "And who shall reap my lands
And bear the tithes to Death for me?

"The nations stilled my thunderings;
  They wearied of my steel despair
  The flames from out my burning hair:
Is there an ending of such things?"

Low laughed the Earth, and answered: "When
  Was any changeless law I gave
  Changed by my sons intent to save,
By puny pitying hands of men?

"I feel no ruth for some I bear. . . .
  The swarming, hungering overflow
  Of crowded millions, doomed to go,
They must destroy who chained you there.

"For some bright stone or shining praise
  They stint a million bodies' breath,
  And sell the women, shamed, to death,
And send the men brief length of days.

"They kill the bodies swift for me,
  And kill the souls you gave to peace. . . .
  You were more merciful than these,
Old master of my cruelty.

"Lo, souls are scarred and virtues dim:
  Take back thy scourge of ministry,
  Rise from thy silence suddenly,
Lest these still take Death's toll to him!"

The War God snapped his golden chain:
  His mercies thundered down the world,
  And lashing battle lines uncurled
And scourged the crouching lands again.

AN INDIAN UPON GOD

WILLIAM B. YEATS

I passed along the water's edge, below the humid trees
My spirit rocked in evening light, the rushes round my knees,
My spirit rocked in sleep and sighs; and saw the moor-fowl
    pace

All dripping on a glassy slope, and saw them cease to chase
Each other round in circles, and heard the eldest speak:
"Who holds the world between His bill and made us strong
    or weak
Is an undying moor-fowl, and He lives beyond the sky.
The rains are from His dripping wing, the moonbeams from
    His eye."
I passed a little further on and heard a lotus talk:
"Who made the world and ruleth it, He hangeth on a stalk,
For I am in his image made, and all this tinkling tide
Is but a sliding drop of rain between his petals wide."
A little way within the gloom a roe-buck raised his eyes
Brimful of starlight, and he said: "The Stamper of the skies,
He is a gentle roe-buck; for how else, I pray, could He
Conceive a thing so sad and soft, a gentle thing like me?"
I passed a little further on and heard a peacock say:
"Who made the grass and made the worms and made my
    feathers gay
He is a monstrous peacock, and he waveth all the night
His languid tail above us, lit with myriad spots of light."

JEHOVAH

Israel Zangwill

"Destroying and making alive, and causing salvation to spring
      forth."—Jewish Prayer Book.

I sing the uplift and the up-welling,
I sing the yearning toward the sun,
And the blind sea that lifts white hands of prayer.
I sing the wild battle cry of warriors
And the sweet whispers of lovers,
And the dear word of the hearth and the altar,
Aspiration, Inspiration, Compensation,
           God!

The hint of beauty behind the turbid cities,
The eternal laws that cleanse and cancel.
The pity through the savagery of nature,
The love atoning for the brothels,
The Master-Artist behind His tragedies
Creator, Destroyer, Purifier, Avenger,
                              God!

Come into the circle of Love and Justice,
Come into the brotherhood of Pity,
Of Holiness and Health!
Strike out glad limbs upon the sunny water,
Or be dragged down amid the rotting weeds
The festering bodies.
Save thy soul from sandy barrenness,
Let it blossom with roses and gleam with living waters.

Blame not, nor reason of your Past,
Nor explain to Him your congenital weakness,
But come, for He is remorseless,
Call Him unjust, but come.
Do not mock or defy Him, for He will prevail;
He regardeth not you: He hath swallowed the worlds and
    the nations;
He hath humor, too: disease and death for the snugly pros-
    perous.

For such is the Law, stern, unchangeable, shining,
Making dung from souls and souls from dung.
Thrilling the dust to holy beautiful spirit,
And returning the spirit to dust,
Come and ye shall know Peace and Joy.
Let what ye desire of the universe penetrate you,
Let Loving-kindness and Mercy pass through you,
And Truth be the Law of your mouth.
For so ye are channels of the divine sea,
Which may not flood the earth but only steal in
Through rifts in your souls.

AT THE WORST

ISRAEL ZANGWILL

"And Man is left alone with Man." 'Tis well!
The shapes that in the dusky background fell
From Man's bright soul are laid by morning's spell.

Why stay the Present 'gainst the Past to poise?
Man grown to Manhood spurns his childish toys
And wakes to grander fears and hopes and joys.

If aught is lost that we should long to keep,
'Tis Manhood's part to work and not to weep.
Old age comes on, and everlasting sleep.

We are—whatever we have been before;
We have whatever gold *was* in the ore;
God lives as much as in the days of yore.

In fires of human work and love and song,
In wells of human tears that pitying throng,
In thunder-clouds of human wrath at wrong.

The burning bush doth not the more consume,
New branches shoot where old no more illume,
Eternal splendor flames upon the gloom.

Though Hell and Heaven were a dream forgot,
And unregarded sacrifice our lot,
We serve God better, deeming He is not.

Perchance, O ye that toil on, though forlorn
By your souls' travail, your own noble scorn,
The very God you crave is being born.

Nor yet hath Man of faith and courage failed,
Albeit dazzled for a space and paled
By glimpse of Truth—God's awful face unveiled.

No change need be in all that we hold dear;
Love, Virtue, Knowledge, Beauty—all are here,
One Hope is gone—but in its train one Fear.

The sea wind blows as fresh; the ocean heaves
As blue and buoyant: Nature nowhere grieves;
As bright a green is on the forest leaves.

Larks sing and roses still are odorous,
Art, Poetry and Music are still for us,
And Woman just as fair and marvellous.

And if the earth with endless fray is rife,
Acknowledge in the universal strife,
The zest of this, the seed of higher, life.

Evil is here? That's work for us to do.
The Old is dying? Let's beget the New.
And Death awaits us? Rest is but our due.

IV. Faith

PROVIDENCE

Light Shining Out of Darkness

WILLIAM COWPER

God moves in a mysterious way
  His wonders to perform;
He plants his footsteps in the sea,
  And rides upon the storm.

Deep in unfathomable mines
  Of never-failing skill
He treasures up his bright designs,
  And works his sovereign will.

Ye fearful saints, fresh courage take,
  The clouds ye so much dread
Are big with mercy, and shall break
  In blessings on your head.

Judge not the Lord by feeble sense,
  But trust him for his grace:
Behind a frowning providence
  He hides a smiling face.

His purposes will ripen fast,
  Unfolding every hour;
The bud may have a bitter taste
  But sweet will be the flower.

Blind unbelief is sure to err,
  And scan his work in vain;
God is his own interpreter
  And he will make it plain.

A LITTLE BIRD I AM

Madame Guyon

(Written in the Bastille)

Translated by Prof. T. C. Upham

A little bird I am,
  Shut in from fields of air,
And in my cage I sit and sing,
  To him who placed me there;
Well pleased a prisoner to be,
Because, my God, it pleases thee!

Naught have I else to do,
  I sing the whole day long;
And he whom I most love to please
  Doth listen to my song;
He caught and bound my wandering wing,
And still he bends to hear me sing.

Thou hast an ear to hear,
  A heart to love and bless;
And though my notes were e'er so rude,
  Thou wouldst not hear the less;
Because thou knowest as they fall,
That love, sweet love, inspires them all.

My cage confines me round,
  Abroad I cannot fly;
But though my wing is closely bound,
  My heart's at liberty;
My prison walls cannot control
The flight, the freedom of the soul.

Oh, it is good to soar,
  These bolts and bars above,
To him whose purpose I adore,
  Whose providence I love;
And in thy mighty will to find
The joy, the freedom of the mind.

TO GOD

ROBERT HERRICK

Lord, I am like to mistletoe,
Which has no root and cannot grow
Or prosper, but by that same tree
It clings about: so I by thee.
What need I then to fear at all
So long as I about thee crawl?
But if that tree should fall and die,
Tumble shall heaven, and so down will I.

THE FLYING WHEEL

KATHARINE TYNAN HINKSON

When I was young the days were long,
O, long the days when I was young:
So long from morn to evenfall
As they would never end at all.

Now I grow old Time flies, alas!
I watch the years and seasons pass.
Time turns him with his fingers thin
A wheel that whirls while it doth spin.

There is no time to take one's ease,
For to sit still and be at peace:
Oh, whirling wheel of Time, be still,
Let me be quiet if you will!

Yet still it turns so giddily,
So fast the years and seasons fly,
Dazed with the noise and speed I run
And stay me on the Changeless One.

I stay myself on Him who stays
Ever the same through nights and days:
The One Unchangeable for aye,
That was and will be: the one Stay,

O'er whom Eternity will pass
But as an image in a glass;
To whom a million years are nought,—
I stay myself on a great Thought.

I stay myself on the great Quiet
After the noises and the riot;
As in a garnished chamber sit
Far from the tumult of the street.

Oh, wheel of Time, turn round apace!
But I have found a resting place.
You will not trouble me again
In the great peace where I attain

THE INCOMPREHENSIBLE

Isaac Watts

Far in the Heavens my God retires:
My God, the mark of my desires.
    And hides His lovely face;
When He descends within my view,
He charms my reason to pursue,
But leaves it tired and fainting in th' unequal chase.

Or if I reach unusual height
    Till near His presence brought,
There floods of glory check my flight

Cramp the bold pinions of my wit,
　　And all untune my thought;
Plunged in a sea of light I roll,
Where wisdom, justice, mercy, shines;
Infinite rays in crossing lines
Beat thick confusion on my sight, and overwhelm my soul.

Great God! behold my reason lies
Adoring: yet my love would rise
　　On pinions not her own:
Faith shall direct her humble flight,
Through all the trackless seas of light,
To Thee, th' Eternal Fair, the Infinite Unknown.

GOD MAKES A PATH

Roger Williams

God makes a path, provides a guide,
　　And feeds a wilderness;
His glorious name, while breath remains,
　　O that I may confess.

Lost many a time, I have had no guide,
　　No house but a hollow tree!
In stormy winter night no fire,
　　No food, no company;

In Him I found a house, a bed,
　　A table, company;
No cup so bitter but's made sweet,
　　Where God shall sweetening be.

b. MODERN FAITH

THE DOUBTER'S PRAYER

ANNE BRONTË

Eternal Power, of earth and air!
  Unseen, yet seen in all around;
Remote, but dwelling everywhere;
  Though silent heard in every sound;

If e'er thine ear in Mercy lent,
  When wretched mortals cried to Thee,
And if indeed, Thy Son was sent,
  To save lost sinners such as me:

Then hear me now, while kneeling here,
  I lift to thee my heart and eye,
And all my soul ascends in prayer,
  Oh, give me—Give me Faith! I cry.

While Faith is with me, I am blest;
  It turns my darkest night to day;
But while I clasp it to my breast,
  I often feel it slide away.

Then, cold and dark, my spirit sinks,
  To see my light of life depart;
And every friend of Hell, methinks,
  Enjoys the anguish of my heart.

What shall I do if all my love,
  My hopes, my toil, are cast away,
And if there be no God above,
  To hear and bless me while I pray?

If this be vain delusion all,
  If death be an eternal sleep
And none can hear my secret call,
  Or see the silent tears I weep!

O help me God! for Thou alone
   Canst my distracted soul relieve;
Forsake it not, it is Thine own,
   Though weak, yet longing to believe.

WAITING

JOHN BURROUGHS

Serene, I fold my hands and wait,
   Nor care for wind, nor tide, nor sea;
I rave no more 'gainst time or fate,
   For, lo! mine own shall come to me.

I stay my haste, I make delays,
   For what avails this eager pace?
I stand amid the eternal ways,
   And what is mine shall know my face.

Asleep, awake, by night or day,
   The friends I seek are seeking me;
No wind can drive my bark astray,
   Nor change the tide of destiny.

What matter if I stand alone?
   I wait with joy the coming years;
My heart shall reap where it has sown,
   And garner up its fruit of tears.

The waters know their own, and draw
   The brook that springs in yonder heights;
So flows the good with equal law
   Unto the soul of pure delights.

The stars come nightly to the sky;
   The tidal wave comes to the sea;
Nor time, nor space, nor deep, nor high,
   Can keep my own away from me.

THERE IS NO UNBELIEF

Elizabeth York Case

There is no unbelief;
Whoever plants a seed beneath the sod
And waits to see it push away the clod—
He trusts in God.

There is no unbelief;
Whoever says when clouds are in the sky,
"Be patient, heart; light breaketh by and by,"
Trusts the Most High.

There is no unbelief;
Whoever sees 'neath winter's field of snow,
The silent harvest of the future grow—
God's power must know.

There is no unbelief;
Whoever lies down on his couch to sleep,
Content to lock each sense in slumber deep,
Knows God will keep.

There is no unbelief;
Whoever says "tomorrow," "the unknown,"
"The future," trusts the power alone
He dares disown.

There is no unbelief;
The heart that looks on when the eye-lids close,
And dares to live when life has only woes,
God's comfort knows.

There is no unbelief;
For thus by day and night unconsciously
The heart lives by that faith the lips deny,
God knoweth why!

HOPE EVERMORE AND BELIEVE

Arthur Hugh Clough

Hope evermore and believe, O man, for e'en as thy thought
So are the things that thou seest; e'en as thy hope and belief.
Cowardly thou art, and timid? They rise to provoke thee
    against them.
Hast thou courage? Enough, see them exulting to yield.
Yea, the rough rock, the dull earth, the wild sea's furying
    waters
(Violent, sayst thou, and hard, mighty, thinkst thou, to destroy),
All with ineffable longing, are waiting their Invader,
All, with one varying voice, call to him, Come and subdue;
Still for their conqueror call, and but for the joy of being
    conquered
(Rapture they will not forego) dare to resist and rebel;
Still, when resisting and raging, in soft undervoice say to him,
Fear not, retire not, O Man; hope evermore and believe.

Go from the east and the west, as the sun and stars direct
    thee,
Go with the girdle of man, go and encompass the earth.
Not for the gain of the gold; for the getting, the hoarding,
    the having,
But for the joy of the deed; but for the duty to do.
Go with the spiritual life, the higher volition and action,
With the great girdle of God, go and encompass the earth.

Go; say not in thy heart, And what then were it accomplished,
Were the wild impulse allayed, what were the use or the good?
Go, when the instinct is stilled, and when the deed is accom-
    plished,
What thou hast done, and shalt do, shall be declared to thee,
    then.
Go with the sun and the stars, and yet evermore in thy spirit
Say to thyself: It is good: yet there is better than it.
This that I see is not all, and this that I do is but little;
Nevertheless it is good, though there is better than it.

WITH WHOM IS NO VARIABLENESS, NEITHER SHADOW OF TURNING

Arthur Hugh Clough

It fortifies my soul to know
That though I perish, truth is so;
That, howsoe'er I stray and range,
Whate'er I do, Thou dost not change.
I steadier step when I recall
That, if I slip, Thou dost not fall.

ADRIFT

Mrs. Edward Dowden

Unto my faith as to a spar, I bind
  My love—and Faith and Love adrift I cast
On a dim sea. I know not if at last
They the eternal shore of God shall find.

I know that neither waves nor wind
  Can sunder them; the cords are tied so fast
  That faith shall never—doubts and dangers past—
Come safe to land and Love be left behind.

THE TIDE OF FAITH

George Eliot

So faith is strong
Only when we are strong, shrinks when we shrink.
It comes when music stirs us, and the chords,
Moving on some grand climax, shake our souls
With influx new that makes new energies.
It comes in swellings of the heart and tears
That rise at noble and at gentle deeds.

It comes in moments of heroic love,
Unjealous joy in joy not made for us;
In conscious triumph of the good within,
Making us worship goodness that rebukes.
Even our failures are a prophecy,
Even our yearnings and our bitter tears
After that fair and true we cannot grasp.
Presentiment of better things on earth
Sweeps in with every force that stirs our souls
To admiration, self-renouncing love.

BRAHMA

RALPH WALDO EMERSON

If the red slayer think he slays,
  Or if the slain think he is slain,
They know not well the subtle ways
  I keep, and pass, and turn again.

Far or forgot to me is near;
  Shadow and sunlight are the same;
The vanished gods to me appear;
  And one to me are shame and fame.

They reckon ill who leave me out;
  When me they fly, I am the wings;
I am the doubter and the doubt,
  And I the hymn the Brahmin sings.

The strong gods pine for my abode,
  And pine in vain the sacred Seven;
But thou, meek lover of the good!
  Find me, and turn thy back on heaven.

EACH AND ALL

RALPH WALDO EMERSON

Little thinks, in the field, yon red-cloaked clown
Of thee from the hill-top looking down;
The heifer that lows in the upland farm,
Far-heard, lows not thine ear to charm;
The sexton, tolling his bell at noon,
Deems not that great Napoleon
Stops his horse and lists with delight,
Whilst his files sweep round yon Alpine height;
Nor knowest thou what argument
Thy life to thy neighbor's creed has lent.
All are needed by each one;
Nothing is good or fair alone.
I thought the sparrow's note from heaven,
Singing at dawn on the alder bough;
I brought him home in his nest at even;
He sings the song but it cheers not now,
For I did not bring home the river and sky;—
He sang to my ear,—they sang to my eye.

The delicate shells lay on the shore;
The bubbles of the latest wave
Fresh pearls to their enamel gave,
And the bellowing of the savage sea
Greeted their safe escape to me.
I wiped away the weeds and foam,
I fetched my sea-born treasures home;
But the poor, unsightly, noisome things
Had left their beauty on the shore,
With the sun and the sand and the wild uproar.

The lover watched his graceful maid,
As 'mid the virgin train she strayed;
Nor knew her beauty's best attire
Was woven still by the snow-white choir.

At last she came to his hermitage,
Like the bird from the woodlands to the cage;—
The gay enchantment was undone,
A gentle wife, but fairy none.

Then I said, "I covet truth;
Beauty is unripe childhood's cheat;
I leave it behind with the games of youth."—
As I spoke, beneath my feet
The ground-pine curled its pretty wreath,
Running over the club-moss burrs;
I inhaled the violet's breath;
Around me stood the oaks and firs;
Pine-cones and acorns lay on the ground;
Over me soared the eternal sky,
Full of light and of deity;
Again I saw, again I heard,
The rolling river, the morning bird;—
Beauty through my senses stole;
I yielded myself to the perfect whole.

THE STREAM OF FAITH

William Channing Gannett

From heart to heart, from creed to creed,
    The hidden river runs;
It quickens all the ages down,
    It binds the sires to sons,—
The stream of Faith, whose source is God,
    Whose sound, the sound of prayer,
Whose meadows are the holy lives
    Upspringing everywhere.

And still it moves, a broadening flood;
    And fresher, fuller grows.
A sense as if the sea were near
    Towards which the river flows.

O thou who art the secret Source
That rises in each soul,
Thou art the Ocean, too,—thy charm,
That ever-deepening roll!

DOUBT

FERNAND GREGH

From *Poets of Modern France*

By Ludwig Lewisohn

Upon the topmost branches dies
A last ray of the setting sun;
A glimmer of strange gilding lies
Upon the leaves' vermilion.

From the pale sky the colors fade
'Tis grey even as grey waters are.
There glide like sudden shafts of shade
The living wings of birds afar.

From all things comes a charm so deep,
So sweet and glad, so void of strife,
Calm as the peacefulness of sleep,
Spreads the divinely cosmic life.

The sounds of the far city roll
On fitful winds to my retreat—
Why falls there sudden on my soul
A feeling beyond speaking sweet?

Dear God, how all the sense of doom
Vanishes in the face of things!
How one is like poor men to whom
Some chance a day of feasting brings!

How one adores in childlike mood
And finds thee where the shadows fall,
Here is life's holy amplitude
Thee who, perhaps art not at all!

A SONG OF DOUBT

Josiah Gilbert Holland

The day is quenched, and the sun is fled;
  God has forgotten the world!
The moon has gone, and the stars are dead:
  God has forgotten the world!

Evil has won in the horrid feud
  Of ages with the throne;
Evil stands on the neck of Good,
  And rules the world alone.

There is no good: there is no God.
  And faith is a heartless cheat
Who bares the back for the devil's rod
  And scatters thorns for the feet.

What are prayers in the lips of death,
  Filling and chilling with hail?
What are prayers but wasted breath,
  Beaten back by the gale?

The day is quenched, and the sun has fled;
  God has forgotten the world!
The moon is gone and the stars are dead,
  God has forgotten the world!

A SONG OF FAITH

Josiah Gilbert Holland

Day will return with a fresher boon;
  God will remember the world!
Night will come with a newer moon;
  God will remember the world!

Evil is only the slave of good;
  Sorrow the servant of joy;
And the soul is mad that refuses food
  Of the meanest in God's employ.

The fountain of joy is fed by tears,
  And love is lit by the breath of sighs;
The deepest griefs and the wildest fears
  Have holiest ministries;

Strong grows the oak in the sweeping storm;
  Safely the flower sleeps under the snow;
And the farmer's hearth is never warm
  Till the cold wind starts to blow.

Day will return with a fresher boon;
  God will remember the world!
Night will come with a newer moon;
  God will remember the world!

FAITH

WILLIAM DEAN HOWELLS

If I lay waste and wither up with doubt
The blessed fields of heaven where once my Faith
Possessed itself serenely safe from death;
If I deny the things past finding out;
Or if I orphan my own soul of One
That seemed a Father, and make void the place
Within me where He dwelt in Power and Grace,
What do I gain by that I have undone?

THE POET'S SIMPLE FAITH

VICTOR HUGO

You say, "Where goest Thou?" I cannot tell,
And still go on. If but the way be straight
I cannot go amiss: before me lies

Dawn and the day: the night behind me: that
Suffices me: I break the bounds: I see,
And nothing more; believe and nothing less.
My future is not one of my concerns.
Translated by Prof. Edward Dowden.

DOUBT

Helen Hunt Jackson

They bade me cast the thing away,
They pointed to my hands all bleeding,
They listened not to all my pleading;
   The thing I meant I could not say;
  I knew that I should rue the day
   If once I cast that thing away.

   I grasped it firm, and bore the pain;
The thorny husks I stripped and scattered;
If I could reach its heart, what mattered
   If other men saw not my gain,
   Or even if I should be slain?
  I knew the risks; I chose the pain.

   O, had I cast that thing away,
I had not found what most I cherish,
A faith without which I should perish,—
   The faith which, like a kernel, lay
   Hid in the husks which on that day
  My instinct would not throw away!

THE BEGINNINGS OF FAITH

Sir Lewis Morris

All travail of high thought,
  All secrets vainly sought,
All struggles for right, heroic, perpetually fought;

Faint gleams of purer fire,
Conquests of gross desire,
Whereby the fettered soul ascends continually higher;

Pure cares for love or friend
Which ever upward tend,
Too deep and heavenward and true to have on earth their end;

Vile hearts malign and fell,
Lives which no tongue may tell,
So dark and dread and shameful that they breathe a present
        hell;

What mountain, deep-set lake,
Sea wastes which surge and break,
Fierce storms which, roaring from the north, the midnight
        forests shake;

Fair morns of summer days,
Rich harvest eves that raise
The soul and heart o'erburdened to an ecstasy of praise;

Low whispers, vague and strange,
Which through our being range,
Breathing perpetual presage of some mighty coming change:

These in the soul do breed
Thoughts which, at last, shall lead
To some clear, firm assurance of a satisfying creed.

FAITH

Alexander Pope

For modes of faith let graceless Zealots fight;
He can't be wrong whose life is in the right;
In faith and hope the world will disagree,
But all mankind's concern is charity:

All must be false that thwart this one great end;
And all of God that bless mankind, or mend.
Man, like the generous vine, supported lives:
The strength he gains is from the embrace he gives.

IF THIS WERE FAITH

ROBERT LOUIS STEVENSON

God, if this were enough,
That I see things bare to the buff
And up to the buttocks in mire;
That I ask not hope nor hire,
Not in the husk,
Nor dawn beyond the dusk,
Nor life beyond death:
God, if this were faith?

Having felt thy wind in my face
Spit sorrow and disgrace,
Having seen thine evil doom
In Golgotha and Khartoum,
And the brutes, the work of thine hands,
Fill with injustice lands
And stain with blood the sea:
If still in my veins the glee
Of the black night and the sun
And the lost battle, run:
If, an adept,
The iniquitous lists I still accept
With joy, and joy to endure and be withstood,
And still to battle and perish for a dream of good:
God, if that were enough?

If to feel, in the ink of the slough,
And the sink of the mire,
Veins of glory and fire
Run through and transpierce and transpire,

And a secret purpose of glory in every part,
And the answering glory of battle fill my heart;
To thrill with the joy of girded men
To go on forever and fail and go on again,
And be mauled to the earth and arise,
And contend for the shade of a word and a thing not seen
    with the eyes;
With the half of a broken hope for a pillow at night
That somehow the right is the right
And the smooth shall bloom from the rough:
Lord, if that were enough?

FAITH

John B. Tabb

In every seed to breathe the flower,
In every drop of dew
To reverence a cloistered star
Within the distant blue;
To wait the promise of the bow
Despite the cloud between,
Is Faith—the fervid evidence
Of loveliness unseen.

From IN MEMORIAM

Alfred Tennyson

Proem

Strong Son of God, immortal Love,
  Whom we, that have not seen thy face,
  By faith, and faith alone, embrace,
Believing where we cannot prove;

Thine are these orbs of light and shade;
  Thou madest Life in man and brute;
  Thou madest Death; and, lo, thy foot
Is on the skull which thou hast made.

Thou wilt not leave us in the dust:
  Thou madest man, he knows not why,
  He thinks he was not made to die;
And thou hast made him: thou art just.

Thou seemest human and divine,
  The highest, holiest manhood, thou;
  Our wills are ours, we know not how:
Our wills are ours, to make them thine.

Our little systems have their day;
  They have their day and cease to be:
  They are but broken lights of thee,
And thou, O Lord, art more than they.

We have but faith: we cannot know;
  For knowledge is of things we see;
  And yet we trust it comes from thee,
A beam in darkness: let it grow.

Let knowledge grow from more to more,
  But more of reverence in us dwell:
  That mind and soul, according well,
May make one music as before,

But vaster. We are fools and slight;
  We mock thee when we do not fear:
  But help thy foolish ones to bear;
Help thy vain worlds to bear thy light.

Forgive what seemed my sin in me,
  What seemed my worth since I began;
  For merit lives from man to man,
And not from man, O Lord, to thee.

Forgive my grief for one removed,
  Thy creature, whom I found so fair.
  I trust he lives in thee, and there
I find him worthier to be loved.

Forgive these wild and wandering cries,
  Confusions of a wasted youth;
  Forgive them where they fail in truth,
And in thy wisdom make me wise.

THE ANCIENT SAGE

ALFRED TENNYSON

Thou canst not prove that thou art body alone,
Nor canst thou prove that thou art spirit alone,
Nor canst thou prove that thou art both in one,
Thou canst not prove thou art immortal, no,
Nor yet that thou art mortal—nay, my son,
Thou canst not prove that I, who speak with thee,
Am not thyself in converse with thyself,
For nothing worthy proving can be proven,
Nor yet disproven. Wherefore thou be wise,
Cleave ever to the sunnier side of doubt,
And cling to Faith beyond the forms of Faith!
She reels not in the storm of warring words,
She brightens at the clash of 'Yes' and 'No,'
She sees the best that glimmers through the worst,
She feels the sun is hid but for a night,
She spies the summer through the winter bud,
She tastes the fruit before the blossom falls,
She hears the lark within the songless egg,
She finds the fountain where they wailed 'Mirage!'

THE HIGHER PANTHEISM

ALFRED TENNYSON

The sun, the moon, the stars, the seas, the hills and the plains,—
Are not these, O Soul, the Vision of Him who reigns?

Is not the Vision He? Tho' He be not that which He seems?
Dreams are true while they last, and do we not live in dreams?

Earth, these solid stars, this weight of body and limb,
Are they not sign and symbol of thy division from Him?

Dark is the world to thee: thyself art the reason why;
For is He not all but thou, that hast power to feel "I am I?"

Glory about thee, without thee; and thou fulfillest thy doom,
Making Him broken gleams and a stifled splendor and gloom.

Speak to Him thou for He hears, and Spirit with Spirit can
    meet—
Closer is He than breathing, and nearer than hands and feet.

God is law, say the wise; O Soul, and let us rejoice,
For if He thunder by law the thunder is yet His voice.

ADJUSTMENT

JOHN GREENLEAF WHITTIER

The tree of Faith its bare dry boughs must shed
    That nearer heaven the living ones may climb;
    The false must fail, though from our shores of time
The old lament be heard,—"Great Pan is dead!"
That wail is Error's, from his high place hurled;
    This sharp recoil is Evil undertrod;
    Our time's unrest, an angel sent of God,
Troubling with life the waters of the world,
Even as they list the winds of the Spirit blow
    To turn or break our century-rusted vanes;
    Sands shift and waste; the rock alone remains
Where, led of Heaven, the strong tides come and go,
    And storm-clouds, rent by thunder-bolt and wind,
    Leave, free of mist, the permanent stars behind.

Therefore I trust, although to outward sense
    Both true and false seem shaken; I will hold
    With newer light my reverence for the old,
And calmly wait the births of Providence.

No gain is lost; the clear-eyed saints look down
  Untroubled on the wreck of schemes and creeds;
  Love yet remains, its rosary of good deeds
Counting in task-field and o'er peopled town;
Truth has charmed life; the Inward Word survives,
  And, day by day, its revelation brings.
  Faith, hope, and charity, whatsoever things
Which cannot be shaken, stand. Still holy lives
  Reveal the Christ of whom the letter told,
  And the new gospel verifies the old.

THE WAITING

JOHN GREENLEAF WHITTIER

I wait and watch: before my eyes
  Methinks the night grows thin and gray;
I wait and watch the eastern skies
To see the golden spears uprise
  Beneath the oriflamme of day!

Like one whose limbs are bound in trance
  I hear the day sounds swell and grow,
And see across the twilight glance,
Troop after troop in swift advance,
  The shining ones with plumes of snow!

I know the errand of their feet,
  I know what mighty work is theirs;
I can but lift up hand unmeet,
The threshing-floors of God to beat,
  And speed them with unworthy prayers.

I will not dream in vain despair
  The steps of progress wait for me:
The puny leverage of a hair
The planet's impulse well may spare,
  A drop of dew the tided sea.

The loss, if loss there be, is mine,
  And yet not mine, if understood;
For one shall grasp and one resign,
One drink life's rue and one its wine,
  And God shall make the balance good.

O power to do! O baffled will!
  O prayer and action! ye are one!
Who may not strive may yet fulfil
The harder task of standing still,
  And good but wished with God is done!

THE ETERNAL GOODNESS

John Greenleaf Whittier

O Friends! with whom my feet have trod
  The quiet aisles of prayer,
Glad witness to your zeal for God
  And love of man I bear.

I trace your lines of argument;
  Your logic linked and strong
I weigh as one who dreads dissent,
  And fears a doubt as wrong.

But still my human hands are weak
  To hold your iron creeds:
Against the words ye bid me speak
  My heart within me pleads.

Who fathoms the Eternal Thought?
  Who talks of scheme and plan?
The Lord is God! He needeth not
  The poor device of man.

I walk with bare, hushed feet the ground
  Ye tread with boldness shod;
I dare not fix with mete and bound
  The love and power of God.

Ye praise His justice; even such
　His pitying love I deem:
Ye seek a king; I fain would touch
　The robe that hath no seam.

Ye see the curse which overbroods
　A world of pain and loss;
I hear our Lord's beatitudes
　And prayer upon the cross.

More than your schoolmen teach, within
　Myself, alas! I know:
Too dark ye cannot paint the sin,
　Too small the merit show.

I bow my forehead to the dust,
　I veil mine eyes for shame,
And urge, in trembling self-distrust,
　A prayer without a claim.

I see the wrong that round me lies,
　I feel the guilt within;
I hear, with groan and travail-cries,
　The world confess its sin.

Yet, in the maddening maze · of things,
　And tossed by storm and flood,
To one fixed trust my spirit clings;
　I know that God is good!

Not mine to look where cherubim
　And seraphs may not see,
But nothing can be good in Him
　Which evil is in me.

The wrong that pains my soul below
　I dare not throne above;
I know not of His hate,—I know
　His goodness and His love.

FAITH

I dimly guess from blessings known
　Of greater out of sight,
And, with the chastened Psalmist, own
　His judgments too are right.

I long for household voices gone,
　For vanished smiles I long,
But God hath led my dear ones on,
　And He can do no wrong.

I know not what the future hath
　Of marvel or surprise,
Assured alone that life and death
　His mercy underlies.

And if my heart and flesh are weak
　To bear an untried pain,
The bruised reed He will not break,
　But strengthen and sustain.

No offering of my own I have,
　Nor works my faith to prove;
I can but give the gifts He gave,
　And plead His love for love.

And so beside the Silent Sea
　I wait the muffled oar;
No harm from Him can come to me
　On ocean or on shore.

I know not where His islands lift
　Their fronded palms in air;
I only know I cannot drift
　Beyond His love and care.

O brothers! if my faith is vain,
　If hopes like these betray,
Pray for me that my feet may gain
　The sure and safer way.

And Thou, O Lord! by whom are seen
Thy creatures as they be,
Forgive me if too close I lean
My human heart on Thee!

c. NEW VOICES

MY FAITH

SRI ANANDA ACHARYA

All this is one
Though the earth is dark and the stars are bright,
This is my faith: there is a hidden light in man.
Though disease we fear and old age we dread, this is my faith:
the soul is brave.
Though the sun of life has risen and will as surely set, this
is my faith: the sun of life shines ever in its place,
unmoving.
Though the royal swans fly and the storms smite their head,
this is my faith: they will reach their home in the Mansa
lake.
Though the mountains stand mute and the birds sing merrily,
this is my faith: the pole-star is firm.
Though friends greet like strangers and strangers are unkind,
this is my faith: love will wake in their souls.
Though all men have different faces, different minds, this is
my faith: one heart moves them all.
Though atoms, forces, lives, fates, graces, times, each from the
other differs, each fighting for supremacy—this is my
faith: all are traveling, under the cloud of unknowing-
ness, to the
All-soul's temple of rest.

VICTORY

(Found on the body of an Australian soldier)

Ye that have faith to look with fearless eyes
    Beyond the tragedy of a world at strife,
And know that out of death and night shall rise
    The dawn of ampler life:
Rejoice, whatever anguish rend the heart,
    That God has given you the priceless dower
To live in these great times and have your part
    In Freedom's crowning hour,
That ye may tell your sons who see the light
    High in the heavens—their heritage to take—
"I saw the powers of darkness take their flight;
    I saw the morning break."

HAVE FAITH

Edward Carpenter

Do not hurry; have faith.

Remember that if you become famous you can never share the lot of those who pass by unnoticed from the cradle to the grave, nor take part in the last heroism of their daily life;

If you seek and encompass wealth and ease the divine outlook of poverty cannot be yours—nor shall you feel all your days the loving and constraining touch of Nature and Necessity;

If you are successful in all you do, you cannot also battle magnificently against odds;

If you have fortune and good health and a loving wife and children, you cannot also be of those who are happy without these things.

Covet not overmuch. Let the strong desires come and go; refuse them not, disown them not; but think not that in them lurks finally the thing you want.

Presently they will fade away and into the intolerable light will dissolve like gossamers before the sun.

Do not hurry; have faith.
(Whither indeed should we hurry? is it not well here?
A little shelter from the storm, a stack of fuel for winter use,
A few handfuls of grain and fruit—
And, lo! the glory of all the earth is ours.)
The main thing is that the messenger is perhaps even now at
    your door—and to see that you are ready for his arrival.

Likely whoever it is his coming will upset all your carefully
    laid plans;
Your most benevolent designs will likely have to be laid aside,
    and he will set you to some quite common-place business,
    or perhaps of dubious character—
  Or send you on a long and solitary journey; perhaps he
will bring you letters of trust to deliver—perhaps the prince
himself will appear—
  Yet see that you are ready for his arrival.

  Is your present experience hard to bear?
Yet remember that never again perhaps in all your days
Will you have another chance at the same.
  Do not fly the lesson, but have a care that you maintain it
while you have the opportunity.

  On all sides God surrounds you, staring out upon you from
the mountains and from the face of the rocks, and of men, and
of animals.
  Will you rush past forever insensate and blindfold—hurrying
breathless from one unfinished task to another, and to catch your
ever-departing trains—as if you were a very Cain flying from
His face?

IN THE HOSPITAL

Arthur Guiterman

Because on the branch that is tapping my pane
    A sun-wakened, leaf-bud uncurled,
Is bursting its rusty brown sheathing in twain,
    I know there is spring in the world.

Because through the sky-patch whose azure and white
  My window frames all the day long,
A yellow bird dips for an instant of flight,
  I know there is song.

Because even here, in this Mansion of Woe,
  Where creep the dull hours, leaden-shod,
Compassion and tenderness aid me, I know
  There is God.

GOD THE ARCHITECT

Harry Kemp

Who Thou art I know not
  But this much I know;
Thou hast set the Pleiades
  In a silver row;

Thou hast sent the trackless winds
  Loose upon their way;
Thou hast reared a colored wall
  Twixt the night and day;

Thou hast made the flowers to bloom
  And the stars to shine;
Hid rare gems of richest ore
  In the tunneled mine;

But chief of all thy wondrous works
  Supreme of all thy plan,
Thou hast put an upward reach
  Into the heart of man.

THE DEAD FAITH

FANNY HEASLIP LEA

She made a little shadow-hidden grave
  The day Faith died;
Therein she laid it, heard the clod's sick fall,
  And smiled aside—
"If less I ask," tear-blind, she mocked, "I may
  Be less denied."

She set a rose to blossom in her hair,
  The day Faith died—
"Now glad," she said, "and free, at last, I go,
  And life is wide."
But through long nights she stared into the dark,
  And knew she lied.

From THE REBEL

IRENE RUTHERFORD McLEOD

Beyond the murk that swallows me
There is an Eye that follows me,
There is an Ear that waits and strains
To catch the echoes of my pains,
There is a Hand outstretched to take
Utmost toll for each mistake:
These Three have stalked me down the years
To mock the passion of my tears.
I fling you scorn, unholy spy!
Though living give my faith the lie,
Though loving clip the wings of Love,
Though men humanity disprove,
Though all my suns and moons go out,
Though tongues of all the ages shout
That only death may not deceive—
I'll not believe! I'll not believe!

FAITH

With ardour passionate in my breath
I'll sing my undefeated faith!
O take me, break me, peaceless life!
My soul was born to welcome strife!
O sap my heart of its deep blood,
If blood be beauty's precious food!
There is no thing I would not give,
There is no hour I dare not live,
There is no hell I'll not explore
To find a hidden heavenly door!

SONNETS

John Masefield

O little self, within whose smallness lies
All that a man was, and is, and will become,
Atom unseen that comprehends the skies
And tells the tracks by which the planets roam.
That, without moving, knows the joy of wings,
The tiger's strength, the eagle's secrecy,
And in the hovel can consort with kings,
Or clothe a god with his own mystery.
O, with what darkness do we cloak thy light,
What dusty folly gather thee for food,
Thou who alone art knowledge and delight,
The heavenly bread, the beautiful, the good.
O living self, O god, O morning star,
Give us thy light, forgive us what we are.

If I could get within this changing I,
This ever altering thing which yet persists,
Keeping the features it is reckoned by,
While each component atom breaks or twists,
If, wandering past strange groups of shifting forms,
Cells at their hidden marvels hard at work,
Pale from much toil, or red from sudden storms,
I might attain to where the Rulers lurk.

If, pressing past the guards in those grey gates,
The brain's most folded intertwisted shell,
I might attain to that which alters fates,
The King, the Supreme Self, the Master Cell,
Then, on Man's earthly peak, I might behold
The unearthly self beyond, unguessed, untold.

How many ways, how many times
The tiger Mind has clutched at what it sought,
Only to prove supposèd virtues crimes,
The imagined godhead but a form of thought.
How many restless brains have wrought and schemed,
Padding their cage, or built, or brought to law,
Made in outlasting brass the something dreamed,
Only to prove themselves the things of awe.
Yet, in the happy moment's lightning blink
Comes scent, or track, or trace, the game goes by,
Some leopard thought is pawing at the brink,
Chaos below, and up above, the sky.
Then the keen nostrils scent, about, about,
To prove the Thing within a Thing Without.

There is no God, as I was taught in youth,
Though each, according to his stature, builds
Some covered shrine for what he thinks the truth,
Which, day by day, his reddest heart-blood gilds.
There is no God; but death, the clasping sea,
In which we move like fish, deep over deep,
Made of men's souls that bodies have set free,
Floods to a justice, though it seems asleep.
There is no God, but still, behind the veil,
The hurt thing works, out of its agony.
Still, like a touching of a brimming Grail,
Return the pennies given to passers by.
There is no God, but we, who breathe the air,
Are God ourselves and touch God everywhere.

SENSE AND SPIRIT

GEORGE MEREDITH

The senses loving Earth or well or ill
Ravel yet more the riddle of our lot.
The mind is in their trammels, and lights not
By trimming fear-bred tales; nor does the will
To find in nature things which less may chill
An ardour that desires, unknowing what.
Till we conceive her living we go distraught,
At best but circle-windsails of a mill.
Seeing she lives, and of her joy of life
Creatively has given us blood and breath
For endless war and never wound unhealed,
The gloomy Wherefore of our battlefield
Solves in the Spirit, wrought of her through strife
To read her own and trust her down to death.

From A FAITH ON TRIAL

GEORGE MEREDITH

'The dream is the thought in the ghost;
'The thought sent flying for food;
'Eyeless, but sprung of an aim
'Supernal of Reason, to find
'The great Over-Reason we name
'Beneficence: mind seeking Mind.
'Dream of the blossom of Good,
'In its waver and current and curve,
'With the hopes of my offspring enscrolled!
'Soon to be seen of a host
'The flag of the Master I serve!
'And life in them doubled on Life,
'As flame upon flame, to behold,
'High over Time-tumbled sea,
'The bliss of his headship of strife,
'Him through handmaiden me.'

FAITH

GEORGE SANTAYANA

O world, thou choosest not the better part!
It is not wisdom to be only wise,
And on the inward vision close the eyes,
But it is wisdom to believe the heart.
Columbus found a world and had no chart,
Save one that faith deciphered in the skies;
To trust the soul's invincible surmise
Was all his science and his only art.
Our knowledge is a torch of smoky pine
That lights the pathway but one step ahead
Across a void of mystery and dread.
Bid, then, the tender light of faith to shine
By which alone the mortal heart is led
Unto the thinking of the thought divine.

V. God in Nature

V. GOD IN NATURE

a. IMMANENCE IN NATURE IN GENERAL

HORA CHRISTI

ALICE BROWN

Sweet is the time for joyous folk
  Of gifts and minstrelsy;
Yet, I, O lowly-hearted One
  Crave but Thy company,
O lonesome road, beset with dread,
  My questing lies afar,
I have no light save in the east,
  The gleaming of Thy Star.

In cloistered aisles they keep today
  Thy feast, O living Lord!
With pomp of banner, pride of song,
  And stately sounding word.
Mute stand the kings of power and place,
  While priests of holy mind
Dispense Thy blessed heritage
  Of peace to all mankind.

I know a spot where budless twigs
  Are bare above the snow,
And where sweet winter-loving birds
  Flit softly to and fro;
There, with the sun for altar-fire,
  The earth for kneeling-place,
The gentle air for chorister,
  Will I adore Thy face.

Lord, underneath the great blue sky,
  My heart shall pean sing,
The gold and myrrh of meekest love
  Mine only offering.
Bliss of Thy birth shall quicken me,
  And for Thy pain and dole
Tears are but vain, so I will keep
  The silence of the soul.

REVELATION

ALICE BROWN

From *The Road to Castaly*

Down in the meadow, sprent with dew
  I saw the Very God
Look from a flower's limpid blue,
  Child of a starveling sod.

DISGUISES

THOMAS EDWARD BROWN

High stretched upon the swinging yard,
I gather in the sheet;
But it is hard
And stiff, and one cries haste.
Then He that is most dear in my regard
Of all the crew gives aidance meet;
But from His hands, and from His feet,
A glory spreads wherewith the night is starred:

Moreover of a cup most bitter-sweet
With fragrance as of nard,
And myrrh, and cassia spiced,
He proffers me to taste.
Then I to Him:—'Art Thou the Christ?'
He saith—'Thou say'st.'

Like to an ox
That staggers 'neath the mortal blow,
She grinds upon the rocks:—
Then straight and low
Leaps forth the levelled line, and in our quarter locks.
The cradle's rigged; with swerving of the blast
We go,
Our Captain last—
Demands
'Who fired that shot?' Each silent stands—
Ah, sweet perplexity!
This too was He.

I have an arbour wherein came a toad
Most hideous to see—
Immediate, seizing staff or goad,
I smote it cruelly.
Then all the place with subtle radiance glowed—
I looked, and it was He!

Song from PIPPA PASSES

ROBERT BROWNING

The year's at the spring
The day's at the morn;
Morning's at seven;
The hillside's dew-pearled;
The lark's on the wing;
The snail's on the thorn;
God's in his heaven—
All's right with the world.

THE HERETIC

Bliss Carman

One day as I sat and suffered,
A long discourse upon sin,
At the door of my brain I listened
And heard this speech within:

One whisper of the Holy Ghost
   Outweighs for me a thousand tomes;
And I must heed that private word,
   Not Plato's, Swedenborg's, nor Rome's.

The voice of beauty and of power
   Which came to the beloved John
In age upon his lonely isle,
   That voice I will obey, or none.

Let not tradition fill my ears
   With prate of evil and of good.
Nor superstition cloak my sight
   Of beauty with a bigot's hood.

Give me the freedom of the earth,
   The leisure of the light and air,
That this enduring soul some part
   Of their serenity may share!

The word that lifts the purple shaft
   Of crocus and of hyacinth
Is more to me than platitudes
   Rethundering from groin and plinth.

And at the first clear, careless strain
   Poured from the wood-bird's silver throat
I have forgotten all the lore
   The preacher bade me get by rote.

Beyond the shadow of the porch,
    I hear the wind among the trees
The river babbling in the clove.
    And the great sound that is the seas.

Let me have brook and flower and bird
    For counselors, that I may learn
The very accent of their tongue,
    And its least syllable discern.

For I, my brother, so would live
    That I may keep the elder law
Of beauty and of certitude,
    By daring love and blameless awe.

SOME KEEP SUNDAY GOING TO CHURCH

EMILY DICKINSON

Some keep Sunday going to church
    I keep it staying at home,
With a bobolink for a chorister,
    And an orchard for a throne.

Some keep Sabbath in surplice,
    I just wear my wings
And instead of tolling the bell for church,
    Our little sexton sings.

God preaches, a noted clergyman,
    And the sermon is never long,
So instead of going to heaven at last
    I'm going all along.

FORBEARANCE

RALPH WALDO EMERSON

Hast thou named all the birds without a gun?
Loved the wood-rose, and left it on its stalk?
At rich men's tables eaten bread and pulse?
Unarmed, faced danger with a heart of trust?
And loved so well a high behavior,
In man or maid, that thou from speech refrained,
Nobility more nobly to repay?
O, be my friend, and teach me to be thine!

GOOD-BYE, PROUD WORLD

RALPH WALDO EMERSON

GOOD-BYE, proud world! I'm going home:
Thou art not my friend, and I'm not thine.
Long through thy weary crowds I roam;
A river-ark on the ocean brine,
Long I've been tossed like the driven foam;
But now, proud world! I'm going home.

Good-bye to Flattery's fawning face;
To Grandeur with his wise grimace;
To upstart Wealth's averted eye;
To supple Office, low and high;
To crowded halls, to court and street;
To frozen hearts and hasting feet;
To those who go and those who come;
Good-bye, proud world! I'm going home.

I am going to my own hearth-stone,
Bosomed in yon green hills alone,—
A secret nook in a pleasant land,
Whose groves the frolic fairies planned;
Where arches green, the livelong day,

Echo the blackbird's roundelay,
And vulgar feet have never trod
A spot that is sacred to thought and God.

O, when I am safe in my sylvan home,
I tread on the pride of Greece and Rome;
And when I am stretched beneath the pines,
Where the evening star so holy shines,
I laugh at the lore and the pride of man,
At the sophist schools and the learned clan;
For what are they all, in their high conceit,
When man in the bush with God may meet?

MUSIC

RALPH WALDO EMERSON

Let me go where'er I will
I hear a sky-born music still:
It sounds from all things old,
It sounds from all things young,
From all that's fair, from all that's foul,
Peals out a cheerful song.

It is not only in the rose,
It is not only in the bird,
Not only where the rainbow glows,
Nor in the song of woman heard,
But in the darkest, meanest things
There alway, alway something sings.

'Tis not in the high stars alone,
Nor in the cup of budding flowers,
Nor in the red-breast's mellow tone,
Nor in the bow that smiles in showers,
But in the mud and scum of things
There alway, alway something sings.

WALDEINSAMKEIT

RALPH WALDO EMERSON

I do not count the hours I spend
In wandering by the sea;
The forest is my loyal friend,
Like God it useth me.

In plains that room for shadows make
Of skirting hills to lie,
Bound in by streams which give and take
Their colors from the sky;

Or on the mountain-crest sublime,
Or down the oaken glade,
O what have I to do with time?
For this the day was made.

Cities of mortals woe-begone
Fantastic care derides,
But in the serious landscape lone
Stern benefit abides.

Sheen will tarnish, honey cloy,
And merry is only a mask for sad,
But, sober on a fund of joy,
The woods at heart are glad.

There the great Planter plants
Of fruitful worlds the grain,
And with a million spells enchants
The souls that walk in pain.

Still on the seeds of all he made
The rose of beauty burns;
Through times that wear and forms that fade,
Immortal youth returns.

The black ducks mounting from the lake,
The pigeon in the pines,
The bittern's boom, a desert make
Which no false art refines.

Down in yon watery nook,
Where bearded mists divide,
The gray old gods whom Chaos knew,
The sires of Nature, hide.

Aloft, in secret veins of air,
Blows the sweet breath of song,
O, few to scale those uplands dare,
Though they to all belong!

See thou bring not to field or stone
The fancies found in books;
Leave authors' eyes, and fetch your own,
To brave the landscape's looks.

Oblivion here thy wisdom is,
Thy thrift, the sleep of cares;
For a proud idleness like this
Crowns all thy mean affairs.

HYMN OF THE WORLD WITHOUT

Psalm CIV

From Moulton's *Modern Readers' Bible*

Bless the Lord, O my soul.
  O Lord my God, thou art very great;
Thou art clothed with honour and majesty:
  Who coverest thyself with light as with a garment;
Who stretchest out the heavens like a curtain;
  Who layeth the beams of his chambers in the waters;
Who maketh the clouds his chariot;
  Who walketh upon the wings of the wind;

Who maketh winds his messengers;
  His ministers a flaming fire.

Who laid the foundations of the earth,
  That it should not be moved forever.
Thou coverest it with the deep as with a vesture;
  The waters stood above the mountains.
At thy rebuke they fled;
  At the voice of thy thunder they hasted away;
They went up by the mountains, they went down by the valleys,
  Unto the place which thou hadst founded for them.
Thou hast set a bound that they may not pass over;
  That they turn not again to cover the earth.

He sendeth forth springs into the valleys;
  They run among the mountains:
They give drink to every beast of the field;
  The wild asses quench their thirst.
By them the fowl of heaven have their habitation,
  They sing among the branches.
He watereth the mountains from His chambers:
  The earth is satisfied with the fruit of thy works.
He causeth the grass to grow for the cattle,
  And herb for the service of man.

That he may bring forth food out of the earth,
  And wine that maketh glad the heart of man,
And oil to make his face to shine,
  And bread that strengtheneth man's heart.
The trees of the Lord are satisfied;
  The cedars of Lebanon, which he hath planted:
Where the birds make their nests;
  As for the stork, the fir trees are her house;
The high mountains are for the wild goats;
  The rocks are a refuge for the conies.

He appointeth the moon for seasons:
  The sun knoweth his going down.
Thou maketh darkness, and it is night;
  Wherein all the beasts of the forest do creep forth.

The young lions roar after their prey,
  And seek their meat from God.
The sun ariseth, they get them away,
  And lay them down in their dens.
Man goeth forth unto his work
  And to his labor until the evening.

O Lord, how manifold are thy works!
In wisdom hast thou made them all.

OMNIPRESENCE

Edward Everett Hale

A thousand sounds, and each a joyful sound;
The dragon flies are humming as they please,
The humming birds are humming all around,
The clithra all alive with buzzing bees,
Each playful leaf its separate whisper found,
As laughing winds went rustling through the grove;
And I saw thousands of such sights as these,
And heard a thousand sounds of joy and love.

And yet so dull I was, I did not know
That He was there who all this love displayed,
I did not think how He who loved us so
Shared all my joy, was glad that I was glad;
And all because I did not hear the word
In English accents say, "It is the Lord."

THE EPITAPH

Katharine Tynan Hinkson

Write on my grave when I am dead,
  Whatever road I trod
That I admired and honourèd
  The wondrous works of God.

That all the days and years I had,
   The greatest and the least,
Each day with grateful heart and glad
   I sat me to a feast.

That not alone for body's meat
   Which takes the lowest place
I gave Him grace when I did eat
   And with a shining face.

But for the spirit filled and fed
   That else must waste and die,
With sun and stars replenishèd
   And dew and evening sky.

The beauty of the hills and seas
   Brimmed that immortal cup;
And when I went by fields and trees
   My heart was lifted up.

Lap me in the green grass and write
   Upon the daisied sod
That still I praised with all my might
   The wondrous works of God.

IMMANENCE

RICHARD HOVEY

Enthroned above the world although he sit,
Still is the world in him and he in it;
   The self-same power in yonder sunset glows
That kindled in the words of Holy Writ.

TRANSCENDENCE

Richard Hovey

Though one with all that sense or soul can see,
Not imprisoned in his own creations, he,
   His life is more than stars or winds or angels—
The sun doth not contain him nor the sea.

SONGS OF KABIR

Kabir

Translated by Rabindranath Tagore

Tell me, O Swan, your ancient tale.
From what land do you come, O Swan? to what shore will
   you fly?
Where would you take your rest, O Swan, and what do you
   seek?

Even this morning, O Swan, awake, arise, follow me!
There is a land where no doubt nor sorrow have rule: where
   the terror of Death is no more.
There the woods of spring are a-bloom, and the fragrant scent
   "He is I" is borne on the wind:
There the bee of the heart is immersed, and desires no other
   joy.

O Lord Increate, who will serve Thee?
Every votary offers his worship to the God of his own creation:
   each day he receives service—
None seek Him, the Perfect: Brahma, the Indivisible Lord.
They believe in ten Avatars; but no Avatar can be the Infinite
   Spirit, for he suffers the results of his deeds:
The Supreme One must be other than this.
The Yogi, the Sanyasi, the Ascetics, are disputing with another:
Kabir says, "O brother! he who has seen that radiance of love,
   he is saved."

The river and its waves are one surf: where is the difference
  between the river and its waves?
When the wave rises, it is the water; and when it falls, it is
  the same water again.   Tell me, Sir, where is the dis-
  tinction?
Because it has been named as wave shall it no longer be con-
  sidered as water?

Within the Supreme Brahma, the worlds are being told like
  beads:
Look upon that rosary with the eyes of wisdom.

Where Spring, the lord of the seasons, reigneth, there the
  Unstruck Music sounds of itself,
There the streams of light flow in all directions;
Few are the men who can cross to that shore!
There, where the millions of Krishnas stand with their hands
  folded,
Where millions of Vishnus bow their heads,
Where millions of Brahmas are reading the Vedas,
Where millions of Shivas are lost in contemplation,
Where millions of Indras dwell in the sky,
Where the demi-gods and the munis are unnumbered,
Where millions of Saraswatis, Goddess of Music, play on the
  vina—
There is my Lord self-revealed: and the scent of sandal and
  flowers dwells in those deeps.

THE ANCIENT THOUGHT

Watson Kerr

The round moon hangs like a yellow lantern in the trees
That lie like lace against the sky,
Oh, still the night! Oh, hushed the breeze—
  Surely God is nigh.

THE MARSHES OF GLYNN

Sidney Lanier

Glooms of the live-oaks, beautiful-braided and woven
With intricate shades of the vines that myriad-cloven
    Clamber the forks of the multiform boughs,—
            Emerald twilights,—
            Virginal shy lights,
Wrought of the leaves to the whisper of vows,
When lovers pace timidly down through the green colonnades
Of the dim sweet woods, of the dear dark woods,
    Of the heavenly woods and glades,
That run to the radiant marginal sand beach within
    The wide sea-marshes of Glynn;—

Beautiful glooms, soft dusks in the noon-day fire,—
Wildwood privacies, closets of lone desire,
Chamber from chamber parted with wavering arras of leaves,—
Cells for the passionate pleasure of prayer to the soul that
            grieves,
Pure with a sense of the passing of saints through the wood,
Cool for the dutiful weighing of ill with good;—

O braided dusks of the oak and woven shades of the vine,
While the riotous noon-day sun of the June-day long did shine
Ye held me fast in your heart and I held you fast in mine:
But now when the moon is no more, and riot is rest,
And the sun is await at the ponderous gate of the West,
And the slant yellow beam down the wood-aisle doth seem
Like a lane into heaven that leads from a dream,—
Ay, now, when my soul all day hath drunken the soul of the
            oak,
And my heart is at ease from men, and the wearisome sound
        of the stroke
    Of the scythe of time and the trowel of trade is low,
    And belief overmasters doubt, and I know that I know,
    And my spirit is grown to a lordly great compass within,
That the length and the breadth and the sweep of the marshes
        of Glynn

Will work me no fear like the fear they have wrought me
      of yore
When length was fatigue, and when breadth was bitterness
      sore,
And when terror and shrinking and dreary unnamable pain
Drew over me out of the merciless miles of the plain,—

Oh, now, unafraid, I am fain to face
     The vast sweet visage of space.
To the edge of the wood I am drawn, I am drawn,
Where the gray beach glimmering runs, as a belt of the dawn,
     For a mete and a mark
     To the forest-dark :—
         So:
Affable live-oak, leaning low,—
Thus—with your favor—soft, with a reverent hand,
(Not lightly touching your person, Lord of the land!)
Bending your beauty aside, with a step I stand
On the firm-packed sand,
        Free
By a world of marsh that borders a world of sea.

Sinuous southward and sinuous northward the shimmering band
Of the sand beach fastens the fringe of the marsh to the folds
      of the land.
Inward and outward to northward and southward the beach-
      lines linger and curl
As a silver-wrought garment that clings to and follows the
      firm sweet limbs of a girl.
Vanishing, swerving, evermore curving again into sight,
Softly the sand-beach wavers away to a dim gray looping of
      light.
And what if behind me to westward the wall of the woods
      stands high
The world lies east: how ample, the marsh and the sea and the
      sky!
A league and a league of marsh-grass, waist-high, broad in
      the blade,
Green, and all of a height, and unflecked with a light or a
      shade,

Stretch leisurely off, in a pleasant plain,
To the terminal blue of the main.

Oh, what is abroad in the marsh and the terminal sea?
    Somehow my soul seems suddenly free
From the weighing of fate and the sad discussion of sin,
By the length and the breadth and the sweep of the marshes
        of Glynn.

Ye marshes, how candid and simple and nothing-withholding
        and free
Ye publish yourselves to the sky and offer yourselves to the sea!
Tolerant plains, that suffer the sea and the rains and the sun,
Ye spread and span like the catholic man who hath mightily
        won
God out of knowledge and good out of infinite pain
And sight out of blindness and purity out of a stain.

As the marsh-hen secretly builds on the watery sod,
Behold I will build me a nest on the greatness of God:
I will fly in the greatness of God as the marsh-hen flies
In the freedom that fills all the space 'twixt the marsh and the
        skies:
By so many roots as the marsh-grass sends in the sod
I will heartily lay me a-hold on the greatness of God:
Oh, like to the greatness of God is the greatness within
The range of the marshes, the liberal marshes of Glynn.

And the sea lends large, as the marsh: lo, out of his plenty
        the sea
Pours fast: full soon the time of the flood-tide must be:
Look how the grace of the sea doth go
About and about through the intricate channels that flow
    Here and there,
            Everywhere,
Till his waters have flooded the uttermost creeks and the low-
        lying lanes,
And the marsh is meshed with a million veins,
That like as with rosy and silvery essences flow
    In the rose-and-silver evening glow.
            Farewell, my lord Sun!

The creeks overflow: a thousand rivulets run
'Twixt the roots of the sod; the blades of the marsh-grass
    stir;
Passeth a hurrying sound of wings that westward whirr;
Passeth and all is still; and the currents cease to run;
And the sea and the marsh are one.

How still the plains of the waters be!
The tide is in his ecstasy.
The tide is at his highest height:
    And it is night.

And now from the Vast of the Lord will the waters of sleep
Roll in on the souls of men,
But who will reveal to our waking ken
The forms that swim and the shapes that creep
    Under the waters of sleep?
And I would I could know what swimmeth below when the tide
    comes in
On the length and the breadth of the marvellous marshes of
    Glynn.

A STRIP OF BLUE

Lucy Larcom

I do not own an inch of land,
    But all I see is mine,—
The orchards and the mowing-fields,
    The lawns and gardens fine.
The winds my tax collectors are,
    They bring me tithes divine,—
Wild scents and subtle essences,
    A tribute rare and free;
And, more magnificent than all,
    My window keeps for me
A glimpse of blue immensity,—
    A little strip of sea.

Richer am I than he who owns
  Great fleets and argosies;
I have a share in every ship
  Won by the inland breeze,
To loiter on yon airy road
  Above the apple trees.
I freight them with my untold dreams;
  Each bears my own picked crew;
And nobler cargoes wait for them
  Than ever India knew,—
My ships that sail into the East
  Across that outlet blue.

Sometimes they seem like living shapes,—
  The people of the sky,—
Guests in white raiment coming down
  From heaven, which is close by;
I call them by familiar names,
  As one by one draws nigh,
So white, so light, so spirit-like
  From violet mists they bloom!
The aching wastes of the unknown
  Are half reclaimed from gloom,
Since on life's hospitable sea
  All souls find sailing room.

The ocean grows a weariness
  With nothing else in sight;
Its east and west, its north and south,
  Spread out from morn to night;
We miss the warm, caressing shore,
  Its brooding shade and light.
A part is greater than the whole;
  By hints are mysteries told.
The fringes of eternity,—
  God's sweeping garment-fold,
In that bright shred of glittering sea,
  I reach out for, and hold.

The sails, like flakes of roseate pearl,
  Float in upon the mist;
The waves are broken precious stones,—
  Sapphire and amethyst,
Washed from celestial basement walls,
  By suns unsetting kissed.
Out through the utmost gates of space,
  Past where the grey stars drift,
To the widening Infinite, my soul
  Glides on, a vessel swift,
Yet loses not her anchorage
  In yonder azure rift.

Here I sit as a little child
  The threshold of God's door
Is that clear band of chrysoprase;
  Now the vast temple floor,
The blinding glory of the dome
  I bow my head before.
Thy universe, O God, is home,
  In height or depth, to me;
Yet here upon thy footstool green
  Content I am to be.
Glad, when is opened unto my need
  Some sea-like glimpse of thee.

From THE FIRE BRINGER

WILLIAM VAUGHN MOODY

Pandora Speaks

I stood within the heart of God;
It seemed a place that I had known:
(I was blood-sister to the clod,
Blood-brother to the stone.)

I found my love and labor there,
My house, my raiment, meat and wine,

My ancient rage, my old despair,—
Yea, all things that were mine.

I saw the spring and summer pass,
The trees grow bare, and winter come;
All was the same as once it was
Upon my hills at home.

Then suddenly in my own heart
I felt God walk and gaze about;
He spoke; His words seemed held apart
With gladness and with doubt.

"Here is my meat and wine," He said,
"My love, my toil, my ancient care;
Here is my cloak, my book, my bed,
And here my old despair;

"Here are my seasons; winter, and spring,
Summer the same, and autumn spills
The fruits I look for; everything
As on my heavenly hills."

THE WORD

RICHARD REALF

O Earth! Thou hast not any wind that blows
Which is not music; every weed of thine
Pressed rightly flows in aromatic wine;
And humble hedge-row flower that grows,
And every little brown bird that doth sing,
Hath something greater than itself, and bears
A living word to every living thing,
Albeit holds the message unawares.
All shapes and sounds have something which is not
Of them: a spirit broods amid the grass;
Vague outlines of the Everlasting Thought
Lie in the melting shadows as they pass;
The touch of an eternal presence thrills
The fringes of the sunsets and the hills.

DUST

GEORGE WILLIAM RUSSELL (*A. E.*)

I heard them in their sadness say
  "The earth rebukes the thought of God;
We are but embers wrapped in clay,
  A little nobler than the sod."

But I have touched the lips of clay,
  Mother, thy rudest sod to me
Is thrilled with fire of hidden day,
  And haunted by all mystery.

THE GREAT BREATH

GEORGE WILLIAM RUSSELL (*A. E.*)

Its edges foamed with amethyst and rose
Withers once more the old blue flower of day:
There where the ether like a diamond glows
Its petals fall away.

A shadowy tumult stirs the dusky air;
Sparkle the delicate dews, the distant snows;
The great deep thrills, for through it everywhere
The breath of Beauty blows.

I saw how all the trembling ages past,
Molded to her by deep and deeper breath,
Neared to the hour when Beauty breathes her last
And knows herself in death.

GOD IS AT THE ANVIL

LEW SARETT

God is at the anvil, beating out the sun;
  Where the molten metal spills,
  At His forge among the hills
He has hammered out the glory of a day that's done.

God is at the anvil, welding golden bars;
  In the scarlet-streaming flame
  He is fashioning a frame
For the shimmering silver beauty of the evening stars.

MADONNA NATURA

WILLIAM SHARP (*Fiona Macleod*)

I love and worship thee in that thy ways
Are fair, and that the glory of past days
  Haloes thy brightness with a sacred hue.
Within thine eyes are dreams of mystic things,
Within thy voice a subtler music rings
  Than ever mortal from the keen reeds drew;
Thou weav'st a web which men have callèd Death
But Life is in the magic of thy breath.

The secret things of Earth thou knowest well;
Thou seest the wild bee build his narrow cell,
  The lonely eagle wing through lonely skies,
The lion on the desert roam afar,
The glow-worm glitter like a fallen star,
  The hour-lived insect as it hums and flies;
Thou seest men like shadows come and go,
And all their endless dreams drift to and fro.

In thee is strength, endurance, wisdom, truth;
Thou art above all mortal joy and ruth,

Thou hast the calm and silence of the night;
Mayhap thou seest what we cannot see,
Surely far off thou hear'st harmoniously
    Echoes of flawless music infinite,
Mayhap thou feel'st thrilling through each sod
Beneath thy feet the very breath of God.

Monna Natura, fair and grand and great,
I worship thee, who art inviolate:
    Through thee I reach to things beyond this span
Of mine own puny life, through thee I learn
Courage and hope, and dimly can discern
    The ever noble grades awaiting man:
Madonna, unto thee I bend and pray—
Saviour, Redeemer thou, whom none can slay!

No human fanes are dedicate to thee,
But thine the temples of each tameless sea,
    Each mountain height and forest glade and plain:
No priests with daily hymns thy praises sing,
But far and wide the wild winds chanting swing,
    And dirge the sea waves on the changeless main,
While songs of birds fill all the fields and woods,
And cries of beasts the savage solitudes.

Hearken, Madonna, hearken to my cry;
Teach me through metaphors of liberty,
    Till strong and fearing nought in life or death
I feel thy sacred freedom through me thrill,
Wise, and defiant, with unquenched will
    Unyielding, though succumb the mortal breath—
Then if I conquer, take me by the hand
And guide me onward to thy Promised Land!

THE VOICE OF GOD

James Stephens

I bent unto the ground
And I heard the quiet sound
Which the grasses make when they
Come up laughing from the clay.

"We are the voice of God," they said:
Thereupon I bent my head
Down again that I might see
If they truly spoke to me.

But around me everywhere
Grass and tree and mountain were
Thundering in a mighty glee,
"We are the voice of deity."

And I leapt from where I lay,
I danced upon the laughing clay,
And to the rock that sang beside,
"We are the voice of God," I cried.

THE WHISPERER

James Stephens

The moon was round,
And as I walked along
There was no sound,
Save where the wind with long
Low hushes whispered to the ground
    A snatch of song.

No thought had I
Save that the moon was fair,
And fair the sky,
And God was everywhere.

I chanted as the wind went by
  A poet's prayer.

Then came a voice—
'Why is it that you praise
And thus rejoice,
O stranger to the ways
Of providence? God has no choice
  In this sad maze.

'His law he laid
Down at the dread beginning,
When He made
The world and set it spinning,
And his casual hand betrayed
  Us into sinning.

'I fashion you,
And then for weal or woe,
My business through,
I care not how you go,
Or struggle, win or lose, nor do
  I want to know.

'Is no appeal,
For I am far from sight,
And cannot feel
The rigour of your plight;
And if ye faint just when ye kneel,
  That, too, is right.

'Then do not sing,
O poet in the night,
That everything
Is beautiful and right.
What if some wind come now and fling
  At thee in spite?'

All in amaze
I listened to the tone
Mocking my praise:
And then I heard the groan

That old tormented nature did upraise
From tree and stone.

And as I went
I heard it once again,
That harsh lament:
And fire came into my brain;
Deep anger unto me was lent
To write this strain.

AUTUMN

RABINDRANATH TAGORE

Today the peace of autumn pervades the world.
In the radiant noon, silent and motionless, the wide stillness
rests like a tired bird spreading over the deserted fields
to all horizons its wings of golden green.
Today the thin thread of the river flows without song, leaving
no mark on its sandy banks.
The many distant villages bask in the sun with eyes closed in
idle and languid slumber.
In the stillness I hear in every blade of grass, in every speck
of dust, in every part of my own body, in the visible and
invisible worlds, in the planets, the sun, and the stars, the
joyous dance of the atoms through endless time—the myriad
murmuring waves of Rhythm surrounding Thy throne.

FRAGMENT

HENRY VAUGHAN

Walk with thy fellow-creatures: note the hush
And whispers among them. There is not a spring
Or leaf but hath his morning hymn; each bush
And oak doth know I AM. Canst thou not sing?
O leave thy cares and follies! go this way,
And thou art sure to prosper all the day.

ODE IN MAY

William Watson

Let me go forth, and share
  The overflowing Sun
  With one wise friend, or one
Better than wise, being fair,
Where the pewit wheels and dips
  On heights of bracken and ling,
And Earth, unto her leaflet tips,
  Tingles with the Spring.

What is so sweet and dear
  As a prosperous morn in May,
  The confident prime of the day,
And the dauntless youth of the year,
When nothing that asks for bliss,
  Asking aright, is denied,
And half of the world a bridegroom is,
  And half of the world a bride?

The Song of Mingling flows,
  Grave, ceremonial, pure,
  As once, from lips that endure,
The cosmic descant rose,
When the temporal lord of life,
  Going his golden way,
Had taken a wondrous maid to wife
  That long had said him nay.

For of old the Sun, our sire,
  Came wooing the mother of men,
  Earth, that was virginal then,
Vestal fire to his fire.
Silent her bosom and coy,
  But the strong god sued and pressed;
And born of their starry nuptial joy
  Are all that drink of her breast.

And the triumph of him that begot,
  And the travail of her that bore,
  Behold they are evermore
As warp and weft in our lot.
  We are children of splendour and flame,
  Of shuddering, also, and tears.
Magnificent out of the dust we came,
  And abject from the Spheres.

O bright irresistible lord!
  We are fruit of Earth's womb, each one,
  And fruit of thy loins, O Sun,
Whence first was the seed outpoured.
To thee as our Father we bow,
  Forbidden thy Father to see,
Who is older and greater than thou, as thou
  Art greater and older than we.

Thou art but as a word of his speech,
  Thou art but as a wave of his hand;
  Thou art brief as a glitter of sand
'Twixt tide and tide on his beach;
Thou art less than a spark of his fire,
  Or a moment's mood of his soul:
Thou art lost in the notes on the lips of his choir
  That chant the chant of the Whole.

LINES COMPOSED A FEW MILES ABOVE
TINTERN ABBEY

WILLIAM WORDSWORTH

                    The sounding cataract
Haunted me like a passion; the tall rock,
The mountain, and the deep and gloomy wood,
Their colors and their forms, were then to me
An appetite; a feeling and a love,
That had no need of a remoter charm,
By thought supplied, nor any interest

Unborrowed from the eye.—That time is past,
And all its aching joys are now no more,
And all its dizzy raptures. Not for this
Faint I, nor mourn, nor murmur; other gifts
Have followed; for such loss, I would believe,
Abundant recompense. For I have learned
To look on Nature, not as in the hour
Of thoughtless youth; but hearing oftentimes
The still, sad music of humanity,
Nor harsh nor grating, though of ample power
To chasten and subdue. And I have felt
A presence that disturbs me with the joy
Of elevated thoughts; a sense sublime,
Of something far more deeply interfused,
Whose dwelling is the light of setting suns,
And the round ocean and the living air,
And the blue sky, and in the mind of man;
A motion and a spirit, that impels
All thinking things, all objects of all thought,
And rolls through all things. Therefore am I still
A lover of the meadows and the woods,
And mountains; and of all that we behold
From this green earth; of all the mighty world
Of eye and ear,—both what they half create,
And what perceive; well pleased to recognize
In nature and the language of the sense,
The anchor of my purest thoughts, the nurse,
The guide, the guardian of my heart, and soul
Of all my moral being.

THE WORLD IS TOO MUCH WITH US

William Wordsworth

The world is too much with us: late and soon,
Getting and spending, we lay waste our powers:
Little we see in Nature that is ours;
We have given our hearts away, a sordid boon!
This sea that bares her bosom to the moon;

The winds that will be howling at all hours,
And are up-gathered now like sleeping flowers;
For this, for everything we are out of tune;
It moves us not.—Great God! I'd rather be
A Pagan suckled in a creed outworn;
So might I, standing on this pleasant lea,
Have glimpses that would make me less forlorn;
Have sight of Proteus rising from the sea,
Or hear old Triton blow his wreathed horn.

b. THE COUNTRY

OUT IN THE FIELDS WITH GOD

ELIZABETH BARRETT BROWNING

The little cares that fretted me
  I lost them yesterday,
Among the fields above the sea,
  Among the winds at play,
Among the lowing of the herds,
  The rustling of the trees,
Among the singing of the birds,
  The humming of the bees.

The foolish fears of what might happen,
  I cast them all away
Among the clover-scented grass,
  Among the new-mown hay,
Among the husking of the corn,
  Where drowsy poppies nod
Where ill thoughts die and good are born—
  Out in the fields with God.

THE COUNTRY FAITH

Norman Gale

Here in the country's heart
Where the grass is green,
Life is the same sweet life
As it e'er hath been.

Trust in a God still lives,
And the bell at morn
Floats with a thought of God
O'er the rising corn.

God comes down in the rain,
And the crop grows tall—
This is the country faith,
And best of all!

FARMERS

William Alexander Percy

I watch the farmers in their fields
    And marvel secretly.
They are so very calm and sure,
    They have such dignity.

They know such simple things so well,
    Although their learning's small,
They find a steady, brown content
    Where some find none at all.

And all their quarrelings with God
    Are soon made up again;
They grant forgiveness when He sends
    His silver, tardy rain.

Their pleasure is so grave and full
  When gathered crops are trim,
You know they think their work was done
  In partnership with Him.

c. TREES

GOOD COMPANY

Karle Wilson Baker

Today I have grown taller from walking with the trees,
The seven sister-poplars who go softly in a line;
And I think my heart is whiter for its parley with a star
That trembled out at nightfall and hung above the pine.

The call-note of a red bird from the cedars in the dusk
Woke his happy mate within me to an answer free and fine;
And a sudden angel beckoned from a column of blue smoke—
Lord, who am I that they should stoop—these holy folk of
        thine?

THE HAPPY TREE

Gerald Gould

There was a bright and happy tree;
  The wind with music laced its boughs,
Thither across the houseless sea
  Came singing birds to house.

Men grudged the tree its happy eves,
  Its happy dawns of eager sound;
So all that crown and tower of leaves
  They levelled with the ground.

They made an upright of the stem,
　A crosspiece of a bough they made:
No shadow of their deed on them
　The fallen branches laid.

But blithely, since the year was young
　When they a fitting hill did find,
There on the happy tree they hung
　The Savior of mankind.

OF AN ORCHARD

Katharine Tynan Hinkson

Good is an orchard, the saint saith,
To meditate on life and death,
With a cool well, a hive of bees,
A hermit's grot below the trees.

Good is an orchard: very good,
Though one should wear no monkish hood;
Right good when spring awakes her flute,
And good in yellowing time of fruit:

Very good in the grass to lie
And see the net-work 'gainst the sky,
A living lace of blue and green
And boughs that let the gold between.

The bees are types of souls that dwell
With honey in a quiet cell;
The ripe fruit figures goldenly
The soul's perfection in God's eye.

Prayer and praise in a country home
Honey and fruit: a man might come
Fed on such meats to walk abroad
And in his Orchard talk with God.

TREES

JOYCE KILMER

I think that I shall never see
A poem lovely as a tree.

A tree whose hungry mouth is pressed
Against the earth's sweet flowing breast;

A tree that looks at God all day,
And lifts her leafy arms to pray;

A tree that may in summer wear
A nest of robins in her hair;

Upon whose bosom snow has lain;
Who intimately lives with rain.

Poems are made by fools like me,
But only God can make a tree.

A BALLAD OF THE TREES AND THE MASTER

SIDNEY LANIER

Into the woods my Master went,
Clean forspent, forspent.
Into the woods my Master came,
Forspent with love and shame,
But the olives they were not blind to Him;
The little gray leaves were kind to Him;
The thorn-tree had a mind to Him,
When into the woods He came.

Out of the woods my Master went,
And He was well content.
Out of the woods my Master came,
Content with death and shame.
When Death and Shame would woo Him last,
From under the trees they drew Him last:

'Twas on a tree they slew Him—last
When out of the woods He came.

A PRAYER

Edwin Markham

Teach me, Father, how to go
  Softly as the grasses grow;
Hush my soul to meet the shock
  Of the wild world as a rock;
But my spirit, propped with power,
  Make as simple as a flower.

. . . .

Teach me, Father, how to be
  Kind and patient as a tree.
Joyfully the crickets croon
  Under the shady oak at noon;
Beetle, on his mission bent,
  Tarries on that cooling tent.
Let me, also, cheer a spot,
  Hidden field or garden grot—
Place where passing souls can rest
  On the way and be their best.

d. GARDENS AND FLOWERS

MY GARDEN

Thomas Edward Brown

A garden is a lovesome thing, God wot!
  Rose plot,
    Fringed pool,
  Ferned grot—
    The veriest school
    Of peace: and yet the fool

Contends that God is not—
Not God! In gardens! When the eve is cool?
　Nay but I have a sign:
　'Tis very sure God walks in mine.

GOD'S GARDEN

Richard Burton

The years are flowers and bloom within
　Eternity's wide garden;
The rose for joy, the thorn for sin,
　The gardener, God, to pardon
All wilding growths, to prune, reclaim,
　And make them rose-like in His name.

AMONG THE FERNS

Edward Carpenter

I lay among the ferns,
Where they lifted their fronds, innumerable, in the greenwood
　wilderness, like wings winnowing the air;
And their voices went by me continually.

And I listened, and Lo! softly inaudibly raining I heard not
　the voices of the ferns only, but of all living creatures:
Voices of mountain and star,
Of cloud and forest and ocean,
And of little rills tumbling among the rocks,
And of the high tops where the moss-beds are and the springs
　arise.
As the wind at midday rains whitening over the grass,
As the night-bird glimmers a moment, fleeting between the
　lonely watcher and the moon,
So softly inaudibly they rained,
While I sat silent.

And in the silence of the greenwood I knew the secret of the
    growth of the ferns;
I saw their delicate leaflets tremble breathing an undescribed
    and unuttered life;
And, below, the ocean lay sleeping;
And round them the mountains and the stars dawned in glad
    companionship forever.

And a voice came to me, saying:
In every creature, in forest and ocean, in leaf and tree and bird
    and beast and man, there moves spirit other than its mortal
    own,
Pure, fluid, as air—intense as fire,
Which looks abroad and passes along the spirits of all other
    creatures, drawing them close to itself,
Nor dreams of other law than that of perfect equality;
And this is the spirit of immortality and peace.

And whatsoever creature hath this spirit, to it
No harm can befall, for wherever it goes it has its nested home,
    and to it every loss comes charged with an equal gain;
It gives—but to receive a thousand-fold;
It yields its life—but at the hands of love;
And death is the law of its eternal growth.

And I saw that was the law of every creature—that this spirit
    should enter in and take possession of it,
That it might have no more fear nor doubt or be at war within
    itself any longer.
And, lo! in the greenwood all around me it moved,
Where the sunlight floated fragrant under the boughs,
And the fern-fronds winnowed the air;
In the oak-leaves dead of last year, and the small shy things
    that rustled among them;
In the songs of the birds, and the broad shadowing leaves
    overhead;
In the fields sleeping below, and in the river and the high
    dreaming air;
Gleaming ecstatic it moved—with joy incarnate.

And it seemed to me, as I looked, that it penetrated these things,
    suffusing them;
And wherever it penetrated, behold! there was nothing left
    down to the smallest atom which was not winged spirit
    instinct with life.

. . . .

Who shall understand the words of the ferns lifting their
    fronds unnumerable?
What man shall go forth into the world, holding his life in his
    open palm—
With high adventurous joy from sunrise to sunset—
Fearless, in his sleeve laughing, having outflanked his enemies?
His heart like nature's garden—that all men abide in—
Free, where the great winds blow, rains fall, and the sun shines,
And manifold growths come forth and scatter their fragrance?
Who shall be like a grave, where men may bury
Sin and sorrow and shame, to rise in the new day
Glorious out of their grave? who, deeply listening,
Shall hear through all his soul the voices of all creation,
Voices of mountain and star, voices of old men
Softly audibly raining?—shall seize and fix them,
Rivet them fast with love, no more to lose them?
Who shall *be* that spirit of deep fulfillment,
Himself, self-centred? Yet evermore from that centre
Over the world expanding, along all creatures
Loyally passing—with love, with perfect equality?

Him immortality crowns. In him all sorrow
And mortal passion of death shall pass from creation.
They who sit by the road and are weary shall rise up
As he passes. Those who despair shall arise.

. . . .

Who shall understand the words of the ferns winnowing the
    air?
    Death shall change as the light in the morning changes:
    Death shall change as the light 'twixt moonset and dawn.

THE HOLY OF HOLIES

GILBERT K. CHESTERTON

"Elder Father, though thine eyes
Shine with hoary mysteries,
Canst thou tell what in the heart
Of a cowslip blossom lies?"

"Smaller than all lives that be,
Secret as the deepest sea,
Stands a little house of seeds
Like an elfin's granary."

"Speller of the stones and weeds
Skilled in Nature's crafts and creeds,
Tell me what is in the heart
Of the smallest of the seeds."

"God Almighty, and with Him
Cherubim and Seraphim,
Filling all eternity,
Adonai Elohim!"

CONSIDER THE LILIES

WILLIAM CHANNING GANNETT

He hides within the lily
  A strong and tender care,
That wins the earth-born atoms
  To glory of the air:
He weaves the shining garments
  Unceasingly and still,
Along the quiet waters,
  In niches of the hill.

We linger at the vigil
    With him who bent the knee,
To watch the old-time lilies
    In distant Galilee;
And still the worship deepens
    And quickens into new,
As brightening down the ages
    God's secret thrilleth through.

O toiler of the lily,
    Thy touch is in the Man!
No leaf that dawns to petal
    But hints the angel-plan.
The flower horizon's open!
    The blossom vaster shows!
We hear thy wide world's echo,—
    See how the lily grows!

THE LORD GOD PLANTED A GARDEN

Dorothy Frances Gurney

The Lord God planted a garden
    In the first white days of the world,
And He set there an angel warden
    In a garment of light enfurled.

So near to the peace of Heaven,
    That the hawk might nest with the wren,
For there in the cool of the even
    God walked with the first of men.

And I dream that these garden closes
    With their shade and their sun-flecked sod
And their lilies and bowers of roses,
    Were laid by the hand of God.

The kiss of the sun for pardon,
    The song of the birds for mirth,—
One is nearer God's heart in a garden
    Than anywhere else on earth.

TO A DAISY

Alice Meynell

Slight as thou art, thou art enough to hide
  Like all created things, secrets from me,
  And stand a barrier to eternity,
And I, how can I praise thee well and wide

From where I dwell—upon the hither side?
  Thou little veil for so great mystery,
  When shall I penetrate all things and thee,
And then look back? For this I must abide,

Till thou shalt grow and fold and be unfurled
Literally between me and the world.
  Then shall I drink from in beneath a spring,

And from a poet's side shall read his book.
O daisy mine, what will it be to look
  From God's side even of such a simple thing?

THE SECRET GARDEN

Robert Nichols

There is somewhere a Secret Garden, which none hath seen
In a place apart
But amid the bramble-bound world, the thicket, the screen
To the enunderstanding of heart.

There is somewhere a Secret Garden, where none hath been,
Where Night and Day
Commingle; where the sun and the starlight's sheen
Shines ever; where ever the moony fountains play
Lifting their lily-like throats, tossing their spray;
Where over the rainbow meets red-hued serene;
Where the flame-dripping branches are brighter green;
Where the Gardener walks in His Garden unheard, unseen.

There is somewhere a Secret Garden: a door in a wall,
Opened: how shine within
Flower and fruit and torrent of blossoms which cannot fall!
Whence a jubilant din
Floats abroad of birds of scintillant feather
Swelling ecstatic throats in chorus together;
Or the cry of one, crying alone a sad and a silver call
Rings from the Secret Garden where none hath been.

There everlastingly the Gardener walks
Unseen, unmarked, unheard
Save as He goes
Humbled and hushed and happy falls each bird,
Each fountain throws
Gentlier upward, changing from blue to rose,
And there is seen
Glimpse of a radiant robe, a darkling mien
'Twixt the sheeted light and the sparkling drift where it blows.

There the flowers wait,
Abasing each noble head,
Till He draw nigh,
Then exalt their lovely faces to Him, rose little, rose great,
Flowers of pale and flowers of passionate dye,
Under His eye
Till softly He lift a hand and the hand is spread
Blessing their beauty, their peace with a word like a sigh.

There is somewhere a Secret Garden, where none hath been,
Or, glimpsed, lost to his grief,
There would I bide, though I ever abode unseen:
A snail or a stone under the lowliest leaf.

THE GARDEN

Rose Parkwood

Two of Thy children one summer day worked in their garden,
    Lord;
They chopped the weeds of yesterday and you sent down a
    golden smile.

Two of Thy children one sunny day worked in their garden,
    Lord;
They hoed the furrow straight for the earthy bed and you
    whispered a singing smile.
Two of Thy children one windy day worked in their garden,
    Lord;
They pressed out the lumps from the clayey soil and you closed
    your shining eyes;
Two of Thy children one cloudy day worked in their garden,
    Lord;
They dropped in the seeds with a song in their hearts and you
    sent a soothing tear.
Two of Thy children one rainy day turned from their garden,
    Lord—
Your Smile and your Sigh and your Tear entered into their
    hearts.
Two of Thy children all the days of their life will work in Thy
    Garden, Lord!

I SEE HIS BLOOD UPON THE ROSE

Joseph Mary Plunkett

I see His blood upon the rose
    And in the stars the glory of His eyes,
His body gleams amid eternal snows
    His tears fall from the skies.

I see His face in every flower;
    The thunder and the surging of the birds
Are but His voice—and carven by His power
    Rocks are His written words.

All pathways by His feet are worn,
    His strong heart stirs the ever-beating sea,
His crown of thorns is twined with every thorn
    His cross is every tree.

FLOWER IN THE CRANNIED WALL

ALFRED TENNYSON

Flower in the crannied wall,
I pluck you out of the crannies;—
Hold you here, root and all, in my hand,
Little flower—but if I could understand
What you are, root and all, and all in all,
I should know what God and man is.

e. ANIMALS

From AUGURIES OF INNOCENCE

WILLIAM BLAKE

To see the world in a grain of sand,
And a Heaven in a wild flower,
Hold Infinity in the palm of your hand,
And Eternity in an hour.
A robin redbreast in a cage
Puts all Heaven in a rage.
A dove-house fill'd with doves and pigeons
Shudders Hell through all its regions.
A dog starved at his master's gate
Predicts the ruin of the State.
A horse misus'd upon the road
Calls to Heaven for human blood.
Each outcry of the hunted hare
A fibre from the brain does tear.
A skylark wounded on the wing,
Doth make a cherub cease to sing.

.   .   .   .

A riddle or the cricket's cry,
Is to doubt a fit reply.

The emmet's inch and eagle's mile
Make lame Philosophy to smile.
He who doubts from what he sees
Will ne'er believe, do what you please.
If the sun and moon should doubt,
They'd immediately go out.

.   .   .   .

God appears and God is Light,
To those poor souls who dwell in night;
But does a human form display
To those who dwell in realms of Day.

THE LAMB

WILLIAM BLAKE

Little lamb, who made thee?
Dost thou know who made thee?
Gave thee life and bade thee feed
By the stream and o'er the mead;
Gave thee clothing of delight,
Softest clothing, woolly, bright;
Gave thee such a tender voice,
Making all the vales rejoice?
Little lamb, who made thee?
Dost thou know who made thee?

Little lamb, I'll tell thee;
Little lamb, I'll tell thee;
He is callèd by thy name,
For he calls himself a lamb.
He is meek and he is mild,
He became a little child,—
I a child and thou a lamb,
We are callèd by his name.
Little lamb, God bless thee!
Little lamb, God bless thee!

THE TIGER

WILLIAM BLAKE

Tiger, tiger, burning bright
In the forests of the night,
What immortal hand or eye
Could frame thy fearful symmetry?

In what distant deeps or skies
Burnt the fire of thine eyes?
On what wings dare he aspire?
What the hand dare seize the fire?

And what shoulder and what art
Could twist the sinews of thy heart?
And, when thy heart began to beat,
What dread hand and what dread feet?

What the hammer? What the chain?
In what furnace was thy brain?
What the anvil? What dread grasp
Dare its deadly terrors clasp?

When the stars threw down their spears,
And watered heaven with their tears,
Did he smile his work to see?
Did he who made the lamb make thee?

Tiger, tiger, burning bright
In the forests of the night,
What immortal hand or eye
Dare frame thy fearful symmetry?

TO A WATERFOWL

WILLIAM CULLEN BRYANT

Whither, midst falling dew,
While glow the heavens with the last steps of day,
Far, through their rosy depths, dost thou pursue
Thy solitary way?

Vainly the fowler's eye
Might mark thy distant flight to do thee wrong,
As, darkly painted on the crimson sky,
Thy figure floats along.

Seek'st thou the plashy brink
Of weedy lake, or marge of river wide,
Or where the rocking billows rise and sink
On the chafed ocean-side?

There is a Power whose care
Teaches thy way along that pathless coast—
The desert and illimitable air—
Lone wandering, but not lost.

All day thy wings have fanned,
At that far height, the cold, thin atmosphere,
Yet stoop not, weary, to the welcome land,
Though the dark night is near.

And soon that toil shall end;
Soon shalt thou find a summer home, and rest,
And scream among thy fellows; reeds shall bend,
Soon o'er thy sheltered nest.

Thou'rt gone, the abyss of heaven
Hath swallowed up thy form; yet, on my heart
Deeply has sunk the lesson thou hast given,
And shall not soon depart.

He who, from zone to zone,
Guides through the boundless sky thy certain flight,
In the long way that I must tread alone,
Will lead my steps aright.

THE SONGS OF THE BIRDS

EDWARD CARPENTER

The rocks flow and the mountain shapes flow,
And the forests swim over the lands like cloud-shadows.
The lines of the seeming everlasting sea are changed,
And its waves beat on unmapped phantom shores:
'Not here, not here!'
All creatures fade from the embraces of their names,
(And you and I slow, slowly disentangling,)
The delicate hairbells quivering in the light,
The gorse, the heather and the fox-gloves tall,
The meadows and the river, rolling, fade:
Fade from their likenesses: fade crying, 'Follow!
Follow, forever follow!'
Who hears? who sees?
Who hears the word of Nature?
The word of her eternal breathing, whispered wherever one
    shall listen,
The word of the birds in the high trees calling,
Of the wind running over the grass,
The word of the glad prisoners, the tender footless creatures,
    the plants of the earth,
Rushing, too, bright-eyed, out·of their momentary masks!
'Not here! Not here!'

But over all the world, shadowing, shadowing:
The dream! the vast and ever-present miracle of all time!
The long forgotten, never forgotten goal!
Over your own heart, out of its secretest depths:
In crystalline beauty!
Out of all creatures, cloud and mountain and river:
Exhaling, ascending!

From plant and bird and man and planet up-pouring:
Thousand-formed, One,
The ever-present, only present reality, source of all illusion,
The Self, the disclosure, the transfiguration of each creature,
And goal of its age-long pilgrimage.

THE DONKEY

GILBERT K. CHESTERTON

When fishes flew and forests walked
  And figs grew upon thorn,
Some moment when the moon was blood
  Then surely I was born:

With monstrous head and sickening cry
  And ears like errant wings,
The devil's walking parody
  On all four-footed things;

The tattered outlaw of the earth
  Of ancient crooked will:
Starve, scourge, deride me: I am dumb,
  I keep my secret still.

Fools! For I also had my hour;
  One far fierce hour and sweet:
There was a shout about my ears,
  And palms before my feet.

TO A DOG

JOSEPHINE PRESTON PEABODY

So, back again?
            —And is your errand done,
Unfailing one?
How quick the gray world, at your morning look,
Turns wonder-book!

Come in,—O guard and guest;
Come O you breathless from a life-long quest!
Search here my heart; and if a comfort be,
Ah, comfort me!
You eloquent one, you best
Of all diviners, so to trace
The weather-gleams upon a face;
With wordless, querying paw,
Adventuring the law!
You shaggy loveliness,
What call was it?—What dream beyond a guess,
Lured you, gray ages back,
From that lone bivouac
Of the wild pack?—
Was it your need, or ours?—The calling trail
Of faith that should not fail?—
Of hope dim understood?—
That should follow our poor humanhood,
Only because you would!
To search and circle, follow and outstrip,
Men and their fellowship;
And keep your heart no less,
Your to-and-fro of hope and wistfulness,
Through all world-weathers and against all odds!

Can you forgive us now?—
Your fallen Gods?

SONG OF MYSELF

WALT WHITMAN

From *Leaves of Grass*

I think I could turn and live with animals, they are so placid
    and self-contained,
I stand and look at them sometimes an hour at a stretch.

They do not sweat and whine about their condition,
They do not lie awake in the dark and weep for their sins,
They do not make me sick discussing their duty to God,
No one is dissatisfied—not one is demented with the mania of
  owning things,
Not one kneels to another, nor to his kind that lived thousands
  of years ago,
Not one is respectable or industrious over the whole earth.

f. THE HEAVENS

PSALM XIX

Joseph Addison

The spacious firmament on high,
With all the blue ethereal sky,
And spangled heavens, a shining frame,
Their great Original proclaim.
The unwearied sun, from day to day,
Does his Creator's power display,
And publishes to every land
The work of an Almighty hand.

Soon as the evening shades prevail,
The moon takes up the wondrous tale,
And nightly to the listening earth
Repeats the story of her birth;
Whilst all the stars that round her burn,
And all the planets in their turn,
Confirm the tidings as they roll,
And spread the truth from pole to pole.

What though in solemn silence all
Move round the dark terrestrial ball;
What though no real voice or sound
Amidst their radiant orbs be found;

In reason's ear they all rejoice,
And utter forth a glorious voice,
Forever singing as they shine,
"The hand that made us is divine."

THE HEAVENS ABOVE AND THE LAW WITHIN

Psalm XIX

From Moulton's *Modern Readers' Bible*

The heavens declare the glory of God;
And the firmament showeth his handiwork.
Day unto day uttereth speech,
And night unto night sheweth knowledge.
There is no speech nor language;
Their voice cannot be heard.
Their line is gone out through all the earth,
And their words to the end of the world.

In them hath he set a tabernacle for the sun,
Which is as a bridegroom coming out of his chamber,
And rejoiceth as a strong man to run his course.
His going forth is from the end of the heaven,
And his circuit unto the ends of it:
And there is nothing hid from the heat thereof.

The law of the Lord is perfect, restoring the soul:
The testimony of the Lord is sure, making wise the simple.
The precepts of the Lord are right, rejoicing the heart;
The commandment of the Lord is pure, enlightening the eyes.
The fear of the Lord is clean, enduring for ever:
The judgments of the Lord are true, and righteous altogether.
More to be desired are they than gold, yea, than much fine gold:
Sweeter also than honey and the honeycomb.

Moreover by them is thy servant warned:
In keeping of them there is great reward.
Who can discern his errors? Clear thou me from hidden
    faults.

Keep back thy servant also from presumptuous sins; let them
    not have dominion over me:
Then shall I be perfect,
And I shall be clear from the great transgression.

.   .   .   .

Let the words of my mouth and the meditations of my heart be
    acceptable in thy sight,
O Lord, my rock and my redeemer.

THE INVISIBLE

Richard Watson Gilder

Such pictures of the heavens were never seen.
We stood at the steep edge of the abyss
And looked out on the making of the suns.
The skies were powdered with the white of stars
And the pale ghosts of systems yet to be;
While here and there a nebulous spiral told,
Against the dark, the story of the orbs—
From the impalpable condensing slow
Through ages infinite.

               Each mighty shape
Seemed as the shape of speed—a whirling wheel
Stupendously revolving,
And yet no eye of man may see it stir.
(That moveless motion brings to the human brain
A hint of the large measurements of time—
Eternity made present.)

               Such new sense
Of magnitudes that make our world an atom
Might crush the soul, did not this saving thought
Leap to the mind and lift it to clear heights:—
" 'Tis but the unseen that grows not old nor dies,
Suffers not change, nor waning, nor decay.
This that we see—this casual glimpse within
The seething pit of space; these million stars

And worlds in making, these are naught but matter;
These are all but the dust of our feet,
And we who gaze forth fearless on the sight
Find not one equal, facing from the vast
Our sentient selves. Not one, sole, lonely star
In all that infinite glitter and deep light
Can make one conscious movement; all are slaves
To law material, immutable—
That Power immense, mysterious, intense,
Unseen as our own souls, but which must be
Like them, the home of thought, with will and might
To stamp on endless matter the soul's will.
Yea, in these souls of ours triumphant dwells
Some segment of the large creative Power—
A thing beyond the things of sight and sense;
A strength to think, a force to conquer force.
One are we with the ever-living One."

THE PATH OF THE STARS

Thomas S. Jones, Jr.

Down through the spheres there came the Name of One
  Who is the Law of Beauty and Light
  He came, and as He came the waiting Night
Shook with gladness of a Day begun;
And as He came, He said: "Thy Will be Done
  On Earth"; and all His vibrant words were white
  And glistening with silver, and their might
Was of the glory of a rising sun.
Unto the Stars sang out His Living Words
  White and with silver, and their rhythmic sound
    Was a mighty symphony unfurled;
And back from out the Stars like homing birds
  They fell in love upon the sleeping ground
    And were forever in a wakened world.

g. MOUNTAINS

HYMN BEFORE SUNRISE IN THE VALE OF CHAMOUNIX

SAMUEL TAYLOR COLERIDGE

Hast thou a charm to stay the morning star
In his steep course? So long he seems to pause
On thy bald, awful head, O sovran Blanc!
The Arve and the Arveiron at thy base
Rave ceaselessly; but thou, most awful Form!
Risest from forth thy silent sea of pines,

How silently! Around thee and above,
Deep is the air and dark, substantial, black,
An ebon mass. Methinks thou piercest it,
As with a wedge! But when I look again,
It is thine own calm home, thy crystal shrine,
Thy habitation from eternity!
O dread and silent Mount! I gazed upon thee,
Till thou, still present to the bodily sense,
Didst vanish from my thought. Entranced in prayer
I worshipp'd the Invisible alone.

Yet, like some sweet beguiling melody,
So sweet, we know not we are listening to it,
Thou, the meanwhile, wast blending with my thought,
Yea, with my life and life's own secret joy:
Till the dilating Soul, enwrapt, transfused,
Into the mighty vision passing—there,
As in her natural form, swell'd vast to Heaven!

Awake, my soul! not only passive praise
Thou owest! not alone these swelling tears,
Mute thanks and secret ecstasy! awake,
Voice of sweet song! Awake, my heart, awake!
Green vales and icy cliffs, all join my Hymn.

Thou first and chief, sole sovran of the vale!
O, struggling with the darkness all the night,
And visited all night by troops of stars,
Or when they climb the sky or when they sink:
Companion of the morning-star at dawn,
Thyself earth's rosy star, and of the dawn
Co-herald! O wake, and utter praise!
Who sank thy sunless pillars deep in the Earth?
Who fill'd thy countenance with rosy light?
Who made thee parent of perpetual streams?

And you, ye five wild torrents, fiercely glad!
Who call'd you forth from night and utter death,
From dark and icy caverns call'd you forth,
Down those precipitous, black, jagged rocks,
Forever shatter'd and the same forever?
Who gave you your invulnerable life,
Your strength, your speed, your fury, and your joy,
Unceasing thunder and eternal foam?
And who commanded (and the silence came),
Here let the billows stiffen, and have rest?

Ye ice-falls! ye that from the mountain's brow
Adown enormous ravines slope amain—
Torrents, methinks, that heard a mighty voice,
And stopp'd at once amid their maddest plunge!
Motionless torrents! silent cataracts!
Who made you glorious as the gates of Heaven
Beneath the keen full moon? Who bade the sun
Clothe you with rainbows? Who, with loving flowers
Of loveliest blue, spread garlands at your feet?—
God! let the torrents, like a shout of nations,
Answer! and let the ice-plains echo, God!
God! sing, ye meadow-streams, with gladsome voice!
Ye pine-groves, with soft and soul-like sounds!
And they too have a voice, yon piles of snow,
And in their perilous fall shall thunder, God!

Ye living flowers that skirt the eternal frost!
Ye wild goats sporting round the eagle's nest!

Ye eagles, playmates of the mountain storm!
Ye lightnings, the dread arrows of the clouds!
Ye signs and wonders of the elements!
Utter forth God, and fill the hills with praise!

Thou too, hoar Mount! with thy sky-pointing peaks,
Oft from whose feet the avalanche, unheard,
Shoots downward, glittering through the pure serene,
Into the depths of clouds that veil thy breast—
Thou, too, again, stupendous Mountain! Thou
That, as I raise my head, awhile bow'd low
In adoration, upward from thy base
Slow-travelling with dim eyes suffused with tears,
Solemnly seemest, like a vapory cloud,
To rise before me—Rise, O ever rise!
Rise, like a cloud of incense from the Earth!
Thou kingly spirit throned among the hills,
Thou dread ambassador from earth to heaven,
Great hierarch! tell thou the silent sky,
And tell the stars and tell yon rising sun,
Earth, with her thousand voices, praises God.

SILENCE

CHARLES HANSON TOWNE

I need not shout my faith. Thrice eloquent
  Are quiet trees and the green listening sod;
Hushed are the stars, whose power is never spent;
  The hills are mute: yet how they speak of God!

h. THE OCEAN

TO THE OCEAN

LORD BYRON

From *Childe Harold's Pilgrimage*

Roll on, thou deep and dark blue Ocean—roll!
Ten thousand fleets sweep over thee in vain;
Man marks the earth with ruin,—his control
Stops with the shore; upon the watery plain
The wrecks are all thy deed, nor doth remain
A shadow of man's ravage, save his own,
When for a moment, like a drop of rain,
He sinks into thy depths with bubbling groan—
Without a grave, unknelled, uncoffined and unknown.

His steps are not upon thy paths,—thy fields
Are not a spoil for him,—thou dost arise
And shake him from thee; the vile strength he wields
For earth's destruction, thou dost all despise,
Spurning him from thy bosom to the skies,
And send'st him, shivering in thy playful spray,
And howling to his gods, where haply lies
His petty hope in some near port or bay,
And dashest him again to earth; there let him lay.

The armaments which thunderstrike the walls
Of rock-built cities, bidding nations quake,
And monarchs tremble in their capitals,
The oak leviathans, whose huge ribs make
Their clay creator the vain title take
Of Lord of thee and Arbiter of War—
These are thy toys, and, as the snowy flake,
They melt into thy yeast of waves, which mar
Alike the Armada's pride, and spoils of Trafalgar.

Thy shores are empires, changed in all save thee—
Assyria, Greece, Rome, Carthage, what are they?
Thy waters washed them power while they were free,
And many a tyrant since; their shores obey
The stranger, slave, or savage; their decay
Has dried up realms to deserts: not so thou;
Unchangeable, save to thy wild waves' play,
Time writes no wrinkle on thine azure brow:
Such as creation's dawn beheld, thou rollest now.

Thou glorious mirror, where the Almighty's form
Glasses itself in tempests; in all time,—
Calm or convulsed, in breeze or gale or storm,
Icing the pole, or in the torrid clime
Dark-heaving—boundless, endless and sublime,
The image of eternity, the throne
Of the Invisible; even from out thy slime
The monsters of the deep are made; each zone
Obeys thee; thou goest forth, dread, fathomless, alone.

And I have loved thee, Ocean! and my joy
Of youthful sports was on thy breast to be
Borne, like thy bubbles, onward: from a boy
I wantoned with thy breakers; they to me
Were a delight; and, if the freshening sea
Made them a terror—'twas a pleasing fear;
For I was as it were a child of thee
And trusted to thy billows far and near,
And laid my hand upon thy mane—as I do here.

THE OCEAN

Psalm CVII, 23-33

From Moulton's *Modern Readers' Bible*

They that go down to the sea in ships,
That do business in great waters;
These see the works of the Lord,
And his wonders in the deep.

For he commandeth and raiseth the stormy wind,
Which lifteth up the waves thereof.
They mount up to heaven,
They go down again to the depths:
Their soul melteth because of trouble.
They reel to and fro,
And stagger like a drunken man,
And are at their wit's end.
Then they cry unto the Lord in their trouble,
And he bringeth them out of their distresses.
He maketh the storm a calm,
So that the waves thereof are still.
Then they are glad because they be quiet;
So he bringeth them unto the haven where they would **be.**
Oh that men would praise the LORD for his goodness,
And for his wonderful works to the children of men!
Let them exalt him also in the assembly of the people,
And praise him in the seat of the elders.

ROCKED IN THE CRADLE OF THE DEEP

EMMA WILLARD

Rocked in the cradle of the deep
I lay me down in peace to sleep;
Secure I rest upon the wave,
For thou, O Lord, hast power to save.
I know thou wilt not slight my call,
For thou dost mark the sparrow's fall;
And calm and peaceful shall I sleep,
Rocked in the cradle of the deep.

When in the dead of night I lie
And gaze upon the trackless sky,
The star-bespangled heavenly scroll,
The boundless waters as they roll,—
I feel thy wondrous power to save
From perils of the stormy wave:
Rocked in the cradle of the deep
I calmly rest and soundly sleep.

And such the trust that still were mine,
Though stormy winds swept o'er the brine,
Or though the tempest's fiery breath
Roused me from sleep to wreck and death.
In ocean cave still safe with Thee
The gem of immortality!
And calm and peaceful shall I sleep
Rocked in the cradle of the deep.

VI. God in the Life of Man
   a. immanent in the soul
   b. revealed in the life of Jesus Christ
      1. *Mediæval and Modern*
      2. *Recent*
   c. revealed in the guidance of individual lives
   d. revealed in historical events
   e. revealed in groups or organizations of individuals
      1. *In the Family*
      2. *In the City*
      3. *In the Church*

VI. God in the Life of Man

a. Immanent in the Soul

REAL PRESENCE

Ivan Adair

Not on an Altar shall mine eyes behold Thee,
   Tho' Thou art sacrifice, Thou too art Priest;
Bend, that the feeble arms of Love enfold Thee,
   So Faith shall bloom, increased.

Not on a Cross, with passion buds around Thee,
   Thorn-crowned and lonely, in Thy suffering;
Nay, but as watching Mary met and found Thee,
   Dawn-robed, the Risen King.

Not in the past, but in the present glorious,
   Not in the future, that I cannot span,
Living and breathing, over death victorious,
   My God . . . my Brother-Man.

IN HIM

James Vila Blake

Though the bee
Miss the clover
Fly it by and know it not:
Though the sea
Wash not oar

283

On the sands a wounded spot;
  Heart, O heart!
  Thou wilt part
From the all-hold on thee, and lose thy way,
  Never, never;
  Nor wilt give
The sweet life from the life of night and day.
  Thou in Him
  Liest as dim
As yellow wings in golden atmosphere,
Or in the sea each watery spiritual sphere.

THE DIVINE IMAGE

William Blake

To Mercy, Pity, Peace, and Love
All pray in their distress;
And to these virtues of delight
Return their thankfulness.

For Mercy, Pity, Peace, and Love
Is God, our Father dear,
And Mercy, Pity, Peace, and Love
Is Man, His child and care.

For Mercy has a human heart,
Pity a human face,
And Love, the human form divine,
And Peace, the human dress.

Then every man, of every clime,
That prays in his distress,
Prays to the human form divine,
Love, Mercy, Pity, Peace.

And all must love the human form,
In heathen, Turk, or Jew;
Where Mercy, Love, and Pity dwell,
There God is dwelling too.

HARVEST

Eva Gore Booth

Though the long seasons seem to separate
Sower and reaper or deeds dreamed and done,
Yet when a man reaches the Ivory Gates
Labour and life and seed and corn are one.

Because thou art the doer and the deed,
Because thou art the thinker and the thought,
Because thou art the helper and the need,
And the cold doubt that brings all things to naught;

Therefore in every gracious form and shape
The world's dear open secret thou shalt find,
From the one beauty there is no escape
Nor from the sunshine of the eternal mind.

The patient laborer, with guesses dim,
Follows this wisdom to its secret goal.
He knows all deeds and dreams exist in him,
And all men's God in every human soul.

LIFE

Margaret Deland

By one great heart the universe is stirred;
  By Its strong pulse, stars climb the darkening blue;
  It throbs in each fresh sunset's changing hue,
And thrills through the low sweet song of every bird.

By It the plunging blood reds all men's veins;
  Joy feels that heart against his rapturous own
  And on It, Sorrow breathes her deepest groan;
It bounds through gladnesses and deepest pains.

Passionless beating through all Time and Space,
  Relentless, calm, majestic in Its march,
  Alike, though Nature shake heaven's endless arch,
Or man's heart break, because of some dead face!

'Tis felt in sunshine greening the soft sod,
  In children's smiling as in mothers' tears,
  And, for strange comfort, through the aching years,
Men's hungry souls have called that great Heart, GOD!

THE INFORMING SPIRIT

RALPH WALDO EMERSON

There is no great and no small
To the Soul that maketh all:
And where it cometh, all things are;
And it cometh everywhere.

I am owner of the sphere,
Of the seven stars and the solar year,
Of Cæsar's hand, and Plato's brain,
Of Lord Christ's heart, and Shakespeare's strain.

From VOLUNTARIES

RALPH WALDO EMERSON

Stainless soldier on the walls,
Knowing this,—and knows no more,—
Whoever fights, whoever falls,
Justice conquers evermore,
Justice after as before,—
And he who battles on her side,
God, though he were ten times slain,
Crowns him victor glorified,
Victor over death and pain.

Blooms the laurel which belongs
To the valiant chief who fights;
I see the wreath, I hear the songs
Lauding the Eternal Rights,
Victors over daily wrongs:
Awful victors, they misguide
Whom they will destroy,
And their coming triumph hide
In our downfall, or our joy:

They reach no term, they never sleep,
In equal strength through space abide;
Though, feigning dwarfs, they crouch and creep,
The strong they slay, the swift outstride:
Fate's grass grows rank in valley clods,
And rankly on the castled steep,—
Speak it firmly, these are gods,
All are ghosts beside.

THE HYMN OF THE WORLD WITHIN

PSALM CIII

From Moulton's *Modern Readers' Bible*

Bless the Lord, O my soul,
    And all that is within me, bless his holy name.
Bless the Lord, O my soul,
    And forget not all his benefits:
Who forgiveth all thine iniquities;
    Who healeth all thy diseases;
Who redeemeth thy life from destruction;
    Who crowneth thee with loving kindness and tender
        mercies:
Who satisfieth thy mouth with good things;
    So that thy youth is renewed like the eagle.

The Lord executeth righteous acts,
    And judgements for all that are oppressed.

He made known his ways unto Moses,
>His doings unto the children of Israel.
The Lord is full of compassion, and gracious,
>Slow to anger and plenteous in mercy.
He will not always chide;
>Neither will he keep his anger forever.
He hath not dealt with us after our sins,
>Nor rewarded us after our iniquities.

For as the heaven is high above the earth,
>So great is his mercy toward them that fear him.
As far as the east is from the west,
>So far hath he removed our transgressions from us.
Like as a father pitieth his children,
>So the Lord pitieth them that fear him.
For he knoweth our frame;
>He remembereth that we are dust.

As for man, his days are as grass;
>As a flower of the field, so he flourisheth.
For the wind passeth over it and it is gone:
>And the place thereof shall know it no more.
But the mercy of the Lord is from everlasting to everlasting
>upon them that fear him.
>And his righteousness unto childrens' children,
To such as keep his covenant,
>And to those that remember his precepts to do them.

The Lord hath established his throne in the heavens;
>And his kingdom ruleth over all.
Bless the Lord, ye angels of his,
>Ye mighty in strength;
That fulfill his word,
>Hearkening unto the voice of his word.
Bless the Lord, all ye his hosts;
>Ye ministers of his, that do his pleasure.
Bless the Lord, all ye his works,
>In all places of his dominion.

THE SEARCHER OF HEARTS IS THY MAKER

Psalm CXXXIX

From Moulton's *Modern Readers' Bible*

O Lord, thou hast searched me and known me.
  Thou knowest my downsitting and mine uprising,
  Thou understandest my thought afar off.
Thou searchest out my path and my lying down,
  And art acquainted with all my ways.
For there is not a word in my tongue,
  But Lo, O Lord, thou knowest it altogether.
Thou hast beset me behind and before,
  And laid thine hand upon me.
Such knowledge is too wonderful for me;
  It is high, I cannot attain unto it.
Whither shall I go from thy spirit?
  Or whither shall I flee from thy presence?
If I ascend up into heaven, thou art there:
  If I make my bed in Sheol, behold thou art there.
If I take the wings of the morning,
  And dwell in the uttermost parts of the sea;
Even there shall thy hand lead me,
  And thy right hand shall hold me.
If I say, Surely the darkness shall overwhelm me,
  And the light about me shall be night;
Even the darkness hideth not from thee,
  But the night shineth as the day:
  The darkness and the light are both alike to thee.
For thou hast possessed my reins:
  Thou hast covered me in my mother's womb.
I will give thanks unto thee; for I am fearfully and wonderfully
    made:
  Wonderful are thy works;
  And that my soul knoweth right well.
My frame was not hidden from thee,
  When I was made in secret,
  And curiously wrought in the lowest parts of the earth.

Thine eyes did see my unperfect substance,
    And in thy book were all my members written,
Which day by day were fashioned,
    When as yet there was none of them.
How precious also are thy thoughts unto me, O God!
    How great is the sum of them!
If I should count them, they are more in number than the sand:
    When I awake, I am still with thee.
Surely thou wilt slay the wicked, O God:
    Depart from me, therefore, ye bloodthirsty men.
For they speak against thee wickedly,
    And thine enemies take thy name in vain.
Do I not hate them, O Lord, that hate thee?
    And am I not grieved with those that rise up against thee?
I hate them with perfect hatred:
    I count them mine enemies,
Search me, O God, and know my heart:
    Try me and know my thoughts;
And see if there be any way of wickedness in me,
    And lead me in the way everlasting.

NODES

ALICE CORBIN HENDERSON

The endless, foolish merriment of stars
Beside the pale cold sorrow of the moon,
Is like the wayward noises of the world
Beside my heart's uplifted silent tune.

The little broken glitter of the waves
Beside the golden sun's intense white blaze,
Is like the idle chatter of the crowd
Beside my heart's unwearied song of praise.

The sun and all the planets in the sky
Beside the sacred wonder of dim space,
Are notes upon a broken tarnished lute
That God will some day mend and put in place.

And space, beside the little secret joy
Of God that sings forever in the clay,
Is smaller than the dust we cannot see,
That yet dies not, till time and space decay.

And as the foolish merriment of stars
Beside the cold pale sorrow of the moon,
My little song, my little joy, my praise,
Beside God's ancient everlasting rune.

From THE CHERUBIM

THOMAS HEYWOOD

I have wandered like a sheep that's lost,
To find Thee out in every coast.
Without I have long seeking been,
Whilst Thou the while abidst *within*.
Through every broad street and strait lane
Of this world's city, but in vain,
I have inquired.   The reason Why?
I sought Thee ill; for how could I
Find Thee *abroad*, when Thou, mean space,
Hadst made *within* thy dwelling-place?

I sent my messengers about
To try if they could find Thee out.
But all was to no purpose still,
Because, indeed, they sought Thee ill;
For how could they discover Thee
That saw not when thou enteredst me?

Mine eyes could tell me?   If He were
Not coloured, sure He came not there.
If not by sound, my ears could say
He doubtless did not pass my way.
My nose could nothing of Him tell,
Because my God He did not smell.
None such I relished, said my taste,

And therefore me He never passed.
My feeling told me that none such
There entered for He did none touch.
Resolved by them how should I be,
Since none of all these are in Thee?

In Thee! My God, Thou hast no hue
That man's frail optic sense can view;
No sound the ear hears; odour none
The smell attracts; all taste is gone
At Thy appearance; where doth fail
A body, how can touch prevail?
Yet when I seek my God, I enquire
For Light, the sun and moon much higher.
More clear and splendrous, 'bove all light,
Which eye receives not, 'Tis so bright.
I seek a voice beyond degree
Of all melodious harmony;

.   .   .   .

So far this Light the rays extends
As that no place it comprehends.

.   .   .   .

This light, this sound, this savoring grace,
This tasteful sweet, this strict embrace,
No place contains, no eye can see,
My God is, and there's none but HE.

THE LIVING TEMPLE

Oliver Wendell Holmes

Not in the world of light alone,
Where God has built his blazing throne.
Nor yet alone in earth below,
With belted seas that come and go,
And endless isles of sunlit green,
Is all thy Maker's glory seen:
Look in upon thy wondrous frame,—
Eternal wisdom still the same!

The smooth, soft air with pulse-like waves
Flows murmuring through its hidden caves,
Whose streams of brightening purple rush,
Fired with a new and livelier blush,
While all their burden of decay
The ebbing current steals away,
And red with Nature's flame they start
From the warm fountains of the heart.

No rest that throbbing slave may ask,
Forever quivering o'er his task,
While far and wide a crimson jet
Leaps forth to fill the woven net
Which in unnumbered crossing tides
The flood of burning life divides,
Then, kindling each decaying part,
Creeps back to find the throbbing heart.

But warmed with that unchanging flame
Behold the outward moving frame,
Its living marbles jointed strong
With glistening band and silvery thong,
And linked to reason's guiding reins
By myriad rings in trembling chains,
Each graven with the threaded zone
Which claims it as the master's own.

See how yon beam of seeming white
Is braided out of seven-hued light,
Yet in those lucid globes no ray
By any chance shall break astray.
Hark how the rolling surge of sound,
Arches and spirals circling round,
Wakes the hushed spirit through thine ear
With music it is heaven to hear.

Then mark the cloven sphere that holds
All thought in its mysterious folds;
That feels sensation's faintest thrill,
And flashes forth the sovereign will;

Think on the stormy world that dwells
Locked in its dim and clustering cells!
The lightning gleams of power it sheds
Along its hollow glassy threads!

O Father! grant thy love divine
To make these mystic temples thine!
When wasting age and wearying strife
Have sapped the leaning walls of life,
When darkness gathers over all,
And the last tottering pillars fall,
Take the poor dust thy mercy warms,
And mould it into heavenly forms!

THE INDWELLING GOD

Frederick Lucian Hosmer

Go not, my soul, in search of Him;
    Thou wilt not find Him there—
Or in the depths of shadow dim,
    Or heights of upper air.

For not in far-off realms of space
    The Spirit hath its throne;
In every heart it findeth place
    And waiteth to be known.

Thought answereth alone to thought
    And Soul with soul hath kin;
The outward God he findeth not,
    Who finds not God within.

And if the vision come to thee
    Revealed by inward sign,
Earth will be full of Deity
    And with his glory shine!

Thou shalt not want for company,
   Nor pitch thy tent alone;
The Indwelling God will go with thee,
   And show thee of his own.

O gift of gifts, O grace of grace,
   That God should condescend
To make thy heart His dwelling-place—
   And be thy daily Friend!

Then go not thou in search of Him
   But to thyself repair;
Wait thou within the silence dim
   And thou shalt find Him there.

SONGS OF KABIR

KABIR

Translated by Rabindranath Tagore

I. 83

The moon shines in my body, but my blind eyes cannot see it:
The moon is within me, and so is the sun.
The unstruck drum of Eternity is sounded within me; but my
   deaf ears cannot hear it.

So long as man clamours for the *I* and the *Mine,* his works
   are as naught:
When all love of the *I* and the *Mine* is dead, then the work
   of the Lord is done.
For work has no other aim than the getting of knowledge:
When that comes, then work is put away.

The flower blooms for the fruit: when the fruit comes, the
   flower withers.
The musk is in the deer, but it seeks it not within itself: it
   wanders in quest of grass.

I. 85

When He Himself reveals Himself, Brahma brings into mani-
festation That which can never be seen.
As the seed is in the plant, as the shade is in the tree, as the
void is in the sky, as infinite forms are in the void—
So from beyond the Infinite, the Infinite comes; and from the
Infinite the finite extends.

The creature is in Brahma, and Brahma is in the creature: they
are ever distinct, yet ever united.
He Himself is the tree, the seed, and the germ.
He Himself is the flower, the fruit, and the shade.
He Himself is the sun, the light, and the lighted.
He Himself is Brahma, creature, and Maya.
He Himself is the manifold form, the infinite space;
He is the breath, the word, and the meaning.
He Himself is the limit and the limitless: and beyond both the
limited and the limitless is He, the Pure Being.
He is the Immanent Mind in Brahma and in the creature.

The Supreme Soul is seen within the soul,
The Point is seen within the Supreme Soul,
And within the Point, the reflection is seen again.
Kabir is blest because he has this supreme vision!

I. 101

Within the earthen vessel are bowers and groves, and within
it is the Creator:
Within this vessel are the seven oceans and the unnumbered
stars.
The touchstone and the jewel-appraiser are within;
And within this vessel the Eternal soundeth, and the spring
wells up.

Kabir says: "Listen to me, my Friend! My beloved Lord is
within."

I. 104

O how may I ever express that secret word?
O how can I say He is not like this, and He is like that?
If I say that He is within me, the universe is ashamed:

If I say that He is without me, it is falsehood.
He makes the inner and the outer worlds to be indivisibly
  one;
The conscious and the unconscious, both are His footstools.
He is neither manifest nor hidden, He is neither revealed nor
  unrevealed:
There are no words to tell that which He is.

I. 121

To Thee Thou hast drawn my love, O Fakir!
I was sleeping in my own chamber, and Thou didst awaken
  me; striking me with Thy voice, O Fakir!
I was drowning in the deeps of the ocean of this world, and
  Thou didst save me: upholding me with Thine arm, O
  Fakir!
Only one word and no second—and Thou hast made me tear
  off all my bonds, O Fakir!
Kabir says, "Thou hast united Thy heart to my heart, O Fakir!"

I. 131

I played day and night with my comrades, and now I am
  greatly afraid.
So high is my Lord's palace, my heart trembles to mount its
  stairs; yet I must not be shy, if I would enjoy His love.
My heart must cleave to my Lover; I must withdraw my veil,
  and meet Him with all my body:
Mine eyes must perform the ceremony of the lamps of love.
Kabir says: "Listen to me, friend: he understands who loves.
  If you feel not love's longing for your Beloved One, it
  is vain to adorn your body, vain to put unguent on your
  eyelids."

From WITHIN AND WITHOUT

George Macdonald

My soul leans toward Him; stretches out its arms,
And waits expectant. Speak to me, my God:

And let me know the living Father cares
For me, even me; for this one of His children.
Hast Thou no word for me? I am Thy thought.
GOD, let Thy mighty heart beat into mine,
And let mine answer as a pulse of Thine.

.   .   .   .

I am an emptiness for Thee to fill;
My soul a cavern for Thy sea. I lie
Diffus'd, abandoning myself to Thee. . . .
I will look up, if life should fail in looking!
Ah, me! A stream cut from my parent spring!
Ah, me! A life lost from its father life!

.   .   .   .

Lord of Thyself and me, through the sore grief
Which thou didst bear to bring us back to God,
Or, rather, bear in being unto us
Thy own pure shining self of love and truth!
When I have learnt to think Thy radiant thoughts,
To live the truth beyond the power to know it,
To bear my light as Thou Thy heavy cross,
Nor ever feel a martyr for Thy sake,
But an unprofitable servant still—
My highest sacrifice my simplest duty
Imperative and unavoidable,
Less than which *all* were nothingness and waste;
When I have lost myself in other men,
And found myself in Thee—the Father then
Will come with Thee, and will abide with me.

HAIL MAN!

Angela Morgan

This flesh is but the symbol and the shrine
Of an immense and unimagined beauty,
Not mortal, but divine;
Structure behind our structure,
Lightning within the brain,

Soul of singing nerve and throbbing vein,
A giant blaze that scorches through our dust,
Fanning our futile "might be" with its "must";
Bearing upon its breast our eager span—
Beyond, above and yet the self of man!

Look how the glow-worm with its feeble might
Signals the presence of celestial fire:
How phosphorus upon the sea at night,
And the swift message o'er the radiant wire,
Proclaim the awesome thing existence covers;
Eternity emerging through our husk,
Sky through our vapor,
Glory through our dusk.

Behold the slender scarlet line that hovers
Between close fingers held against the sun,
Each life a swift and beaming taper
Afire from one.
And how each seems the token
Of a great mystery no man has spoken,
Wherein we walk and work and do our tasks,
Nor dream within what light the spirit basks.

This creaking tent we call the universe,
One motion in a mighty caravan
Whose million million orbits but rehearse
The miracle that swings the heart of man
Is but the outward breathing, of that Source—
Call it by whatever sounding name—
God or Jehovah, Life or Primal Force—
While like a vast impalpable pure flame,
Bears up the visible as 'twere, a toy;
Props with its permanence our mortal screen;
Hotter than hissing fire, than light more keen;
Solid as stone, simple and clean as glass;
Fluid as flashing waves that leap and pass . . .

Yet doth obscuring flesh
Infinity enmesh.

While soul within its prison speaks to soul,
Hailing the habitation as the whole!
This flesh is but the visible out-pouring
Of a portentous and mighty thing,
Whereof each mortal knowing,
Becomes a king.

PROVIDENCE

CALE YOUNG RICE

When I was far from the sea's voice and vastness
I looked for God in the days and hours and seasons.
But now, by its large and eternal tides surrounded
I know I shall only find Him in the greater swing of the years.

For all the seas are His mysteries, not to be learned from a
    single surf-beat,
No wave suffices Him for a revelation.
How like the seas that dower all lands with green and the
    breath of blossoms,
With dews that never have heard its deathless surges.

Let me be patient, then, sure that stars are not jetsam tossing,
Or meaningless waste waters of omnipotence.
Let me be patient even when man is sunk in the storm of His
    purpose
And swirled, a strangled corpse, under His Ages.

From THE HYMN OF MAN

ALGERNON CHARLES SWINBURNE

Thou and I and he are not gods made men for a span,
For God, if a God there be, is the substance of men which is
    man.
Our lives are as pulses or pores of his manifold body and
    breath;

As waves of his sea on the shores where birth is the beacon
    of death.
We men, the multiform features of man, whatsoever we be,
Recreate him of whom we are creatures, and all we only are he.
Not each man of all men is God, but God is the fruit of the
    whole;
Indivisible spirit and blood, indiscernible body from soul.
Not men's but man's is the glory of godhead, the kingdom of
    time,
The mountainous ages made hoary with snows for the spirit to
    climb.
A God with the world inwound whose clay to his foot sole
    clings;
A manifold God fast-bound as with the iron of adverse things.
A soul that labors and lives, an emotion, a strenuous breath,
From the flame that its own mouth gives reillumed, and
    refreshed with death.
In the sea whereof centuries are waves the live God plunges
    and swims;
His bed is in all men's graves, but the worm hath not hold on
    his limbs.
Night puts not out his eyes, nor time sheds change on his head;
With such fire as the stars of the skies are the roots of his
    heart fed.
Men are the thoughts passing through it, the veins that fulfil
    it with blood,
With spirit of sense to renew it as springs fulfilling a flood.
Men are the heartbeats of man, the plumes that feather his
    wings,
Storm-worn, since being began, with the wind and thunder of
    things.
Things are cruel and blind; their strength detains and deforms:
And the wearying wings of the mind still beat up the stream
    of their storms.
Still, as swimming up stream, they strike out blind in the
    blast,
In thunders of vision and dream, and lightnings of future and
    past.
We are baffled and caught in the current and bruised upon
    edges of shoals;

As weeds or as reeds in the torrent of things are the wind-
   shaken souls.
Spirit by spirit goes under, a foam-bell's bubble of breath,
That blows and opens in sunder and blurs not the mirror of
   death.
For a worm or a thorn in his path is a man's soul quenched as
   a flame;
For his lust of an hour or his wrath shall the worm and
   the man be the same.

.   .   .   .

By the spirit are things overcome; they are stark, and the spirit
   hath breath:
It hath speech, and their forces are dumb; it is living, and
   things are of death.

.   .   .   .

Space is the soul's to inherit; the night is hers as the day;
Lo, saith man, this is my spirit; how shall not the worlds make
   way?
Space is thought, and the wonders thereof, and the spectre of
   space;
Is thought not more than the thunders and lightnings? Shall
   thought give place?
Is the body not more than the vesture? The life not more than
   the meat?
The will than the word or the gesture, the heart than the hands
   or the feet?
Is the tongue not more than the speech is? the head not more
   than the crown?
And if higher than is heaven be the reach of the soul, shall
   not heaven bow down?
Time, father of life, and more great than the life it begat and
   began,
Earth's keeper and heaven's and their fate, lives, thinks, and
   hath substance in man.

.   .   .   .

The seal of his knowledge is sure, the truth and his spirit are
   wed;
Men perish, but man shall endure; lives die, but the life is not
   dead.

.   .   .   .

Thou art smitten, thou God, thou art smitten; thy death is upon
    Thee, O Lord.
And the love-song of earth as thou diest resounds through the
    wind of her wings—
Glory to Man in the highest! for Man is the master of things.

From GITANJALI

Rabindranath Tagore

10

Here is thy footstool and there rest thy feet where live the
    poorest, and lowliest, and best.
When I try to bow to thee, my obeisance cannot reach down
    to the depth where thy feet rest among the poorest,
    and lowliest, and lost.

Pride can never approach to where thou walkest in the
    clothes of the humble among the poorest, and lowliest,
    and lost.
My heart can never find its way to where thou keepest
    company with the companionless among the poorest,
    the lowliest, and the lost.

11

Leave this chanting and singing and telling of beads!
Whom dost thou worship in this dark corner of a temple with
    doors all shut?
Open thine eyes and see thy God is not before thee!
He is there where the tiller is tilling the hard ground and
    where the path-maker is breaking stones. He is with
    them in sun and in shower, and his garment is covered
    with dust. Put off thy holy mantle even like him and
    come down on the dusty soil!
Deliverance? Where is this deliverance to be found? Our
    master himself has joyfully taken upon him the bonds
    of creation; he is bound with us all forever.

Come out of thy meditations and leave aside thy flowers
and incense ; What harm is there if thy clothes become
tattered and stained ? Meet him and stand by him in
toil and in the sweat of thy brow.

From IN MEMORIAM

ALFRED TENNYSON

CXXIV

That which we dare invoke to bless;
  Our dearest faith; our ghastliest doubt;
  He, They, One, All; within, without;
The Power in darkness Whom we guess.

I found Him not in world or sun,
  Or eagle's wings, or insect's eye;
  Nor through the questions men may try,
The petty cobwebs we have spun.

If e'er when faith had fallen asleep,
  I heard a voice 'Believe no more'
  And heard an ever-breaking shore
That tumbled in the godless deep;
A warmth within the breast would melt
  The freezing reason's colder part,
  And like a man in wrath the heart
Stood up and answered 'I have felt.'

I SEEK THEE IN THE HEART ALONE

HERBERT TRENCH

Fountain of Fire whom all divide
We haste asunder like the spray,
But waneless doth thy flame abide
Whom every torch can take away!

I seek Thee in the heart alone,
I shall not find in hill or plain;
Our rushing star must keep its moan,
Our nightly soul its homeward pain.

Song beyond thought, Light beyond power,
Even the consumings of this breast
Advance the clearness of that hour
When all shall poise, and be at rest.

It cracks at last—the glowing sheath
The illusion—Personality—
Absorbed and interwoven with death
The myriads are dissolved in Thee.

INTROVERSION

EVELYN UNDERHILL (Mrs. Stuart Moore)

What do you seek within, O soul, my brother?
  What do you seek within?
I seek a life that shall never die,
    Some haven to win
    From mortality.

What do you find within, O soul, my brother?
  What do you find within?
I find great quiet where no noises come.
    Without, the world's din;
    Silence in my home.

Whom do you find within, O soul, my brother?
  Whom do you find within?
I find a friend that in secret came:
    His scarred hands within
    He shields a faint flame.

What would you do within, O soul, my brother?
  What would you do within?

Bar door and window that none may see:
That alone we may be
(Alone! face to face,
In that flame-lit place!)
When first we begin
To speak one with another.

SUPERSENSUAL

EVELYN UNDERHILL

When first the busy, clumsy tongue is stilled,
Save that some childish, stammering words of love
The coming birth of man's true language prove:
When, one and all,
The wistful, seeking senses are fulfillèd
With strange, austere delight:
When eye and ear
Are inward turned to meet the flooding light,
The cadence of thy coming quick to hear:
When on thy mystic flight,
Thou Swift yet Changeless, herald breezes bring
To scent the heart's swept cell
With incense from the thurible of spring,
The fragrance which the lily seeks in vain:
When touch no more may tell
The verities of contact unexpressed,
And, deeply pressed,
To that surrender which is holiest pain,
We taste thy very rest—
Ah, then we find
Folded about by kindly-nurturing night,
Instinct with silence sweetly musical,
The rapt communion of the mind with Mind.
Then may the senses fall
Vanquished indeed, nor dread
That this their dear defeat be counted sin:
For every door of flesh shall lift its head,
Because the King of Life is entered in.

THEOPHANY

Evelyn Underhill

Deep cradled in the fringed mow to lie
And feel the rhythmic flux of life sweep by,
This is to know the easy heaven that waits
Before our timidly-embattled gates:
To show the exultant leap and thrust of things
Outward toward perfection, in the heart
Of every bud to see the folded wings,
Discern the patient whole in every part.

THE DWELLING PLACE

Henry Vaughan

What happy secret fountain,
Fair shade or mountain,
Whose undiscovered virgin glory
Boasts it this day, though not in story,
Was then thy dwelling? did some cloud
Fix'd to a tent, descend and shroud
My distrest Lord? or did a star,
Beckoned by thee, though high and far,
In sparkling smiles haste gladly down
To lodge light and increase her own?
My dear, dear God! I do not know
What lodged thee then, nor where, nor how;
But I am sure thou now dost come
Oft to a narrow, homely room,
Where thou too hast but the least part,
My God, I mean *my sinful heart.*

HEALTH OF BODY DEPENDENT ON SOUL

JONES VERY

Not from the earth, or skies,
    Or seasons as they roll,
Come health and vigor to the frame,
    But from the living soul.

Is this alive to God,
    And not the slave to sin?
Then will the body, too, receive
    Health from the soul within.

But if disease has touched
    The spirit's inmost part,
In vain we seek from outward things
    To heal the deadly smart.

The mind, the heart unchanged,
    Which clouded e'en our home,
Will make the outward world the same,
    Where'er our feet may roam.

The fairest scenes on earth,
    The mildest, purest sky,
Will bring no vigor to the step,
    No lustre to the eye.

For He who formed our frame
    Made man a perfect whole,
And made the body's health depend
    Upon the living soul.

THE LIGHT FROM WITHIN

JONES VERY

I saw on earth another light
  Than that which lit my eye
Come forth as from my soul within,
  And from a higher sky.

Its beams shone still unclouded on,
  When in the farthest west
The sun I once had known had sunk
  Forever to his rest.

And on I walked, though dark the night,
  Nor rose his orb by day;
As one who by a surer guide
  Was pointed out the way.

'Twas brighter far than noonday's beam;
  It shone from God within,
And lit, as by a lamp from heaven,
  The world's track of sin.

SONG OF MYSELF

WALT WHITMAN

From *Leaves of Grass*

I hear and behold God in every object, yet understand God
  not in the least,
Nor do I understand who there can be more wonderful than
  myself.

Why should I wish to see God better than this day?
I see something of God each hour of the twenty-four, and
  each moment then,

In the faces of men and women I see God, and in my own
    face in the glass,
I find letters from God dropped in the street—and every one is
    signed by God's name,
And I leave them where they are, for I know that others will
    punctually come forever and ever.

b. REVEALED IN THE LIFE OF JESUS CHRIST

1. *Mediæval and Modern*

KARSHISH, THE ARAB PHYSICIAN

Being an Epistle

Containing His Strange Medical Experience

ROBERT BROWNING

Karshish, the picker-up of learning's crumbs,
The not-incurious in God's handiwork
(This man's-flesh He hath admirably made,
Blown like a bubble, kneaded like a paste,
To coop up and keep down on earth a space
That puff of vapor from His mouth, man's soul)
—To Abib, all-sagacious in our art,
Breeder in me of what poor skill I boast,
Like me inquisitive how pricks and cracks
Befall the flesh through too much stress and strain,
Whereby the wily vapor fain would slip
Back and rejoin its source before the term,—
And aptest in contrivance, under God,
To baffle it by deftly stopping such:—
The vagrant Scholar to his Sage at home
Sends greeting (health and knowledge, fame with **peace)**
Three samples of true snake-stone—rarer still,
One of the other sort, the melon-shaped,

(But fitter, pounded fine, for charms than drugs)
And writeth now the twenty-second time.

My journeyings were brought to Jericho:
Thus I resume. Who studious in our art
Shall count a little labor unrepaid?
I have shed sweat enough, left flesh and bone
On many a flinty furlong of this land.
Also the country-side is all on fire
With rumors of a marching hitherward—
Some say Vespasian cometh, some his son.
A black lynx snarled and pricked a tufted ear;
Lust of my blood inflamed his yellow balls:
I cried and threw my staff and he was gone.
Twice have the robbers stripped and beaten me,
And once a town declared me for a spy,
But at the end I reach Jerusalem,
Since this poor covert where I pass the night,
This Bethany, lies scarce the distance thence
A man with plague-sores at the third degree
Runs till he drops down dead. Thou laughest here!
'Sooth, it elates me, thus reposed and safe,
To void the stuffing of my travel-scrip
And share with thee whatever Jewry yields.
A viscid choler is observable
In tertians, I was nearly bold to say,
And falling-sickness hath a happier cure
Than our school wots of: there's a spider here
Weaves no web, watches on the ledge of tombs,
Sprinkled with mottles on an ash-gray back;
Take five and drop them . . . but who knows his mind,
The Syrian runagate I trust this to?
His service payeth me a sublimate
Blown up his nose to help the ailing eye.
Best wait I reach Jerusalem at morn,
There set in order my experiences,
Gather what most deserves and give thee all—
Or, I might add, Judea's gum-tragacanth
Scales off in purer flakes, shines clearer-grained,
Cracks 'twixt the pestle and the porphyry,

In fine, exceeds our produce. Scalp-disease
Confounds me, crossing so with leprosy—
Thou hadst admired one sort I gained at Zoar—
But zeal outruns discretion. Here I end.

Yet stay: my Syrian blinketh gratefully,
Protesteth his devotion is my price—
Suppose I write what harms not, though he steal?
I half resolve to tell thee, yet I blush,
What set me off a-writing first of all.
An itch I had, a sting to write, a tang!
For, be it this town's barrenness—or else
The Man had something in the look of him—
His case has struck me far more than 'tis worth.
So, pardon if—(lest presently I lose
In the great press of novelty at hand
The care and pains this somehow stole from me)
I bid thee take the thing while fresh in mind,
Almost in sight—for, wilt thou have the truth?
The very man is gone from me but now,
Whose ailment is the subject of discourse.
Thus, then, and let thy better wit help all.

'Tis but a case of mania—subinduced
By epilepsy, at the turning-point
Of trance prolonged unduly some three days,
When by the exhibition of some drug
Or spell, exorcisation, stroke of art
Unknown to me and which 'twere well to know,
The evil thing out-breaking all at once
Left the man whole and sound of body indeed,—
But, flinging, so to speak, life's gates too wide,
Making a clear house of it too suddenly,
The first conceit that entered might inscribe
Whatever it was minded on the wall
So plainly at that vantage, as it were,
(First come, first served) that nothing subsequent
Attaineth to erase the fancy-scrawls
Which the returned and new-established soul
Hath gotten now so thoroughly by heart
That henceforth she will read or these or none.

And first—the man's own firm conviction rests
That he was dead (in fact they buried him)
—That he was dead and then restored to life
By a Nazarene physician of his tribe:
—'Sayeth, the same bade "Rise," and he did rise.
"Such cases are diurnal" thou wilt cry.
Not so this figment:—not, that such a fume,
Instead of giving way to time and health,
Should eat itself into the life of life,
As saffron tingeth flesh, blood, bones and all!
For see, how he takes up the after-life,
The man—it is one Lazarus, a Jew,
Sanguine, proportioned, fifty years of age,
The body's habit wholly laudable,
As much, indeed, beyond the common health
As he were made and put aside to show.
Think, could we penetrate by any drug
And bathe the wearied soul and worried flesh,
And bring it clear and fair, by three days' sleep!
Whence has the man the balm that brightens all?
This grown man eyes the world now like a child.
Some elders of his tribe, I should premise,
Led in their friend, obedient as a sheep,
To bear my inquisition. While they spoke,
Now sharply, now with sorrow,—told the case,—
He listened not except I spoke to him,
But folded his two hands and let them talk,
Watching the flies that buzzed: and yet no fool.
And that's a sample how his years must go.
Look, if a beggar, in fixed middle-life,
Should find a treasure, can he use the same
With straightened habits and with tastes starved small,
And take at once to his impoverished brain
The sudden element that changes things,
That sets the undreamed-of rapture at his hand,
And puts the old cheap joy in the scorned dust?
Is he not such an one as moves to mirth—
Warily parsimonious, when no need,
Wasteful as drunkenness at undue times?
All prudent counsel as to what befits

The golden mean, is lost on such an one.
The man's fantastic will is the man's law.

. . . .

And oft the man's soul springs into his face
As if he saw again and heard again
His sage that bade him "Rise" and he did rise.
Something—a word, a tick o' the blood within
Admonishes—then back he sinks at once
To ashes, that was very fire before,
In sedulous recurrence to his trade
Whereby he earneth him the daily bread—
And studiously the humbler for that pride,
Professedly the faultier that he knows
God's secret while he holds the thread of life.
Indeed the especial marking of the man
Is prone submission to the heavenly will—
Seeing it, what it is, and why it is.
—'Sayeth, he will wait patient to the last
For that same death which must restore his being
To equilibrium, body loosening soul
Divorced even now by premature full growth:
He will live, nay, it pleaseth him to live
So long as God please, and just how God please. . . .
Hence I perceive not he affects to preach
The doctrine of his sect whate'er it be—
Make proselytes as madmen thirst to do.
How can he give his neighbor the real ground,
His own conviction? ardent as he is—
Call his great truth a lie, why still the old
"Be it as God please" reassureth him.
I probed the sore as thy disciple should—
"How, beast," said I, "this stolid carelessness
Sufficeth thee, when Rome is on her march
To stamp out like a little spark thy town,
Thy tribe, thy crazy tale and thee at once?"
He merely looked with his large eyes on me.
The man is apathetic, you deduce?
Contrariwise, he loves both old and young,
Able and weak—affects the very brutes
And birds, how say I? flowers of the field—

As a wise workman recognizes tools
In a master's workshop, loving what they make.
Thus is the man as harmless as a lamb:
Only impatient, let him do his best,
At ignorance and carelessness and sin—
An indignation which is promptly curbed:
As when in certain travels I have feigned
To be an ignoramus in our art
According to some preconceived design,
And happed to hear the land's practitioners
Steeped in conceit sublimed by ignorance,
Prattle fantastically on disease,
Its cause and cure—and I must hold my peace!

Thou wilt object—why have I not ere this
Sought out the sage himself, the Nazarene
Who wrought this cure, inquiring at the source,
Conferring with the frankness that befits?
Alas! it grieveth me, the learned leech
Perished in a tumult many years ago,
Accused,—our learning's fate,—of wizardry,
Rebellion, to the setting up a rule
And creed prodigious as described to me.
His death which happened when the earthquake fell
(Prefiguring, as soon appeared, the loss
To occult learning in our lord the sage
That lived there in the pyramid alone)
Was wrought by the mad people,—that's their wont—
On vain recourse, as I conjecture it,
To his tried virtue, for miraculous help—
How could he stop the earthquake? That's their way!
The other imputations must be lies:
But take one—though I loathe to give it thee,
In mere respect for any good man's fame!
(And after all, our patient Lazarus
Is stark mad—should we count on what he says?
Perhaps not—though in writing to a leech
'Tis well to keep back nothing of a case.)
This man so cured regards the curer then,
As—God forgive me—who but God himself,

Creator and Sustainer of the world,
That came and dwelt in flesh on it awhile!
—'Sayeth that such an One was born and lived,
Taught, healed the sick, broke bread at his own house,
Then died, with Lazarus by, for aught I know,
And yet was . . . what I said nor choose repeat,
And must have so avouched himself, in fact,
In hearing of this very Lazarus
Who saith—but why all this of what he saith?
Why write of trivial matters, things of price
Calling at every moment for remark?
I noticed on the margin of a pool
Blue-flowering borage, the Aleppo sort,
Aboundeth, very nitrous.   It is strange!

Thy pardon for this long and tedious case,
Which, now that I review it, needs must seem
Unduly dwelt on, prolixly set forth.
Nor I myself discern in what is writ
Good cause for the peculiar interest
And awe indeed this man has touched me with.
Perhaps the journey's end, the weariness
Had wrought upon me first.   I met him thus—
I crossed a ridge of short sharp broken hills
Like an old lion's cheek-teeth.   Out there came
A moon made like a face with certain spots
Multiform, manifold, and menacing:
Then a wind rose behind me. So we met
In this old sleepy town at unaware,
The man and I.   I send thee what is writ.
Regard it as a chance, a matter risked
To this ambiguous Syrian—he may lose,
Or steal, or give it thee with equal good.
Jerusalem's repose shall make amends
For time this letter wastes, thy time and mine,
Till when, once more they pardon and farewell!

The very God! think, Abib; dost thou think?
So, the All-Great were the All-Loving, too—
So, through the thunder comes a human voice

Saying, "O heart I made, a heart beats here!
Face, my hands fashioned, see it in myself.
Thou hast no power nor mayst conceive of mine,
But love I gave thee, with myself to love,
And thou must love me who have died for thee!"
The madman saith He said so: it is strange.

THE HOLY NATIVITY OF OUR LORD GOD

RICHARD CRASHAW

A Hymn as Sung by the Shepherds

Chorus

Come, we shepherds, whose blest sight
Hath met Love's noon in Nature's night;
Come, we lift up our loftier song
And wake the sun that lies too long.

To all our world of well-stol'n joy
He slept, and dreamt of no such thing;
While we found our Heaven's fairer eye
And kissed the cradle of our King.
Tell him he rises now, too late
To show us aught worth looking at.

Tell him we now can show him more
Than he e'er showed to mortal sight;
Than he himself e'er saw before;
Which to be seen needs not his light.
Tell him, Tityrus, where th' hast been
Tell him, Thyrsis, what th' hast seen.

Tityrus

Gloomy night embraced the place
Where the noble Infant lay.
The Babe looked up and showed His face;
In spite of darkness it was day.

It was Thy day, Sweet! and did rise
Not from the east, but from Thine eyes.

Chorus

It was Thy day, Sweet . . .

Thyrsis

Winter chid aloud; and sent
The angry North to wage his wars.
   The North forgot his fierce intent;
And left perfumes instead of scars.
   By those sweet eyes' persuasive powers,
Where he meant frost he scattered flowers.

Chorus

By those sweet eyes . . .

Both

We saw Thee in Thy balmy nest,
Young Dawn of our Eternal Day!
   We saw Thine eyes break from the East
And chase the trembling shades away.
   We saw Thee and we blest the sight,
We saw Thee by Thine own sweet light.

Tityrus

Poor World, said I, what wilt thou do
To entertain this starry Stranger?
   Is this the best thou canst bestow?
A cold. and not too cleanly, manger?
   Contend, the powers of heaven and earth,
To fit a bed for this huge birth!

Chorus

Contend the powers . . .

Thyrsis

Proud World, said I; cease your contest
And let the mighty Babe alone;
  The phœnix builds the phœnix' nest,
Love's architecture is his own;
  The Babe whose birth embraves this morn,
Made His own bed ere He was born.

Chorus

  The Babe whose . . .

Tityrus

I saw the curl'd drops, soft and slow,
Come hovering o'er the place's head;
  Offering their whitest sheets of snow
To furnish the fair Infant's bed.
  Forbear, said I; be not too bold;
Your fleece is white, but 'tis too cold.

Chorus

  Forbear, said I . . .

Thyrsis

I saw the obsequious seraphim
Their rosy fleece of fire bestow,
  For well they now can spare their wings
Since Heaven itself lies here below.
  Well done, said I; but are you sure
Your down so warm, will pass for pure?

Chorus

  Well done, said I . . .

Tityrus

No, no, your King's not yet to seek
Where to repose His royal head;

See, see how soon His new-bloomed cheek
'Twixt mother's breasts is gone to bed!
Sweet choice, said we! no way but so
Not to lie cold, yet sleep in snow.

Chorus

Sweet choice, said we . . .

Both

We saw Thee in Thy balmy nest,
Bright Dawn of our Eternal Day!
We saw Thine eyes break from their east
And chase the trembling shades away.
We saw Thee, and we blest the sight,
We saw Thee by Thine own sweet light.

Chorus

We saw Thee . . .

Full Chorus

Welcome, all wonders in one night!
Eternity shut in a span,
Summer in winter, day in night,
Heaven in earth, and God in man.
Great Little One! Whose all-embracing birth
Lifts earth to heaven, stoops heaven to earth.

Welcome—though nor to gold nor silk,
To more than Cæsar's birthright is;
Two sister-seas of virgin-milk
With many a rarely-tempered kiss
That breathes at once both maid and mother,
Warms in the one, cools on the other.

Welcome—though not to those gay flies
Gilded i' th' beams of earthly kings,
Slippery souls in smiling eyes—
But to poor shepherds, homespun things,

Whose wealth's their flock, whose wit's to be
Well read in this simplicity.

Yet, when young April's husband show'rs
Shall bless the fruitful Maia's bed,
  We'll bring the first-born of her flow'rs
To kiss Thy feet and crown Thy head.
  To Thee, dread Lamb! Whose love must keep
The shepherds, more than they the sheep.

To Thee, meek Majesty! soft King
Of simple graces and sweet loves!
  Each of us his lamb will bring,
Each his pair of silver doves!
  Till burnt at last in the fire of Thy fair eyes,
Ourselves become our own best sacrifice!

A CHRISTMAS HYMN

Alfred Domett

It was the calm and silent night!
  Seven hundred years and fifty-three
Had Rome been growing up to might,
  And now was Queen of land and sea.
No sound was heard of clashing wars;
  Peace brooded o'er the hushed domain;
Apollo, Pallas, Jove and Mars
  Held undisturbed their ancient reign,
      In the solemn midnight
        Centuries ago.

'Twas in the calm and silent night!
  The Senator of haughty Rome,
Impatient urged his chariot's flight,
  In lordly revel, rolling home:
Triumphal arches gleaming swell
  His breast with thoughts of boundless sway;
What recked the Roman what befell

A paltry province far away,
In the solemn midnight
Centuries ago!

Within that province far away
Went plodding home a weary boor:
A streak of light before him lay,
Fall'n through a half-shut stable door
Across his path. He passed—for naught
Told what was going on within;
How keen the stars! his only thought;
The air how calm and cold and thin,
In the solemn midnight
Centuries ago!

O strange indifference!—low and high
Drowsed over common joys and cares:
The earth was still—but knew not why;
The world was listening—unawares.
How calm a moment may precede
One that shall thrill the world forever!
To that still moment none would heed,
Man's doom was linked, no more to sever,
In the solemn midnight
Centuries ago.

It *is* the calm and solemn night!
A thousand bells ring out and throw
Their joyous peal abroad, and smite
The darkness, charmed and holy now.
The night, that erst no name had worn,
To it a happy name is given:
For in that stable lay new-born,
The peaceful Prince of Earth and Heaven,
In the solemn midnight
Centuries ago.

EXCELLENCY OF CHRIST

Giles Fletcher

He is a path, if any be misled;
  He is a robe, if any naked be;
If any chance to hunger, he is bread;
  If any be a bondman he is free;
  If any be but weak, how strong is he!
To dead men life he is, to sick men health;
To blind men sight, and to the needy wealth;
A pleasure without loss, a treasure without stealth.

THE SONG OF A HEATHEN

Richard Watson Gilder

(Sojourning in Galilee, A.D. 32)

If Jesus Christ is a man,—
  And only a man,—I say
That of all mankind I cleave to him,
  And to him will I cleave alway.

If Jesus Christ is a god,—
  And the only God,—I swear
I will follow Him through heaven and hell,
  The earth, the sea, and the air!

EASTER CHORUS FROM FAUST

Goethe

Translated by Bayard Taylor

Christ is arisen!
Joy to the Mortal One,
Whom the unmerited

Clinging, inherited
Needs did imprison.

. . . . .

Christ is ascended!
Bliss hath invested him,—
Woes that molested him,
Trials that tested him,
Gloriously ended!

. . . . .

Christ is arisen
Out of Corruption's womb
Burst ye the prison,
Break from your gloom!
Praising and pleading him,
Lovingly needing him,
Brotherly feeding him,
Preaching and speeding him,
Blessing, succeeding Him,
Thus is the Master near,—
Thus is He here!

SECOND SEEING

Louis Golding

If He be truly Christ
The Sacrificed,
    When I am deaf and blind as they
Who hung Him up between
The two thieves mean,
    In Calvary upon a moaning day.

If I not recognize
Within His eyes
    The slow blood fall down pools of pain,
Nor on contracted brows
The thorns that house
    Their swords about the anguish of His brain.

If I do not perceive
His mother grieve
  Below the rood where He hangs crossed,
Nor hear the sea and wind
Cry, "Thou hast sinned!"
  Then woe is me that I am doubly lost.

This is not He alone
Whom I have known,
  This is all Christs since time began.
The blood of all the dead
His veins have shed,
  For He is God and Ghost and Everyman.

REALITY

Frances Ridley Havergal

  Reality, reality.
Lord Jesus Christ Thou art to me!
From the spectral mist and the driving clouds,
From the shifting shadows and phantom crowds
From unreal words and unreal lives,
Where truth with falsehood feebly strives;
From the passings away, the chance and change,
Flickerings, vanishings, swift and strange,
      I turn to my glorious rest in Thee,
      Who art the grand Reality!

      Reality in greatest need,
Lord Jesus Christ Thou art indeed!
Is the pilot real who alone can guide
The drifting ship o'er the midnight tide?
Is the life-boat real, as it nears the wreck,
And the saved ones leap from the parting deck?
Is the haven real, where the barque may flee
From the autumn gales of the wild north sea?
      Reality indeed art Thou,
      My pilot, life-boat, haven now.

Reality, reality,
In the brightest days art Thou to me!
Thou art the sunshine of my mirth,
Thou art the heaven above my earth,
The spring of love of all my heart,
And the fountain of my song Thou art;
For dearer than the dearest now,
And better than the best art Thou,
    Beloved Lord, in whom I see
    Joy-giving, glad Reality.

Reality, reality,
Lord Jesus Thou hast been to me,
When I thought the dream of life was past
And "the Master's home-call" come at last;
When I thought I had only to wait
A little while at the Golden Gate,—
Only another day or two,
Till Thou Thyself shouldst bear me through;
    How real Thy presence was to me!
    How precious Thy Reality!

Reality, reality,
Lord Jesus Christ Thou art to me;
Thy name is sweeter than songs of old,
Thy words are better than "most fine gold,"
Thy deeds are greater than hero-glory,
Thy life is grander than poet story;
But Thou, Thyself for aye the same
Art more than words and life and name!
    Thyself Thou hast revealed to me,
    In glorious reality.

Reality, reality,
Lord Jesus Christ is crowned in Thee,
In Thee is every type fulfilled,
In Thee is every yearning stilled
For perfect beauty, truth and love:
For Thou art always far above
The grandest glimpse of our Ideal,

Yet more and more we know Thee real,
  And marvel more and more to see
  Thine infinite Reality.

  Reality, reality,
Lord Jesus Christ Thou art to me!
My glorious king, my Lord, my God,
Life is too short for half the laud,
For half the debt of praise I owe,
For this blest knowledge that "I know
The reality of Jesus Christ,"—
Unmeasured blessing, gift unpriced!
    Will I not praise Thee when I see
    In the long noon of Eternity
      Unveiled, Thy "bright reality"?

THAT HOLY THING

George MacDonald

They all were looking for a king
  To slay their foes and lift them high:
Thou cam'st, a little baby thing
  That made a woman cry.

O son of Man, to right my lot
  Naught but thy presence can avail;
Yet on the road thy wheels are not,
  Nor on the seas thy sail.

ON THE MORNING OF CHRIST'S NATIVITY

John Milton

This is the month, and this the happy morn,
Wherein the Son of Heaven's eternal King,
Of wedded maid and virgin mother born,
Our great redemption from above did bring;

For so the holy sages once did sing,
That he our deadly forfeit should release,
And with his Father work us a perpetual peace.

That glorious form, that light unsufferable,
And that far-beaming blaze of majesty,
Wherewith he wont at Heaven's high council-table
To sit the midst of Trinal Unity,
He laid aside; and here with us to be,
Forsook the courts of everlasting day,
And chose with us a darksome house of mortal clay.

Say, Heavenly Muse, shall not thy sacred vein
Afford a present to the Infant God?
Hast thou no verse, no hymn, or solemn strain,
To welcome him to this his new abode,
Now while the heaven, by the sun's team untrod,
Hath took no print of the approaching light,
And all the spangled host keep watch in squadrons bright?

See how from far upon the eastern road
The star-led wisards haste with odours sweet!
Oh! run, prevent them with thy humble ode,
And lay it lowly at his blessed feet;
Have thou the honour first my Lord to greet,
And join thy voice unto the angel quire,
From out his secret altar touched with hallowed fire.

The Hymn

It was the winter wild,
While the heaven-born child
All meanly wrapt in the rude manger lies;
Nature, in awe to him,
Had doffed her gaudy trim,
With her great Master so to sympathize:
It was no season then for her
To wanton with the sun, her lusty paramour.

Only with speeches fair
She woos the gentle air
To hide her guilty front with innocent snow,

And on her naked shame,
Pollute with sinful blame,
   The saintly veil of maiden white to throw;
Confounded, that her Maker's eyes
Should look so near upon her foul deformities.

But he, her fears to cease,
Sent down the meek-eyed Peace:
   She, crowned with olive green, came softly sliding
Down through the turning sphere,
His ready harbinger,
   With turtle wing the amorous clouds dividing;
And waving wide her myrtle wand,
She strikes a universal peace through sea and land.

No war, or battle's sound,
Was heard the world around;
   The idle spear and shield were high uphung;
The hooked chariot stood
Unstained with hostile blood;
   The trumpet spake not to the armed throng;
And kings sat still with awful eye,
As if they surely knew their sovran lord was by.

But peaceful was the night
Wherein the Prince of Light
   His reign of peace upon the earth began:
The winds, with wonder whist,
Smoothly the waters kissed,
   Whispering new joys to the mild ocean,
Who now hath quite forgot to rave,
While birds of calm sit brooding on the charmed wave.

The stars, with deep amaze,
Stand fixed in steadfast gaze,
   Bending one way their precious influence,
And will not take their flight,
For all the morning light,
   Or Lucifer that often warned them thence;
But in their glimmering orbs did glow,
Until their Lord himself bespake and bid them go.

And though the shady gloom
Had given day her room,
    The sun himself withheld his wonted speed,
And hid his head for shame,
As his inferior flame
    The new-enlightened world no more should need:
He saw a greater Sun appear
Than his bright throne or burning axletree could bear.

The shepherds on the lawn,
Or ere the point of dawn,
    Sat simply chatting in a rustic row;
Full little thought they than,
That the mighty Pan
    Was kindly come to live with them below:
Perhaps their loves, or else their sheep,
Was all that did their silly thoughts so busy keep.

When such music sweet
Their hearts and ears did greet
    As never was by mortal finger strook,
Divinely-warbled voice
Answering the stringed noise,
    As all their souls in blissful rapture took:
The air, such pleasure loath to lose,
With thousand echoes still prolongs each heavenly close.

Nature, that heard such sound
Beneath the hollow round
    Of Cynthia's seat the airy region thrilling,
Now was almost won
To think her part was done,
    And that her reign had here its last fulfilling:
She knew such harmony alone
Could hold all heaven and earth in happier union.

At last surrounds their sight
A globe of circular light,
    That with long beams the shame-faced night arrayed:

The helmed cherubim
And sworded seraphim
      Are seen in glittering ranks with wings displayed,
Harping in loud and solemn quire,
With unexpressive notes, to Heaven's new-born heir.

Such music (as 'tis said)
Before was never made,
      But when of old the sons of morning sung,
While the Creator great
His constellations set,
      And the well-balanced world on hinges hung,
And cast the dark foundations deep,
And bid the weltering waves their oozy channel keep.

Ring out, ye crystal spheres!
Once bless our human ears
      (If ye have power to touch our senses so),
And let your silver chime
Move in melodious time;
      And let the bass of heaven's deep organ blow;
And with your ninefold harmony
Make up full consort to the angelic symphony.

For if such holy song
Enwrap our fancy long,
      Time will run back and fetch the age of gold;
And speckled Vanity
Will sicken soon and die,
      And leprous Sin will melt from earthly mould;
And Hell itself will pass away,
And leave her dolorous mansions to the peering day.

Yea, Truth and Justice then
Will down return to men,
      Orbed in a rainbow; and, like glories wearing.
Mercy will sit between,
Throned in celestial sheen,
      With radiant feet the tissued clouds down steering;
And Heaven, as at some festival,
Will open wide the gates of her high Palace Hall.

But wisest Fate says no,
This must not yet be so;
      The Babe lies yet in smiling infancy
That on the bitter cross
Must redeem our loss,
      So both himself and us to glorify:
Yet first, to those ychained in sleep,
The wakeful trump of doom must thunder through the
      deep.

With such a horrid clang
As on Mount Sinai rang,
      While the red fire and smouldering clouds outbrake;
The aged earth, aghast
With terror of that blast,
      Shall from the surface to the center shake,
When at the world's last sessiön,
The dreadful Judge in middle air shall spread his throne.

And then at last our bliss
Full and perfect is,
      But now begins; for from this happy day
The old Dragon underground,
In straiter limits bound,
      Not half so far casts his usurpèd sway;
And wroth to see his kingdom fail,
Swinges the scaly horror of his folded tail.

The oracles are dumb;
No voice or hideous hum
      Runs through the archèd roof in words deceiving.
Apollo from his shrine
Can no more divine,
      With hollow shriek the steep of Delphos leaving.
No nightly trance, or breathèd spell,
Inspires the pale-eyed priest from the prophetic cell.

The lonely mountains o'er,
And the resounding shore,
      A voice of weeping heard and loud lament;

From haunted spring, and dale
Edgèd with poplar pale,
    The parting Genius is with sighing sent;
With flower-inwoven tresses torn
The Nymphs in twilight shade of tangled thickets mourn.

In consecrated earth,
And on the holy hearth,
    The Lars and Lemures moan with midnight plaint;
In urns and altars round,
A drear and dying sound
    Affrights the flamens at their service quaint;
And the chill marble seems to sweat,
While each peculiar power forgoes his wonted seat.

Peor and Baälim
Forsake their temples dim,
    With that twice-battered god of Palestine;
And mooned Ashtaroth,
Heaven's queen and mother both,
    Now sits not girt with tapers' holy shine;
The Libyc Hammon shrinks his horn;
In vain the Tyrian maids their wounded Thammuz mourn.

And sullen Moloch, fled,
Hath left in shadows dread
    His burning idol all of blackest hue;
In vain with cymbals' ring
They call the grisly king,
    In dismal dance about the furnace blue;
The brutish gods of Nile as fast,
Isis and Orus and the dog Anubis, haste.

Nor is Osiris seen
In Memphian grove or green,
    Trampling the unshowered grass with lowings loud;
Nor can he be at rest
Within his sacred chest;
    Naught but profoundest Hell can be his shroud;
In vain, with timbrelled anthems dark,
The sable-stoled sorcerers bear his worshipped ark.

He feels from Juda's land
The dreaded Infant's hand;
  The rays of Bethlehem blind his dusky eyn;
Nor all the gods beside
Longer dare abide,
  Not Typhon huge ending in snaky twine:
Our Babe, to show his Godhead true,
Can in his swaddling bands control the damned crew.

So when the sun in bed,
Curtained with cloudy red,
  Pillows his chin upon an orient wave,
The flocking shadows pale
Troop to the infernal jail,
  Each fettered ghost slips to his several grave,
And the yellow-skirted fays
Fly after the night-steeds, leaving their moon-loved maze.

But see! The Virgin blest
Hath laid her Babe to rest.
  Time is our tedious song should here have ending:
Heaven's youngest-teemed star
Hath fixed her polished car
  Her sleeping Lord with handmaid lamp attending;
And all about the courtly stable
Bright-harnessed angels sit in order serviceable.

THE WAY, THE TRUTH, AND THE LIFE

Theodore Parker

O thou great Friend to all the sons of men,
Who once appear'dst in humblest guise below,
Sin to rebuke, to break the captive's chain,
To call thy brethren forth from want and woe!—
Thee would I sing. Thy truth is still the light
Which guides the nations groping on their way,
Stumbling and falling in disastrous night,
Yet hoping ever for the perfect day.

Yes, thou art still the life; thou art the way
The holiest know,—light, life, and way of heaven;
And they who dearest hope and deepest pray
Toil by the truth, life, way that thou hast given;
And in thy name aspiring mortals trust
To uplift their bleeding brothers rescued from the dust.

MARY'S GIRLHOOD

Gabriel Charles Dante Rossetti

This is that blessed Mary, pre-elect
  God's virgin. Gone is a great while, and she
    Dwelt young in Nazareth of Galilee.
Unto God's will she brought devout respect,
  Profound simplicity of intellect
    And supreme patience. From her mother's knee
    Faithful and hopeful; wise in charity;
Strong in grave peace; in pity circumspect.

So held she through her girlhood; as it were
  An angel-watered lily, that near God
    Grows and is quiet. Till, one dawn at home
She woke in her white bed, and had no fear
  At all,—yet wept till sunshine, and felt awed:
    Because the fullness of the time was come.

DOMINE QUO VADIS?

William Watson

Darkening the azure roof of Nero's world,
From smouldering Rome the smoke of ruin curled;
And the fierce populace went clamoring—
"These Christian dogs, 'tis they have done this thing!"
So to the wild wolf Hate were sacrificed
The panting, huddled flock whose crime was Christ.

Now Peter lodged in Rome, and rose each morn
Looking to be ere night in sunder torn
By those blind hands that with inebriate zeal
Burned the strong saints, or broke them on the wheel,
Or flung them to the lions to make mirth
For dames that ruled the lords that ruled the earth.

And unto him their towering rocky hold,
Repaired those sheep of the Good Shepherd's fold
In whose white fleece as yet no blood or foam
Bear witness to the ravening fangs of Rome.
"More light, more cheap," they cried, "we hold our lives
Than chaff the flail or dust the whirlwind drives:
As chaff they are winnowed and as dust are blown;
Nay, they are nought; but priceless is thine own.
Not in yon streaming shambles must thou die;
We counsel, we entreat, we charge thee, fly!"
And Peter answered: "Nay, my place is here;
Through the dread storm, this ship of Christ I steer.
Blind is the tempest, deaf the roaring tide,
And I, His pilot, at the helm abide."

Then One stood forth, the flashing of whose soul
Enrayed his presence like an aureole.
Eager he spake; his fellows, ere they heard,
Caught from his eyes the swift and leaping word:
"Let *us* His vines, be in the wine-press trod,
And poured a beverage for the lips of God;

"Or, ground as wheat of His eternal field,
Bread for His table let our bodies yield.
Behold, the church hath other use for thee;
Thy safety is her own, and thou must flee.
Ours be the glory at her call to die,
But quick and whole God needs His great ally."

And Peter said: "Do lords of spear and shield
Thus leave their hosts uncaptained on the field,
And from some mount of prospect watch afar
The havoc of the hurricane of war?

Yet, if He wills it . . . Nay, my task is plain,—
To serve, and to endure, and to remain.
But weak I stand, and I beseech you all
Urge me no more, lest at a touch I fall."
There knelt a noble youth at Peter's feet,
And like a viol's strings his voice was sweet.
A suppliant angel might have pleaded so,
Crowned with the splendor of some suppliant woe.
He said: "My sire and brethren yesterday
The heathen did with ghastly torments slay.
Pain, like a worm, beneath their feet they trod.
Their souls went up like incense unto God.
An offering richer yet, can Heaven require?
O live, and be my brethren and my sire."
And Peter answered: "Son, there is no small need
That thou exhort me to the easier deed.
Rather I would that thou and these had lent
Strength to uphold, not shatter, my intent.
Already my resolve is shaken sore.
I pray thee, if thou love me, say no more."

And even as he spake, he went apart,
Somewhat to hide the brimming of his heart,
Wherein a voice came flitting to and fro,
That now said "Tarry!" and anon said "Go!"
And louder every moment, "Go!" it cried,
And "Tarry!" to a whisper sank and died.
And as a leaf when summer is o'erpast
Hangs trembling ere it fall in some chance blast,
So hung his trembling purpose and fell dead;
And he arose and hurried forth and fled,
Darkness conniving, through the Capuan gate,
From all that heaven of love, that hell of hate,
To the Campania glimmering wide and still,
And strove to think he did his Master's will.

But spectral eyes and mocking tongues pursued,
And with vague hands he fought a phantom brood.
Doubts, like a swarm of gnats, o'erhung his flight,
And, "Lord," he prayed, "Have I not done aright?"

Can I not, living, more avail for Thee
Than whelmed in yon red storm of agony?
The tempest, it shall pass and I remain,
Not from its fiery sickle saved in vain.
Are there no seeds to sow, no desert lands
Waiting the tillage of these eager hands,
That I should beastlike 'neath the butcher fall,
More fruitlessly than oxen from the stall?
Is earth so easeful, is men's hate so sweet,
Are thorns so welcome unto sleepless feet,
Have death and heaven so feeble lures, that I,
Choosing to live, should win rebuke thereby?
Not mine the dread of pain, the lust of bliss!
Master, who judgest, have I done amiss?"

Lo, on the darkness brake a wandering ray:
A vision flashed along the Appian Way,
Divinely in the pagan night it shone—
A mournful Face—a Figure hurrying on—
Though haggard and dishevelled, frail and worn,
A King, of David's lineage, crowned with thorn.
"Lord, whither farest?" Peter, wondering, cried.
"To Rome," said Christ, "to be re-crucified."

Into the night the vision ebbed like breath;
And Peter turned, and rushed on Rome and death.

THE LEPER

NATHANIEL P. WILLIS

"Room for the leper! Room!" and as he came
The cry passed on. "Room for the leper! Room!"
And aside they stood—
Matron, and child, and pitiless manhood—all
Who met him on his way—and let him pass.
And onward through the open gate he came,
A leper, with ashes on his brow,
Sackcloth about his loins, and on his lip

A covering—stepping painfully and slow,
And with difficult utterance, like one
Whose heart is with an iron nerve put down,
Crying, "Unclean! unclean!"
        For Helon was a leper!

Day was breaking,
When at the altar of the temple stood
The holy priest of God. The incense lamp
Burned with a struggling light, and a low chant
Swelled through the hollow arches of the roof,
Like an articulate wail; and there, alone,
Wasted to ghastly thinness, Helon knelt.
The echoes of the melancholy strain
Died in the distant aisles, and he rose up,
Struggling with weakness; and bowed his head
Unto the sprinkled ashes, and put off
His costly raiment for the leper's garb,
And with the sackcloth round him, and his lip
Hid in the loathsome covering, stood still,
        Waiting to hear his doom:—

"Depart! depart, O child
Of Israel from the temple of thy God!
For he has smote thee with his chastening rod,
And to the desert wild,
From all thou lovest, away thy feet must flee,
That from thy plague his people may be free.

"Depart! and come not near
The busy mart, the crowded city more;
Nor set thy foot a human threshold o'er;
    And stay thou not to hear
Voices that call thee in the way, and fly
From all who in the wilderness pass by.

"Wet not thy burning lip
In streams that to a human dwelling glide;
Nor rest thee where the covert fountains hide;
    Nor kneel thee down to dip

The water where the pilgrim bends to drink,
By desert well, or river's grassy brink.

"And pass thou not between
The weary traveller and the cooling breeze;
And lie not down to sleep beneath the trees
    Where human tracks are seen.
Nor milk the goat that browseth on the plain,
Nor pluck the standing corn, or yellow grain.

"And now, depart! and when
Thy heart is heavy, and thine eyes are dim,
Lift up thy prayer beseechingly to Him
    Who, from the tribes of men,
Selected thee to feel His chastening rod:—
Depart, O leper, and forget not God!"

And he went forth,—alone! Not one, of all
The many whom he loved, nor she whose name
Was woven in the fibres of his heart,
Breaking within him now, to come and speak
Comfort unto him. Yea, he went his way,
Sick and heart-broken and alone,—to die!
For God had cursed the leper!
                    It was noon,
And Helon knelt beside a stagnant pool
In the lone wilderness, and bathed his brow,
Hot with the burning leprosy, and touched
The loathsome water to his fevered lips,
Praying he might be so blessed,—to die!
Footsteps approached, and, with no strength to flee
He drew the covering closer on his lip,
Crying, "Unclean, unclean!" and, in the folds
Of the coarse sackcloth, shrouding up his face,
He fell upon the earth till they should pass.
Nearer the stranger came, and bending o'er
The leper's prostrate form, pronounced his name,
"Helon! Arise!" The voice was like the master-tone
Of a rich instrument,—most strangely sweet;
And the dull pulses of disease awoke,

And for a moment beat beneath the hot
And leprous scales with a restoring thrill.
"Helon, Arise!"   And he forgot his curse,
And rose, and stood before him. Love and awe
Mingled in the regard of Helon's eye
As he beheld the stranger. He was not
In costly raiment clad, nor on his brow
The symbol of a princely lineage wore;
No followers at his back, nor in his hand
Buckler, sword, or spear; yet in his mien
Command sat throned serene, and, if he smiled,
A kingly condescension graced his lips,
The lion would have crouched to in his lair.
His garb was simple, and his sandals worn;
His statue modelled with a perfect grace;
His countenance the impress of a God,
Touched with the open innocence of a child;
His eye was blue and calm, as is the sky
In the serenest noon; his hair unshorn
Fell to his shoulders; and his curling beard
The fullness of perfected manhood bore.
He looked on Helon earnestly awhile,
As if his heart was moved, and, stooping down,
He took a little water in his hand
And laid it on his brow and said, "Be clean!"
And lo! the scales fell from him, and his blood
Coursed with delicious coolness through his vei
And his dry palms grew moist, and on his br
The dewy softness of an infant stole.
His leprosy was cleansed, and he fell down
Prostrate at Jesus' feet and worshipped him.

2. Recent

TO THE CHRISTIANS

FRANCIS ADAMS (English Poet and Rebel)

Take, then, your paltry Christ,
    Your gentleman God.
We want the carpenter's son,
    With his saw and hod.

We want the man who loved
    The poor and the oppressed,
Who hated the Rich man and the King
    And the Scribe and the Priest.

We want the Galilean
    Who knew the cross and rod.
It's your "good taste" that prefers
    A bastard "God."

THE KINGS OF THE EAST

KATHARINE LEE BATES

I

The Kings of the East are riding
    To-night to Bethlehem.
The sunset glows dividing,
The Kings of the East are riding;
A star their journey guiding,
    Gleaming with gold and gem
The Kings of the East are riding
    To-night to Bethlehem.

II

To a strange sweet harp of Zion
  The starry host troops forth;
The golden glaived Orion
To a strange sweet harp of Zion;
The Archer and the Lion,
  The watcher of the North;
To a strange sweet harp of Zion
  The starry host troops forth.

III

There beams above a manger
  The child-face of a star;
Amid the stars a stranger,
It beams above a manger;
What means this ether-ranger
  To pause where poor folk are?
There beams above a manger
  The child-face of a star.

CRUCIFIXION

EVA GORE BOOTH

In the crowd's multitudinous mind
  Terror and passion embrace,
Whilst the darkness heavily blind
  Hides face from horror-struck face;
And all men, huddled and dumb,
  Shrink from the death-strangled cry,
And the hidden terror to come,
  And the dead men hurrying by.
White gleams from the limbs of the dead
  Raised high o'er the blood-stained sod,
And the soldier shuddered and said,
  'Lo, this was the Son of God.'
Nay, but all Life is one,
  A wind that wails through the vast,

And this deed is never done,
  This passion is never past.
When any son of man by man's blind doom
  On any justest scaffold strangled dies,
Once more across the shadow-stricken gloom
  Against the sun the dark-winged Horror flies,
A lost voice cries from the far olive trees
  Weary and harsh with pain, a desolate cry,
What ye have done unto the least of these
  Is done to God in Heaven, for earth and sky,
And bird and beast, green leaves and golden sun,
  Men's dreams, the starry dust, the bread, the wine,
Rivers and seas, my soul and his, are one
  Through all things flows one life austere, divine,
Strangling the murderer you are slaying me,
  Scattering the stars and leaves like broken bread,
Casting dark shadows on the sun-lit sea,
  Striking the swallows and the sea-gulls dead,
Making the red rose wither to its fall,
  Darkening the sunshine, blasting the green sod,—
Wounding one soul, you wound the soul of all,
  The unity of Life, the soul of God.

A VIRILE CHRIST

Rex Boundy

Give us a virile Christ for these rough days!
You painters, sculptors, show the warrior bold
And you who turn mere words to gleaming gold,
Too long your lips have sounded in the praise
Of patience and humility. Our ways
Have parted from the quietude of old;
We need a man of strength with us to hold
The very breach of Death without amaze.
Did He not scourge from temple courts the thieves?
And make the arch-fiend's self again to fall?
And blast the fig-tree that was only leaves?
And still the raging tumult of the sea?

Did He not bear the greatest pain of all,
Silent, upon the cross on Calvary?

THE POET

WITTER BYNNER

A poet lived in Galilee
  Whose mother dearly knew him—-
And his beauty like a cooling tree
  Drew many people to him.

He loved the speech of simple men
  And little children's laughter;
He came, they always came again,
  He went—they followed after.

He had sweet-hearted things to say,
  And he was solemn only
When people were unkind . . . that day:
  He'd stand there straight and lonely

And tell them what they ought to do;
  "Love other folk," he pleaded,
"As you love me and I love you!"
  But almost no one heeded.

A poet died in Galilee
  They stared at him and slew him . . .
What would they do to you and me
  If we should say we knew him?

COMRADE JESUS

SARAH N. CLEGHORN

Thanks to St. Matthew, who had been
At mass-meetings in Palestine,
We knew whose side was spoken for
When Comrade Jesus took the floor.

"Where sore they toil and hard they lie,
Among the great unwashed, dwell I:—
The tramp, the convict, I am he;
Cold-shoulder him, cold-shoulder me."

By Dives' door, with thoughtful eye,
He did tomorrow prophesy:—
"The kingdom's gate is low and small;
The rich can scarce wedge through at all."

"A dangerous man," said Caiaphas,
"An ignorant demagogue, alas!
Friend of low women, it is he
Slanders the upright Pharisee."

For law and order, it was plain,
For Holy Church, he must be slain.
The troops are there to awe the crowd:
And violence was not allowed.

Their clumsy force with force to foil
His strong, clean hands he would not soil.
He saw their childishness quite plain
Between the lightnings of his pain.

Between the twilights of his end,
He made his fellow-felon friend:
With swollen tongue and blinded eyes,
Invited him to paradise.

Ah, let no Local him refuse!
Comrade Jesus hath paid his dues.
Whatever other be debarred,
Comrade Jesus hath his red card.

CHRIST, THE MAN

William Henry Davies

Lord, I say nothing: I profess
    No faith in Thee nor Christ Thy Son:
Yet no man ever heard me mock
    A true believing one.

If knowledge is not great enough
  To give a man believing power,
Lord he must wait in Thy great hand
  Till revelation's hour.

Meanwhile he'll follow Christ the man
  In that humanity He taught
Which to the poor and the oppressed,
  Gives its best time and thought.

THE JEW TO JESUS

FLORENCE KIPER FRANK

O Man of mine own people, I alone
Among these alien ones can know thy face,
I who have felt the kinship of thy race
Burn in me, as I sit where they intone
Thy praises,—those who, striving to make known
A God for sacrifice, have missed the grace
Of thy sweet human meaning in its place,
Thou who art of our blood-bond and our own.

Are we not sharers of thy passion? Yea,
In spirit-anguish closely by thy side
We have drained the bitter cup, and, tortured, felt
With thee the bruising of each heavy welt.
Every land is our Gethsemane.
A thousand times have we been crucified.

THE SECOND CRUCIFIXION

RICHARD LE GALLIENNE

Loud mockers in the roaring street
  Say Christ is crucified again:
Twice pierced his gospel-bearing feet,
  Twice broken his great heart in vain.

I hear and to myself I smile,
For Christ talks with me all the while.

No angel now to roll the stone
    From off his unawaking sleep,
In vain shall Mary watch alone,
    In vain the soldiers vigil keep.

Yet while they deem my Lord is dead
My eyes are on his shining head.

Ah! nevermore shall Mary hear
    That voice exceeding sweet and low
Within the garden calling clear:
    Her Lord is gone, and she must go.

Yet all the while my Lord I meet
In every London lane and street.

Poor Lazarus shall wait in vain,
    And Bartimeus still go blind;
The healing hem shall ne'er again
    Be touched by suffering humankind.

Yet all the while I see them rest,
The poor and outcast, on His breast.

No more unto the stubborn heart
    With gentle knocking shall he plead,
No more the mystic pity start,
    For Christ twice dead is dead indeed.

So in the street I hear men say,
Yet Christ is with me all the day.

A GUARD OF THE SEPULCHER

EDWIN MARKHAM

I was a Roman soldier in my prime;
Now age is on me and the yoke of time.
I saw your Risen Christ, for I am he
Who reached the hyssop to Him on the tree;
And I am one of two who watched beside
The Sepulcher of Him we crucified.
All that last night I watched with sleepless eyes;
Great stars arose and crept across the skies.
The world was all too still for mortal rest.
For pitiless thoughts were busy in my breast.
The night was long, so long, it seemed at last
I had grown old and a long life had passed.
Far off the hills of Moab, touched with light,
Were swimming in the hollow of the night.
I saw Jerusalem all wrapped in cloud,
Stretched like a dead thing folded in a shroud.

Once in the pauses of our whispered talk
I heard a something on the garden walk.
Perhaps it was a crisp leaf lightly stirred—
Perhaps the dream-note of a waking bird.
Then suddenly an angel burning white
Came down with earthquake in the breaking light,
And rolled the great stone from the Sepulcher,
Mixing the morning with a scent of myrrh.
And lo, the Dead had risen with the day:
The Man of Mystery had gone His way!

Years have I wandered, carrying my shame;
Now let the Tooth of Time eat out my name.
For we, who all the Wonder might have told,
Kept silence, for our mouths were stopped with gold.

CALVARY

Edwin Arlington Robinson

Friendless and faint, with martyred steps and slow,
Faint for the flesh, but for the spirit free
Stung by the mob that came to see the show,
The Master toiled along to Calvary;
We jibed him, as he went, with houndish glee,
Till his dimmed eyes for us did overflow;
We cursed his vengeless hands thrice wretchedly,—
And this was nineteen hundred years ago.

But after nineteen hundred years the shame
Still clings, and we have not made good the loss
That outraged faith has entered in his name.
Ah, when shall come love's courage to be strong!
Tell me, O Lord—tell me, O Lord, how long
Are we to keep Christ writhing on the cross!

TO A CONTEMPORARY BUNKSHOOTER

Carl Sandburg

You come along . . . tearing your shirt . . . yelling
    about Jesus.
Where do you get that stuff?
What do you know about Jesus?
Jesus had a way of talking soft and outside of a few bankers
    and higher-ups among the con men of Jerusalem every-
    body liked to have this Jesus around because he never
    made any fake passes and everything he said went and
    he helped the sick and gave the people hope.

You come along squirting words at us, shaking your fist and
    calling us all damn fools so fierce the froth slobbers over
    your lips . . . always blabbing we're all going to hell
    straight off and you know all about it.

I've read Jesus' words. I know what he said. You don't throw any scare into me. I've got your number. I know how much you know about Jesus.

He never came near clean people or dirty people but they felt cleaner because he came along. It was you crowd of bankers and business men and lawyers who hired the sluggers and murderers who put Jesus out of the running.

I say the same bunch backing you nailed the nails into the hands of this Jesus of Nazareth. He had lined up against him the same crooks and strong-arm men now lined up with you paying your way.

This Jesus was good to look at, smelled good, listened good. He threw out something fresh and beautiful from the skin of his body and the touch of his hands wherever he passed along.

You slimy bunkshooter, you put a smut on every human blossom in reach of your rotten breath belching about hell-fire and hiccupping about this Man who lived a clean life in Galilee.

When are you going to quit making the carpenters build emergency hospitals for women and girls driven crazy with wrecked nerves from your gibberish about Jesus—I put it to you again: where do you get that stuff; what do you know about Jesus?

Go ahead and bust all the chairs you want to. Smash a whole wagon load of furniture at every performance. Turn sixty somersaults and stand on your nutty head. If it wasn't for the way you scare the women and kids I'd feel sorry for you and pass the hat.

I like to watch a good four-flusher work, but not when he starts people puking and calling for the doctors.

I like a man that's got nerve and can pull off a great original performance, but you—you're only a bug-house peddler of second-hand gospel—you're only shoving out a phoney imitation of the goods this Jesus wanted free as air and sunlight.

You tell people living in shanties Jesus is going to fix it up all
     right with them by giving them mansions in the skies
     after they're dead and the worms have eaten 'em.
You tell $6 a week department store girls all they need is
     Jesus; you take a steel trust wop, dead without having
     lived, gray and shrunken at forty years of age, and you
     tell him to look at Jesus on the cross and he'll be all
     right.
You tell poor people they don't need any more money on pay
     day and even if it's fierce to be out of a job, Jesus'll fix
     that up all right, all right—all they gotta do is take
     Jesus the way you say.
I'm telling you Jesus wouldn't stand for the stuff you're handing
     out. Jesus played it different. The bankers and lawyers
     of Jerusalem got their sluggers and murderers to go
     after Jesus just because Jesus wouldn't play their game.
     He didn't sit in with the big thieves.

I don't want a lot of gab from a bunkshooter in my religion.
I won't take my religion from any man who never works except
     with his mouth and never cherishes any memory except
     the face of the woman on the American silver dollar.

I ask you to come through and show me where you're pouring
     out the blood of your life.
I've been to this suburb of Jerusalem they call Golgotha, where
     they nailed Him, and I know if the story is straight it
     was real blood ran from His Hands and the nail-holes,
     and it was real blood spurted in red drops where the
     spear of the Roman soldier rammed in between the ribs of
     this Jesus of Nazareth.

THE REDEEMER

SIEGFRIED SASSOON

DARKNESS: the rain sluiced down; the mire was deep;
It was past twelve on a mid-winter night,
When peaceful folk in beds lay snug asleep;
There, with much work to do before the light,

We lugged our clay-sucked boots as best we might
Along the trench; sometimes a bullet sang,
And droning shells burst with a hollow bang;
We were soaked, chilled and wretched, every one.
Darkness: the distant wink of a huge gun.

I turned in the black ditch, loathing the storm;
A rocket fizzed, and burned with blanching flare,
And lit the face of what had been a form
Foundering in the mirk. He stood before me there:
I say that he was Christ; stiff in the glare,
And leaning forward from his burdening task,
Both arms supporting it; his eyes on mine
Stared from the woful head that seemed a mask
Of mortal pain in Hell's unholy shrine.

No thorny crown, only a woolen cap
He wore—an English soldier, white and strong,
Who loved his time like any simple chap,
Good days of work and sport and homely song;
Now he has learned that nights are very long,
And dawn a watching of the windowed sky.
But to the end, unjudging, he'll endure
Horror and pain, not uncontent to die
That Lancaster on Lune may stand secure.

He faced me, reeling in his weariness,
Shouldering his load of planks, so hard to bear.
I say that he was Christ, who wrought to bless
All groping things with freedom bright as air,
And with His mercy washed and made them fair.
Then the flame sank, and all grew black as pitch,
While we began to struggle along in the ditch;
And someone flung his burden in the muck,
Mumbling: "O Christ Almighty, now I'm stuck."

THE GREAT MAN

EUNICE TIETJENS

I cannot always feel His greatness,
Sometimes He walks beside me, step by step.
And paces slowly in the ways—
The simple, wingless ways
That my thoughts tread. He gossips with me then,
And finds it good;
Not as an eagle might, His great wings folded, be content,
To walk a little, knowing is His choice,
But as a simple man,
And I forget.

Then suddenly a call floats down
From the clear airy spaces,
The great keen, lonely heights of being.
And He who was my comrade hears the call
And rises from my side, and soars,
Deep-chanting, to the heights.
Then I remember.
And my upward gaze goes with him, and I see
Far off against the sky
The glint of golden sunlight on His wings.

A LOST WORD OF JESUS

HENRY VAN DYKE

Hear the word that Jesus spake
    Eighteen centuries ago,
    Where the crimson lilies blow
Round the blue Tiberian lake:
There the bread of Life he brake,
    Through the fields of harvest walking
    With his lowly comrades, talking
Of the secret thoughts that feed

Weary hearts in time of need.
    Art thou hungry?   Come and take;
    Hear the word that Jesus spake.
'Tis tne sacrament of labor; meat and drink divinely blest,
Friendship's food, and sweet refreshment; strength and courage,
    joy and rest.

    Yet this word the Master said,
      Long ago and far away,
      Silent and forgotten lay
    Buried with the silent dead,—
    Where the sands of Egypt spread,
      Sea-like, tawny billows heaping
      Over ancient cities sleeping;
    While the river Nile between
    Rolls its summer flood of green,
      Rolls its autumn flood of red,—
      There the word the Master said
Written on a frail papyrus, scorched by fire, wrinkled, torn,
Hidden in God's hand, was waiting for its resurrection morn.

    Hear the Master's risen word!
      Delving spades have set it free,—
      Wake! the world has need of thee,—
    Rise, and let thy voice be heard,
    Like a fountain disinterred.
      Upward-springing, singing, sparkling;
      Through the doubtful shadows darkling;
    Till the clouds of pain and rage
    Brooding, o'er the toiling age,
      As with rifts of light are stirred
      By the music of the word;
Gospel for the heavy-laden, answer to the labourer's cry;
"Raise the stone and thou shalt find me; cleave the wood, and
    there am I."

A GOOD BISHOP

ANONYMOUS, 10th Century A.D. (Old High German)

Translated by Wm. Taylor

Before St. Anno
Six were sainted
Of our holy bishops.
Like the seven stars
They shall shine from heaven.
Purer and brighter
Is the light of Anno
Than a hyacinth set in a gold ring!

This darling man
We will have for a pattern;
And those that would grow
In virtue and trustiness
Shall dress by him as at a mirror.

As the sun in the air
Between earth and heaven
Glitters to both—
So went Bishop Anno
Between God and man.
Such was his virtue in the palace
That the emperor obeyed him;
He behaved with honour to both sides
And was counted among the first barons.

In his gestures at worship
He was awful as an angel
Many a man knew his goodness.
Hear what were his manners—

His words were frank and open;
He spoke truth fearing no man;
Like a lamb he sat among princes,
Like a lamb he walked among the people:
To the unruly he was sharp;
To the gentle he was mild:
Widows and orphans praised him always.

Preaching and praying
No one could do better.
Happy was Cologne
To be worthy of such a bishop!

RABBI BEN EZRA

ROBERT BROWNING

Grow old along with me!
The best is yet to be,
The last of life, for which the first was made:
Our times are in His hand
Who saith "A whole I planned,
Youth shows but half; trust God: see all, nor be afraid!"

Not that, amassing flowers,
Youth sighed, "Which rose make ours,
Which lily leave and then as best recall!"
Not that, admiring stars,
It yearned "Nor Jove, nor Mars;
Mine be some figured flame which blends, transcends them all!"

Not for such hopes and fears
Annulling youth's brief years,
Do I remonstrate: folly wide the mark!
Rather I prize the doubt
Low kinds exist without,
Finished and finite clods, untroubled by a spark.

Poor vaunt of life indeed,
Were man but formed to feed
On joy, to solely seek and find and feast:
Such feasting ended, then
As sure an end to men;
Irks care the crop-full bird? Frets doubt the maw-crammed
    beast?

Rejoice we are allied
To That which doth provide
And not partake, effect and not receive!
A spark disturbs our clod;
Nearer we hold of God
Who gives, than of His tribes that take, I must believe.

Then, welcome each rebuff
That turns earth's smoothness rough,
Each sting that bids nor sit nor stand but go!
Be our joys three-parts pain!
Strive, and hold cheap the strain;
Learn, nor account the pang; dare, never grudge the throe!

For thence,—a paradox
Which comforts while it mocks,—
Shall life succeed in that it seems to fail:
What I aspired to be,
And was not, comforts me:
A brute I might have been, but would not sink i' the scale.

What is he but a brute
Whose flesh has soul to suit,
Whose spirit works lest arms and legs want play?
To man, propose this test—
Thy body at its best,
How far can that project thy soul on its lone way?

Yet gifts should prove their use:
I own the Past profuse
Of power each side, perfection every turn:
Eyes, ears took in their dole,

Brain treasured up the whole;
Should not the heart beat once "How good to live and learn?"

Not once beat "Praise be Thine!
I see the whole design,
I, who saw power, see now love perfect too:
Perfect I call Thy plan:
Thanks that I was a man!
Maker, remake, complete,—I trust what Thou shalt do!"

For pleasant is this flesh;
Our soul, in its rose-mesh
Pulled ever to the earth, still yearns for rest:
Would we some prize might hold
To match those manifold
Possessions of the brute,—gain most, as we did best!

Let us not always say,
"Spite of this flesh to-day
I strove, made head, gained ground upon the whole!"
As the bird wings and sings,
Let us cry, "All good things
Are ours, nor soul helps flesh more, now, than flesh helps
soul!"

Therefore I summon age
To grant youth's heritage,
Life's struggle having so far reached its term:
Thence shall I pass, approved
A man, for aye removed
From the developed brute; a God tho' in the germ.

And I shall thereupon
Take rest, ere I be gone
Once more on my adventure brave and new:
Fearless and unperplexed,
When I wage battle next,
What weapons to select, what armour to indue.

Youth ended, I shall try
My gain or loss thereby:

Leave the fire ashes, what survives is gold:
And I shall weigh the same,
Give life its praise or blame:
Young, all lay in dispute; I shall know, being old.

For note, when evening shuts,
A certain moment cuts
The deed off, calls the glory from the gray:
A whisper from the west
Shoots—"Add this to the rest,
Take it and try its worth: here dies another day."

So, still within this life,
Tho' lifted o'er its strife,
Let me discern, compare, pronounce at last,
"This rage was right i' the main,
That acquiescence vain:
The Future I may face now I have proved the Past."

For more is not reserved
To man, with soul just nerved
To act to-morrow what he learns to-day:
Here, work enough to watch
The Master work, and catch
Hints of the proper craft, tricks of the tool's true play.

As it was better, youth
Should strive, thro' acts uncouth,
Toward making, than repose on aught found made:
So, better, age, exempt
From strife, should know, than tempt
Further.   Thou waitedst age: wait death, nor be afraid!

Enough now, if the Right
And Good and Infinite
Be named here, as thou callest thy hand thine own,
With knowledge absolute,
Subject to no dispute
From fools that crowded youth, nor let thee feel alone.

Be there, for once and all,
Severed great minds from small,
Announced to each his station in the Past!
Was I, the world arraigned,
Were they, my soul disdained,
Right? Let age speak the truth and give us peace at last!

Now, who shall arbitrate?
Ten men love what I hate,
Shun what I follow, slight what I receive;
Ten, who in ears and eyes
Match me: we all surmise,
They this thing, and I that: whom shall my soul believe?

Not on the vulgar mass
Called "work," must sentence pass,
Things done, that took the eye and had the price;
O'er which, from level stand,
The low world laid its hand,
Found straightway to its mind, could value in a trice:

But all, the world's coarse thumb
And finger failed to plumb,
So passed in making up the main account:
All instincts immature,
All purposes unsure,
That weighed not as his work, yet swelled the man's amount:

Thoughts hardly to be packed
Into a narrow act,
Fancies that broke thro' language and escaped:
All I could never be,
All, men ignored in me,
This, I was worth to God, whose wheel the pitcher shaped.

Ay, note that Potter's wheel,
That metaphor! and feel
Why time spins fast, why passive lies our clay,—
Thou, to whom fools propound,
When the wine makes its round,
"Since life fleets, all is change; the Past gone, seize to-day!"

Fool!   All that is, at all,
Lasts ever, past recall;
Earth changes, but thy soul and God stand sure:
What entered into thee,
That was, is, and shall be:
Time's wheel runs back or stops: Potter and clay endure.

He fixed thee mid this dance
Of plastic circumstance,
This Present, thou forsooth, wouldst fain arrest:
Machinery just meant
To give thy soul its bent,
Try thee and turn thee forth, sufficiently impressed.

What tho' the earlier grooves
Which ran the laughing loves
Around thy base, no longer pause and press?
What tho' about thy rim,
Skull-things in order grim
Grow out, in graver mood, obey the sterner stress?

Look not thou down but up!
To uses of a cup
The festal board, lamp's flash and trumpet's peal,
The new wine's foaming flow,
The Master's lips a-glow!
Thou, heaven's consummate cup, what needst thou with earth's
    wheel?

But I need, now as then,
Thee, God, who mouldest men!
And since, not even while the whirl was worst,
Did I,—to the wheel of life
With shapes and colours rife,
Bound dizzily,—mistake my end, to slake Thy thirst:

So take and use thy work.
Amend what flaws may lurk
What strain o' the stuff, what warpings past the aim!
My times be in Thy hand!
Perfect the cup as planned!
Let age approve of youth and death complete the same!

THE GOOD PARSON

CHAUCER

Translated by H. C. Leonard

The parson of a country town was he
Who knew the straits of humble poverty;
But rich he was in holy thought and work,
Nor less in learning as became a clerk.
The word of Christ most truly did he preach,
And his parishioners devoutly teach.
Benign was he, in labors diligent,
And in adversity was still content—
As proved full oft. To all his flock a friend,
Averse was he to ban or to contend
When tithes were due. Much rather was he fond,
Unto his poor parishioners around,
Of his own substance and his dues to give,
Content on little, for himself to live.
Wide was his parish, scattered far asunder,
Yet none did he neglect, in rain, or thunder.
Sorrow and sickness won his kindly care;
With staff in hand he travelled everywhere.
This good example to his sheep he brought
That first he wrought, and afterwards he taught.
This parable he joined the Word unto—
That, "If gold rust, what shall iron do?"
For if a priest be foul in whom we trust,
No wonder if a common man should rust!
And shame it were, in those the flock who keep
For shepherds to be foul yet clean the sheep.
Well ought a priest example fair to give,
By his own cleanness, how his sheep should live.
He did not put his benefice to hire,
And leave his sheep encumbered in the mire,
Then haste to St. Pauls in London Town,
To seek a chantry where to settle down,
And there at least to sing the daily mass,

Or with a brotherhood his time to pass.
He dwelt at home, with watchful care to keep
From prowling wolves his well-protected sheep
Though holy in himself and virtuous
He still to sinful men was piteous,
Not sparing of his speech, in vain conceit,
But in his teaching kindly and discreet.
To draw his flock to heaven with noble art,
By good example, was his holy art.
Nor less did he rebuke the obstinate,
Whether they were of high or low estate.
For pomp and worldly show he did not care,
No morbid conscience made his rule severe.
The lore of Christ and his apostles twelve
He taught, but first he followed it himself.

HYMN TO ST. TERESA

RICHARD CRASHAW

Love, thou art Absolute sole lord
Of Life and Death.   To prove the word,
We'll now appeal to none of all
Those thy old Soldiers, great and tall
Ripe Men of Martyrdom, that could reach down
With strong arms, their triumphant crown;
Such as could with lusty breath
Speak loud into the face of death
Their great Lord's glorious name, to none
Of those whose spatious Bosomes spread a throne
For Love at large to fill, spare blood and sweat;
And take him to a private seat,
Making his mansion in the mild
And milky soul of a soft child.
   Scarse had she learn'd to lisp the name
Of Martyr; yet she thinks it shame
Life should so long play with that breath
Which spent can buy so brave a death.

She never undertook to know
What death with love should have to doe;
Nor has she e'er yet understood
Why to show love, she should shed blood
Yet though she cannot tell you why,
She can Love, and she can DY.

 Scarse has she Blood enough to make
A guilty sword blush for her sake;
Yet has she a Heart dares hope to prove
How much less strong is Death than Love.

 Be love but there; let six poor yeares
Be posed with the maturest Feares
Man trembles at, you straight shall find
Love knows no nonage, nor the Mind.
'Tis Love, not yeares or Limbs that can
Make the Martyr, or the man.

 Love touch't her Heart, and lo it beates
High, and burnes with such brave heates;
Such thirstes to dy, as dares drink up,
A thousand cold deaths in one cup.
Good reason. For she breathes all fire.
Her (weake) brest heaves with strong desire
Of what she may with fruitless wishes
Seek for amongst her Mother's kisses,

 Since 'tis not to be had at home
She'll travail to a Martyrdom.
No home for hers confesses she
But where she may a Martyr be.

 She'll to the Moores; and trade with them,
For this unvalued Diadem.
She'll offer them here dearest Breath,
With CHRIST's Name in't, in change for death.
She'll bargain with them; and will give
Them GOD; teach them how to live
In him: or, if this they deny,
For him she'll teach them how to DY.
So shall she leave amongst them sown
Her Lord's Blood; or at least her own.

 Farewell then, all the world! Adieu.
TERESA is no more for you.

Farewell, all pleasures, sports and joyes,
(Never till now esteemed toyes,)
(Farewell what ever deare may be,)
Mother's armes or Father's knee.
Farewell house, and farewell home!
She's for the Moores and Martyrdom.

Sweet, not so fast! lo thy fair Spouse
Whom thou seekst with so swift vowes,
Calls thee back, and bids thee come
T'embrace a milder Martyrdom.

Blest powres forbid, Thy tender life;
Should bleed upon a barbarous knife;
Or some base hand have power to race
Thy Brest's chaste cabinet, and uncase
A soul kept there so sweet, O no;
Wise heaven will never have it so.
Thou art love's victime; and must dy
A death more mystical and high.
Into love's armes thou shalt let fall
A still—surviving funerall.
His is the Dart must make the Death
Whose stroke shall taste thy hallow'd breath;
A Dart thrice dipt in that rich flame
Which writes thy spouse's radiant Name
Upon the roof of Heav'n; where ay
It shines, and with a sovereign ray
Beates bright upon the burning faces
Of soules which in that names sweet graces
Find everlasting smiles. So rare,
So spirituall, pure, and fair
Must be th' immortall instrument
Upon whose choice point shall be sent
A life so lov'd; and that there be
Fit executioners for Thee,
The fairest and first-born sons of fire,
Blest Seraphim, shall leave their quire
And turn love's souldiers, upon Thee
To exercise their archerie.

O how oft shalt thou complain
Of a sweet and subtle Pain.

Of intolerable Joyes;
Of a Death, in which who dyes
Loves his death and dyes again.
And would forever be so slain.
And lives, and dyes; and knowes not why
To live, But that he thus may never leave to DY.
   How kindly will thy gentle Heart
Kisse the sweetly-killing dart!
And close in his embraces keep
Those delicious Wounds, that weep
Balsom to heal themselves with. Thus
When These thy Deaths, so numerous,
Shall all at last dy into one,
And melt thy soul's sweet mansion;
Like a soft lump of incense, hasted
By too hot a fire, and wasted
Into perfuming clouds, so fast
Shalt thou exhale to Heav'n at last
In a resolving Sigh, and then
O what? Ask not the Tongues of men.
Angells cannot tell, suffice,
Thyselfe shall feel thine own full joyes
And hold them fast forever there
So soon as you first appear,
The Moon of maiden stars, thy white
Mistresse, attended by such bright
Soules as thy shining self, shall come
And in her first rankes make thee room;
Where mongst her snowy family
Immortal well-comes wait for thee.
   O what delight, when revealed Life shall stand
And teach thy lipps heav'n with his hand;
On which thou now maist to thy wishes
Heap up thy consecrated kisses.
What joyes shall seize thy soul, when she
Bending her blessed eyes on thee
(Those second smiles of Heav'n) shall dart
Her mild rayes through thy melting heart!
   Angels, thy old friends, there shall greet thee
Glad at their own home now to meet thee.

All thy good Workes which went before
And waited for thee at the door,
Shall own thee there; and all in one
Weave a constellation
Of Crowns, with which the King thy spouse
Shall bind up thy triumphant browes.
    All thy old woes shall now smile on thee
And thy paines sitt bright upon thee
All thy Sufferings be divine.
Teares shall take comfort, and turn gemms
And wrongs repent to Diadems.
Ev'n thy Death shall live; and new
Dresse the soul that erst they slew.
Thy wounds shall blush to such bright scarres
As keep account of the Lamb's warres.
    Those rare Workes where thou shalt leave writt,
Love's noble history, with witt
Taught thee by none but him, while here
They feed our soules, shall cloth Thine there.
Each heav'nly word by whose hid flame
Our hard Hearts shall strike fire, the same
Shall flourish on thy browes, and be
Both fire to us and flame to thee;
Whose light shall live bright in thy Face
By glory, in our hearts by grace.
    Thou shalt look round about, and see
Thousands of crowned Soules throng to be
Themselves thy crown. Sons of thy vowes
The virgin-births with which thy sovereign spouse
Made fruitful thy fair soul, goe now
And with them all about thee bow
To Him, put on (He'll say) put on
(My rosy love) That thy rich zone
Sparkling with the sacred flames
Of thousand soules, whose happy names
Heaven keep upon thy score. (Thy bright
Life brought them first to kisse the light
That kindled them to starrs.) And so
Thou with the Lamb, thy lord, shalt goe;
And whereso'er he setts his white

Stepps, walk with Him those wayes of light
Which who in death would live to see,
Must learn in life to dy like thee.

THE SMOOTH DIVINE

TIMOTHY DWIGHT

There smiled the Smooth Divine, unused to wound
The sinner's heart with hell's alarming sound.
No terrors on his gentle tongue attend;
No grating truths the nicest ear offend.
That strange new birth, that methodistic grace,
Nor in his heart nor sermons found a place.
Plato's fine tales he clumsily retold,
Trite, fireside, moral see-saws, dull as old,—
His Christ and Bible placed at good remove,
Guilt hell-deserving, and forgiving love.
'Twas best, he said, mankind should cease to sin:
Good fame required it; so did peace within.
Their honors, well he knew, would ne'er be driven;
But hoped they still would please to go to heaven.
Each week he paid his visitation dues;
Coaxed, jested, laughed; rehearsed the private news;
Smoked with each goody, thought her cheese excelled;
Her pipe he lighted and her baby held.
Or, placed in some great town, with lacquered shoes,
Trim wig, and trimmer gown, and glistening hose,
He bowed, talked politics, learned manners mild,
Most meekly questioned, and most smoothly smiled;
At rich men's jests laughed loud, their stories praised,
Their wives' new patterns gazed, and gazed, and gazed;
Most daintily on pampered turkeys dined,
Nor shrunk with fasting, nor with study pined;
Yet from their churches saw his brethren driven,
Who thundered truth and spoke the voice of heaven.
Chilled trembling guilt in Satan's headlong path,
Charmed the feet back, and roused the ear of death.
"Let fools," he cried, "slave on, while prudent I
Snug in my nest shall live and snug shall die."

THE HIGHWAY

William Channing Gannett

When the night is still and far,
  Watcher from the shadowed deeps!
When the morning breaks its bar,
  Life that shines and wakes and leaps!
When old Bible verses glow,
  Starring all the deep of thought,
Till it fills with quiet dawn
  From the peace our years have brought,—
    Sun within both skies, we see
    How all lights lead back to thee!

'Cross the field of daily work
  Run the footpaths, leading—where?
Run they east or run they west,
  One way all the workers fare.
Every awful thing of earth,—
  Sin and pain and battle-noise;
Every dear thing,—baby's birth,
  Faces, flowers, or lovers' joys,—
    Is a wicket-gate, where we
    Join the great highway to thee!

Restless, restless, speed we on,—
  Whither in the vast unknown?
Not to you and not to me
  Are the sealed orders shown:
But the Hand that built the road,
  And the Light that leads the feet,
And this inward restlessness,
  Are such invitation sweet,
    That where I no longer see,
    Highway still must lead to thee!

THE VILLAGE PARSON

OLIVER GOLDSMITH

From *The Deserted Village*

Near yonder copse, where once the garden smiled,
And still where many a garden-flower grows wild;
There, where a few torn shrubs the place disclose,
The village preacher's modest mansion rose.
A man he was to all the country dear,
And passing rich with forty pounds a year;
Remote from towns he ran his godly race,
Nor e'er had changed, nor wished to change, his place;
Unskillful he to fawn, or seek for power,
By doctrines fashioned to the varying hour;
Far other aims his heart had learned to prize,
More skilled to raise the wretched than to rise.
His house was known to all the vagrant train,
He chid their wanderings but relieved their pain;
The long-remembered beggar was his guest,
Whose beard descending swept his aged breast;
The ruined spendthrift, now no longer proud,
Claimed kindred there, and had his claims allowed;
The broken soldier, kindly bade to stay,
Sat by the fire and talked the night away;
Wept o'er his wounds, or, tales of sorrow done,
Shouldered his crutch and showed how fields were won.
Pleased with his guests, the good man learned to glow,
And quite forgot their vices in their woe;
Careless their merits or their faults to scan,
His pity gave ere charity began.
   Thus to relieve the wretched was his pride,
And e'en his failings leaned to Virtue's side;
But in his duty prompt at every call,
He watched and wept, he prayed and felt for all.
And, as a bird each fond endearment tries
To tempt its new-fledged offspring to the skies,
He tried each art, reproved each dull delay,

Allured to brighter worlds, and led the way.
  Beside the bed where parting life was laid,
And sorrow, guilt and pain by turns dismayed,
The reverend champion stood. At his control
Despair and anguish fled the struggling soul;
Comfort came down the trembling wretch to raise,
And his last faltering accents whispered praise.
  At church with meek and unaffected grace,
His looks adorned the venerable place;
Truth from his lips prevailed with double sway,
And fools who came to scoff, remained to pray.
The service past, around the pious man,
With steady zeal, each honest rustic ran;
Even children followed with endearing wile,
And plucked his gown to share the good man's smile.
His ready smile a parent's warmth expressed;
Their welfare pleased him and their cares distrest;
To them his heart, his love, his griefs were given,
But all his serious thoughts had rest in heaven.
As some tall cliff that lifts its awful form
Swells from the vale and midway leaves the storm,
Tho' round its breast the rolling clouds are spread
Eternal sunshine settles on its head.

From ALL FELLOWS

Laurence Housman

Dear love, when with a two-fold mind
    I pray for better grace;
And from my pit of torment find
    Your breath upon my face,

And hear you without thought of fear
    Bid me to guard you well,
And guide your footsteps to win clear—
    When my feet walk in hell;

I wonder, how can God be glad
    To hear men praise Him so

Who makes His piteous earth so sad
  A lot to undergo?

Or does He too dip Feet in fire
  And share the thirster's thirst;
And listen to man's great desire
  Holding a Heart to burst?

IN THE GARDEN OF THE LORD

Helen Keller

The word of God came unto me,
Sitting alone among the multitudes;
And my blind eyes were touched with light.
And there was laid upon my lips a flame of fire.

I laugh and shout for life is good,
Though my feet are set in silent ways.
In merry mood I leave the crowd
To walk in my garden. Ever as I walk
I gather fruits and flowers in my hands.
And with joyful heart I bless the sun
That kindles all the place with radiant life.
I run with playful winds that blow the scent

Of rose and jessamine in eddying whirls.
At last I come where tall lilies grow,
Lifting their faces like white saints to God.
While the lilies pray, I kneel upon the ground;
I have strayed into the holy temple of the Lord.

From THE VISION OF SIR LAUNFAL

James Russell Lowell

"For Christ's sweet sake, I beg an alms";
  .   .   .   .   .   .
Sir Launfal sees only the grewsome thing,
The leper, lank as the rain-blanched bone,
That cowers beside him, a thing as lone

And white as the ice-isles of the Northern seas
In the desolate horror of his disease.

And Sir Launfal said, "I behold in thee
The image of Him who died on the tree;
Thou also hast had thy crown of thorns,
Thou also hast had the world's buffets and scorns,
And to thy life were not denied
The wounds in the hands and feet and side:
Mild Mary's Son, acknowledge me;
Behold, through him, I give to thee!"

Then the soul of the leper stood up in his eyes
    And looked at Sir Launfal, and straightway he
Remembered in what a haughtier guise
    He had flung an alms to leprosie,
When he girt his young life up in gilded mail
And set forth in search of the Holy Grail.
The heart within him was ashes and dust;
He parted in twain his single crust,
He broke the ice on the streamlet's brink,
And gave the leper to eat and drink,
'Twas a mouldy crust of coarse brown bread,
    'Twas water out of a wooden bowl,—
Yet with fine wheaten bread was the leper fed,
    And 'twas red wine he drank with his thirsty soul.

As Sir Launfal mused with a downcast face,
A light shone round about the place;
The leper no longer crouched at his side
But stood before him glorified,
Shining and tall and fair and straight,
As the pillar that stood by the Beautiful Gate,—
Himself the Gate whereby men can
Enter the temple of God in Man.

His words were shed softer than leaves from the pine,
And they fell on Sir Launfal as snows on the brine,
Which mingle their softness and quiet in one
With the shaggy unrest they float down upon:

And the voice that was calmer than silence said,
  "Lo, it is I, be not afraid!
In many climes, without avail,
Thou has spent thy life for the Holy Grail;
Behold, it is here,—this cup which thou
Didst fill at the streamlet for me but now;
This crust is my body broken for thee,
This water His blood that died on the tree;
The Holy Supper is kept, indeed,
In whatso we share with another's need;
Not what we give, but what we share,
For the gift without the giver is bare;
Who gives himself with his alms feeds three,—
Himself, his hungering neighbor, and Me."

THE MAN WITH THE HOE

Written After Seeing Millet's World-Famous Painting

EDWIN MARKHAM

Bowed by the weight of centuries, he leans
Upon his hoe and gazes on the ground,
The emptiness of ages in his face,
And on his back the burden of the world.
Who made him dead to rapture and despair,
A thing that grieves not and that never hopes,
Stolid and stunned, a brother to the ox?
Who loosened and let down this brutal jaw?
Whose was the hand that slanted back this brow?
Whose breath blew out the light within this brain?

Is this the Thing the Lord God made and gave
To have dominion over sea and land;
To trace the stars and search the heavens for power;
To feel the passion of Eternity?
Is this the Dream He dreamed who shaped the suns
And pillared the blue firmament with light?
Down all the stretch of Hell to its last gulf,
There is no shape more terrible than this—
More tongued with censure of the world's blind greed—

More filled with signs and portents for the soul—
More fraught with menace to the universe.

What gulfs between him and the seraphim!
Slave of the wheel of labour, what to him
Are Plato and the swing of Pleiades?
What the long reaches of the peaks of song,
The rift of dawn, the reddening of the rose?
Through this dread shape the suffering ages look;
Time's tragedy is in that aching stoop;
Through this dread shape humanity betrayed,
Plundered, profaned, and disinherited,
Cries protest to the Judges of the World,
A protest that is also prophesy.

O masters, lords and rulers in all lands,
Is this the handiwork you give to God,
This monstrous thing distorted and soul-quenched?
How will you ever straighten up this shape;
Touch it again with immortality;
Give back the upward looking and the light;
Rebuild in it the music and the dream;
Make right the immemorial infamies,
Perfidious wrongs, immedicable woes?

O masters, lords, and rulers in all lands,
How will the Future reckon with this Man?
How answer his brute questions in that hour
When whirlwinds of rebellion shake the world?
How will it be with kingdoms and with kings—
With those who shaped him to the thing he is—
When this dumb Terror shall reply to God
After the silence of the centuries?

d. REVEALED IN HISTORICAL EVENTS

THE DESTRUCTION OF SENNACHERIB

Lord Byron

The Assyrian came down like the wolf on the fold,
And his cohorts were gleaming in purple and gold;
And the sheen of their spears was like stars on the sea,
When the blue wave rolls nightly on deep Galilee.

Like the leaves of the forest when summer is green,
That host with their banners at sunset were seen;
Like the leaves of the forest when autumn hath blown,
That host on the morrow lay withered and strown.

For the Angel of Death spread his wings on the blast,
And breathed in the face of the foe as he passed;
And the eyes of the sleepers waxed deadly and chill,
And their hearts but once heaved, and forever grew still!

And there lay the steed with his nostril all wide,
But through it there rolled not the breath of his pride:
And the foam of his gasping lay white on the turf,
And cold as the spray of the rock-beating surf.

And there lay the rider distorted and pale,
With the dew on his brow and the rust on his mail;
And the tents were all silent, the banners alone,
The lances unlifted, the trumpet unblown.

And the widows of Ashur are loud in their wail,
And the idols are broke in the temple of Baal;
And the might of the Gentile, unsmote by the sword,
Hath melted like snow in the glance of the Lord!

BOSTON HYMN

RALPH WALDO EMERSON

The word of the Lord by night
To the watching Pilgrims came,
As they sat by the seaside,
And filled their hearts with flame.

God said, I am tired of kings,
I suffer them no more;
Up to my ear the morning brings
The outrage of the poor.

Think ye I made this ball
A field of havoc and war,
Where tyrants great and tyrants small
May harry the weak and poor?

My angel,—his name is Freedom,—
Choose him to be your king;
He shall cut pathways east and west,
And fend you with his wing.

Lo! I uncover the land
Which I hid of old time in the West,
As the sculptor uncovers the statue
When he has wrought his best;

I show Columbia, of the rocks
Which dip their foot in the seas
And soar to the air-borne flocks
Of clouds and the boreal fleece.

I will divide my goods;
Call in the wretch and slave:
None shall rule but the humble,
And none but Toil shall have.

I will have never a noble,
No lineage counted great;
Fishers and choppers and plowmen
Shall constitute a state.

Go, cut down trees in the forest
And trim the straightest boughs;
Cut down trees in the forest
And build me a wooden house.

Call the people together
The young men and the sires,
The digger in the harvest field,
Hireling and him that hires.

And here in a pine state-house
They shall choose men to rule
In every needful faculty,
In church and state and school.

Lo, now! if these poor men
Can govern the land and sea
And make just laws below the sun,
As planets faithful be.

And ye shall succor men;
'Tis nobleness to serve;
Help them who cannot help again:
Beware from right to swerve.

I break your bonds and masterships,
And I unchain the slave:
Free be his heart and hand henceforth
As wind and wandering wave.

I cause from every creature
His proper good to flow;
As much as he is and doeth
So much he shall bestow.

But, lay hands on another
To coin his labor and sweat,
He goes in pawn for his victim
For eternal years in debt.

Today unbind the captive,
So only are ye unbound;
Lift up a people from the dust,
Trump of their rescue, sound!

Pay ransom to the owner
And fill the bag to the brim.
Who is the owner? The slave is owner,
And ever was. Pay him.

O North! Give him beauty for rags
And honor, O South! for his shame;
Nevada! Coin thy golden crags
With Freedom's image and name.

Up! and the dusky race
That sat in darkness long,—
Be swift their feet as antelopes,
And as Behemoth strong.

Come, East and West and North,
By races, as snow flakes,
And carry my purpose forth,
Which neither halts nor shakes.

My will fulfilled shall be,
For, in daylight or in dark,
My thunderbolt has eyes to see
His way home to the mark.

WHO FOLLOWS IN HIS TRAIN?

REGINALD HEBER

The Son of God goes forth to war,
  A kingly crown to gain;
His blood-red banner streams afar;
  'Who follows in his train?
Who best can drink his cup of woe,
  Triumphant over pain,
Who patient bears his cross below:
  He follows in his train!

That martyr first, whose eagle eye
  Could pierce beyond the grave;
Who saw his master in the sky,
  And called on him to save;
Like him with pardon on his tongue,
  In midst of mortal pain,
He prayed for those that did the wrong;
  Who follows in his train?

A glorious band, the chosen few,
  On whom the Spirit came;
Twelve valiant saints their hope they knew,
  And mocked the cross and flame;
They met the tyrant's brandished steel,
  The lion's gory mane,
They bowed their necks the death to feel!
  Who follows in their train?

A noble army, men and boys,
  The matron and the maid,
Around the Saviour's throne rejoice,
  In robes of light arrayed.

They climbed the steep ascent of heaven,
  Through peril, toil, and pain;
Oh God, to us may grace be given
  To follow in their train!

THE AGE IS GREAT AND STRONG

Victor Hugo

Translated by W. J. Robertson

The age is great and strong. Her chains are riven.
Thoughts on the march of man her mission sends;
Toil's clamor mounts on human speech to heaven
And with the sound divine of nature blends.

In cities and in solitary stations
Man loves the milk wherewith we nourish him;
And in the shapeless block of somber nations
Thought molds in dreams new peoples grand and dim.

New days draw nigh. Hushed is the riot's clangor.
The Greve is cleansed, the old scaffold crumbling lies.
Volcano torrents, like the peoples' anger,
First devastate and after fertilize.

New mighty poets, touched by God's own finger,
Shed from inspired brows their radiant beams.
Art has fresh valleys where our souls may linger,
And drink deep draughts of song from sacred streams.

Stone upon stone, remembering antique manners,
In times that shake with every storm-tossed wild,
The thinker rears these columns crowned with banners—
Respect for gray old age, love for child.

Beneath our roof-tree Duty and Right his father
Dwell once again august and honored guests.
The outcasts that around our threshold gather
Come with less flaming eyes, less hateful breasts.

No longer truth closes her austere portals,
Deciphered is each word, each scroll unfurled,
Learning the book of Life enfranchised mortals
Find a new sense's secret in the world.

O poets! Iron and steam with fiery forces
Lift from the earth, while yet your dreams float round,
Time's ancient load, that clogged the chariot's courses
Crushing with heavy wheels the hard rough ground.

Man by his puissant will subdues blind matter;
Thinks, seeks, creates; with living breath fulfilled
The seeds that nature's hand store up and scatter
Thrill as the forest leaves by winds are thrilled.

Yea, all things move and grow. The fleet hours flying
Leave each their track. The age has risen up great
And now between its luminous banks, far-lying,
Man like a broadened river sees his fate.

But in this boasted march of wrong and error,
'Mid the vast splendor of an age that glows,
One thing, O Jesus, fills my heart with terror;
The echo of Thy voice still feebler grows!

CRANMER'S PROPHECY OF QUEEN ELIZABETH

WILLIAM SHAKESPEARE

From *Henry VIII*

                    Let me speak, sir,
For Heaven now bids me; and the words I utter
Let none think flattery, for they'll find them truth.
This royal infant, (Heaven still move about her!)
Though in her cradle, yet now promises
Upon this land a thousand thousand blessings,
Which time shall bring to ripeness: She shall be
(But few now living, can behold that goodness)

A pattern to all princes, living with her,
And all, that shall succeed: Sheba was never
More covetous of wisdom and fair virtue
Than this pure soul shall be: all princely graces,
That mould up such a mighty piece as this is,
With all the virtues that attend the good,
Shall still be doubled on her: Truth shall nurse her,
Holy and heavenly thoughts still counsel her:
She shall be loved and fear'd: Her own shall bless her:
Her foes shake like a field of beaten corn,
And hang their heads with sorrow: Good grows with her:
In her days, every man shall eat in safety
Under his own vine, what he plants; and sing
The merry songs of peace to all his neighbours:
God shall be truly known; and those about her
From her shall read the perfect ways of honour,
And by those claim their greatness, not by blood.
Nor shall this peace sleep with her: But as when
The bird of wonder dies, the maiden phœnix,
Her ashes new create another heir,
As great in admiration as herself;
So shall she leave her blessedness to one,
(When heaven shall call her from this cloud of darkness,)
Who, from the sacred ashes of her honour,
Shall star-like rise, as great in fame as she was,
And so stand fix'd: Peace, plenty, love, truth, terror,
That were the servants to this chosen infant,
Shall then be his, and like a vine grow to him;
Wherever the bright sun of heaven shall shine,
His honour and the greatness of his name
Shall be, and make new nations: He shall flourish,
And, like a mountain cedar, reach his branches
To all the plains about him:—Our children's children
Shall see this, and bless Heaven.   25—v. 4.

THE COTTER'S SATURDAY NIGHT

ROBERT BURNS

The cheerfu' supper done, wi' serious face,
They, round the ingle, form a circle wide;
The sire turns o'er wi' patriarchal grace,
The big ha' Bible, ance his father's pride.
His bonnet reverently is laid aside,
His lyart haffets wearing thin and bare;
Those strains that once did sweet in Zion glide,
He wales a portion with judicious care;
And, "Let us worship God!" he says, with solemn air.

They chant their artless notes in simple guise,
They tune their hearts, by far the noblest aim;
Perhaps *Dundee's* wild-warbling measures rise,
Or plaintive *Martyrs,* worthy of the name;
Or noble *Elgin* beats the heaven-ward flame,
The sweetest far of Scotia's holy lays:
Compar'd with these, Italian trills are tame;
The tickl'd ear no heart-felt raptures raise;
Nae unison hae they with our Creator's praise.

The priest-like father reads the sacred page,—
How Abram was the friend of God on high;
Or, Moses bade eternal warfare wage
With Amalek's ungracious progeny;
Or, how the royal Bard did groaning lie
Beneath the stroke of heaven's avenging ire;
Or Job's pathetic plaint and wailing cry;
Or rapt Isaiah's wild, seraphic fire;
Or other holy Seers that tune the sacred lyre.

Perhaps the Christian volume is the theme:
How guiltless blood for guilty man was shed;
How He, who bore in heaven the second name
Had not on earth whereon to lay His head;
How His first followers and servants sped;
How precepts sage they wrote to many a land;
How He, who lone in Patmos banished,
Saw in the sun a mighty angel stand,
And heard great Bab'lon's doom pronounc'd by Heaven's
                    Command.

Then kneeling down to Heaven's Eternal King,
The saint, the father, and the husband prays;
Hope 'springs exulting on triumphant wing,'
That thus they all shall meet in future days,
There, ever bask in uncreated rays,
No more to sigh or shed the bitter tear,
Together hymning their Creator's praise,
In such society, yet still more dear;
While circling time moves round in an eternal sphere.

Compar'd to this, how poor Religion's pride,
In all the pomp of method and of art;
When men display to congregations wide
Devotion's ev'ry grace except the heart!
The Power, incens'd, the pageant will desert,
The pompous strain, the sacerdotal stole;
But haply, in some cottage far apart,
May hear, well-pleas'd, the language of the soul,
And in His Book of Life the inmates poor enroll.

Then homeward all take off their sev'ral way;
The youngling cottagers retire to rest:
The parent pair their secret homage pay,
And proffer up to Heaven the warm request,
That He who stills the raven's clam'rous nest,
And decks the lily fair in flow'ry pride,
Would, in the way His wisdom sees the best,
For them and for their little ones provide;
But, chiefly, in their hearts with grace divine preside.

From scenes like these, old Scotia's grandeur springs,
That makes her lov'd at home, rever'd abroad:
Princes and lords are but the breath of kings,
'An honest man's the noblest work of God.'
And certes, in fair Virtue's heavenly road,
The cottage leaves the palace far behind:
What is a lordling's pomp? A cumbrous load,
Disguising oft the wretch of human kind,
Studied in arts of Hell, in wickedness refin'd!

O Scotia! my dear, my native soil!
For whom my warmest wish to heaven is sent!
Long may thy hardy sons of rustic toil
Be blest with health, and peace, and sweet content!
And oh! may Heaven their simple lives prevent
From Luxury's contagion, weak and vile!
Then, howe'er crowns and coronets be rent,
A virtuous populace may rise the while,
And stand a wall of fire around their much-lov'd isle.

O THOU! who pour'd the patriotic tide,
That stream'd through Wallace's undaunted heart,
Who dar'd to nobly stem tyrannic pride,
Or nobly die, the second glorious part;
(The patriot's God, peculiarly thou art,
His friend, inspirer, guardian, and reward!)
O never, never Scotia's realm desert;
But still the patriot, and the patriot-bard
In bright succession raise, her ornament and guard!

LOVE'S VISION

Edward Carpenter

At night in each other's arms,
Content, overjoyed, resting, deep, deep, down in the darkness,
Lo, the heavens opened and He appeared—
Whom no mortal eye may see,
Whom no eye clouded with Care,

Whom none who seeks after this or that, whom none who has
    not escaped from self.

There—in the region of Equality, in the world of Freedom no
    longer limited,
Standing as a lofty peak in heaven above the clouds,
From below hidden, yet to all who pass into that region most
    clearly visible—
He the Eternal appeared.

2. *In the City*

CALM SOUL OF ALL THINGS

Matthew Arnold

Calm soul of all things! be it mine
    To feel amid the city's jar,
That there abides a peace of thine
    Man did not make and cannot mar!

The will to neither strive nor cry
    The power to feel with others give!
Calm, calm me more! nor let me die
    Before I have begun to live!

EAST LONDON

Matthew Arnold

'Twas August, and the fierce sun overhead
Smote on the squalid streets of Bethnal Green,
And the pale weaver, through his windows seen
In Spitalfields, look'd thrice dispirited.

I met a preacher there I knew, and said:
"Ill and o'er-worked, how fare you in this scene?"—
"Bravely!" said he; "for I of late have been
Much cheered with thoughts of Christ, *the living bread.*"

O human soul! as long as thou canst so
Set up a mark of everlasting light,
Above the howling senses' ebb and flow,

To cheer thee, and to right thee if thou roam—
Not with lost toil thou laborest through the night!
Thou mak'st the heaven thou hop'st indeed thy home.

OVER THE GREAT CITY

Edward Carpenter

Over the great city
Where the wind rushes through the parks and gardens,
In the air, the high clouds brooding,
In the lines of street perspective, the lamps, the traffic,
The pavements and the innumerable feet upon them,
I AM: make no mistake—do not be deluded.

Think not because I do not appear at first glance—because the
    centuries have gone by and there is no assured tidings of
    me that therefore I am not there.
Think not because all goes its own way that therefore I do not
    go my own way through all.

The fixed bent of hurrying faces in the street—each turned
    toward its own light, seeing no other—yet I am the Light
    towards which they all look.
The toil of so many hands towards so many multifarious ends,
    yet my hands know the touch and twining of them all.

All come to me at last.
There is no love like mine;
For all other love takes one and not another;
And other love is pain, but this is joy eternal.

THE CITY'S CROWN

DUDLEY FOULKE

What makes a city great? Huge piles of stone
  Heaped heavenward? Vast multitudes who dwell
Within wide circling walls? Palace and throne
  And riches past the count of man to tell,
And wide domain? Nay, these the empty husk!
  True glory dwells where great deeds are done,
Where glorious men rise whose names a'thwart the dusk
  Of misty centuries gleam like the sun!
In Athens, Sparta, Florence, 'twas the soul
  That was the city's bright immortal part,
The splendor of the spirit was their goal,
  Their jewel the unconquerable heart!
So may the city that I love be great
'Till every stone shall be articulate.

THE CITY

GEORGE WILLIAM RUSSELL (*A. E.*)

Full of Zeus the cities: full of Zeus the harbors: full of Zeus are
  all the ways of men.

What domination of what darkness dies this hour,
And through what new, rejoicing, winged, ethereal power
O'erthrown, the cells opened, the heart released from fear?
Gay twilight and grave twilight pass. The stars appear
O'er the prodigious, smouldering, dusky, city flare.
The hanging gardens of Babylon were not more fair
Then these blue-flickering glades, where childhood in its glee
Re-echoes with fresh voice the heaven-lit ecstasy.
Yon girl whirls like an eastern dervish. Her dance is
No less a god-intoxicated dance than his,
Though all-unknowing the arcane fire that lights her feet,
What motions of what starry tribes her limbs repeat.
I too, fire-smitten, cannot linger: I know there lies

Open somewhere this hour a gate to Paradise,
Its blazing battlements with watchers thronged, O where?
I know not, but my flame-winged feet shall lead me there.
O, hurry, hurry, unknown shepherd of desires,
And with thy flock of bright imperishable fires
Pen me within the starry fold, ere night falls
And I am left alone below immutable walls.
Or am I there already, and is it Paradise
To look on mortal things with an immortal's eyes?
Above the misty brilliance, the streets assume
A night-dilated blue magnificence of gloom
Like many-templed Nineveh tower beyond tower;
And I am hurried on in this immortal hour.
Mine eyes beget new majesties: my spirit greets
The trams, the high-built glittering galleons of the streets
The flow through twilight rivers from galaxies of light.
Nay, in the Fount of Days they rise, they take their flight,
And wend to the great deep, the Holy Sepulcher.
Those dark misshapen folk to be made lovely there
Hurry with me, not all ignoble as we seem,
Lured by some inexpressible and gorgeous dream.
The earth melts in my blood. The air that I inhale
Is like enchanted wine poured from the Holy Grail.
What was that glimmer then? Was it the flash of wings
As through the blinded mart rode on the King of Kings?
O stay, departing glory, stay with us but a day,
And burning Seraphim shall leap from out our clay,
And plumed and crested hosts shall shine where men have been,
Heaven hold no lordlier court than earth at College Green.
Ah, no, the wizardry is over; the magic flame
That might have melted all in beauty fades as it came.
The stars are far and faint and strange. The night draws
    down.
Exiled from light, forlorn, I walk in Dublin town.
Yet had I might to lift the veil, the will to dare,
The fiery rushing chariots of the Lord are there,
The whirlwind path, the blazing gates, the trumpets blown,
The halls of heaven, the majesty of throne by throne,
Enraptured faces, hands uplifted, welcome sung
By the throned gods. tall, golden-coloured, joyful, young.

THE GARDEN OF GOD

George William Russell (*A. E.*)

Within the iron cities
One walked unknown for years,
In his heart the pity of pities
That grew for human tears.

When love and grief were ended
The flower of pity grew:
By unseen hands 'twas tended
And fed with holy dew.

Though in his heart were barred in
The blooms of beauty blown,
Yet he who grew the garden
Could call no flower his own.

For by the hands that watered,
The blooms that opened fair
Through frost and pain were scattered
To sweeten the dead air.

THE GOSPEL OF LABOR

Henry van Dyke

But I think the king of that country comes out from his tireless
host
And walks in this world of the weary, as if he loved it the
most:
For here in the dusty confusion, with eyes that are heavy and
dim
He meets again the laboring men who are looking and longing
for Him.

He cancels the curse of Eden, and brings them a blessing
instead,

Blessed are they that labor for Jesus partakes of their bread,
He puts His hand to their burdens, He enters their homes at
    night:
Who does his best shall have as his guest the Master of life
    and light.

And courage will come with His presence, and patience return
    at His touch,
And manifold sins be forgiven to those who love Him much:
And the cries of envy and anger will change to the songs of
    cheer,
For the toiling age will forget its rage when the Prince of
    Peace draws near.

This is the gospel of labor, ring it, ye bells of the kirk,—
The Lord of Love comes down from above to live with the men
    who work,
This is the rose that he planted, here in the thorn-cursed soil—
Heaven is blessed with perfect rest, but the blessing of earth
    is toil.

IN THE CITY

ISRAEL ZANGWILL

Sudden amid the slush and rain,
I know not how, I know not why,
A rose unfolds within my brain,
And all the world is at July.

A trumpet sounds, green surges splash
And daffodillies dance i' the sun;
Through tears fair pictures flit and splash
Upon the city's background dun.

Women are true and men are good,
Concord sleeps at the heart of strife,
How sweet is human brotherhood,
And all the common daily life!

3. *In the Church*

A NEW ENGLAND CHURCH

WILSON AGNEW BARRETT

The white church on the hill
   Looks over the little bay—
A beautiful thing on the hill
   When the mist is gray;
When the hill looks old, and the air turns cold
   With the dying day!

The white church on the hill—
   The Greek in a Puritan town—
Was built on the brow of the hill
   For John Wesley's God's renown,
And a conscience old set a steeple cold
   On its Grecian crown.

In a storm of faith on the hill
   Hands raised it over the bay.
When the night is clear on the hill,
   It stands up strong and gray;
But its door is old, and its tower points cold
   To the Milky Way.

The white church on the hill
   Looks lonely over the town.
Dim to them under the hill
   Is its God's renown,
And its Bible old, and its creed grown cold,
   And the letters brown.

THE LATEST DECALOGUE

Arthur Hugh Clough

Thou shalt have one God only; who
Would be at the expense of two?

No graven images may be
Worship'd, except the currency:

Swear not at all; for, for thy curse
Thine enemy is none the worse:

At church on Sunday to attend
Will serve to keep the world thy friend:

Honour thy parents; that is, all
From whom advancement may befall;

Thou shalt not kill; but needst not strive
Officiously to keep alive:

Do not adultery commit;
Advantage rarely comes of it:

Thou shalt not steal; an empty feat,
Where 'tis so lucrative to cheat:

Bear not false witness; let the lie
Have time on its own wings to fly:

Thou shalt not covet, but tradition
Approves all forms of competition.

THE IMPERCIPIENT

(At a Cathedral Service)

THOMAS HARDY

That with this bright believing band
    I have no claim to be,
That faiths by which my comrades stand,
    Seem fantasies to me,
And mirage-mists their Shining Land,
    Is a strange destiny.

Why thus my soul should be consigned
    To Infelicity, ˙
Why always I must feel as blind
    To sights my brethren see,
Why joys they've found I cannot find,
    Abides a mystery.

Since heart of mine knows not that ease
    Which they know; since it be
That He who breathes All's-Well to these
    Breathes no All's-Well to me,
My lack might move their sympathies
    And Christian charity!

I am like a gazer who should mark
    An inland company
Standing upfingered with, "Hark! hark!
    The glorious distant sea!"
And feel, "Alas, 'tis but yon dark
    And wind-swept pine to me!"

Yet I would bear my shortcomings
    With meet tranquillity,
But for the charge that blessed things,
    I'd liefer not have be.
O, doth a bird deprived of wings

Go earth-bound wilfully!
Enough! As yet disquiet clings
About us. Rest shall we.

THE CITY CHURCH

E. H. K.

There is a sentinel before the gate
Who guards it night and day. And on his face
There ever lurks a scornful, sceptic smile,
Which mocks the hallowed precincts, and invites
The teeming millions of humanity
To jeer in unison with him, and press
Their busy footsteps quicker. And without,
The flags are worn and hollowed by the tread
Of men and women, but within they lie
Untrodden, smooth and true, as on the day
When God first found His temple made with hands,
And came and dwelt there. Yet men dare not pass
The guardian at the gateway, for they dread
The jesting of their fellows, and they steel
Their hearts against the summons of their souls,
And hasten past the portal—for they know
The sentinel is Satan. But within
The throbbing of the pulses of the world
Is silenced, and the soul is free to roam
At random through the mansions of the mind.
For in the quiet of the shadowed aisle,
The tired eyes are lifted to behold
The blessed Cross, illumined by the gleam
Of crimson from the sanctuary lamp,
Hung in the chancel by a silver chain,
Burning for ever. And amid the gloom
The soul can leave the body and ascend
The stair that leads from earth through flame and cloud
Up to God's heaven, and forget man's hell—
For still the grinning guardian keeps the gate,
And still men fear the sneer that curls his lip,
And still they stab their souls and slink away.

PRIEST OR POET

SHANE LESLIE

O Lord, why must thy poets peak and pine
  Why fall thy singers into fate?
When all thy priests do sup on amber wine
  And walk in purples delicate?

Thy Prophets of the desert honey sip,
  And sate their souls with loneliness,
Yet breakest Thou Thy flame upon their lip
  And givest camel's hair for dress.

To Poets, Lord, Thou givest neither drink
  Nor raiment, fire nor peace nor food;
Enhungered, thirsting as they daily sink
  Beneath the trampling multitude.

THE CHURCH

EDWIN FORD PIPER

The blinding sun at ten o'clock
Glares on the white walls of the little church,—
The shingles silver-gray, the shutters green,
Sunflowers man-high in bloom against the wall,—
And glares on dingy wagons trailed by dust,
Slow-jolting to the platform at the door.
Women alight and enter, while the men
Tie sweating teams to the much-gnawed hitching posts.
How drowsily the horses stamp at flies!
The landscape wavers in the shimmering heat.

Come in from the strong sunlight. The pine pews
Are filled with settlers. Men with grizzled beards,
And faces weathered rough by sun and wind—
Wind that would wear down granite—listless stand

Awkwardly easing muscles now relaxed
Longer than is their use. The women move
Graceful and gracious, whether pale or tanned,
Thin, nervous, or in rosy health. Their eyes
Are bright, and bearing cheerful. Least at ease
Are growing girls and boys. Welcomes go round,
And gossips buzz until the organ wails
The slow, sad measures of the opening hymn.

Beside the window, dreamily,
A sunflower pokes its stiff and oily head
Droned over by a hairy bumble-bee.
An awkward boy sits gazing; does not hear
The text or sermon; only sees the flower
Nod in the breeze, and finds the pew grow hard,
While muscles twitch and ache for liberty.

A little church; the settlers come for miles.
Some few, unhearing, sit in selfish dreams;
For life is vilely mingled, sweetly mixed,
Scanty or bounteous in vital force;
But here the most are really worshippers
Seeking in fellowship a sympathy
With God. Their simple faces plainly show
What feelings stir the heart, for hard looks melt,
And thin, worn wretchedness in garb grotesque
Is eased of ugliness while it feeds
On love and hope. This meager hour may lift
Some grovelling face to see the blessed sky;
Master a soul, and yield it back to life
Tempered against the evil days to be.

A little thing, this church? Remove its roots
Ossa upon Pelion would not fill the pit.

THE CHURCH

JULES ROMAIN

Translated by Jethro Bithell

The self-deceit of having wrought the light

People arrive to worship in their church.
Though it is getting tired and insecure,
The monument can make a gathering yet
With people poured into it by the roads.
It sifts them as they enter through its porch,
And gently it removes from each the thoughts
Which might not melt so well as all the rest,
Replacing them by others left behind
By those who came to Mass in days of old.

The crowd which tramples on the flags outside
Bears nosegays of ideas new and bright;
The fresh dreams of to-day spread over them,
Rosy and blue as sunshades which in their
Own manner dye the radiance of the sky.

Inside there are no nosegays and no sunshades.

The naves and aisles are overflowing with
A crowd the pillars intimately know,
Their contact is as ancient as the church,
And every summer Sunday when the sun
Begins to lick the windows by one edge,
And in the winter of discoloured lamps,
For centuries this crowd has been reborn
On every following Sunday still the same.

Women and men are entering in file.

The crowd is borne in haste by all the doors,
Rumbling an instant, ordered, then appeased;

It has not changed its shape; it is already
Moulded unto the contours of the walls;
Faithfully bodies lean on the same chairs.
Now it is born again while ring the bells.

But the dark power
That gives it life
On the seventh day
Of every week,
Softens at last
Like an old spring,
Little by little
Born less far
From death.

It is a group
Worn out with use
Whose flesh grows flabby.
And in the winter
It is cold
Under the roof.
In olden days,
In the city

It was the greatest of unanimous beings,
And all the city was transfused in it.
But now the workshops have arisen,
The workshops full of youth!

They live in ardour.
Their smoke soars higher than the sound of bells.
They do not fear to hide the sun,
For their machines make sunshine.

Like a dog that comes out of a pool and sneezes,
The workshop shivering scatters round it drops
Of energy that wake the town to life.

But the senile group
Sprouts not with bristling
Wires and cables.

No electricity
Rustles from it
To countless houses.

It is feeble,
Its chinks are stopped,
It is gathered in.

But it preserves with pride its fixed idea:
Others may swell with sap and ramify;
And shadow with a foliage of green forces
                All the massed houses;
The humble group would tenderly, heart to heart,
Speak to the infinite group benevolent words.
For it is sure a soul stands o'er the world.

It knows God's finger painlessly from Heaven
Leads the leash of natural forces;
That God sees all, and that His tender eyes
Wrap up the form and penetrate the essence of things.

      The group is sure of it.

                But fears
Lest having to keep watch o'er all these minds
And bodies, all these angels, beasts, and deaths,
Ant-hills, cities, forests,
Planets and planetary systems,
God see no more the little auditory
Which listens to the Mass in pillared shade.

It calls Him; makes to Him the holy signs.
In olden days God taught His creatures words
Which force Him to give heed and to vouchsafe.

The group that mumbles them knows not their meaning,
But knows the priest before the altar knows:
The illuminated summit of the group.

Upon the murmurs serving it as rollers
Slowly the common thought advances, like
A boat that fishers launch into the sea;
    And onward floats the thought to God.

From hearts the fervour passes to the walls,
The rising fluid magnetizes
The steeple, and the steeple brings down God.

    God approaches, God descends;
    He is quite near; the air
    Weighs heavier.
    Something compresses, heats it;
    The choir is filled with incense
    So that, arriving, God
    Shall find here clouds
    Like those He dwells in,
    And feels less strange.

He is quite near, quite near. You can whisper to Him,
Tell Him what you would dare tell no man, ask Him
For anything you like. And even if God
Refuse, He is so good you cannot vex Him.

"O God in Heaven, vouchsafe to cure my leg!
  Matter burst from it yesterday. My God,
Vouchsafe to fill my shop with customers!
—Help me find out if my servant John
Is robbing me!—O, God, cure my sore eyes!
—Save me, my God, from being drunk so often!
—Lord, let my son pass his examination!
He is so shy. Thou shalt have a great big candle.
—Help me to make her fall in love with me,
I will put ninepence in St. Anthony's box.
—My God, if only I could get some work!
—He makes a martyr of me. Let him die!
—My God, my God, I am certain I am pregnant;
O let the child go rotten in my belly."

It is like a hamlet at the hour of noon.
On every soul's hearth they have kindled fire,
Which casts its smoke and yields it to the wind.
God sees the bluish prayers climb up to Him.

They are a perfume which delight Him. He
Comes nearer. The crowd rises, touches Him.
Their longing to caress serves them for arm.
They seize on God to press Him close to them;
To be alone and to possess Him all.

This morning, God, the conscience of the universe,
Has from the universe withdrawn, like blood
Out of a bull's limbs bleeding at the head.
All the world's soul, the whole of God is here;
The church is the glad vase that gathers Him.

God now can think but of the little crowd;
The things they wish He too must wish, since He
In them is incarnated and their breath.

> Then in mystical servitude;
> Drunk with alcohol
> Hid in the organ notes,
> The light of the rose-window,
> And the stained glass;
> Clad with incense like
> A scented sleep that bends and swoons;
> By old, magnetic rites
> Plunged in hypnotic sleep
> Whence mount, like bubbles
> Crossing stagnant waters,
> Memories and mouldiness
> And age-old madness;
> Forgetting that beyond these walls
> There is the town, and earth,
> And then infinity;
> The group so old, so little,
> Which withers, which is scarce alive,
> Dreams aloud that it is God.

LILLIUM REGIS

Francis Thompson

O Lily of the King! low lies thy silver wing,
  And long has been the hour of thine unqueening;
And thy scent of Paradise on the night wind spills its sighs,
  Nor any take the secrets of its meaning.
O Lily of the King! I speak a heavy thing,
  O Patience, most sorrowful of daughters!
Lo, the hour is at hand for the troubling of the land,
  And red shall be the breaking of the waters.

Sit fast upon thy stalk, when the blast shall with thee talk,
  With the mercies of the king for thine awning;
And the just understand that thine hour is at hand,
  Thine hour at hand with power in the dawning.
When the nations lie in blood, and their kings a broken brood,
  Look up, O most sorrowful of daughters!
Lift up thine head and hark what sounds are in the dark,
  For his feet are coming to thee on the waters.

O Lily of the King! I shall not see, that sing,
  I shall not see the hour of thy queening!
But my Song shall see, and wake like a flower that dawn-winds
    shake,
  And sigh with joy the odors of its meaning.
O Lily of the King, remember then the thing
  That this dead mouth sang; and thy daughters,
As they dance before His way, sing there on the Day
  What I sang when the Night was on the waters!

THE CHURCH TODAY

William Watson

Outwardly splendid as of old—
Inwardly sparkless, void and cold—
Her force and fire all spent and gone—
Like the dead moon she still shines on.

VII. Prayers

a. DESCRIPTIONS OF PRAYER

THE PEAKS

STEPHEN CRANE

In the night
Gray heavy clouds muffled the valleys
And the peaks looked toward God alone:
    "O Master, that movest the wind with a finger,
    Humble, idle, futile peaks are we,
    Grant that we may run swiftly across the world
    To huddle in worship at Thy feet."

In the morning
A noise of men at work came through the clear blue miles,
And the little black cities were apparent.
    "O Master, that knowest the meaning of raindrops,
    Humble, idle, futile peaks are we,
    Give voice to us, we pray, O Lord,
    That we may sing thy goodness to the sun."

In the evening,
The far valleys were sprinkled with tiny lights,
    O Master
    Thou that knowest the value of kings and birds,
    Thou hast made us humble, idle, futile peaks.
    Thou only needest eternal patience;
    We bow to Thy wisdom, O Lord—
    Humble, idle, futile peaks."

In the night
Gray, heavy clouds muffled the valleys
And the peaks looked toward God alone.

THE RIGHT USE OF PRAYER

Sir Aubrey de Vere

Therefore, when thou wouldst pray, or dost thine alms,
    Blow not a trump before thee: Hypocrites
    Do thus, vaingloriously; the common streets
Boast of their largess, echoing their psalms.
On such the laud of men, like unctuous balms,
    Falls with sweet savor. Impious Counterfeits!
    Prating of heaven, for earth their bosom beats!
Grasping at weeds, they lose immortal palms!

God needs not iteration nor vain cries:
    That man communion with his God might share
    Below, Christ gave the ordinance of prayer:
Vague ambages, and witless ecstasies,
    Avail not: ere a voice to prayer be given
    The heart should rise on wings of love to heaven.

WHAT IS PRAYER?

James Montgomery

Prayer is the soul's sincere desire,
    Uttered or unexpressed—
The motion of a hidden fire,
    That kindles in the breast.

Prayer is the burthen of a sigh,
    The falling of a tear—
The upward glancing of an eye,
    When none but God is near.

Prayer is the simplest form of speech
    That infant lips can try—
Prayer the sublimest strains that reach
    The majesty on high.

Prayer is the contrite sinner's voice
   Returning from his ways,
While angels in their songs rejoice,
   And cry, "Behold! He prays!"

Prayer is the Christian's vital breath—
   The Christian's native air—
His watchword at the gates of death—
   He enters heaven with prayer.

The saints in prayer appear as one
   In words and deed and mind,
Where with the Father and the Son
   Sweet fellowship they find.

Nor prayer is made by man alone—
   The holy spirit pleads—
And Jesus, on the eternal throne,
   For sinners intercedes.

O Thou by whom we come to God—
   The Life, the Truth, the Way!
The path of prayer Thyself hast trod;
   Lord, teach us how to pray!

GOD PRAYS

ANGELA MORGAN

Last night I tossed and could not sleep
When sodden heavens weep and weep,
As they have wept for many a day,
One lies awake to fear and pray,
One thinks of bodies blown like hail
Across the sky where angels quail;
One's sickened pulses leap and hark
To hear the horror in the dark.
What is thy will for the people, God?
Thy will for the people, tell it me!

For war is swallowing up the sod
And still no help from Thee,
Thou, who art mighty, hast forgot;
And art Thou God, or art Thou not?
When wilt Thou come to save the earth
Where death has conquered birth?

And the Lord God whispered and said to me,
"These things shall be, these things shall be,
Nor help shall come from the scarlet skies,
Till the people rise!
Till the people rise, my arm is weak;
I cannot speak till the people speak;
When men are dumb, my voice is dumb—
I cannot come till my people come."
And the Lord God's presence was white, so white,
Like a pillar of stars against the night,
"Millions on millions pray to me
Yet hearken not to hear me pray;
Nor comes there any to set me free
Of all who plead from night to day.
So God is mute and Heaven is still
While the nations kill."

"Thy people have travailed much," I cried,
"I travail even as they," God sighed.
"I have cradled their woe since the stars were young—
My infant planets were scarcely hung
When I dreamed the dream of my liberty
And planned a people to utter me.
I am the pang of their discontent,
The passion of their long lament;
I am the purpose of their pain,
I writhe beneath their chain."
"But Thou art mighty, and needst no aid.
Can God, the Infinite, be afraid?"
"They, too, are God, yet know it not.
'Tis they, not I, who have forgot.
And war is drinking the living sod,"
Said God.

"Thy people are fettered by iron laws
And each must follow a country's cause
And all are sworn to avenge their dead
How may the people rise?" I said.
And then God's face! It was white, so white,
With the grief that sorroweth day and night.

"Think you I planted my image there
That men should trample it to despair?
Who fears the throe that rebellion brings?"
"Help them stand, O Christ!" I prayed.
Thy people are feeble and sore afraid."
"My people are strong," God whispered me,
"Broad as the land, great as the sea;
They will tower as tall as the tallest skies
Up to the level of my eyes,
When they dare to rise.
Yea, all my people every where!
Not in one land of black despair
But over the flaming earth and sea
Wherever wrong and oppression be
The shout of my people must come to me.
Not till their spirit break the curse
May I claim my own in the universe;
And this the reason of war and blood
That men may come to their angelhood.
If the people rise, if the people rise,
I will answer them from the swarming skies
Where Herculean hosts of night
Shall spring to splendor over night,
Blazing systems of sun and star
Are not so great as my people are,
Nor chanting angels so sweet to hear
As the voice of nations, freed from fear.
They are my mouth, my breath, my soul!
I wait their summons to make me whole."

All night long I toss and cannot sleep;
When shattered heavens weep and weep,
As they have wept for many days.
I know at last 'tis God who prays.

ENVOI

John G. Neihardt

Oh, seek me not within a tomb—
  Thou shalt not find me in the clay!
I pierce a little wall of gloom
  To mingle with the day!

I brothered with the things that pass,
  Poor giddy joy and puckered grief;
I go to brother with the grass
  And with the sunning leaf.

Not death can sheathe me in a shroud;
  A joy-sword whetted keen with pain,
I join the armies of the cloud,
  The lightning and the rain.

Oh, subtle in the sap a-thrill,
  Athletic in the glad uplift,
A portion of the cosmic will,
  I pierced the planet-drift.

My God and I shall interknit
  As rain and ocean, breath and air;
And, oh, the luring thought of it
  Is prayer!

PRAYER

Alfred Tennyson

From *Idylls of the King*

Pray for my soul. More things are wrought by prayer
Than this world dreams of. Wherefore let thy voice
Rise like a fountain for me night and day.
For what are men better than sheep or goats

That nourish a blind life within the brain,
It, knowing God, they lift not hands of prayer
Both for themselves and those who call them friends?
For so the whole round earth is every way
Bound by gold chains about the feet of God.

A FAR CRY TO HEAVEN

Edith M. Thomas

What! dost thou pray that the outgone tide be rolled back on
    the strand,
The flame be rekindled that mounted away from the smoul-
    dering brand,
The past-summer harvest flow golden through stubble-lands
    naked and sere,
The winter-gray woods upgather and quicken the leaves of last
    year?—
Thy prayers are as clouds in a drouth; regardless, unfruitful,
    they roll;
For this, that thou prayest vain things, 'tis a far cry to Heaven,
    my soul,—
           Oh, a far cry to Heaven!
Thou dreamest the word shall return, shot arrow-like into the
    air,
The wound in the breast where it lodged be balmed and closed
    for thy prayer,
The ear of the dead be unsealed, till thou whisper a boon once
    denied,
The white hour of life be restored, that passed thee unprized,
    undescribed!—
Thy prayers are as runners that faint, that fail, within sight
    of the goal,
For this, that thou cravest fond things, 'tis a far cry to Heaven,
    my soul,
           Oh, a far cry to Heaven!
And cravest thou fondly the quivering sands shall be firm to
    thy feet,

The brackish pool of the waste to thy lips be made wholesome
    and sweet?
And cravest thou subtly the bane thou desirest be wrought to
    thy good,
As forth from a poisonous flower a bee convoyeth safe food?
For this, that thou prayest ill things, thy prayers are an anger-
    rent scroll,
The chamber of audit is closed,—'tis a far cry to Heaven, my
    soul,—
        Oh, a far cry to Heaven!

PRAYER

RICHARD C. TRENCH

Lord, what a change within us one short hour
  Spent in Thy presence will avail to make!
  What heavy burdens from our bosoms take!
  What parched grounds refresh as with a shower!
We kneel, and all around us seems to lower;
  We rise, and all, the distant and the near,
  Stands forth in sunny outline, brave and clear;
We kneel, how weak! we rise, how full of power!
Why, therefore, should we do ourselves this wrong,
Or others—that we are not always strong—
  That we are sometimes overborne with care—
  That we should ever weak or heartless be,
Anxious or troubled—when with us is prayer,
  And joy and strength and courage are with Thee?

PRAYER

THOMAS WASHBOURNE

What a commanding power
There is in prayer! which can **tower**
As high as heaven, and tie the hands
Of God Himself in bands,

That He unable is to loose the reins
To Justice, till released from these chains!
Samson could break his cords
As tow, and yet the Lord of Lords
Who gave that strength to Samson, can not
Break the cords of Man.

BARTER

MARGARET WIDDEMER

If in that secret place
Where thou has cherished it, there yet is lying
Thy dearest bitterness, thy fondest sin,
Though thou hast guarded it with hurt and crying
Lift now thy face
Unlock the bolted door and let God in
And lay it in his holy hands to take:

How such an evil gift can please Him so
I do not know,
But, keeping it for wages, he shall make
Thy foul room sweet for thee with blowing wind
(He is so serviceable and so kind)
And set sweet water for thy thirst's distress
Instead of what thou hadst of bitterness;
And he shall bend and spread
Green balsam boughs to make a springing bed
Where thine own thorns pricked in;

Who would not pay away his dearest sin
To let such service in?

UNANSWERED PRAYERS

Ella Wheeler Wilcox

Like some school master, kind in being stern,
Who hears the children crying o'er their slates
And calling, "Help me, master!" yet helps not,
Since in his silence and refusal lies
Their self-development, so God abides
Unheeding many prayers. He is not deaf
To any cry sent up from earnest hearts;
He hears and strengthens when he must deny.
He sees us weeping o'er life's hard sums,
But should he give the key and dry our tears,
What would it profit us when school were done
And not one lesson mastered?
                              What a world
Were this if all our prayers were answered. Not
In famed Pandora's box were such vast ills
As lie in human hearts. Should our desires,
Voiced one by one in prayer, ascend to God
And come back as events shaped to our wish,
What Chaos would result!
                         In my fierce youth
I sighed out breath enough to move a fleet,
Voicing wild prayers to heaven for fancied boons
Which were denied; and that denial bends
My knee to prayers of gratitude each day
Of my maturer years. Yet from those prayers
I rose always regirded for the strife
And conscious of new strength. Pray on, sad heart,
That which thou pleadest for may not be given,
But in the lofty attitude where souls
Who supplicate God's grace are lifted, there
Thou shalt find help to bear thy daily lot
Which is not elsewhere found.

b. GENERAL PRAYERS

DESIRE

MATTHEW ARNOLD

Thou, who dost dwell alone;
Thou, who dost know thine own,
Thou, to whom all are known,
From the cradle to the grave,—
Save, O Save!

From the world's temptations,
From tribulations,
From that fierce anguish
Wherein we languish,
From that torpor deep
Wherein we lie asleep,
Heavy as death, cold as the grave,—
Save, O Save!

When the soul, growing clearer,
Sees God no nearer;
When the soul, mounting higher,
To God comes no nigher;
But the arch-fiend Pride
Mounts at her side,
Foiling her high emprise,
Sealing her eagle eyes,
And when she fain would soar,
Makes idols to adore,
Changing the pure emotion
Of her high devotion
To a skin-deep sense
Of her own eloquence;
Strong to deceive, strong to enslave,—
Save, O Save!

From the ingrained fashion
Of this earthly nature
That mars thy creature;
From grief that is but passion,
From mirth that is but feigning,
From tears that bring no healing,
From wild and weak complaining,—
Thine old strength revealing,
    Save, O Save!

From doubt, where all is double,
Where wise men are not strong,
Where comfort turns to trouble,
Where just men suffer wrong;
Where sorrow treads on joy,
Where sweet things soonest cloy,
Where faiths are built on dust,
Where love is half mistrust,
Hungry and barren, and sharp as the sea—
    O set us free!

O let the false dream fly
Where our sick souls do lie
Tossing continually!
O where thy voice doth come
Let all doubts be dumb,
Let all words be mild,
All strifes be reconciled,
All pains beguiled!
Light bring no blindness,
Love no unkindness,
Knowledge no ruin,
Fear no undoing!
From the cradle to the grave,—
    Save, O Save!

PAGAN PRAYER

ALICE BROWN

You that uphold the world
Uphold me.
You that light the sun,
Make me see,
Bear with me my sorrow:
Help me meet the morrow,
Patiently.

O'er the road we may know not
To end we must fear not,
Guide us, O mighty One!
March with us, heroes!

THE LARGER PRAYER

EDNAH D. CHENEY

At first I prayed for Sight:
  Could I but see the way,
How gladly, swiftly would I walk
  To everlasting day!

And next I prayed for Strength:
  That I might tread the road
With firm, unfaltering feet, and win
  The heaven's serene abode.

And then I asked for Faith:
  Could I but trust my God,
I'd live enfolded in His peace,
  Though foes were all abroad.

But now I pray for Love:
  Deep love to God and man
A living love that will not fail,
  However dark his plan.

And Light and Strength and Faith
Are opening everywhere,
God waited for me till
I prayed the larger prayer.

PRAYER

Thomas Ellwood

Oh! that mine eye might closed be
To what concerns not me to see;
That deafness might possess my ear
To what concerns not me to hear:
That truth my tongue might ever tie
From speaking words of vanity:
That no vain thought might ever rest
Or be conceived within my breast;
So that in deed and word and thought,
Glory may unto God be wrought.
But what are wishes? Lord, mine eye
Is fixed on Thee, to Thee I cry!
Cleanse, Lord, and purify my heart
And make it clean in every part;
And when 'tis pure, Lord keep it so,
For that is more than I can do.

GIFTS

Emma Lazarus

"O World-God, give me Wealth!" the Egyptian cried.
His prayer was granted. High as heaven, behold
Palace and pyramid; the brimming tide
Of lavish Nile washed all his land with gold.
Armies of slaves toiled ant-wise at his feet,
World-circling traffic roared through mart and street,
His priests were gods, his spice-balmed kings enshrined,
Set death at nought in rock-ribbed charnels deep.

Seek Pharaoh's race today and ye shall find
Rust and the moth, silence and dusty sleep.

"O World-God, give me beauty!" cried the Greek.
His prayer was granted. All the earth became
Plastic and vocal to his sense; each peak,
Each grove, each stream, quick with Promethean flame,
Peopled the world with imaged grace and light.
The lyre was his, and his the breathing might
Of the immortal marble, his the play
Of diamond-pointed thought and golden tongue.
Go seek the sunshine race. Ye find today
A broken column and a lute unstrung.

"O World-God, give me Power!" the Roman cried.
His prayer was granted. The vast world was chained
A captive to the chariot of his pride.
The blood of myriad provinces was drained
To feed that fierce, insatiable red heart.
Invulnerably bulwarked every part
With serried legions and with close-meshed Code.
Within, the burrowing worm had gnawed its home,
A roofless ruin stands where once abode
The imperial race of everlasting Rome.

"O Godhead, give me Truth!" the Hebrew cried.
His prayer was granted; he became the slave
Of the Idea, a pilgrim far and wide,
Cursed, hated, spurned, and scourged with none to save.
The Pharaohs knew him, and when Greece beheld,
His wisdom wore the hoary crown of Eld.
Beauty he hath forsworn, and wealth and power.
Seek him today, and find in every land.
No fire consumes him, neither floods devour;
Immortal through the lamp within his hand.

THE POET'S PRAYER

Stephen Philipps

That I have felt the rushing wind of Thee:
That I have run before thy blast to sea;
That my one moment of transcendent strife
Is more than many years of listless life;
Beautiful Power, I praise Thee: yet I send
A prayer that sudden strength be not the end.
Desert me not when from my flagging sails
Thy breathing dies away, and virtue fails:
When Thou hast spent the glory of that gust,
Remember still the body of this dust.
Not then when I am boundless, without bars,
When I am rapt in hurry to the stars;
When I anticipate an endless bliss,
And feel before my time the final kiss,
Not then I need Thee: for delight is wise,
I err not in the freedom of the skies;
I fear not joy, so joy might ever be,
And rapture finish in felicity.
But when Thy joy is past, comes in the test,
To front the life that lingers after zest:
To live in mere negation of Thy light,
A more than blindness after more than sight.
'Tis not in flesh so swiftly to descend,
And sudden from the spheres with earth to blend;
And I, from splendour thrown, and dashed from dream,
Into the flare pursue the former gleam.
Sustain me in that hour with Thy left hand,
And aid me, when I cease to soar, to stand;
Make me Thy athlete even in my bed,
Thy girded runner though the course be sped;
Still to refrain that I may more bestow,
From sternness to a larger sweetness grow.
I ask not that false calm which many feign,
And call that peace which is a dearth of pain.
True calm doth quiver like the calmest star;

It is that white where all the colours are;
And for its very vestibule doth own
The tree of Jesus and the pyre of Joan.
Thither I press: but O do Thou meanwhile
Support me in privations of Thy smile.
Spaces Thou hast ordained the stars between,
And silences where melody hath been:
Teach me those absences of fire to face,
And Thee no less in silence to embrace,
Else shall Thy dreadful gift still people Hell,
And men not measure from what height I fell.

THE UNIVERSAL PRAYER

ALEXANDER POPE

Father of all! In every age,
  In every clime adored,
By saint, by savage, and by sage
  Jehovah, Jove, or Lord!

Thou Great First Cause, least understood,
  Who all my sense confined
To know but this, that thou art good,
  And that myself am blind!

Yet gave me, in this dark estate,
  To see the good from ill;
And, binding nature fast in fate,
  Left free the human will.

What conscience dictates to be done,
  Or warns me not to do,
This teach me more than hell to shun,
  That more than heaven pursue.

What blessings thy free bounty gives,
  Let me not cast away;
For God is paid when man receives;
  To enjoy is to obey.

Yet not to earth's contracted span
  Thy goodness let me bound,
Or think thee Lord alone of man,
  When thousand worlds are round.

Let not this weak, unknowing hand
  Presume thy bolts to throw,
And deal damnation round the land
  On each I judge thy foe.

If I am right, thy grace impart
  Still in the right to stay;
If I am wrong, Oh, teach my heart
  To find the better way!

Save me alike from foolish pride,
  And impious discontent,
At aught thy wisdom has denied,
  Or aught thy goodness lent.

Teach me to feel another's woe,
  To hide the fault I see;
That mercy I to others show,
  That mercy show to me.

Mean though I am, not wholly so,
  Since quickened by thy breath;
Oh, lead me wheresoe'er I go,
  Through this day's life or death.

This day be bread and peace my lot;
  All else beneath the sun
Thou knowest if best bestowed or not,
  And let thy will be done.

To thee, whose temple is all space,—
  Whose altar, earth, sea, skies,—
One chorus let all beings raise!
  All Nature's incense rise!

A LITANY FOR LATTER-DAY MYSTICS

CALE YOUNG RICE

Out of the Vastness that is God
   I summon the power to heal me.
It comes with peace ineffable
   And patience, to anneal me.
Ajar I set my soul-doors
   Toward unbounded Life
And let the infinitudes of it
   Flow through me, vigour-rife.

Out of the Vastness that is God
   I summon the power to still me.
It comes from inner deeps divine
   With destinies that thrill me;
It follows the hush of every wrong;
   And every vain unrest
It banishes; and leaves a bliss
   Before all unpossessed.

Out of the Vastness that is God
   I summon the strength to keep me,
And from all fleshly fears that fret
   With spirit-winds to sweep me.
I summon the faith that puts to flight
   All impotence and ills,
And that, thro' the wide universe,
   Well-being's breath distills.

THE FOOL'S PRAYER

EDWARD ROWLAND SILL

The royal feast was done; the king
   Sought some new sport to banish care,
And to his jester cried: "Sir Fool,
   Kneel now, and make for us a prayer!"

The jester doffed his cap and bells,
  And stood the mocking court before;
They could not see the bitter smile
  Behind the painted grin he wore.

He bowed his head, and bent his knee
  Upon the monarch's silken stool;
His pleading voice arose: "O Lord,
  Be merciful to me, a fool!

"No pity, Lord, could change the heart
  From red with wrong, to white as wool;
The rod must heal the sin; but, Lord,
  Be merciful to me, a fool!

" 'Tis not by guilt the onward sweep
  Of truth and right, O Lord, we stay;
'Tis by our follies that so long
  We hold the earth from heaven away.

"These clumsy feet, still in the mire,
  Go crushing blossoms without end;
These hard, well-meaning hands we thrust
  Among the heart-strings of a friend.

"The ill-timed truth we might have kept—
  Who knows how sharp it pierced and stung!
The word we had not sense to say—
  Who knows how grandly it had rung?

"Our faults no tenderness should ask,
  The chastening stripes must cleanse them all;
But for our blunders—oh, in shame
  Before the eyes of heaven we fall.

"Earth bears no balsam for mistakes;
  Men crown the knave, and scourge the tool
That did his will; but Thou, O Lord,
  Be merciful to me, a fool!"

The room was hushed; in silence rose
  The King, and sought his gardens cool,
And walked apart, and murmured low,
  "Be merciful to me, a fool!"

PRAYER

Henry van Dyke

These are the gifts I ask of thee,
                    Spirit serene—
Strength for the daily task;
Courage to face the road;
Good cheer to help me bear the traveller's load;
And for the hours of rest that come between,
An inward joy in all things heard and seen.

These are the sins I fain would have thee take away—
Malice and cold disdain;
Hot anger, sullen hate;
Scorn of the lowly, envy of the great;
And discontent that casts a shadow gray
On all the brightness of a common day.

A CONFESSION

Paul Verlaine

Translated by Arthur Symons

O my God, thou hast wounded me with love,
Behold the wound that is still vibrating,
O my God, thou hast wounded me with love.

O my God, thy fear hath fallen upon me,
Behold the burn is there, and it throbs aloud.
O my God, thy fear hath fallen upon me,

O my God, I have known all that is vile,
And thy glory hath stationed itself in me,
O my God, I have known all that is vile.

Drown my soul in floods, floods of thy wine,
Mingle my life with the body of thy bread.
Drown my soul in floods, floods of thy wine.

Take my blood that I have not poured out,
Take my flesh unworthy of thy suffering,
Take my blood that I have not poured out.

Take my brow that has only learned to blush,
To be the footstool of thine adorable feet,
Take my brow that has only learned to blush.

Take my hands because they have labored not,
For coals of fire and for rare frankincense,
Take my hands because they have labored not.

Take my heart that has beaten for vain things,
To throb under the thorns of Calvary,
Take my heart that has beaten for vain things.

Take my feet, frivolous travellers,
That they may run to the crying of thy grace,
Take my feet, foolish travellers.

Take my voice, a harsh and lying noise,
For the reproaches of thy penitence,
Take my voice, a harsh and lying noise.

Take mine eyes, luminaries of deceit,
That they may be extinguished in the tears of prayer,
Take mine eyes, luminaries of deceit.

Ah, thou God of pardon and promises,
What is the pit of mine ingratitude!
Ah, thou God of pardon and promises.

God of terror and God of holiness,
Alas, my sinfulness is a black abyss,
God of terror and holiness.

Thou God of peace, of joy and delight,
All my tears, all my ignorances,
Thou God of peace, of joy and delight.

Thou, O God, knowest all this, all this,
How poor I am, poorer than any man,
Thou, O God, knowest all this, all this.

And what I have, my God, I give to thee.

c. PRAYERS OF INVOCATION

VENI CREATOR

Bliss Carman

I

Lord of the grass and hill,
Lord of the rain,
White Overlord of will,
Master of pain,

I who am dust and air
Blown through the halls of death,
Like a pale ghost of prayer,—
I am thy breath.

Lord of the blade and leaf,
Lord of the bloom,
Sheer Overlord of grief,
Master of doom.

Lonely as wind or snow,
Through the vague world and **dim,**
Vagrant and glad I go;
I am thy whim.

Lord of the storm and lull,
Lord of the sea,
I am thy broken gull,
Blown far alee.

Lord of the harvest dew,
Lord of the dawn,
Star of the paling blue
Darkling and gone,

Lost on the mountain height
Where the first winds are stir**red,**
Out of the wells of night
I am thy word.

Lord of the haunted hush,
Where raptures throng,
I am thy hermit thrush,
Ending no song.

Lord of the frost and cold,
Lord of the North,
When the red sun grows old
And day goes forth,

I shall put off this girth,—
Go glad and free,
Earth to my mother earth,
Spirit to thee.

II

Lord of my heart's elation,
Spirit of things unseen,
Be thou my aspiration
Consuming and serene!

Bear up, bear out, bear onward
This mortal soul alone,
To selfhood or oblivion,
Incredibly thine own,—

As the foamheads are loosened
And blown along the sea,
Or sink and merge forever
In that which bids them be.

HYMN TO ZEUS

Cleanthes (From the Greek)

Translated by Plumptre

Most glorious of all the Undying, many-named, girt round with
   awe!
Jove, author of Nature, applying to all things the rudder of
   law,—
Hail! Hail! For it justly rejoices the races whose life is a
   span
To lift unto thee their voices—the Author and Framer of man.
For we are thy sons; thou didst give us the symbols of speech
   at our birth,
Alone of all the things that live and mortal move upon earth.
Wherefore thou shalt find me extolling and ever singing thy
   praise;
Since thee the great Universe, rolling on its path round the
   world, obeys—
Obeys thee, wherever thou guidest, and gladly is bound in thy
   hands,
So great is the power thou confidest, with strong, invincible
   hands,
To thy mighty ministering servant, the bolt of the thunder, that
   flies
Two-edged, like a sword, and fervent, that is living and never
   dies.
All nature, in fear and dismay, doth quake in the path of its
   stroke,

What time thou preparest the way for the one Word thy lips
    have spoke,
Which blends with lights smaller and greater, which pervadeth
    and thrilleth all things.
So great is thy power and thy nature—in the Universe Highest
    of Kings!
On earth, of all deeds that are done, O God! there is none
    without thee;
In the holy ether not one, nor one on the face of the sea;
Save the deeds that evil men, driven by their own blind folly
    have planned;
But things that have grown uneven are made even again by
    thy hand;
And things unseemly grow seemly, the unfriendly are friendly
    to thee;
For no good and evil supremely thou hast blended in one by
    decree.
For all thy decree is one, ever,—a word that endureth for
    aye,
Which mortals, rebellious, endeavor to flee from and shun to
    obey—
Ill-fated, that, worn with proneness for the lordship of all
    goodly things,
Neither hear nor behold, in its oneness, the law that divinity
    brings;
Which men with reason obeying, might attain unto glorious life,
No longer aimlessly straying in the paths of ignoble strife.
There are men with a zeal, unblest, that are wearied with
    following fame,
And men with a baser quest, that are turned to lucre and shame,
There are men, too, that pamper and pleasure the flesh with
    delicate stings;
All these desire beyond measure to be other than all these
    things.

Great Jove, all-giver, dark-clouded, great Lord of the thunder-
    bolt's breath!
Deliver the men that are shrouded in ignorance dismal as death.
O father, dispel from their souls the darkness, and grant them
    the light

Of reason, thy stay, when the whole wide world thou rulest
   with might,
That we, being honored, may honor thy name with the music
   of hymns,
Exalting the deeds of the Donor, unceasing, as rightly
   beseems
Mankind; for no worthier trust is awarded to God or to Man
Than forever to glory with justice in the law that endures and
   is One.

O, THOU ETERNAL ONE!

Derzhavin

Translated by Sir John Bowring

(Secretary of State under Catherine II)

O Thou Eternal One! whose presence bright
All space doth occupy, all motions guide;
Unchanged through time's all-devastating flight:
Thou only God! There is no God beside!
Being of all beings! Mighty One!
Whom none could comprehend and none explore;
Who fillst existence with Thyself alone:
Embracing all, supporting, ruling o'er,—
Being whom we call God, and know no more!

In its sublime research philosophy
May measure out the ocean deeps, may count
The sands or the sun's rays; but God! for thee
There is no weight nor measure: none can mount
Up to thy mysteries. Reason's brightest spark,
Though kindled by thy light, in vain would try
To trace thy counsels, infinite and dark;
And thought is lost ere thought can soar so high.
Even like past moments in eternity.

Thou from primeval nothingness didst call
First chaos, then existence: Lord, on thee

Eternity had its foundation; all
Sprung from thee,—of light, joy, harmony,
Sole origin: all life, all beauty thine.
Thy word created all and doth create;
Thy splendor fills all space with rays divine.
Thou wert and art and shalt be! Glorious! Great!
Light-giving, life-sustaining Potentate!

Thy chains the unmeasured universe surround,
Upheld by thee, by thee inspired with breath!
Thou the beginning with the end hast bound,
And beautifully mingled life and death!
As sparks mount upward from the fiery blaze,
So suns are born, so worlds spring forth from thee,
And as the spangles in the sunny rays
Shine round the silver snow, the pageantry
Of heaven's bright army glitters in thy praise.

A million torches lighted by thy hand
Wander unwearied through the blue abyss:
They own thy power, accomplish thy command,
All gay with life, all eloquent with bliss.
What shall we call them? Piles of crystal light,
A glorious company of golden streams,
Lamps of celestial ether burning bright,
Suns lighting systems with their joyous beams?
But thou to these art as the noon to night.

Yes! As a drop of water in the sea,
All this magnificence in thee is lost:
What are ten thousand worlds compared to thee?
What am I, then? Heaven's unnumbered host,
Though multiplied by myriads, and arrayed
In all the glory of sublimest thought,
Is but an atom in the balance, weighed
Against thy greatness, is a cipher brought
Against infinity! Oh, what am I, then? Nought!

Nought, yet the effulgence of thy light divine,
Pervading worlds, hath reached my bosom. too:

Yes! In my spirit doth thy spirit shine,
As shines the sunbeam in a drop of dew.
Nought! Yet I live, and on hope's pinions fly
Eager toward thy presence; for in thee
I live and breathe and dwell; aspiring high,
Even to the throne of thy divinity.
I am, O God! and surely Thou must be!

Thou art! directing, guiding all, thou art!
Direct my understanding, then, to thee;
Control my spirit, guide my wandering heart:
Though but an atom midst immensity,
Still I am something, fashioned by thy hand!
I hold a middle rank twixt heaven and earth,
On the last verge of mortal being stand,
Close to the realm where angels have their birth,
Just on the boundaries of the spirit land!

The chain of being is complete in me;
In me is matter's last gradation lost,
And the next step is spirit—Deity!
I can command the lightning and am dust!
A monarch and a slave; a worm, a god!
Whence came I here? and how so marvellously
Constructed and conceived? Unknown! This clod
Lives surely through some higher energy;
For from itself alone it could not be!

Creator! yes, thy wisdom and thy word
Created me! Thou Source of life and good!
Thou Spirit of my Spirit, and my Lord!
Thy light, thy love, in their bright plenitude
Filled me with an immortal soul, to spring
Over the abyss of death, and bade it wear
The garments of eternal day, and wing
Its heavenly flight beyond this little sphere,
Even to its source—to thee—its Author there.

O thoughts ineffable! O visions blest!
Though worthless our conceptions all of thee,

Yet shall thy shadowed image fill our breast,
And waft its homage to thy Deity.
God! thus alone my lonely thoughts can soar;
Thus seek thy presence, Being wise and good!
Midst thy vast works admire, obey, adore;
And when the tongue is eloquent no more,
The soul shall speak in tears of gratitude!

INVOCATION

Max Eastman

Truth, be more precious to me than the eyes
Of happy love; burn hotter in my throat
Than passion, and possess me like my pride;
More sweet than freedom, more desired than joy,
More sacred than the pleasing of a friend.

THE PRAYER

Alfred Tennyson

From *In Memoriam CXXXI*

O living will that shall endure
    When all that seems shall suffer shock,
    Rise in the spiritual rock,
Flow through our deeds and make them pure,

That we may lift from out the dust
    A voice as unto him that hears,
    A cry above the conquered years
To one that with us works, and trust

With faith that comes from self-control,
    The truths that never can be proved
    Until we close with all we loved,
And all we flow from. soul in soul.

d. PRAYERS FOR COMFORT IN PROSPECT OF DEATH

A PRAYER IN THE PROSPECT OF DEATH

ROBERT BURNS

O Thou unknown, Almighty Cause
　Of all my hope and fear!
In whose dread presence, ere an hour,
　Perhaps I must appear!

If I have wander'd in those paths
　Of life I ought to shun—
As something loudly in my breast,
　Remonstrates I have done—

Thou know'st that Thou hast formèd me
　With passions wild and strong;
And list'ning to their witching voice
　Has often led me wrong.

Where human weakness has come short,
　Or frailty stept aside,
Do thou, All-Good—for such Thou art—
　In shades of darkness hide.

Where with intention I have err'd,
　No other plea I have,
But, Thou art good; and Goodness still
　Delighteth to forgive.

PRAYER BEFORE EXECUTION

MARY QUEEN OF SCOTS

O Domine Deus! Speravi in te,
O care mi Jesu, nunc libera me!
In dura catena, in misera poena,
　Desidero te!
Languendo, gemendo, et genuflectendo,
Adoro, imploro, ut liberes me!

(Translation by John Fawcett, 1782.)

O merciful Father, my hope is in thee!
O gracious Redeemer, deliver thou me!
My bondage bemoaning, with sorrowful groaning,
   I long to be free;
Lamenting, relenting, and humbly repenting,
O Jesu, my Savior, I languish for thee!

e. PRAYERS FOR GUIDANCE

A PRAYER

JOHN DRINKWATER

Lord, not for light in darkness do we pray,
Not that the veil be lifted from our eyes,
Nor that the slow ascension of our day
    Be otherwise.

Not for a clearer vision of the things
Whereof the fashioning shall make us great,
Not for remission of the peril and stings
    Of time and fate.

Not for a fuller knowledge of the end
Whereto we travel, bruised yet unafraid,
Nor that the little healing that we lend
    Shall be repaid.

Not these, O Lord. We would not break the bars
Thy wisdom sets about us; we shall climb
Unfetter'd to the secrets of the stars
    In Thy good time.

We do not crave the high perception swift
When to refrain were well, and when fulfill,
Nor yet the understanding strong to sift
    The good from ill.

Not these, O Lord. For these Thou hast revealed,
We know the golden season when to reap
The heavy-fruited treasure of the field,
    The hour to sleep.

Not these. We know the hemlock from the rose,
The pure from stained, the noble from the base,
The tranquil holy light of truth that glows
    On Pity's face.

We know the paths wherein our feet should press,
Across our hearts are written Thy decrees:
Yet now, O Lord, be merciful to bless
    With more than these.

Grant us the will to fashion as we feel,
Grant us the strength to labor as we know,
Grant us the purpose, ribb'd and edg'd with steel,
    To strike the blow.

Knowledge we ask not,—knowledge Thou hast lent,
But, Lord, the will,—there lies our bitter need,
Give us to build above the deep intent
    The deed, the deed.

THE CRY OF THE AGE

HAMLIN GARLAND

What shall I do to be just?
What shall I do for the gain
Of the world—for its sadness?
Teach me, O Seers that I trust!
Chart me the difficult main
Leading me out of my sorrow and madness;
Preach me out of the purging of pain.

Shall I wrench from my finger the ring
To cast to the tramp at my door?
Shall I tear off each luminous thing
To drop in the palm of the poor?

What shall I do to be just?
Teach me, O Ye in the light,
Whom the poor and the rich alike trust:
My heart is aflame to be right.

TWO PRAYERS

Charlotte Perkins Gilman

Only for these I pray,
　Pray with assurance strong;
Light to discover the way,
　Power to follow it long.

Let me have light to see,
　Light to be sure and know,
When the road is clear to me
　Willingly I go.

Let me have power to do,
　Power of the brain and nerve,
Though the task is heavy and new
　Willingly I will serve.

My prayers are lesser than three,
　Nothing I pray but two;
Let me have light to see,
　Let me have power to do.

THE ELIXIR

George Herbert

Teach me, my God and King,
　In all things thee to see;
And what I do in anything,
　To do it as for thee.

Not rudely, as a beast,
  To run into an action;
But still to make thee prepossessed,
  And give it his perfection.

A man that looks on glass
  On it may stay his eye;
Or, if he pleaseth, through it pass,
  And then the heaven espy.

All may of thee partake,
  Nothing can be so mean,
Which, with this tincture, for thy sake
  Will not grow bright and clean.

A servant with this clause,
  Makes drudgery divine;
Who sweeps a room as for thy laws,
  Makes that, and the action, fine.

This is the famous stone
  That turneth all to gold;
For that which God doth touch and own
  Cannot for less be told.

THE PILLAR OF THE CLOUD

John Henry Newman

Lead, kindly light, amid the encircling gloom,
  Lead thou me on!
The night is dark and I am far from home;
  Lead thou me on!
Keep thou my feet; I do not ask to see
The distant scene; one step enough for me.

I was not ever thus, nor prayed that thou
  Shouldst lead me on;
I loved to choose and see my path; but now
  Lead thou me on!
I loved the garish day, and, spite of fears
Pride ruled my will: remember not past years!

So long thy power has blest me, sure it still
  Will lead me on
O'er moor and fen, o'er crag and torrent till
  The night is gone,
And with the morn those angel faces smile
Which I have loved long since and lost awhile!

THE MYSTIC'S PRAYER

WILLIAM SHARP (*Fiona Macleod*)

Lay me to sleep in sheltering flame
  O Master of the Hidden Fire!
Wash pure my heart, and cleanse for me
  My soul's desire.

In flame of sunrise bathe my mind,
  O Master of the Hidden Fire,
That, when I wake, clear-eyed may be
  My soul's desire.

THE INWARD LIGHT

HENRY SEPTIMUS SUTTON

I have a little inward light, which still
All tenderly I keep, and ever will.
I think it never wholly dies away;
But oft it seems as if it could not stay,
And I do strive to keep it if I may.

Sometimes the wind gusts push it sore aside:
Then closely to my breast my light I hide,
And for it make a tent of my two hands,
And though it scarce might on the lamp abide,
It soon recovers and uprightly stands.

Sometimes it seems there is no flame at all;
I look quite close, because it is so small:
Then all for sorrow do I weep and sigh;
But Some One seems to listen when I cry,
And the light burns up and I know not why.

O God! O Father! hear thy child who cries!
Who would not quench thy flame; who would not dare
To let it dwindle in a sinful air;
Who does feel how all-precious such a prize,
And yet, alas! is feeble and not wise.

Oh, hear, dear Father! For thou knowst the need:
Thou knowst what awful height there is in Thee,—
How very low I am; oh, do Thou feed
Thy light, that it burn ever, and succeed
My life to deepest holiness to lead.

f. PRAYERS OF GRATITUDE

A THANKSGIVING TO GOD

Robert Herrick

Lord, thou hast given me a cell
   Wherein to dwell;
A little house, whose humble roof
   Is weather-proof;
Under the sparres of which I lie,
   Both soft and drie;
Where thou, my chamber for to ward,
   Hast set a guard
Of harmless thoughts, to watch and keep
   Me while I sleep.
Low is my porch, as is my Fate,
   Both void of state;
And yet the threshold of my door,
   Is worn by the poore,
Who hither come and freely get
   Good words, or meat:
Like as my parlour, so my hall
   And kitchen's small;
A little butterie, and therein
   A little bin,

Which keeps my little loaf of bread
  Unchipt, unflead:
Some brittle sticks of thorn and brier
  Make me a fire,
Close by whose loving coals I sit,
  And glow like it.
Lord I confess, too, when I dine
  The pulse is thine,
And all those other bits that bee
  There placed by Thee;
The worts, the purslane and the messe
  Of watercresse,
Which of thy kindness thou hast sent;
  And my content
Makes those and my belovèd beet
  To be more sweet.
'Tis Thou that crownst my glittering hearth
  With guiltless mirth;
And giv'st me wassaile bowles to drink,
  Spiced to the brink.
Lord 'tis Thy plenty-dropping hand
  That soiles my land,
And giv'st me for my bushel sowne
  Twice ten for one:
Thou mak'st my teeming hen to lay
  Her egg each day;
Beside my healthful ewes to bear
  Me twins each yeare;
The while the conduits of my kine
  Run creame for wine.

All these and better thou dost send
  Me to this end,—
That I should render, for my part,
  A thankful heart;
Which, fired with incense, I resigne
  As wholly Thine;
But the acceptance, that must be,
  MY CHRIST, by thee.

A PRAYER

William Dean Howells

Lord, for the erring thought
Not into evil wrought;
Lord, for the wicked will,
Betrayed and baffled still;
For the heart from itself kept,
Our thanksgiving accept!
For ignorant hopes that were
Broken at our blind prayer;
For pain, death, sorrow sent,
Unto our chastisement;
For all loss of seeming good,
Quicken our gratitude!

PRAYER

Harry Kemp

I kneel not now to pray that Thou
  Make white one single sin,—
I only kneel to thank the Lord
  For what I have not been;

For deeds which sprouted in my heart
  But ne'er to bloom were brought,
For monstrous vices which I slew
  In the shambles of my thought—

Dark deeds the world has never guessed
  By hell and passion bred,
Which never grew beyond the bud
  That cankered in my head.

Some said I was a righteous man—
  Poor fools! the gallows tree
(If Thou hadst let one foot to slip)
  Had held a limb for me.

So for the man I might have been
  My heart must cease to mourn,
'Twere best to praise the living God
  For monsters never born;

To bend—the spiritual knee
  (Knowing myself within)
And thank the kind, benignant God
  For what I have not been!

GOD, YOU HAVE BEEN TOO GOOD TO ME

CHARLES WHARTON STORK

God, you have been too good to me,
You don't know what you've done.
A clod's too small to drink in all
The treasure of the sun.

The pitcher fills the lifted cup
And still the blessings pour
They overbrim the shallow rim
With cool refreshing store.

You are too prodigal with joy,
Too careless of its worth,
To let the stream with crystal gleam
Fall wasted on the earth.

Yet many thirsty lips draw near
And quaff the greater part!
There still will be too much for me
To hold in one glad heart.

g.   WAR PRAYERS

VICARIOUS ATONEMENT

RICHARD ALDINGTON

There is an old and very cruel god

.   .   .   .

We will endure;
We will try not to wince
When he crushes and rends us.

If indeed it is for your sakes,
If we perish or moan in torture,
Or stagger under sordid burdens
That you may live—
Then we can endure.

If our wasted blood
Makes bright the page
Of poets yet to be;
If this our tortured life
Saved from destruction's nails
Gold words of a Greek long dead;
Then we can endure,
Then hope,
Then watch the sun rise
Without utter bitterness.
But, O thou old and very cruel god,
Take if thou canst,
This bitter cup from us.

PRAYER

Gilbert Keith Chesterton

O God of earth and altar,
Bow down and hear our cry,
Our earthly rulers falter,
Our people drift and die;
The walls of gold entomb us,
The swords of scorn divide,
Take not Thy thunder from us
But take away our pride!

From all that terror teaches,
From lies of tongue and pen,
From all the easy speeches
That comfort cruel men,
From sale and profanation
Of honor and the sword,
From sleep and from damnation
Deliver us, Good Lord!

Tie in a living tether
The priest and prince and thrall,
Bind all our lives together,
Smite us and save us all;
From ire and exultation
A-flame with faith and free
Lift up a living nation
A single sword to thee!

BEFORE ACTION

WILLIAM NOEL HODGSON

By all the glories of the day,
And the cool evening's benison;
By the last sunset touch that lay
Upon the hills when the day was done:
By beauty lavishly outpoured,
And blessing carelessly received,
By all the days that I have lived,
Make me a soldier, Lord.

By all of all men's hopes and fears,
And all the wonders poets sing,
The laughter of unclouded years,
And every sad and lovely thing:
By the romantic ages stored
With high endeavor that was his,
By all his mad catastrophes,
Make me a man, O Lord.

I, that on my familiar hill,
Saw with uncomprehending eyes
A hundred of thy sunsets spill
Their fresh and sanguine sacrifice,
Ere the sun swings his noon-day sword
Must say goodbye to all of this:—
By all delights that I shall miss,
Help me to die, O Lord!

A PRAYER OF THE PEOPLES

Percy Mackaye

God of us who kill our kind!
Master of this blood-tracked Mind
Which from wolf and Caliban
Staggers toward the star of man—
Now, on Thy cathedral stair,
God, we cry to Thee in prayer!

Where our stifled anguish bleeds
Strangling through Thine organ reeds,
Where our voiceless songs suspire
From the corpses in Thy choir—
Through Thy charred and shattered nave,
God, we cry on Thee to save!

Save us from our tribal gods!
From the racial powers, whose rods—
Wreathed with stinging serpents—stir
Odin and old Jupiter
From their ancient hells of hate
To invade Thy dawning state.

Save us from their curse of kings!
Free our souls' imaginings
From the feudal dreams of war;
Yea, God, let us nevermore
Make, with slaves idolatry
Kaiser, King or Czar of *Thee!*

We who, craven in our prayer,
Would lay off on Thee our care—
Lay instead on *us* Thy load;
On our minds Thy spirit's goad,
On our laggard wills Thy whips
And Thy passion on our lips!

Fill us with the reasoned faith
That the prophet lies, who saith

All this web of destiny,
Torn and tangled, cannot be
Newly wove and redesigned
By the Godward human mind.

Teach us: so, no more to call
Guidance supernatural
To our help, but—heart and will—
Know ourselves responsible
For our world of wasted good
And our blinded brotherhood.

Lord, our God! to whom from clay,
Blood and mire, Thy peoples pray—
Not from Thy cathedral's stair
Thou hearest:—Thou criest *through* our prayer
For our prayer is but the gate:
We, who pray, ourselves are fate.

h. PRAYERS FOR SPECIAL THINGS

FOR INSPIRATION

MICHELANGELO BUONAROTTI

Translated by William Wordsworth

The prayers I make will then be sweet indeed,
  If thou the spirit give by which I pray;
  My unassisted heart is barren clay,
Which of its native self can nothing feed;
Of good and pious works thou art the seed
  Which quickens where thou say'st it may;
  Unless thou show us then thine own true way,
No man can find it! Father, Thou must lead!
Do thou, then, breathe those thoughts into my mind
  By which such virtue may in me be bred
  That in thy holy footsteps I may tread:
The fetters of my tongue do thou unbind,
  That I may have the power to sing of thee
  And sound thy praises everlastingly.

A VOYAGER'S PRAYER

CHIPPEWA INDIANS

Translated by Tanner

O Great Spirit!
Thou hast made this lake;
Thou hast also created us as Thy children;
Thou art able to make this water calm
Until we have safely passed over.

FOR FORGIVENESS

JOHN DONNE

Wilt thou forgive that sin where I begun,
  Which was my sin, though it were done before?
Wilt thou forgive that sin, through which I run
  And do run still, though still I do deplore?
    When Thou hast done, Thou hast not done;
      For I have more.

Wilt Thou forgive that sin which I have won
  Others to sin, and made my sins their door?
Wilt Thou forgive that sin which I did shun
  A year or two, but wallowed in a score?
    When Thou hast done, Thou hast not done;
      For I have more.

I have a sin of fear, that when I have spun
  My last thread, I shall perish on the shore;
But swear by thyself, that at my death Thy Son
  Shall shine as He shines now and heretofore;
    And, having done that, Thou hast done;
      I fear no more.

TO A SACRED COW

EAST INDIAN TODA

Translated by W. E. Mashiel

What a fine cow your predecessor was!
How well she supported us with her milk!
Will you not supply us in like manner?
You are a God amongst us—
Do not let the sacred place go to ruin;
Let one become a thousand:
Let all be well:
Let us have plenty of milk!

PRAYER FOR RAIN

KALEVALA

(From the Finnish)

Rise, O earth, from out thy slumber,
Field of the Creator, rouse thee,
Make the blade arise and flourish,
Let the stalks grow up and lengthen,
That the ears may grow by thousands,
Yet a hundredfold increasing,
By my ploughing and my sowing,
In return for all my labour.
Ukko, then, of Gods the highest,
Father, thou in heaven abiding,
Thou to whom the clouds are subject,
Of the scattered clouds the ruler,
All thy clouds do thou assemble,
In the light make clear thy counsel,
Send thou forth a cloud from eastward,
In the north-west let one gather,

Send thou others from the westward,
Let them drive along from southward,
Send the light rain forth from heaven,
Let the clouds distil with honey,
That the corn may sprout up strongly,
And the stalks may wave and rustle.
Ukko, then, of Gods the highest,
Father of the highest heaven,
Heard, and all the clouds assembled,
In the light made clear his counsel,
And he sent a cloud from eastward,
In the north-west let one gather,
Others, too, he sent from westward,
Let them drive along from southward,
Linked them edge to edge together,
And he closed the rifts between them,
Then he sent the rain from heaven,
And the clouds distilled sweet honey,
That the corn might sprout up stronger,
And the stalks might wave and rustle,
Thus the sprouting germ was nourished,
And the rustling stalks grew upward,
From the soft earth of the cornfield,
Though the toil of Vainamoinen.

EPITAPH

George MacDonald

Here lie I, Martin Elginbrodde;
Hae mercy o' my soul, Lord God,
As I wad do, were I Lord God,
An' ye were Martin Elginbrodde.

PRAYER TO THE MOUNTAIN SPIRIT

Navajo Indians

Translated by Cronyn

Lord of the Mountain,
Reared with the mountain,
Young man, Chieftain,
Hear a young man's prayer!
Hear a prayer for cleanness.
Keeper of the strong rain,
Drumming on the mountain;
Lord of the small rain
That restores the earth in newness;
Keeper of the clean rain,
Hear a prayer for wholeness.

Young man, Chieftain,
Hear a prayer for fleetness.
Keeper of the deer's way,
Reared among the eagles,
Clear my feet of slothness.
Keeper of the paths of men,
Hear a prayer for straightness.

Hear a prayer for courage.
Lord of the peaks,
Reared amid the thunders;
Keeper of the headlands
Holding up the harvest,
Keeper of the strong rocks
Hear a prayer for staunchness
Young man, Chieftain,
Spirit of the Mountain!

PRAYER FOR PAIN

John G. Neihardt

I do not pray for peace nor ease,
Nor truce from sorrow:

No suppliant on servile knees
  Begs here against tomorrow!

Lean flame against lean flame we flash,
  O Fates that meet me fair;
Blue steel against blue steel we clash—
  Lay on, and I shall dare!

But Thou of deeps the awful Deep,
  Thou Breather in the clay,
Grant this my only prayer—Oh, keep
  My soul from turning gray!

For until now, whatever wrought
  Against my sweet desires,
My days were smitten harps strung taut,
  My nights were slumberous lyres.

And howsoe'er the hard blow rang
  Upon my battered shield,
Some lark-like, soaring spirit sang
  Above my battlefield.

And through my soul of stormy night
  The zigzag blue flame ran.
I asked no odds—I fought my fight—
  Events against a man.

But now—at last—the gray mist chokes
  And numbs me. *Leave me pain!*
Oh, let me feel the biting strokes,
  That I may fight again!

A DANCE CHANT

Osage Indians

Translated by D. G. Brinton

O Wahkonda (Master of Life) pity me!
I am very poor:
Give me what I need:

Give me success against my enemies:
May I be able to take scalps!
May I be able to take horses!

PRAYER

Louis Untermeyer

God, although this life is but a wraith,
  Although we know not what we use;
Although we grope with little faith,
  God, give me the heart to fight—and lose.

Ever insurgent let me be,
  Make me more daring than devout;
From sleek contentment keep me free
  And fill me with a buoyant doubt.

Open my eyes to visions girt
  With beauty, and with wonder lit,—
But let me always see the dirt,
  And all that spawn and die in it.

Open my ears to music, let
  Me thrill with Spring's first flutes and drums
But never let me dare forget
  The bitter ballads of the slums.

From compromise and things half-done,
  Keep me, with stern and stubborn pride;
But when at last the fight is won,
  God, keep me still unsatisfied.

PRAYER OF COLUMBUS

Walt Whitman

A batter'd, wreck'd old man,
Thrown on this savage shore, far, far from home,
Pent by the sea, and dark rebellious brows, twelve dreary months,
Sore, stiff with many toils, sickened, and nigh to death.

I take my way along the island's edge,
Venting a heavy heart.

I am too full of woe!
Haply I may not live another day;
I cannot rest, O God, I cannot eat or drink or sleep,
Till I put forth myself, my prayer, once more to Thee,
Breathe, bathe myself once more in Thee, commune with Thee,
Report myself once more to Thee.

Thou knowest my years entire, my life,
(My long and crowded life of active work, not adoration merely),
Thou knowest the prayers and vigils of my youth,
Thou knowest my manhood's solemn and visionary meditations,
Thou knowest how, before I commenced, I devoted all to come
    to Thee,
Thou knowest I have in age ratified all those vows, and strictly
    kept them,
Thou knowest I have not once lost nor faith nor ecstasy in Thee,
In shackles, prison'd, in disgrace, repining not,
Accepting all from Thee, as duly come from Thee.

All my emprises have been filled with Thee,
My speculations, plans, begun and carried on in thoughts of
    Thee,
Sailing the deep or journeying the land for Thee;
Intentions, purports, aspirations mine—leaving results to Thee.

O I am sure they really come from Thee!
The urge, the ardor, the unconquerable will,
The potent, felt, interior command, stronger than words,
A message from the Heavens whispering to me even in sleep.
These sped me on.

By me and these the work so far accomplished (for what has
    been, has been),
By me earth's elder cloyed and stifled lands, uncloyed, unloosed.
By me the hemispheres rounded and tied, the unknown to the
    known.

The end I know not, it is all in Thee;
Or small or great I know not—haply what broad fields, what
    lands,

Haply the brutish measureless human undergrowth I know,
Transplanted there may rise to stature, knowledge worthy Thee.
Haply the swords I know may there indeed be turned to reaping-
     tools;
Haply the lifeless cross I know, Europe's dead cross, may bud
     and blossom there.

One effort more, my altar this bleak sand;
That Thou, O God, my life hast lighted,
With ray of light, steady, ineffable, vouchsafed of Thee,
(Light rare, untellable, lighting the very light!
Beyond all signs, descriptions, languages!)
For that, O God—be it my latest word, here on my knees,
Old, poor, and paralyzed—I thank Thee.

My terminus near,
The clouds already closing in upon me,
The voyage balked, the course disputed, lost,
I yield my ships to Thee.

Steersman unseen! henceforth the helms are Thine;
Take Thou command—(what to my petty skill Thy naviga-
     tion?)
My hands, my limbs grow nerveless;
My brain feels racked, bewildered;
Let the old timbers part—I will not part,
I will cling fast to Thee, O God, though the waves buffet me;
Thee, Thee, at least I know.

Is it the prophet's thought I speak, or am I raving?
What do I know of life? What of myself?
I know not even my own work past or present;
Dim, ever-shifting guesses of it spread before me,
Of newer, better worlds, their mighty parturition
Mocking, perplexing me.

And these things I see suddenly—what mean they?
As if some miracle, some hand divine unsealed mine eyes,
Shadowy vast shapes smile through the air and sky,
And on the distant waves sail countless ships,
And anthems in new tongues I hear saluting me.

VIII. Worship

VIII. Worship

a. PRE-CHRISTIAN PERIOD

From HYMN TO MARDUK

Assyrian, c. 2000 B.C.

O MIGHTY, powerful, strong one of Ashur,
O exalted prince, first-born of Nu-Dim-Nud,
O Marduk, terrible one, who maketh Eturra to rejoice,
Lord of Esagila, support of Babylon, lover of Ezida,
Protector of all living, patron of E-mahtila, renewer of life,
Protection of the land, benefactor of peoples, far and wide.
Forever the ruler of the shrines,
Forever is thy name acceptable in the mouth of the people,
O Marduk, great lord * * *
By thy illustrious command, Let me live, let me prosper and
Let me honour thy divinity!
When I plan, let me attain (my plan),
Establish truth in my mouth,
Put (?) kindness in my heart,
Return and be established. May they proclaim favours to me!
May my god stand at my right hand!
May my goddess stand at my left hand!
May my god, my benefactor, establish himself at my side,
To give and to command, to hearken and to show favour!
Let the word I speak, when I speak, be propitious.
O Marduk, great lord, command life,
The life of my life do thou command!
When I bow myself before thee joyfully, may I be satisfied!
May Bel be thy light, may Ae make thee to rejoice!

May the gods of the world be tributary to thee!
May the great gods please thy heart!

Another HYMN TO MARDUK

O Marduk, lord of countries, terrible one * * *
Powerful, independent, perfect * * *
Exalted, lofty, whose * * * cannot be changed
   (The next eight lines are too badly broken to translate.)
Lord of the fountains, mountains, and seas, overseer of the
   mountains,
Lord of * * * and fortresses, who directeth the course of the
   rivers,
Bestower of corn and grain (?), grower of wheat and barley
   (?), who maketh the green herb to spring forth.
Thou createst what god and goddess create, in the midst of
   their * * * art thou.
Ruler of Anunnaki, leader of the Igigi,
Wise one, first-born of Ea, creator of all mankind,
Lord art thou, and like a father and a mother in * * * art
   thou,
And thou, like the Sun-god, makest light their darkness.
               (Twenty-four lines omitted.)
O my lord, stand by me at this time, and hear my cry, pronounce
   judgment and determine fate.
The sickness of * * * do thou destroy and the disease of my
   body do thou take away.
O my god and goddess, judge mankind and * * *
By command of thy mouth, may no evil approach me, the magic
   of the sorcerer and sorceress!

PENITENTIAL PSALM TO THE GODDESS ANUNIT

BABYLONIAN, c. 2000 B.C.

IV

May the wrath of the heart of my god be pacified!
May the god who is unknown to me be pacified;
May the goddess who is unknown to me be pacified;
May the known and unknown god be pacified!
May the known and unknown goddess be pacified!
May the heart of my god be pacified!
May the heart of my goddess be pacified!
May the god or goddess known or unknown be pacified!
May the god who is angry with me be pacified!
May the goddess who is angry with me be pacified
The sin which I have committed I know not.
The misdeed which I have committed I know not.
A gracious name may my god announce!
A gracious name may my goddess announce!
A gracious name may my known and unknown god announce!
A gracious name may my known and unknown goddess announce!
Pure food have I not eaten,
Clear water have I not drunk.
An offence against my god have I unwittingly committed.
A transgression against my goddess have I unwittingly done.
O lord, my sins are many, great are my iniquities!
My god, my sins are many, great are my iniquities!
My goddess, my sins are many, great are my iniquities!
Known or unknown god, my sins are many, great are my iniquities!
Known or unknown goddess, my sins are many, great are my iniquities!
The sin, which I have committed I know not.
The iniquity, which I have done, I know not.
The offence, which I have committed, I know not.
The transgression I have done, I know not.
The lord, in the anger of his heart, hath looked upon me.

The god, in the wrath of his heart, hath visited me.

The goddess hath become angry with me, and hath grievously stricken me.

The known or unknown god hath straitened me.

The known or unknown goddess hath brought affliction upon me.

I sought for help, but no one taketh my hand.

I wept, but no one came to my side.

I utter cries, but no one hearkens to me.

I am afflicted, I am overcome, I do not look up.

Unto my merciful god I turn, I make supplication.

I kiss the feet of my goddess and * * *

To known and unknown god, I make supplication.

To known and unknown goddess, I make supplication.

O lord, look with favour upon me, receive my supplication!

O goddess, look with favour upon me, receive my supplication!

Known and unknown god * * *

Known and unknown goddess * * *

How long, my god * * *

How long, my goddess, until thy face be burned toward me?

How long, known or unknown god, until the anger of thy heart be pacified?

How long, known or unknown goddess, until thy unfriendly heart be pacified?

Mankind is perverted and has no judgment.

Of all men who are alive, who knows anything?

They do not know whether they do good or evil.

O lord, do not cast aside thy servant!

He is cast into the mire; take his hand.

The sin which I have sinned, turn to mercy!

The iniquity which I have committed, let the wind carry away!

My many transgressions tear off like a garment!

My god, my sins are seven times seven; forgive my sins!

My goddess, my sins are seven times seven; forgive my sins!

Known and unknown god, my sins are seven times seven; forgive my sins;

Known and unknown goddess, my sins are seven times seven; forgive my sins!

Forgive my sins and I will humble myself before thee.

May thy heart, as the heart of a mother who hath borne children,
be glad!
As a mother who hath borne children, as a father who hath
begotten (them), may it be glad!

PENITENTIAL PSALM

BABYLONIAN, c. 2000 B.C.

Suppliant:

I, thy servant, full of sighs, cry unto thee.
Thou acceptest the fervent prayer of him who is burdened
with sin.
Thou lookest upon a man and that man lives.
O potentate of the world, mistress of mankind!
Merciful one, to whom it is good to turn, who accepteth
supplication!

Priest:

His god and his goddess being angry with him he crieth
unto thee.
Turn thy face toward him and take his hand.

Suppliant:

Besides thee there is no god who guideth aright.
Look with true favour upon me and accept my supplication.
Declare, "how long" (I am to wait), and let thy liver be
pacified.
When, O my mistress, will thy face be turned?
Like the doves do I moan, in sighs do I abound.

Priest:

With woe and grief, full of sighs, is his soul;
Tears doth he weep, laments doth he pour forth.

* * *

See Buddhist Sisters, Section II. a.

HYMN TO AMEN RA, THE SUN GOD

EGYPTIAN, c. 1700 B.C.

Translated by Frank Lloyd Griffith

Praise of Amen Ra!
The bull in Heliopolis, the chief of all the gods,
The beautiful and beloved god
Who giveth life to all warm-blooded things,
To all manner of goodly cattle!

I

Hail to thee, Amen Ra! lord of the thrones of the two lands,
Thou who dwellest in the sanctuary of Karnak.
Bull of his mother, he who dwelleth in his fields,
Wide-ranging in the Land of the South.
Lord of the Mezau, ruler of Pent,
Prince of heaven, heir of earth,
Lord of all things that exist!
Alone in his exploits even amongst the gods,
The goodly bull of the Ennead of the gods,
Chiefest of all the gods,
Lord of truth, father of the gods,
Maker of men, creator of animals,
Lord of the things which are, maker of fruit trees,
Maker of pasture, who causeth the cattle to live!
Image made by Ptah, youth fair of love!
The gods give praise unto him;
Maker of things below and of things above, he illuminateth the
    two lands;
He traverseth the sky in peace.
King of Upper and Lower Egypt, Ra the Justified, chief of the
    two lands.
Great one of valor, lord of awe;
Chief, making the earth in its entirety!
Nobler in thy ways than any god,
The gods rejoice in his beauties!

To him are given acclamations in the Great House,
Glorious celebrations in the House of Flame;
The gods love his odor when he cometh from Punt.
Prince of the dew, he entereth the land of the Mezau!
Fair of face, coming to the Divine Land!
    The gods gather as dogs at his feet,
Even as they recognize his majesty as their lord.
Lord of fear, great one of terror,
Great of soul, lordly in manifestations,
Flourishing of offerings, maker of plenty,
Acclamations to thee, maker of the gods,
Thou who dost upraise the sky, and press down the ground!

·   ·   ·   ·   ·   ·   ·   ·   ·   ·   ·   ·   ·   ·

III

    Ra, exalted in Karnak!
Great of splendor in the House of the Obelisk
Ani, lord of the New Moon festival,
To whom are celebrated the festival of the sixth day and of the
        quarter month.
Liege lord, to whom Life, Prosperity, Health! lord of all the
        gods,
Who see him (?) in the midst of the horizon,
Chief over the Pat and Hades,
His name is more hidden than his birth,
In his name of Amen, the hidden One.
    Hail to thee who art in peace!
Lord of enlargement of heart, lordly in manifestations,
Lord of the uraeus crown, with lofty double plume;
Fair of diadem, with lofty white crown!
The gods love the sight of thee,
The Sekhemt crown is established upon thy forehead.
Thy loveliness is shed abroad over the two lands;
Thy rays shine forth in the eyes of men; fair for the Pat and
        the Rekhyt is thy rising,
Weary are the flocks when thou art radiant.
Thy loveliness is in the southern sky, thy sweetness in the
        northern sky,
Thy beauties conquer hearts,

Thy loveliness maketh arms to droop,
Thy beautiful form maketh hands to fail;
Hearts faint at the sight of thee.
  Sole figure, who didst make all that is!
One and only one, maker of all that are,
From whose eyes mankind issued,
By whose mouth the gods were created,
Who makest the herbage, and makest to live the cattle, goats,
      swine, and sheep,
The fruit trees for the Henememt.
He maketh the life of fishes in the river,
The fowl of the air,
Giving breath to that which is in the egg;
Making the offspring of the serpent to live;
Making to live therewith the flies,
The creeping things, and the leaping things, and the like.
Making provision for the mice in their holes;
Making to live the birds in every tree,
  Hail to thee, maker of all these!
One and only one, with many arms!
At night wakeful while all sleep,
Seeking good for his flock.
Amen-ra establisheth all things!
Tum Horus of the horizon!
Praises be to thee in that all say,
"Acclamations to thee, for that thou outweariest thyself with us!
Obeisance to thee for that thou didst make us!"
  Hail to thee, from all animals!
Acclamations to thee from every land,
To the height of heaven, to the breadth of earth,
To the depth of the great waters!
The gods bow before thy majesty,
Exalting the mighty spirit that formed them!
They rejoice at the coming of him who begat them!
They say unto thee:—"Come, come in peace!
Fathers of the fathers of all the gods,
Thou who dost upraise the sky and press down the ground."
Maker of that which is, former of those which have being,
Liege lord—to whom Life, Prosperity, Health!—chief of the
      gods.

We adore thy mighty spirit even as thou madest us;
Who were made for thee when thou fashionest us.
We give praises unto thee for that thou outweariest thyself
    with us.
  Hail to thee who didst make all that is!
Lord of truth, father of the gods,
Maker of men, fashioner of animals,
Lord of corn,
Making to live the animals of the desert.
Amen, bull fair of face,
Beloved in Thebes,
Great one of splendors in the House of the Obelisk,
Twice crowned in Heliopolis,
Thou who judgest between the twain in the Great Hall!
  Chief of the great Ennead of the gods,
One and only one, without his peer,
Dwelling in Thebes,
Ani in his divine Ennead,
He liveth on truth every day.
God of the horizon, Horus of the East,
Who hath made the hills that have silver, gold,
Real lapis lazuli, at his pleasure:
Gums and incense are mingled for the Mezau,
Fresh incense for thy nostrils.
Fair of face he cometh to Mezau,
Amen Ra, lord of the throne of the two lands,
He who dwelleth in Thebes,
Ani in his sanctuary.

IV

  Sole King is he, even in the midst of the gods;
Many are his names, none knoweth their number.
He riseth on the horizon of the east, he is laid to rest on the
    horizon of the west.
He overthroweth his enemies
In the daily task of every day;
In the morning he is born each day;
Thoth raiseth his eyes,
And propitiateth him with his benefits;

The gods rejoice in his beauties,
Exalting him who is in the midst of adorers!
Lord of the Sekti and of the Madet bark,
Which traverse for thee Nu in peace!
    Thy crew rejoice
When they see the overthrow of the wicked one,
Whose members taste the knife;
The flame devoureth him;
His soul is more punished than his body;
That Nak serpent, he is deprived of movement.
The gods are in exultation,
The crew of Ra are in peace,
Heliopolis is in exultation,
The enemies of Tum are overthrown.
Karnak is in peace, Heliopolis is in exultation.
The heart of the uraeus goddess is glad,
The enemies of her lord are overthrown;
The gods of Kheraha are in acclamation,
The dwellers in the sanctuaries are in obeisance;
They behold him mighty in his power.
Mighty prince of the gods!
Great one of Justice, lord of Karnak,
In this thy name, "Doer of Justice,"
Lord of Plenty, Peaceful Bull;
In this thy name, "Amen, Bull of his Mother,"
    Making mankind,* creating all that is,
In this thy name of "Tum Khepera,"
    Great hawk, adorning the breast!
Fair of face adorning the bosom.
Figure lofty of diadem.
The two uraei fly on wings before him,
The hearts of men run up to him (like dogs),
The illuminated ones turn toward him.
Adorning the two lands by his coming forth,
Hail to thee, Amen Ra, lord of the throne of the two lands!
His city loveth his rising.
                This is the end,
                    in peace,
                as it was found.

HYMN TO ZEUS

ÆSCHYLUS (From the Greek)

First Chorus from Agamemnon

Zeus,—by what name soe'er
  He glories being addressed,
Even by that holiest name
  I name the highest and the Best.
On him I cast my troublous care,
  My only refuge from despair:
Weighing all else, in Him alone I find
Relief from this vain burden of the mind.

One erst appeared supreme,
  Bold with abounding might,
But like a darkling dream
  Vanished in long past night
Powerless to save; and he is gone
  Who flourished since, in turn to own
His conqueror, to whom with soul on fire
Man crying aloud shall gain his soul's desire—,

Zeus who prepared for men
  The path of wisdom, binding fast
Learning to suffering. In their sleep
  The mind is visited again
With memory of affliction past.
  Without the will, reflection deep
Reads lesson that perforce shall last,
Thanks to the power that plies the sovran oar,
Resistless, toward the eternal shore.

CHORUS FROM ŒDIPUS REX

SOPHOCLES, 490-405 B.C.

Strophe I

Oh, may my constant feet not fail,
Walking in paths of righteousness,
　　Sinless in word and deed,—
　　True to those eternal laws
That scale forever the high steep
Of heaven's pure ether, whence they sprang;—
For only in Olympus is their home,
Nor mortal wisdom gave them birth:
And howsoe'er men may forget,
　　They will not sleep;
For the might of the god within them grows not old.

Antistrophe I

Rooted in pride, the tyrant grows;
But pride that with its own too-much
　　Is rashly surfeited,
　　Heeding not the prudent mean,
　　Down the inevitable gulf
From its high pinnacle is hurled,
Where use of feet or foothold there is none.
But, O kind gods, the noble strength
That struggles for the State's behoof
　　Unbend not yet:
In the gods have I put my trust; I will not fear.

Strophe II

But whoso walks disdainfully
　　In act or word,
And fears not Justice, nor reveres
　　The throned gods,—
　　Him let misfortune slay

For his ill-starred wantoning,
  Should he heap unrighteous gains,
Nor from unhallowed paths withhold his feet,
  Or reach rash hands to pluck forbidden fruit.
    Who shall do this, and boast
    That yet his soul is proof
Against the arrows of offended Heaven?
  If honor crowns such deeds as these,
  Not song but silence, then, for me!

Antistrophe II

To earth's dread centre, unprofaned
    By mortal touch,
No more with awe will I repair,
    Nor Abae's shrine,
    Nor the Olympian plain,
If the truth stands not confessed,
Pointed at by all the world.
    O Zeus supreme, if rightly thou art called
    Lord over all, let not these things escape
      Thee and thy timeless sway!
      For now men set at naught
Apollo's word, and cry, "Behold, it fails!"
  His praise is darkened with a doubt;
  And faith is sapped, and Heaven defied.

b. EARLY CHRISTIAN AND MEDIÆVAL PERIODS

INSPIRATION

Ode VI of Solomon

Translated by J. Rendel Harris

As the hand moves over the harp, and the strings speak,
So speaks in my members the Spirit of the Lord,
And I speak by His love.

For He destroys what is foreign, and everything that is bitter:
For thus it was from the beginning and will be to the end,
That nothing should be His adversary,
And nothing should stand up against Him.

The Lord hath multiplied the knowledge of Himself,
And is zealous that these things should be known,
Which by His grace have been given unto us.
And the praise of His name He gave us:
Our spirits praise His holy Spirit.

For there went forth a stream and became a river great and
    broad;
For it flooded and broke up everything and it brought (water)
    to the Temple:
And the restrainers of the children of men were not able to
    restrain it,
Nor the arts of those whose business it is to restrain waters;
For it spread over the face of the whole earth, and filled
    everything:
And all the thirsty upon earth were given to drink of it;
And thirst was relieved and quenched: for from the Most High
    the draft was given.

Blessed then are the ministers of that draft who are en-
    trusted with that water of His:
They have assuaged the dry lips, and the will that had fainted
    they have raised up;
And souls that were near departing they have brought back
    from death:
And limbs that had fallen they straightened and set up:
They gave strength for their feebleness and light to their eyes:
For everyone knew them in the Lord, and they lived by the
    water of life forever.

                            Hallelujah.

TO TRUTH

Translated by J. Rendel Harris

Ode XXXVIII of Solomon

I went up to the light of truth as if into a chariot:
And the Truth took me and led me:
And carried me across pits and gullies;
And from the rocks and waves it preserved me:
And it became to me an instrument of salvation:
And set me on the arms of immortal life:
And it went with me and made me rest, and suffered me not to
    wander, because it was the Truth;
And I ran no risk, because I walked with Him;
And I did not make an error in anything because I obeyed the
    Truth.

For Error flees away from it, and meets it not:
But the Truth proceeds in the right path,
And whatever I did not know, it made clear to me,
All the poisons of error, and the plagues which announce the
    fear of death
And I saw the destroyer of destruction, when the bride who is
    corrupted is adorned;
And the bridegroom who corrupts and is corrupted;
And I asked the Truth, "Who are these?"
And He said to me, This is the deceiver and the error:
And they are alike in the beloved and in His bride:
And they lead astray and corrupt the (whole) world:
And they invite many to the banquet,
And give them to drink the wine of their intoxication,
And remove their wisdom and knowledge,
And (so they) make them without intelligence;
And then they leave them;
And then these go about like madmen corrupting:
Seeing that they are without heart, nor do they seek it.

And I was made wise so as not to fall into the hands of the
    Deceiver;
And I rejoiced in myself because the Truth went with me,

And I was established and lived and was redeemed,
And my foundations were laid on the hand of the Lord:
Because He established me.
For He set the root and watered it and fixed it and blessed it;
And its fruits are forever,
It struck deep and sprung up and spread out, and was full and
    enlarged;
And the Lord alone was glorified in His planting and in His
    husbandry:
By His care and the blessing of His lips, by the beautiful
    planting
              Of His right-hand:
And by the discovery of His planting and by the thought of
    His mind.
           Hallelujah.

EARLIEST CHRISTIAN HYMN

OF

CLEMENT OF ALEXANDRIA, 1st Cent. A.D.

Translated by E. H. Plumptre

Curb for stubborn steed,
Making its will give heed;
Wing that directest right,
The wild bird's wandering flight;
Helm for the ships that keep
Their pathway o'er the deep;
Shepherd of sheep that own
Their Master on the throne,
Stir up thy children meek
With guileless lips to speak,
In hymn and song, thy praise,
Guide of their infant ways.
O King of saints, O Lord,
Mighty, all-conquering Word;
Son of the highest God
Wielding his wisdom's rod;
Our stay when cares annoy,

Giver of endless joy;
Of all our mortal race
Savior, of boundless grace,
    O Jesus, hear!

Shepherd and Sower, thou,
Now helm, and bridle now,
Wing for the heavenward flight
Of flocks all pure and bright,
Fisher of men, the blest,
Out of the world's unrest,
Out of Sin's troubled sea
Taking us, Lord, to thee;
Out of the waves of strife
With bait of blissful life,
With choicest fish, good store,
Drawing thy nets to shore.
Lead us, O shepherd true,
Thy mystic sheep, we sue,
Lead us, O holy Lord,
Who from thy sons dost ward
With all-prevailing charm,
Peril, curse and harm;
O path where Christ has trod,
O way that leads to God,
O Word abiding aye,
O endless Light on high,
Mercy's fresh-springing flood,
Worker of all things good,
O glorious Life of all,
That on their Maker call.
    Christ Jesus, hear!
O Milk of Heaven, that prest
From full, overflowing breast
Of her, the mystic bride,
Thy wisdom hath supplied;
Thine infant children seek
With baby lips all weak,
Filled with the Spirit's dew
From that dear bosom true,

Thy praises pure to sing,
Hymns meet for thee, our King,
   For Thee, the Christ;
Our holy tribute, this,
For wisdom, life and bliss,
Singing in chorus meet,
Singing in concert sweet
   The Almighty Son.
We, heirs of peace unpriced,
We, who are born in Christ,
A people pure from stain,
Praise we our God again,
   Lord of our Peace!

DE PROFUNDIS

Out of the depths have I cried unto Thee, O Lord.

Lord, hear my voice; let Thine ears be attentive to the voice of my supplications.

If Thou, Lord, shouldst mark iniquities, O Lord, who shall stand?

But there is forgiveness with Thee, that Thou mayest be feared.

I wait for the Lord, my soul doth wait, and in His word do I hope.

My soul waiteth for the Lord more than they that watch for the morning; I say more than they that watch for the morning.

Let Israel hope in the Lord for with the Lord there is mercy and with Him is plenteous redemption.

And He shall redeem Israel from all his iniquities.

GLORIA IN EXCELSIS

Glory be to God on high, and on earth peace, good-will towards men.

We praise Thee, we bless Thee, we worship Thee, we glorify Thee.

We give thanks to Thee, for Thy great glory.

O Lord God, heavenly King, God the Father Almighty.

O Lord, the only begotten Son, Jesus Christ.

O Lord God, Lamb of God, Son of the Father,

That takest away the sins of the world, have mercy upon us.

Thou that takest away the sins of the world, have mercy upon us.

Thou that takest away the sins of the world, receive our prayer.

Thou that sittest at the right hand of God the Father, have mercy upon us.

For Thou only art holy, Thou only art the Lord.

Thou only, O Christ, with the Holy Ghost, art most high in the glory of God the Father.

MAGNIFICAT

My soul doth magnify the Lord,

And my spirit hath rejoiced in God my Saviour.

For he hath regarded the low estate of his handmaiden: for behold, from henceforth all generations shall call me blessed.

For he that is mighty hath done to me great things; and holy *is* his name.

And his mercy is on them that fear him from generation to generation.

He hath showed strength with his arm; he hath scattered the proud in the imagination of their hearts.

He hath put down the mighty from *their* seats, and exalted them of low degree.

He hath filled the hungry with good things and the rich he hath sent empty away.

He hath holpen his servant Israel, in remembrance of *his* mercy.

As he spake to our fathers, to Abraham, and to his seed forever.

NUNC DIMITTIS

Lord, now lettest Thou Thy servant depart in peace: according to Thy word.

For mine eyes have seen Thy salvation.

Which Thou hast prepared before the face of all people.
A light to lighten the Gentiles; and the glory of Thy people Israel.

TE DEUM LAUDAMUS

ANONYMOUS

We praise thee, O God; we acknowledge thee to be the Lord.
All the earth doth worship thee, the Father everlasting.
To thee all Angels cry aloud; the Heavens, and all the powers therein.
To thee Cherubim and Seraphim continually do cry,
Holy, Holy, Holy, Lord God of Sabaoth;
Heaven and earth are full of the Majesty of thy Glory.
The glorious company of the Apostles praise thee.
The goodly fellowship of the prophets praise thee.
The noble army of martyrs praise thee.
The holy Church throughout all the world doth acknowledge thee;
The Father of an infinite Majesty;
Thine honorable, true, and only Son;
Also the Holy Ghost, the comforter.
Thou art the King of Glory, O Christ.
Thou art the everlasting Son of the Father.
When thou tookest upon thee to deliver man,
    thou didst not abhor the Virgin's womb.
When thou hadst overcome the sharpness of death,
    thou didst open the kingdom of Heaven to all believers.
Thou sittest at the right hand of God, in the Glory of the Father.
We believe that thou shalt come to be our Judge.
We therefore pray thee, help thy servants, whom thou hast redeemed with the precious blood.
Make them to be numbered with thy Saints in glory everlasting.
O Lord, save thy people, and bless thine heritage.
Govern them, and lift them up forever.
Day by day we magnify thee;
And we worship thy Name ever, world without end.
Vouchsafe, O Lord, to keep us this day without sin.
O Lord, have mercy upon us, have mercy upon us.
O Lord, let thy mercy lighten upon us, as our trust is in thee.
O Lord, in thee have I trusted; let me never be confounded.

STABAT MATER

JACOBUS DE BENEDICTIS

At the cross her station keeping,
Stood the mournful mother weeping
  Close to Jesus to the last;
Through her heart His sorrow sharing,
All His bitter anguish bearing,
  Now at length the sword had passed.

Oh, how sad and sore distressed
Was that Mother highly blessed
  Of the sole-begotten One!
Christ above in torment hangs,
She beneath beholds the pangs
  Of her dying glorious Son.

Is there one who would not weep,
Whelmed in miseries so deep,
  Christ's dear Mother to behold?
Can the human heart refrain
From partaking in her pain,
  In that Mother's pain untold?

Bruised, derided, cursed, defiled,
She beheld her tender child
  All with bloody scourges rent,
For the sins of His own nation,
Saw Him hang in desolation,
  Till His spirit forth He sent.

O thou Mother, fount of love!
Touch my spirit from above,
  Make my heart with thine accord;
Make me feel as thou hast felt;
Make my soul to glow and melt
  With the love of Christ my Lord.

Holy Mother! pierce me through;
In my heart each wound renew
    Of my Saviour crucified:
Let me share with thee His pain,
Who for all my sins was slain,
    Who for me in torments died.

Let me mingle tears with thee,
Mourning Him who mourned for me,
    All the days that I may live:
By the cross with thee to stay,
There with thee to weep and pray,
    Is all I ask of thee to give.

Virgin of all virgins best,
Listen to my fond request:
    Let me share thy grief divine;
Let me, to my latest breath,
In my body bear the death
    Of that dying Son of thine.

Wounded with His every wound,
Steep my soul till it hath swooned
    In His very blood away:
Be to me, O Virgin, nigh,
Lest in flames I burn and die
    In His awful judgment day.

Christ, when thou shalt call me hence,
Be Thy Mother my defence,
    Be Thy cross my victory;
While my body here decays,
May my soul Thy goodness praise,
    Safe in Paradise with Thee.

THE DEER'S CRY

St. Patrick, c. 400 A.D.

I arise today
Through a mighty strength, the invocation of the Trinity,
Through a belief in the threeness,
Through confession of the oneness
Of the Creator of Creation.

I arise today
Through the strength of Christ's birth with His Baptism,
Through the strength of His crucifixion with His burial,
Through the strength of His resurrection with His ascension,
Through the strength of His descent for the judgment of Doom.

I arise today
Through the strength of the love of Cherubim,
In obedience of angels,
In the service of archangels,
In hope of resurrection to meet with reward,
In prayers of patriarchs
In predictions of prophets,
In preachings of apostles,
In faiths of confessors,
In innocence of holy virgins,
In deeds of righteous men.
I arise today
Through the strength of heaven:
Light of sun
Radiance of moon,
Splendour of fire,
Speed of lightning,
Swiftness of wind,
Depth of sea,
Stability of earth,
Firmness of rock.

A arise today
Through God's strength to pilot me:

God's might to uphold me,
God's wisdom to guide me,
God's eye to look before me,
God's ear to hear me,
God's word to speak for me,
God's hand to guard me,
God's way to lie before me,
God's shield to protect me,
God's host to save me
From snares of devils,
From temptations of vices,
From every one who shall wish me ill,
Afar and anear,
Alone and in a multitude.

I summon today all these powers between me and those evils,
Against every cruel merciless power that may oppose my body
    and soul,
Against incantations of false prophets,
Against black laws of pagandom,
Against false laws of heretics,
Against craft of idolatry,
Against spells of women and smiths and wizards,
Against every knowledge that corrupts man's body and soul.

Christ shield me today
Against poison, against burning,
Against drowning, against wounding,
So that there may come to me abundance of reward.
Christ with me, Christ before me, Christ behind me,
Christ in me, Christ beneath me, Christ above me,
Christ on my right, Christ on my left,
Christ when I lie down, Christ when I sit down,
        Christ when I arise,
Christ in the heart of every man who thinks of me,
Christ in the mouth of every one who speaks of me,
Christ in every eye that sees me,
Christ in every ear that hears me.

I arise today
Through a mighty strength, the invocation of the Trinity,

Through a belief in the threeness,
Through a confession of the oneness
Of the Creator of Creation.

MORNING HYMN

Gregory the Great, c. 600 A.D.

Translated by Edward Caswall

Lo, fainter now lie spread the shades of night,
And upward spread the trembling gleams of morn;
Suppliant we bend before the Lord of Light,
    And pray at early dawn,

That his sweet charity may all our sin
Forgive, and make our miseries to cease;
May grant us health, grant us the gift divine
    Of everlasting peace.

Father Supreme, this grace on us confer;
And Thou, O son, by an eternal birth!
With Thee, coequal spirit comforter!
    Whose glory fills the earth.

A HYMN

The Venerable Bede, 735 A.D.

Translated by Elizabeth Charles

A hymn of glory let us sing;
New songs throughout the world shall ring;
By a new way none ever trod
Christ mounteth to the throne of God.

The apostles on the mountain stand,—
The mystic mount, in Holy Land;

They with the virgin mother, see
Jesus ascend in majesty.

The angels say to the eleven:
"Why stand ye gazing into heaven?
This is the Savior, this is He!
Jesus hath triumphed gloriously!"

They said the Lord should come again,
As these beheld him rising then,
Calm soaring through the radiant sky,
Mounting its dazzling summits high.

May our affections thither tend,
And thither constantly ascend,
Where, seated on the Father's throne,
Thee reigning in the heavens we own!

Be thou our present joy, Oh Lord!
Who wilt be ever our reward;
And, as the countless ages flee,
May all our glory be in Thee!

THE SOUL'S BITTER CRY

TAMIL SAIVITE SAINTS, Between 600 and 800 A.D.

In right I have no power to live,
   Day after day I'm stained with sin;
I read, but do not understand;
   I hold Thee not my heart within.
O light, O flame, O first of all,
   I wandered far that I might see,
Athihai Virattanam's Lord,
   Thy flower—like feet of purity.

Daily I'm sunk in worldly sin;
   Naught know I as I ought to know;
Absorbed in vice as 'twere my kin,
   I see no path in which to go.

O Thou with throat one darkling gem,
  Gracious, such grace to me accord,
That I may see Thy beauteous feet,
  Athihai Virattanam's Lord.

My fickle heart one love forsakes,
  And forthwith to some other clings;
Swiftly to some one thing it sways,
  And e'en as swiftly backward swings.
O Thou with crescent in Thy hair,
  Athihai Virattanam's Lord,
Fixed at Thy feet henceforth I lie,
  For Thou hast broken my soul's cord.

The bond of lust I cannot break;
  Desire's fierce torture will not die;
My Soul I cannot stab awake
  To scan my flesh with seeing eye.
I bear upon me load of deeds,
  Load such as I can ne'er lay down.
Athihai Virattanam's Lord,
  Weary of joyless life I've grown.

VENI CREATOR SPIRITUS

Attributed to CHARLEMAGNE, 800 A.D.

Translated by Dryden

Creator Spirit, by whose aid
The world's foundations first were laid,
Come, visit every pious mind,
Come, pour thy joys on humankind;
From sin and sorrow set us free,
And make us temples worthy thee.

O source of uncreated light,
The Father's promised Paraclete;
Thrice holy fount, thrice holy fire,

Our hearts with heavenly love inspire;
Come, and thy sacred unction bring,
To sanctify us while we sing.

Plenteous of grace, descend from high,
Rich in thy seven-fold energy!
Thou strength of his Almighty hand,
Whose power does heaven and earth command;
Proceeding Spirit, our defence,
Who dost the gift of tongues dispense,
And crownedst thy gift with eloquence!

Refine and purge our earthly parts:
But, oh, inflame and fire our hearts:
Our frailties help, our vice control;
Submit the senses to the soul;
And when rebellious they are grown,
Then lay thy hand and hold them down.

Chase from our minds the infernal foe,
And peace, the fruit of love, bestow;
And, lest our feet should step astray,
Protect and guide us on the way.

Make us eternal truths receive,
And practice all that we believe:
Give us thyself that we may see
Thy Father and the Son by thee.

Immortal honor, endless fame,
Attend the Almighty Father's name:
The Savior Son be glorified,
Who for lost man's redemption died:
And equal adoration be,
Eternal Paraclete, to thee!

THE FINISHED COURSE

St. Joseph of the Studium, 850 A.D.

Translated by J. M. Neale

Safe home, safe home in port;
    Strained cordage, shattered deck,
Torn sails, provisions short,
    And only not a wreck;
But oh, the joy, upon the shore
To tell our voyage perils o'er!

The prize, the prize secure!
    The wrestler nearly fell;
Bore all he could endure
    And bore not always well;
But he may smile at troubles gone
Who sets the victor's garland on.

No more the foe can harm;
    No more, of leaguered camp,
And cry of night alarm,
    And need of ready lamp;
And yet how nearly he had failed!
How nearly had the foe prevailed!

The lamb is in the fold,
    In perfect safety penned;
The lion once had hold,
    And thought to make an end,
But One came by with wounded side,
And for the sheep the shepherd died.

The exile is at home;
    O nights and days of tears!
O longings not to roam!
    O sins and doubts and fears!
What matters now? O joyful day!
The King hath wiped all tears away!

O happy, happy bride,
  The widowed hours are past!
The bridegroom at thy side
  Thou all his own at last;
The sorrows of thy former cup
In full fruition swallowed up.

HYMN OF SIVAITE PURITANS

10th CENTURY A.D.

When once I knew the Lord,
What to me were the host
Of pagan deities,
Some fixed in temple shrine
Or carried in the crowd;
Some made of unbaked clay,
And some burnt hard with fire?
With all the lying tales
That fill the sacred books,
They've vanished from my mind.

How many flowers I gave
At famous temple-shrines!
How often told my Cede
And washed the idol's head!
And still with weary feet
Encircled Siva's shrines!
But now at last I know
Where dwells the King of Gods,
And never will adore
A temple made by hands.

But yet I have a shrine—
The mind within my breast.
An image too is there—
The soul that came from God.
I offer ash and flowers—
The praises of my heart;

And all the God-made world
Is frankincense and myrrh.
And thus where'er I go
I ever worship God.

STRENGTH, LOVE, LIGHT

KING ROBERT OF FRANCE, c. 1000 A.D.

O Thou almighty Will
Faint are thy children, till
    Thou come with power:
Strength of our good intents,
In our frail hour, Defence,
Calm of Faith's confidence,
    Come, in this hour!

O Thou most tender Love!
Deep in our spirits move:
    Tarry, dear Guest!
Quench thou our passion's fire,
Raise thou each low desire,
Deeds of brave love inspire,
    Quickener and Rest!

O Light serene and still!
Come and our spirits fill,
    Bring in the day:
Guide of our feeble sight,
Star of our darkest night,
Shine on the path of right,
    Show us the way!

Jerusalem, the Golden, Bernard of Cluny, 1145 *A.D.* (*see Section XII*).

JESUS, THOU JOY OF LOVING HEARTS

St. Bernard of Clairvaux (From the Latin) 1150 A.D.

Jesus, thou joy of loving hearts,
    Thou Fount of life, thou Light of men,
From the best bliss that earth imparts,
    We turn unfilled to thee again.

Thy truth unchanged hath ever stood;
    Thou savest those who on thee call;
To them that seek thee, thou art good,
    To them that find thee, all in all.

We taste thee, O thou living Bread,
    And long to feast upon thee still;
We drink of thee the Fountain-head,
    And thirst, our souls from thee to fill.

Our restless spirits yearn for thee,
    Where'er our changeful lot is cast;
Glad, when thy gracious smile we see,
    Blest, when our faith can hold thee fast.

O Jesus, ever with us stay;
    Make all our moments calm and bright;
Chase the dark night of sin away;
    Shed o'er the world thy holy light.

CANTICLE OF THE SUN

Saint Francis of Assisi, 1225 A.D.

Translated by Maurice Francis Egan

Oh, Most High, Almighty, Good Lord God, to Thee belong
    praise, glory, honor and all blessing.
Praised be my Lord God, with all His creatures, and especially
    our brother the Sun, who brings us the day and who brings
    us the light: fair is he, and he shines with a very great
    splendor.

O Lord, he signifies us to thee!

Praised be my Lord for our sister the Moon, and for the stars, the which He has set clear and lovely in the heaven.

Praised be my Lord for our brother the wind, and for air and clouds, calms and all weather, by which Thou upholdest life and all creatures.

Praised be my Lord for our sister water, who is very serviceable to us, and humble and precious and clean.

Praised be my Lord for our brother fire, through whom thou givest us light in the darkness; and he is bright and pleasant and very mighty and strong.

Praised be my Lord for our mother the earth, the which doth sustain us and keep us, and bringeth forth divers fruits and flowers of many colors, and grass.

Praised be my Lord for all those who pardon one another for love's sake, and who endure weakness and tribulation: blessed are they who peacefully shall endure, for thou, O Most High, wilt give them a crown.

Praised be my Lord for our sister, the death of the body, from which no man escapeth. Woe to him who dieth in mortal sin. Blessed are those who die in thy most holy will, for the second death shall have no power to do them harm.

Praise ye and bless the Lord, and give thanks to Him and serve Him with great humility.

HYMN

ST. THOMAS AQUINAS, c. 1250 A.D.

Sing, my tongue, the Saviour's glory,
Of His flesh the mystery sing;
Of the blood, all price exceeding,
Shed by our Immortal King.
Destined for the world's redemption,
From a noble womb to spring.

Of a pure and spotless Virgin
Born for us on earth below,
He, as Man with man conversing,

Stayed the seeds of truth to sow;
Then He closed in solemn order
Wondrously His life of woe.

On the night of that Last Supper,
Seated with His chosen band,
He the paschal victim eating,
First fulfils the Law's command;
Then, as food to all His brethren,
Gives Himself with His own Hand.

Word made flesh, the bread of nature
By His Word to Flesh He turns;
Wine into His Blood He changes:—
What though sense no change discerns,
Only be the heart in earnest,
Faith her lesson quickly learns.

Down in adoration falling,
Lo! the Sacred Host we hail:
Lo! o'er ancient forms departing,
Newer rites of grace prevail:
Faith for all defects supplying,
Where the feeble senses fail.

To the Everlasting Father,
And the Son who reigns on high,
With the Holy Ghost proceeding
Forth from each eternally,
Be salvation, honour, blessing,
Might and endless majesty. Amen.

Songs of Kabir, 1440 *A.D., Translated by Rabindranath Tagore (See Sections V and VI).*

From NANAK AND THE SIKHS

E. INDIAN, c. 1469 A.D.

How shall I address Thee, O God? how shall I praise Thee?
   how shall I describe Thee? and how shall I know Thee?
Saith Nanak, everybody speaketh of Thee, one wiser than the
   other.
Great is the Lord, great is His name; (it is only) what He doeth
   that cometh to pass.
Nanak, he who is spiritually proud shall not be honoured on
   his arrival in the next world.

Praisers praise God, but have not acquired a knowledge of Him,
As rivers and streams fall into the sea, but know not (its
   extent).
Kings and emperors who possess oceans and mountains of
   property and wealth
Are not equal to the worm which forgetteth not God in its
   heart.

Make contentment thine earrings, modesty and self-respect thy
   wallet, meditation the ashes (to smear on thy body).
Make thy body, which is only a morsel for death, thy beggar's
   coat, and faith thy rule of life and thy staff.
Make association with all thine Ai Panth, and the conquest of
   thy heart the conquest of the world.
Hail! Hail to Him,
The primal, the pure, without beginning, the indestructible, the
   same in every age!

One Maya in union (with) God gave birth to three acceptable
   children.
One of them is the creator, the second the provider, the third
   performeth the function of destroyer.
As it pleaseth God, He directeth them by His orders.
He beholdeth them, but is not seen by them. This is very
   marvellous.

Hail! Hail to Him,
The primal, the pure, without beginning, the indestructible, the
    same in every age!

Make continence thy furnace, forbearance thy goldsmith,
Understanding thy anvil, divine knowledge thy tools,
The fear (of God) thy bellows, austerities thy fire,
Divine love thy crucible, and melt God's name therein.
In such a true mint the Word shall be coined.
This is the practice of those on whom God looketh with an eye
    of favor.
Nanak, the Kind One, by a glance maketh them happy.

The air is the Guru, water our father, and the great earth our
    mother;
Day and night are our two nurses, male and female, who set
    the whole world a-playing.
Merits and demerits shall be read out in the presence of the
    judge.
According to men's acts, some shall be near and others distant
    (from God).
Those who have pondered on the Name and departed after the
    completion of their toil,
Shall have their countenances made bright, O Nanak; how many
    shall be emancipated in company with them!

c. REFORMATION PERIOD

HYMN

MARTIN LUTHER, 1521

Translated by Frederick Hedge

A mighty fortress is our God
A bulwark never failing;
Our helper he amid the flood
Of mortal ills prevailing.

For still our ancient foe,
Doth seek to work us woe;
His craft and power are great,
And, armed with cruel hate
On earth has not his equal.

Did we in our own strength confide,
Our striving would be losing,—
Were not the right man on our side,
The man of God's own choosing.
Dost ask who that may be?
Christ Jesus, it is he,
Lord Sabaoth is his name,
From age to age the same,
And he must win the battle.

And though this world, with devils filled,
Should threaten to undo us,
We will not fear for God hath willed
His truth to triumph through us.
The Prince of darkness grim,
We tremble not for him,
His rage we can endure,
For lo! his doom is sure,
One little word shall fell him.

That word above all earthly powers,
No thanks to them, abideth;
The spirit and the gifts are ours
Through Him who with us sideth.
Let goods and kindred go,
This mortal life also;
The body they may kill,
God's truth abideth still,
His kingdom is forever.

HYMN

St. Francis Xavier, 1550

My God, I love thee, not because
  I hope for heaven thereby;
Nor because they who love thee not
  Must burn eternally.

Thou, O my Jesus, thou didst me
  Upon the cross embrace;
For me didst bear the nails and spear,
  And manifold disgrace;

And griefs and torments numberless;
  And sweat of agony;
E'en death itself,—and all for one
  Who was thine enemy.

Then why, O blessed Jesu Christ!
  Should I not love thee well;
Not for the sake of winning heaven,
  Or of escaping hell:

Not with the hope of gaining aught;
  Not seeking a reward;
But as thyself hast loved me,
  Oh, ever-loving Lord!

E'en so I love thee, and will love
  And in thy praise will sing;
Solely because thou art my God,
  And my eternal King.

SALUTATION TO JESUS CHRIST

John Calvin, 1560

I greet thee, my Redeemer sure,
  I trust in none but thee,
Thou who hast borne such toil and shame
  And suffering for me:
Our hearts from cares and cravings vain
  And foolish fears set free.

Thou art the King compassionate,
  Thou reignest everywhere,
Almighty Lord, reign thou in us,
  Rule all we have and are:
Enlighten us and raise to heaven,
  Amid thy glories there.

Thou art the life by which we live;
  Our stay and strength's in thee;
Uphold us so in face of death,
  What time soe'er it be,
That we may meet it with strong heart,
  And may die peacefully.

The true and perfect gentleness
  We find in thee alone;
Make us to know thy loveliness,
  Teach us to love thee known;
Grant us sweet fellowship with thee,
  And all who are thine own.

Our hope is in none else but thee;
  Faith holds thy promise fast;
Be pleased, Lord, to strengthen us,
  Whom Thou redeemed hast,
To bear all troubles patiently,
  And overcome at last.

Children of Eve and heirs of ill,
  To thee thy banished cry;
To thee in sorrow's vale we bring
  Our sighs and misery;
We take the sinners' place and plead:
  Lord, save us, or we die.

Look Thou, our Daysman and High **Priest**
  Upon our low estate;
Make us to see God's face in peace
  Through thee, our Advocate;
With thee, our Savior may our feet
  Enter at heaven's gate.

Lord Jesus Christ of holy souls,
  The Bridegroom sweet and true,
Meet thou the rage of Anti-Christ,
  Break thou his nets in two;
Grant us thy Spirit's help, thy will
  In every deed to do.

SCOTCH TE DEUM

WILLIAM KETHE, 1560

All people that on earth do dwell,
  Sing to the Lord with cheerful voice;
Him serve with mirth, His praise forth **tell**,
  Come Ye before Him and rejoice.

The Lord ye know is God indeed,
  Without our aid He did us make;
We are His folk, He doth us feed,
  And for His sheep he doth us take.

O enter then His gates with praise,
  Approach with joy His courts unto;
Praise, laud, and bless His name always,
  For it is seemly so to do.

For why? the Lord our God is good,
  His mercy is forever sure;
His truth at all times firmly stood
  And shall from age to age endure.

O MOTHER DEAR, JERUSALEM

"F. B. P.," 1583

O mother dear, Jerusalem!
  When shall I come to thee?
When shall my sorrows have an end?
  Thy joys when shall I see?

O happy harbour of God's saints!
  O sweet and pleasant soil!
In thee no sorrow can be found,
  Nor grief, nor care, nor toil.

No murky cloud o'ershadows thee,
  Nor gloom, nor darksome night;
But every soul shines as the sun;
  For God himself gives light.

O my sweet home, Jerusalem,
  Thy joys when shall I see?
The King that sitteth on thy throne
  In His felicity?

Thy gardens and thy godly walks
  Continually are green,
Where grow such sweet and pleasant flowers
  As nowhere else are seen.

Right through thy streets, with silver sound,
  The living waters flow,
And on the banks, on either side,
  The trees of life do grow.

Those trees for evermore bear fruit,
  And evermore do spring:
There evermore the angels are,
  And evermore do sing.

Jerusalem, my happy home,
  Would God I were in thee!
Would God my woes were at an end,
  Thy joys that I might see!

BATTLE HYMN

Gustavus Adolphus, 1630

Translated by Catherine Winkworth

Fear not, O little flock! the foe
Who madly seeks your overthrow;
  Dread not his rage and power:
What though your courage sometimes faints?
His seeming triumph o'er God's saints
  Lasts but an hour.

Be of good cheer; your cause belongs
To him who can avenge your wrongs;
  Leave it to him, our Lord.
Though hidden now from all our eyes,
He sees the Gideon who shall rise
  To save us, and his word.

As true as God's own word is true,
Not earth or hell with all their crew
  Against us shall prevail.
A jest and byword are they grown;
God is with us, we are his own,
  Our victory cannot fail.

Amen, Lord Jesus; grant our prayer!
Great captain, now thine arm make bare;

Fight for us once again!
So shall the saints and martyrs raise
A mighty chorus to thy praise
World without end! Amen.

d. SEVENTEENTH CENTURY

FAIREST LORD JESUS

ANONYMOUS (From the German)

Fairest Lord Jesus
Ruler of all nature
O thou of God and man the Son!
Thee will I cherish,
Thee will I honor,
Thou my soul's glory, joy and crown.

Fair are the meadows,
Fairer still the woodlands,
Robed in the blooming garb of spring;
Jesus is fairer,
Jesus is purer,
Who makes the woful heart to sing.

Fair is the sunshine,
Fairer still the moonlight,
And all the twinkling, starry host;
Jesus shines fairer,
Jesus shines purer,
Than all the angels heaven can boast.

A MYSTIC SONG

ANONYMOUS (From the French)

Translated by Percy Allen

Out for a walk the other day,
I met sweet Jesus by the way.
My heart flies, flies, flies;
My heart toward heaven flies,

He said to me: "Daughter, what seekest Thou?"
"I was seeking thee, Jesus sweet, and now
My heart toward heaven flies;
Humility and Charity,
And also holy Chastity,
My heart flies, flies, flies,
My heart toward heaven flies.

"The gifts of perfect love are they,
Daughter thine shall they be one day."
My heart flies, flies, flies,
My heart toward heaven flies.

THOU ART OF ALL CREATED THINGS

PEDRO CALDERON DE LA BARCA

Thou art the essence of all created things,
O Lord, the essence and the cause,
The source and center of all bliss;
What are those veils of woven light
Where sun and moon and stars unite,
The purple morn, the spangled night,
But curtains which thy mercy draws
Between the heavenly world and this?
The terrors of the sea and land—

When all the elements conspire,
The earth and water, storm and fire—
Are but the sketches of thy hand;
Do they not all in countless ways—
The lightning's flash, the howling storm,
The dread volcano's awful blaze—
Proclaim thy glory and thy praise?
Beneath the sunny summer showers
Thy love assumes a milder form,
And writes its angel name in flowers;
The wind that flies with winged feet
Around the grassy gladdened earth,
Seems but commissioned to repeat
In echo's accents—silvery sweet—
That Thou, O Lord, didst give it birth.
There is a tongue in every flame,
There is a tongue in every wave;
To these the bounteous Godhead gave
These organs but to praise his name!

LET US WITH A GLADSOME MIND

JOHN MILTON, 1623

Let us with a gladsome mind
Praise the Lord for He is kind;
For His mercies aye endure,
Ever faithful, ever sure.

Let us blaze His name abroad,
For of gods He is the God;
Who by all-commanding might,
Filled the new-made world with light

He the golden tressed sun
Caused all day his course to run;
Th' horned moon to shine by night,
'Mid her spangled sisters bright.

He His chosen race did bless,
In the wasteful wilderness;
He hath, with a piteous eye,
Looked upon our misery.

All things living He doth feed.
His full hand supplies their need;
For His mercies aye endure,
Ever faithful, ever sure.

ADAM'S HYMN IN PARADISE

van Vondel (From the Dutch), c. 1640

Translated by Sir John Bowring

O Father, we approach Thy throne,
Who bidst the Glorious sun arise
All-Good, almighty and all-wise,
Great source of all things, God alone!

We see Thee! Brighter than the rays
Of the bright sun, we see thee shine!
As in a fountain divine,
We see thee, endless fount of days!

We see thee who our frame hast wrought
With one swift word, from senseless clay;
Waked with one glance of heavenly ray,
Our never dying souls from naught.

Those souls Thou lightedst with the spark
At Thy pure fire; and gracious still,
Gavst immortality, free will,
And language not involved in dark!

THE RESTLESS HEART

Psalm of the Maratha Saints

E. Indian, 1608-1649

As on the bank the poor fish lies
  And gasps and writhes in pain,
Or as a man with anxious eyes
  Seeks hidden gold in vain,—
So is my heart distressed and cries
  To come to thee again.

Thou knowest, Lord, the agony
  Of the lost infant's wail,
Yearning his mother's face to see.
  (How oft I tell this tale!)
O at thy feet the mystery
  Of the dark world unveil!

The fire of this harassing thought
  Upon my bosom preys.
Why is it I am thus forgot?
  (O, who can know thy ways?)
Nay, Lord, thou seest my hapless lot;
  Have mercy, Tuka says.

ADAM'S MORNING HYMN

John Milton, 1667

From *Paradise Lost*

"These are thy glorious works, Parent of good,
 Almighty, thine this universal frame,
 Thus wondrous fair; thyself how wondrous then!
 Unspeakable, who sitt'st above these heavens,
 To us invisible, or dimly seen

In these thy lowest works; yet these declare
Thy goodness beyond thought, and power divine.
Speak, ye who best can tell, ye sons of light,
Angels, for ye behold him, and with songs
And choral symphonies, day without night,
Circle his throne rejoicing, ye in heaven,
On earth join all ye creatures to extol
Him first, him last, him midst, and without end.
Fairest of stars, last in the train of night,
If better thou belong not to the dawn,
Sure pledge of day, that crown'st the smiling morn
With thy bright circlet, praise him in thy sphere
While day arises, that sweet hour of prime.
Thou Sun, of this great World both eye and soul,
Acknowledge him thy Greater, sound his praise
In thy eternal course, both when thou climb'st,
And when high noon hast gained, and when thou fall'st
Moon that now meet'st the orient sun, now fliest,
With the fixed stars, fixed in their orb that flies,
And ye five other wandering fires that move
In mystic dance not without song, resound
His praise, who out of darkness called up light.
Air, and ye elements, the eldest birth
Of Nature's womb, that in quaternion run
Perpetual circle, multiform, and mix
And nourish all things, let your ceaseless change
Vary to our great Maker still new praise.
Ye mists and exhalations that now rise
From hill or steaming lake, dusky or gray,
Till the sun paint your fleecy skirts with gold,
In honor to the world's great Author rise,
Whether to deck with clouds the uncoloured sky,
Or wet the thirsty earth with falling showers,
Rising or falling, still advance his praise.
His praise, ye winds, that from four quarters blow,
Breathe soft or loud; and wave your tops, ye pines,
With every plant in every sign of worship wave.
Fountains, and ye that warble as ye flow,
Melodious murmurs, warbling tune his praise.
Join voices, all ye living souls; ye birds

That singing up to heaven-gate ascend,
Bear on your wings and in your notes his praise;
Ye that in waters glide, and ye that walk
The earth, and stately tread, or lowly creep,
Witness if *I* be silent, morn or even,
To hill or valley, fountain or fresh shade,
Made vocal by my song, and taught his praise.
Hail, universal Lord, be bounteous still
To give us only good; and if the night
Have gathered aught of evil, or concealed,
Disperse it, as now light dispels the dark."
So prayed they innocent, and to their thoughts
Firm peace recovered soon and wonted calm.

Book V. Lines 153 to 210.

FROM THE CHORUS OF ATHALIE

JEAN BAPTISTE RACINE, c. 1690

Translated by Charles Randolph

Cho.

The God whose goodness filleth every clime
Let all his creatures worship and adore;
Whose throne was reared before the birth of Time.
To him be glory now and evermore.

One Voice:

The sons of violence in vain
Would check his people's grateful strain,
    And blot his sacred name.
Yet day to day his power declares,
His bounty every creature shares
    His greatness all proclaim.

Another voice:

Dispensing Light and Life at his behest,
Bursts forth the sun by him in splendor drest;
But of almighty love a brighter sign,
Shines forth thy law, pure, perfect and divine.

ADORATION

MADAME GUYON, C. 1700

I love my God, but with no love of mine,
   For I have none to give;
I love thee, Lord, but all that love is thine
   For by thy life I live.
I am as nothing, and rejoice to be
Emptied and lost and swallowed up in thee.

Thou, Lord, alone, art all thy children need
   And there is none beside;
From thee the streams of blessedness proceed;
   In thee the blest abide,
Fountain of life and all-abounding grace,
Our source, our center and our dwelling-place!

e. EVANGELICAL PERIOD (Eighteenth Century)

WHEN I SURVEY THE WONDROUS CROSS

ISAAC WATTS, 1707

When I survey the wondrous Cross,
   On which the Prince of Glory died,
My richest gain I count but loss,
   And pour contempt on all my pride.

Forbid it, Lord, that I should boast,
   Save in the death of Christ, my God;
All the vain things that charm me most,
   I sacrifice them to His Blood.

See, from His head, His hands, His feet,
   Sorrow and love flow mingled down;

Did e'er such love and sorrow meet?
    Or thorns compose so rich a crown?

Were the whole realm of nature mine,
    That were a tribute far too small;
Love so amazing, so divine,
    Demands my soul, my life, my all.

RISE, CROWNED WITH LIGHT, IMPERIAL SALEM RISE!

ALEXANDER POPE, 1712

Rise, crowned with light, imperial Salem rise!
Exalt thy towering head and lift thine eyes!
See heaven its sparkling portals wide display,
And break upon thee in a flood of day.

See a long race thy spacious courts adorn:
See future sons, and daughters yet unborn,
In crowding ranks on every side arise,
Demanding life, impatient for the skies.

See barbarous nations at thy gates attend,
Walk in thy light, and in thy temple bend:
See thy bright altars thronged with prostrate kings,
While every land its joyous tribute brings.

The seas shall waste, the skies to smoke decay,
Rocks fall to dust, and mountains melt away;
But fixed His word, His saving power remains;
Thy realms shall last, thy own Messiah reigns.

JESUS SHALL REIGN WHERE'ER THE SUN

ISAAC WATTS, 1719

Jesus shall reign where'er the sun
Does His successive journeys run;
His kingdom spread from shore to shore,
Till moons shall wax and wane no more.

From north to south the princes meet
To pay their homage at His feet;
While western empires own their Lord,
And savage tribes attend his word.

To Him shall endless prayers be made,
And endless praises crown His head;
His name like sweet perfume shall rise
With every morning sacrifice.

People and realms of every tongue
Dwell on His love with sweetest song;
And infant voices shall proclaim
Their early blessings on his name.

Let every creature rise and bring
Peculiar honors to our King;
Angels descend with songs again,
And earth repeat the loud Amen.

O GOD, OUR HELP IN AGES PAST

ISAAC WATTS, 1719

O God, our help in ages past,
Our hope in years to come,
Our shelter from the stormy blast,
And our eternal home—

Under the shadow of thy throne
Thy saints have dwelt secure;
Sufficient is thine arm alone,
And our defense is sure.

Before the hills in order stood,
Or earth received her frame,
From everlasting thou art God,
To endless years the same.

A thousand ages in thy sight
   Are like an evening gone;
Short as the watch that ends the night
   Before the rising sun.

Time, like an ever-rolling stream
   Bears all its sons away;
They fly, forgotten, as a dream
   Dies at the opening day.

Our God, our help in ages past,
   Our hope in years to come,
Be thou our guard while troubles last,
   And our eternal home.

DIVINE LOVE

CHARLES WESLEY, 1746

Love divine, all love excelling,
   Joy of heaven, to earth come down;
Fix in us thy humble dwelling;
   All thy faithful mercies crown.
Jesus, thou art all compassion,
   Pure, unbounded love thou art;
Visit us with thy salvation,
   Enter every trembling heart.

Breathe, O breathe thy loving spirit
   Into every troubled breast;
Let us all in thee inherit,
   Let us find the promised rest;
Take away the love of sinning,
   Alpha and Omega be,
End of faith, as its beginning,
   Set our hearts at liberty.

Come, Almighty to deliver,
   Let us all thy life receive;
Suddenly return, and never,
   Nevermore thy temples leave.

Thee we would be always blessing;
  Serve thee as thy hosts above;
Pray, and praise thee without ceasing;
  Glory in thy perfect love.

Finish, then, thy new creation,
  Pure and spotless may we be;
Let us see thy great salvation
  Perfectly restored in thee;
Changed from glory into glory,
  Till in heaven we take our place:
Till we cast our crowns before thee,
  Lost in wonder, love, and praise!

JESUS, LOVER OF MY SOUL

Charles Wesley, 1740

Jesus, Lover of my soul,
  Let me to Thy bosom fly,
While the nearer waters roll,
  While the tempest still is high:
Hide me, O my Saviour, hide,
  Till the storm of life is past;
Safe into the haven guide,
  O, receive my soul at last!

Other refuge have I none;
  Hangs my helpless soul on Thee;
Leave, ah, leave me not alone,
  Still support and comfort me!
All my trust on Thee is stayed,
  All my help from Thee I bring;
Cover my defenseless head
  With the shadow of Thy wing.

Thou, O Christ, art all I want;
  More than all in Thee I find:
Raise the fallen, cheer the faint,
  Heal the sick, and lead the blind.

Just and holy is Thy name;
  I am all unrighteousness;
False and full of sin I am,
  Thou art full of truth and grace.

Plenteous grace with Thee is found,
  Grace to cover all my sin;
Let the healing streams abound;
  Make and keep me pure within
Thou of life the fountain art,
  Freely let me take of Thee;
Spring thou up within my heart,
  Rise to all eternity.

CHILDREN OF THE HEAVENLY KING

John Cennick, 1743

Children of the heavenly King,
As ye journey, sweetly sing!
Sing your Saviour's worthy praise,
Glorious in His works and ways!

We are traveling home to God,
In the way the fathers trod:
They are happy now, and we
Soon their happiness shall see.

Lift your eyes, ye sons of light!
Zion's city is in sight:
There our endless home shall be,
There our Lord we soon shall see.

Fear not, brethren; joyful stand
On the borders of your land;
Jesus Christ, your Father's Son,
Bids you undismayed go on.

Lord, obediently we go,
Gladly leaving all below;

Only Thou our leader be,
And we still will follow Thee.

THE CHRISTIAN PILGRIM'S HYMN

WILLIAM WILLIAMS, 1745

Guide me, O thou great Jehovah,
  Pilgrim through this barren land:
I am weak but thou art mighty;
  Hold me with thy powerful hand:
    Bread of heaven! Bread of heaven!
    Feed me now and evermore!

Open now the crystal fountain
  Whence the healing streams do flow;
Let the fiery cloudy pillar
  Lead me all my journey through:
    Strong Deliverer! Strong Deliverer!
    Be thou still my strength and shield.

When I tread the verge of Jordan,
  Bid my anxious fears subside;
Death of deaths, and hell's destruction,
  Land me safe on Canaan's side:
    Songs of praises, songs of praises,
    I will ever give to thee.

Musing on my habitation,
  Musing on my heavenly home,
Fills my soul with holy longing;
  Come, my Jesus, quickly come!
    Vanity is all I see;
    Lord, I long to be with thee!

ADESTE FIDELES

ANONYMOUS, 1751

Translated by Frederick Oakeley

O come, all ye faithful,
  Joyful and triumphant;
O come ye, O come ye to Bethlehem;
  Come and behold Him
  Born, the King of Angels;
  O come, let us adore Him,
  O come, let us adore Him,
O come, let us adore Him, Christ the Lord.

  God of God,
  Light of Light,
Lo! He abhors not the Virgin's womb;
  Very God,
  Begotten, not created;
  O come, let us adore Him,
  O come, let us adore Him,
O come, let us adore Him, Christ the Lord.

  Sing, choirs of angels;
  Sing in exultation,
Sing, all ye citizens of Heav'n above:
  "Glory to God
  All glory in the highest";
  O come, let us adore Him,
  O come, let us adore Him,
O come, let us adore Him, Christ the Lord.

  Yea, Lord, we greet Thee,
  Born this happy morning;
Jesu, to Thee be glory given;
  Word of the Father,
  Now in flesh appearing;
  O come, let us adore Him,
  O come, let us adore Him,
O come, let us adore Him, Christ the Lord.

AWAKE, MY SOUL!

PHILIP DODDRIDGE

Awake, my soul; stretch every nerve,
  And press with vigor on:
A heavenly race demands thy zeal,
  And an immortal crown.

A cloud of witnesses around
  Hold thee in full survey;
Forget the steps already trod,
  And onward urge thy way.

'Tis God's all-animating voice
  That calls thee from on high;
'Tis his own hand presents the prize
  To thine aspiring eye,—

That prize, with peerless glories bright,
  Which shall new lustre boast
When victors' wreaths and monarchs' gems
  Shall blend in common dust.

COME, THOU ALMIGHTY KING

CHARLES WESLEY, c. 1757

Come, Thou almighty King,
Help us Thy name to sing,
  Help us to praise:
Father All-glorious,
O'er all victorious,
Come, and reign over us,
  Ancient of Days.

Come, Thou incarnate Word,
Gird on Thy mighty sword,
  Our prayer attend:

Come, and Thy people bless,
And give Thy word success:
Spirit of holiness,
    On us descend.

Come, holy Comforter
Thy sacred witness bear
    In this glad hour:
Thou who almighty art,
Now rule in every heart,
And ne'er from us depart,
    Spirit of power.

ROCK OF AGES

AUGUSTUS M. TOPLADY, 1776

Rock of Ages, cleft for me,
Let me hide myself in thee;
Let the water and the blood,
From thy wounded side which flowed,
Be of sin the double cure,
Save from wrath and make me pure.

Could my tears forever flow,
Could my zeal no languor know,
These for sin could not atone;
Thou must save and thou alone:
In my hand no price I bring;
Simply to thy cross I cling.

While I draw this fleeting breath,
When my eyes shall close in death,
When I rise to worlds unknown,
And behold thee on thy throne,
Rock of Ages, cleft for me,
Let me hide myself in thee.

CORONATION

(The English Te Deum)

EDWARD PERRONET, 1779

All hail the Power of Jesus' name!
  Let angels prostrate fall;
Bring forth the royal diadem,
  And crown Him Lord of all!

Crown Him, ye martyrs of your God,
  Who from His altar call;
Extol the stem of Jesse's rod,
  And crown Him Lord of all.

Ye seed of Israel's chosen race,
  Ye ransomed from the Fall,
Hail Him who saves you by His grace,
  And crown Him Lord of all.

Sinners, whose love can ne'er forget
  The wormwood and the gall,
Go, spread your trophies at His feet,
  And crown Him Lord of all.

Let every kindred, every tribe,
  On this terrestrial ball,
To Him all majesty ascribe,
  And crown Him Lord of all.

Oh that with yonder sacred throng
  We at His feet may fall,
Join in the everlasting song,
  And crown Him Lord of all!

GLORIOUS THINGS OF THEE ARE SPOKEN

John Newton, 1779

Glorious things of thee are spoken,
  Zion, city of our God;
He, whose word cannot be broken,
  Form'd thee for His own abode;
On the Rock of Ages founded,
  What can shake thy sure repose?
With Salvation's walls surrounded,
  Thou may'st smile at all thy foes.

See, the streams of living waters
  Springing from eternal love,
Well supply thy sons and daughters,
  And all fear of want remove.
Who can faint while such a river
  Ever flows their thirst t'assuage.
Grace, which, like the Lord, the Giver,
  Never fails from age to age?

Round each habitation hovering,
  See the cloud and fire appear
For a glory and a covering,
  Showing that the Lord is near;
Thus deriving from their banner,
  Light by night and shade by day,
Safe they feed upon the manna
  Which he gives them when they pray.

Blest inhabitants of Zion,
  Washed in their Redeemer's blood!
Jesus whom their souls rely on,
  Makes them kings and priests to God.
'Tis his love His people raises
  Over self to reign as kings:
And as priests, His solemn praises
  Each for a thank-offering brings.

HOW FIRM A FOUNDATION

"K." in Rippon's Selections, 1787

How firm a foundation, ye saints of the Lord,
Is laid for your faith in His excellent word!
What more can He say than to you He hath said,
You who unto Jesus for refuge have fled?

"Fear not, I am with thee, O be not dismayed;
I, I am thy God, and will still give thee aid;
I'll strengthen thee, help thee, and cause thee to stand,
Upheld by My righteous, omnipotent hand.

"When through the deep waters I call thee to go,
The rivers of sorrow shall not overflow;
For I will be with thee thy troubles to bless,
And sanctify to thee thy deepest distress.

"When through fiery trials thy pathway shall lie,
My grace, all-sufficient, shall be thy supply,
The flame shall not hurt thee; I only design
Thy dross to consume, and thy gold to refine.

"E'en down to old age all My people shall prove
My sovereign, eternal, unchangeable love;
And when hoary hairs shall their temples adorn,
Like lambs they shall still in My bosom be borne.

"The soul that on Jesus hath leaned for repose,
I will not, I will not desert to his foes;
That soul, though all hell should endeavor to shake,
I'll never, no, never, no, never forsake."

f. NINETEENTH CENTURY

BRIGHTEST AND BEST OF THE SONS OF THE MORNING

REGINALD HEBER, 1811

Brightest and best of the sons of the morning,
  Dawn on our darkness, and lend us thine aid!
Star of the east, the horizon adorning,
  Guide where our infant Redeemer is laid!

Cold on His cradle the dewdrops are shining;
  Low lies His head with the beasts of the stall;
Angels adore Him in slumber reclining,
  Maker and Monarch and Saviour of all.

Say, shall we yield Him, in costly devotion,
  Odors of Edom and offerings divine,
Gems of the mountain and pearls of the ocean,
  Myrrh from the forest, or gold from the mine?

Vainly we offer each ample oblation,
  Vainly with gifts would His favor secure;
Richer by far is the heart's adoration,
  Dearer to God are the prayers of the poor.

Brightest and best of the sons of the morning,
  Dawn on our darkness, and lend us thine aid!
Star of the east, the horizon adorning,
  Guide where our infant Redeemer is laid!

For the Majesty and Mercy of God, by Sir Robert Grant, 1815 (See Section III d).

FROM GREENLAND'S ICY MOUNTAINS

REGINALD HEBER, 1819

From Greenland's icy mountains,
From India's coral strand,
Where Afric's sunny fountains
Roll down their golden sand,
From many an ancient river,
From many a palmy plain,
They call us to deliver
Their land from error's chain.

What though the spicy breezes
Blow soft o'er Ceylon's isle;
Though every prospect pleases,
And only man is vile;
In vain, with lavish kindness,
The gifts of God are strown;
The heathen in his blindness,
Bows down to wood and stone.

Can we, whose souls are lighted
With wisdom from on high,
Can we to men benighted
The lamp of life deny?
Salvation! O salvation!
The joyful sound proclaim,
Till each remotest nation
Has learned Messiah's name.

Waft, waft, ye winds, His story;
And you, ye waters, roll,
Till like a sea of glory,
It spreads from pole to pole;
Till, o'er our ransomed nature,
The Lamb for sinners slain
Redeemer, King, Creator,
In bliss return to reign.

IN THE CROSS OF CHRIST I GLORY

JOHN BOWRING, 1825

In the cross of Christ I glory,
  Towering o'er the wrecks of time;
All the light of sacred story
  Gathers round its head sublime.

When the woes of life o'ertake me,
  Hopes deceive and fears annoy,
Never shall the cross forsake me:
  Lo, it glows with peace and joy.

When the sun of bliss is beaming
  Light and love upon my way,
From the cross the radiance streaming
  Adds more luster to the day.

Bane and blessing, pain and pleasure,
  By thy cross are sanctified;
Peace there is that knows no measure,
  Joys that through all time abide.

In the cross of Christ I glory,
  Towering o'er the wrecks of time;
All the light of sacred story
  Gathers round its head sublime.

ETERNAL LIGHT!

THOMAS BINNEY, 1826

Eternal Light! Eternal Light!
  How pure the soul must be,
When, placed within Thy searching sight
It shrinks not, but, with calm delight
  Can live, and look on thee!

The spirits that surround Thy throne,
　May bear the burning bliss;
But that is surely theirs alone,
Since they have never, never known
　A fallen world like this.

O! how shall I, whose native sphere
　Is dark, whose mind is dim,
Before the Ineffable appear,
And on my naked spirit bear
　That uncreated beam?

There is a way for man to rise
　To that sublime abode:—
An offering and a sacrifice,
A Holy Spirit's energies,
　An Advocate with God:—

These, these prepare us for the sight
　Of Holiness above:
The sons of ignorance and night
May dwell in the Eternal Light,
　Through the Eternal Love! Amen.

FULFILLMENT

WILLIAM A. MUHLENBERG, 1826

Oh, cease, my wandering soul,
　On restless wing to roam:
All this wide world, to either pole,
　Hath not for thee a home.

Behold the ark of God!
　Behold the open door!
Oh, haste to gain that dear abode,
　And rove, my soul, no more.

There safe shalt thou abide
  There sweet shall be thy rest;
And every longing satisfied
  With full salvation blest.

For Who Follows in His Train? *by Reginald Heber.* 1827
(See Section VI d).

THRICE HOLY

REGINALD HEBER, 1827

Holy, Holy, Holy, Lord God Almighty!
  Early in the morning our song shall rise to thee:
Holy, Holy, Holy! Merciful and mighty!
  God in three persons, blessed Trinity!

Holy, Holy, Holy! all the saints adore thee,
  Casting down their golden crowns around the glassy sea;
Cherubim and seraphim falling down before thee,
  Which wert and art and evermore shall be!

Holy, Holy, Holy! though the darkness hide thee,
  Though the eye of sinful man thy glory may not see,
Only thou art Holy, there is none beside thee,
  Perfect in power, in love and purity!

Holy, Holy, Holy! Lord God Almighty!
  All thy works shall praise thy name, in earth and sky and sea:
Holy, Holy, Holy! Merciful and Mighty!
  God in three persons, blessed Trinity!

MY FAITH LOOKS UP TO THEE

RAY PALMER, 1830

My faith looks up to Thee,
Thou Lamb of Calvary,
  Savior Divine;

Now hear me while I pray;
Take all my guilt away;
O, let me from this day
 Be wholly Thine!

May Thy rich grace impart
Strength to my fainting heart,
 My zeal inspire;
As thou hast died for me,
O, may my love to Thee
Pure, warm and changeless be,
 A living fire!

While life's dark maze I tread,
And griefs around me spread,
 Be thou my guide;
Bid darkness turn to day,
Wipe sorrow's tears away,
Nor let me ever stray
 From Thee aside.

When ends life's transient dream,
When death's cold sullen stream
 Shall o'er me roll;
Blest Savior then, in love,
Fear and distrust remove;
O, bear me safe above,
 A ransomed soul!

THE MORNING LIGHT IS BREAKING

Samuel F. Smith, 1832

The morning light is breaking;
 The darkness disappears;
The sons of earth are waking,
 To penitential tears;
Each breeze that sweeps the ocean
 Brings tidings from afar,

Of nations in commotion,
   Prepared for Zion's war.

See heathen nations bending
   Before the God we love,
And thousand hearts ascending
   In gratitude above;
While sinners now confessing,
   The Gospel call obey,
And seek the Saviour's blessing,
   A nation in a day.

Blest river of salvation!
   Pursue thy onward way;
Flow thou to every nation,
   Nor in thy richness stay;
Stay not till all the lowly
   Triumphant reach their home;
Stay not till all the holy
   Proclaim, "The Lord is come!"

THE PILGRIM FATHERS

Leonard Bacon, 1833

Oh, God, beneath thy guiding hand
   Our exiled fathers crossed the sea;
And when they trod the wintry strand,
   With prayer and psalm they worshipped Thee.

Thou heard'st, well pleased, the song, the prayer;
   Thy blessing came and still its power
Shall onward through all ages bear
   The memory of that holy hour.

Laws, freedom, truth, and faith in God
   Came with those exiles o'er the waves,
And where their pilgrim feet have trod,
   The God they trusted guards their graves.

And here thy name, Oh, God of love,
  Their children's children shall adore,
Till these eternal hills remove,
  And spring adorns the earth no more.

THE CHURCH'S ONE FOUNDATION

Samuel J. Stone, 1866

The Church's one foundation
  Is Jesus Christ her Lord;
She is His new creation
  By water and the word;
From heaven He came and sought her
  To be His holy bride;
With His own blood He bought her,
  And for her life He died.

Elect from every nation,
  Yet one o'er all the earth,
Her charter of salvation
  One Lord, one faith, one birth;
One holy name she blesses,
  Partakes one holy food,
And to one hope she presses,
  With every grace endued.

'Mid toil and tribulation,
  And tumult of her war,
She waits the consummation
  Of peace for evermore;
Till with the vision glorious
  Her longing eyes are blest,
And the great church victorious
  Shall be the church at rest.

Yet she on earth hath union
  With Father, Spirit, Son,
And mystic sweet communion
  With those whose rest is won;

O happy ones and holy!
 Lord, give us grace that we,
Like them the meek and lowly,
 On high may dwell with Thee.

NEARER, MY GOD, TO THEE

SARAH FLOWER ADAMS, 1841

Nearer, my God, to Thee,
 Nearer to Thee!
E'en though it be a cross
 That raiseth me;
Still all my song shall be,
Nearer, my God, to Thee,
 Nearer to Thee!

Though like the wanderer,
 The sun gone down,
Darkness be over me,
 My rest a stone;
Yet in my dreams I'd be
Nearer, my God, to Thee,
 Nearer to Thee!

There let my way appear
 Steps unto heaven;
All that Thou sendest me
 In mercy given;
Angels to beckon me
Nearer, my God, to Thee,
 Nearer to Thee!

Then, with my waking thoughts
 Bright with Thy praise,
Out of my stony griefs,
 Altars I'll raise;
So by my woes to be
Nearer, my God, to Thee,
 Nearer to Thee!

Or, if on joyful wing,
  Cleaving the sky,
Sun, moon, and stars forgot,
  Upward I fly,
Still all my song shall be
Nearer, my God, to Thee,
  Nearer to Thee!

HARVEST HOME

HENRY ALFORD, 1844

Come, ye thankful people, come
Raise the song of Harvest Home!
All is safely gathered in,
Ere the winter storms begin;
God, the maker, doth provide,
For our wants to be supplied;
Come to God's own temple, come;
Raise the song of Harvest Home!

What is earth but God's own field,
Fruit unto His praise to yield?
Wheat and tares therein are sown,
Unto joy or sorrow grown;
Ripening with a wondrous power,
Till the final Harvest hour:
Grant, Oh, Lord of life, that we
Holy grain and pure may be.

For we know that thou wilt come,
And wilt take thy people home;
From thy field wilt purge away
All that doth offend, that day;
And thine angels charge at last
In the fires the tares to cast,
But the fruitful ears to store
In thy garner evermore.

Come, then, Lord of mercy, come,
Bid us sing thy Harvest Home!
Let thy saints be gathered in,
Free from sorrow, free from sin;
All upon the golden floor
Praising thee forevermore;
Come, with thousand angels, come;
Bid us sing thy Harvest Home!

ABIDE WITH ME

HENRY F. LYTE, 1847

Abide with me!   Fast falls the eventide,
The darkness deepens: Lord, with me abide!
When other helpers fail, and comforts flee,
Help of the helpless, O, abide with me!

Swift to its close ebbs out life's little day;
Earth's joys grow dim, its glories pass away;
Change and decay in all around I see;
O thou, who changest not, abide with me!

I need thy presence every passing hour;
What but thy grace can foil the tempter's power?
Who, like thyself, my guide and stay can be?
Through cloud and sunshine, Lord, abide with me!

I fear no foe, with thee at hand to bless;
Ills have no weight, and tears no bitterness;
Where is death's sting? where, grave, thy victory?
I triumph still, if thou abide with me.

Hold thou thy cross before my closing eyes;
Shine through the gloom and point me to the skies;
Heaven's morning breaks, and earth's vain shadows flee
In life, in death, O Lord, abide with me!

THERE IS A GREEN HILL FAR AWAY

CECIL F. ALEXANDER, 1848

There is a green hill far away,
  Without a city wall,
Where the dear Lord was crucified,
  Who died to save us all.

We may not know, we cannot tell,
  What pains he had to bear;
But we believe it was for us
  He hung and suffered there.

He died that we might be forgiven,
  He died to make us good,
That we might go at last to heaven,
  Saved by His precious blood.

There was no other good enough
  To pay the price of sin;
He only could unlock the gate
  Of heaven and let us in.

Oh dearly, dearly has He loved,
  And we must love Him, too,
And trust in His redeeming blood,
  And try His works to do.

GOD OUR FATHER

FREDERICK W. FABER, 1854

Souls of men! why will ye scatter
  Like a crowd of frightened sheep?
Foolish hearts! why will ye wander
  From a love so true and deep?
It is God: His love looks mighty

But is mightier than it seems;
'Tis our father; and His fondness
  Goes far out beyond our dreams.

There's a wideness in God's mercy
  Like the wideness of the sea;
There's a kindness in his justice,
  Which is more than liberty.
There is no place where earth's sorrows
  Are more felt than up in heaven:
There is no place where earth's failings
  Have such kindly judgment given.

There is grace enough for thousands -
  Of new worlds as great as this;
There is room for fresh creations
  In that upper home of bliss:
For the love of God is broader
  Than the measure of man's mind,
And the heart of the Eternal
  Is most wonderfully kind.

But we make His love too narrow
  By false limits of our own;
And we magnify His strictness
  With a zeal He will not own.
If our love were but more simple,
  We should take Him at his word;
And our lives would be all sunshine
  In the sweetness of our Lord.

LIFT UP YOUR HEADS, REJOICE!

THOMAS T. LYNCH, 1856

Lift up your heads, rejoice,
  Redemption draweth nigh!
Now breathes a softer air,
  Now shines a milder sky;

The early trees put forth
  Their new and tender leaf;
Hushed is the moaning wind
  That told of winter's grief.

Lift up your heads, rejoice,
  Redemption draweth nigh!
Now mount the leaden clouds,
  Now flames the darkening sky;
The early scattered drops
  Descend with heavy fall,
And to the waiting earth
  The hidden thunders call.

Lift up your heads, rejoice,
  Redemption draweth nigh!
O note the varying signs
  Of earth, and air, and sky;
The God of glory comes
  In gentleness and might,
To comfort and alarm,
  To succor and to smite.

He comes, the wide world's King,
  He comes, the true heart's Friend,
New gladness to begin,
  And ancient wrong to end;
He comes, to fill with light
The weary waiting eye:
Lift up your heads, rejoice,
  Redemption draweth nigh.

HE LEADETH ME

JOSEPH H. GILMORE, 1859

He leadeth me! Oh, blessèd thought!
Oh words with heavenly comfort fraught!
Whate'er I do, where'er I be,
Still 'tis God's hand that leadeth me.

He leadeth me! He leadeth me!
By His own hand He leadeth me;
His faithful follower I would be,
For by His hand He leadeth me.

Sometimes 'mid scenes of deepest gloom,
Sometimes where Eden's bowers bloom,
By waters calm, o'er troubled sea,
Still 'tis God's hand that leadeth me.

Lord, I would clasp Thy hand in mine;
Nor ever murmur nor repine;
Content, whatever lot I see,
Since 'tis God's hand that leadeth me.

And when my task on earth is done,
When, by Thy grace, the victory's won,
E'en death's cold wave I will not flee,
Since Thou through Jordan leadest me.

A SUN-DAY HYMN

OLIVER WENDELL HOLMES, 1860

Lord of all being, throned afar,
Thy glory flames from sun and star:
Center and soul of every sphere,
Yet to each loving heart how near!

Sun of our life, thy quickening ray
Sheds on our path the glow of day;
Star of our hope, thy softened light
Cheers the long watches of the night.

Our midnight is thy smile withdrawn;
Our noontide is thy gracious dawn;
Our rainbow arch thy mercy's sign;
All, save the clouds of sin, are thine.

Lord of all life, below, above
Whose light is truth, whose warmth is love,
Before thy ever-blazing throne
We ask no luster of our own.

Grant us thy truth to make us free,
And kindling hearts that burn for thee,
Till all thy living altars claim
One holy light, one heavenly flame.

CITY OF GOD

SAMUEL JOHNSON, 1860

City of God, how broad and far
  Out-spread thy walls sublime!
The true thy chartered free men are
  Of every age and clime.

One holy Church, one army strong,
  One steadfast high intent,
One working band, one harvest song,
  One King omnipotent!

How purely hath thy speech come down
  From man's primeval youth;
How grandly hath thine empire grown
  Of freedom, love, and truth!

How gleam thy watchfires through the night
  With never-fainting ray!
How rise thy towers, serene and bright,
  To meet the dawning day!

In vain the surge's angry shock,
  In vain the drifting sands:
Unharmed upon the eternal Rock
  The eternal City stands.

O DAY OF REST AND GLADNESS

CHRISTOPHER WORDSWORTH, 1862

O day of rest and gladness,
  O day of joy and light,
O balm of care and sadness,
  Most beautiful, most bright!
On Thee the high and lowly,
  Through ages joined in tune,
Sing, "Holy, holy, holy!"
  To the great God triune.

Thou art a port protected
  From storms that round us rise;
A garden intersected
  With streams of paradise;
Thou art a cooling fountain
  In life's dry dreary sand;
From thee, like Pisgah's mountain,
  We view our promised land.

Today on weary nations
  The heavenly manna falls;
To holy convocations
  The silver trumpet calls;
Where gospel light is glowing
  With pure and radiant beams,
And living water flowing
  With soul-refreshing streams.

A day of sweet reflection
  Thou art,—a day of love,
A day of resurrection
  From earth to things above.
New graces ever gaining
  From this our day of rest.
We reach the rest remaining
  To spirits of the blest.

FUNERAL HYMN

William Walsham Howe, 1864

For all the saints who from their labors rest,
Who thee by faith before the world confessed,
Thy Name, O Jesus, be forever blessed.
        Alleluia.

Thou wast their rock, their fortress and their might:
Thou, Lord, their Captain in the well-fought fight;
Thou in the darkness drear, the one true Light.
        Alleluia.

O may thy soldiers, faithful, true and bold,
Fight as the saints who nobly fought of old,
And win, with them, the victor's crown of gold.
        Alleluia.

O blest communion, fellowship divine!
We feebly struggle; they in glory shine;
Yet all are one in Thee, for all are thine.
        Alleluia.

And when the strife is fierce, the warfare long,
Steals on the ear the distant triumph song,
And hearts are brave again, and arms are strong.
        Alleluia.

The golden evening brightens in the west;
Soon, to faithful warriors cometh rest;
Sweet is the calm of paradise the blest.
        Alleluia.

But lo! there breaks a yet more glorious **day;**
The saints triumphant rise in bright array;
The King of glory passes on His way.
        Alleluia.

From earth's wide bounds, from ocean's farthest coast,
Through gates of pearl streams in the countless host,
Singing to the Father, Son and Holy Ghost,
　　　　Alleluia,　Amen.

FROM OUR MASTER

JOHN GREENLEAF WHITTIER, 1866

Immortal Love, forever full,
　Forever flowing free,
Forever shared, forever whole,
　A never-ebbing sea!

We may not climb the heavenly steeps
　To bring the Lord Christ down;
In vain we search the lowest deeps,
　For Him no depths can drown.

But warm, sweet, tender, even yet
　A present help is He;
And faith has still its Olivet
　And love its Galilee.

The healing of His seamless dress
　Is by our beds of pain;
We touch Him in life's throng and press,
　And we are whole again.

Through Him the first fond prayers are said
　Our lips of childhood frame;
The last low whispers of our dead
　Are burdened with His name.

O Lord and Master of us all!
　Whate'er our name or sign,
We own Thy sway, we hear Thy call,
　We test our lives by thine.

ONWARD, CHRISTIAN SOLDIERS

SABINE BARING-GOULD, 1867

Onward, Christian soldiers,
    Marching as to war,
With the cross of Jesus
    Going on before.
Christ the royal master,
    Leads against the foe;
Forward into battle,
    See his banners go.

At the sound of triumph
    Satan's host doth flee;
On, then, Christian soldiers,
    On to victory!
Hell's foundations quiver
    At the shout of praise;
Brothers lift your voices,
    Loud your anthems raise.

Like a mighty army
    Moves the church of God;
Brethren, we are treading
    Where the saints have trod;
We are not divided,
    All one body, we,
One in hope and doctrine,
    One in charity.

Crowns and thrones may perish,
    Kingdoms rise and wane,
But the church of Jesus
    Constant will remain;
Gates of hell can never
    'Gainst that church prevail;
We have Christ's own promise,
    And that cannot fail.

Onward, then, ye people!
　　Join our happy throng,
Blend with ours your voices,
　　In the triumph song;
Glory laud and honor
　　Unto Christ the king;
This through countless ages
　　Men and angels sing.

PILGRIM'S SONG

BERNARD S. INGEMANN, 1825

Translated by Sabine Baring-Gould, 1867

Thro' the night of doubt and sorrow
　　Onward goes the pilgrim band,
Singing songs of expectation,
　　Marching to the promised land.
Clear before us through the darkness
　　Gleams and burns the guiding light;
Brother clasps the hand of brother,
　　Stepping fearless through the night.

One the light of God's own presence
　　O'er His ransomed people shed,
Chasing far the gloom and terror,
　　Brightening all the path we tread;
One the object of our journey,
　　One the faith which never tires,
One the earnest looking forward,
　　One the hope our God inspires;

One the strain that lips of thousands
　　Lift as from the heart of one;
One the conflict, one the peril,
　　One the march in God begun;
One the gladness of rejoicing
　　On the far eternal shore,
Where the one almighty Father
　　Reigns in love for evermore.

Onward, therefore, pilgrim brothers,
  Onward with the cross our aid!
Bear its shame and fight its battle,
  Till we rest beneath its shade!
Soon shall come the great awaking,
  Soon the rending of the tomb;
Then the scattering of the shadows,
  And the end of toil and gloom.

CHILD'S EVENING HYMN

SABINE BARING-GOULD, 1868

Now the day is over,
  Night is drawing nigh,
Shadows of the evening
  Steal across the sky.

Now the darkness gathers,
  Stars begin to peep,
Birds and beasts and flowers
  Soon will be asleep.

Jesus give the weary
  Calm and sweet repose,
With thy tenderest blessing
  May our eyelids close.

Grant to little children
  Visions bright of thee,
Guard the sailors tossing
  On the deep blue sea.

Comfort every sufferer
  Watching late in pain;
Those who plan some evil
  From their sin restrain.

Through the long night-watches
  May thy angels spread
Their white wings above me,
  Watching round my bed.

When the morning wakens,
  Then may I arise
Pure and fresh and sinless
  In thy holy eyes.

O LITTLE TOWN OF BETHLEHEM

PHILLIPS BROOKS, 1868

O little town of Bethlehem,
  How still we see thee lie!
Above thy deep and dreamless sleep
  The silent stars go by;
Yet in thy dark streets shineth
  The Everlasting Light;
The hopes and fears of all the years
  Are met in thee tonight.

For Christ is born of Mary;
  And, gathered all above,
While mortals sleep, the angels keep
  Their watch of wondering love.
O morning stars, together
  Proclaim the holy birth:
And praises sing to God the King,
  And peace to men on earth.

How silently, how silently,
  The wondrous gift is given!
So God imparts to human hearts
  The blessings of His heaven.
No ear may hear His coming,
  But in this world of sin,
Where meek souls will receive him still,
  The dear Christ enters in.

O holy Child of Bethlehem!
  Descend to us, we pray;
Cast out our sin, and enter in,
  Be born in us today.
We hear the Christmas angels
  The great glad tidings tell;
O come to us, abide with us,
  Our Lord, Immanuel.

THERE WERE NINETY AND NINE

ELIZABETH C. CLEPHANE, 1868

There were ninety and nine that safely lay,
  In the shelter of the fold;
But one was out on the hills away,
  Far off from the gates of gold.
Away on the mountains wild and bare,
Away from the tender shepherd's care.

"Lord, Thou hast here Thy ninety and nine,
  Are they not enough for Thee?"
But the shepherd made answer, "This of Mine
  Has wandered away from Me;
And although the road be rough and steep,
I go to the desert to find my sheep."

But none of the ransomed ever knew
  How deep were the waters crossed;
Nor how dark was the night that the Lord passed
    through,
  Ere he found His sheep that was lost.
Out in the desert He heard its cry,
Sick and helpless, and ready to die.

"Lord, whence are those blood-drops all the way,
  That mark out the mountains' track?"
"They were shed for the one who has gone astray
  Ere the shepherd could bring him back."

"Lord, whence are Thy hands so rent and torn?"
"They are pierced tonight by many a thorn."

And all through the mountains, thunder-riven,
  And up from the rocky steep,
There arose a cry to the gate of heaven,
  "Rejoice! I have found my sheep."
And the angels echoed around the Throne
Rejoice! for the Lord brings back His own."

NOW THE LABOURER'S TASK IS O'ER

John Ellerton, 1871

Now the labourer's task is o'er,
  Now the battle day is past;
Now upon the farther shore
  Lands the voyager at last.
Father, in Thy gracious keeping
Leave we now Thy servant sleeping.

There the tears of earth are dried;
  There its hidden things are clear;
There the work of life is tried
  By a juster Judge than here.
Father, in Thy gracious keeping
Leave we now Thy servant sleeping.

There the penitents, that turn
  To the Cross their dying eyes,
All the love of Christ shall learn
  At His Feet in Paradise.
Father, in Thy gracious keeping
Leave we now Thy servant sleeping.

There no more the powers of hell
  Can prevail to mar their peace;
Christ the Lord shall guard them well,
  He who died for their release.

Father, in Thy gracious keeping
Leave we now Thy servant sleeping.

"Earth to earth, and dust to dust,"
  Calmly now the words we say,
Left behind we wait in trust
  For the Resurrection Day
Father, in Thy gracious keeping
Leave we now Thy servant sleeping.

THOU ART COMING!

FRANCES RIDLEY HAVERGAL, 1873

Thou art coming, O my Savior;
Thou art coming, O my King!
In Thy beauty all-resplendent,
In Thy glory all-transcendent;
  Well may we rejoice and sing;
Coming: in the opening east
  Herald brightness slowly swells;
Coming: O Thou glorious priest!
  Hear we not thy golden bells?

Thou art coming, Thou art coming;
  We shall meet Thee on Thy way;
We shall bless Thee, we shall know Thee,
We shall bless Thee, we shall show Thee
  All our hearts could never say;
What an anthem that will be,
  Music rapturously sweet
Pouring out our love to Thee
  At Thine own all-glorious feet.

Thou art coming; we are waiting
  With a hope that cannot fail;
Asking not the day nor hour,
Resting on Thy word of power,
  Anchored safe within the veil.

Time appointed may be long,
　　But the vision must be sure;
Certainty shall make us strong
　　Joyful patience can endure.

Oh, the joy to see Thee reigning,
　　Thee, our own beloved Lord!
Every tongue Thy name confessing,
　　Worship, honor, glory, blessing
Brought to Thee with one accord;
　　Thee, our Master, and our Friend,
Vindicated and enthroned;
　　Unto earth's remotest end
Glorified, adored and owned!

PEACE, PERFECT PEACE

EDWARD HENRY BICKERSTETH, 1875

Peace, perfect peace, in this dark world of sin?
The blood of Jesus whispers peace within.

Peace, perfect peace, by thronging duties pressed?
To do the will of Jesus, this is rest.

Peace, perfect peace, with sorrows surging round?
On Jesus' bosom naught but calm is found.

Peace, perfect peace, with loved ones far away?
In Jesus' keeping we are safe, and they.

Peace, perfect peace, the future all unknown?
Jesus we know, and He is on the throne.

Peace, perfect peace, death shadowing us and ours?
Jesus has vanquished death and all its powers.

It is enough; earth's struggles soon shall cease,
And Jesus call us to Heaven's perfect peace.

THE DAY IS DYING IN THE WEST

MARY A. LATHBURY, 1877

Day is dying in the west;
Heaven is touching earth with rest;
Wait and worship while the night
Sets the evening lamps alight,
    Through all the sky.

Refrain

            Holy, holy, holy, Lord God of hosts!
            Heaven and earth are full of Thee;
            Heaven and earth are praising Thee,
                O Lord most high!

Lord of life, beneath the dome
Of the universe, Thy home,
Gather us, who seek Thy face
To the fold of Thy embrace,
    For Thou art nigh.

While the deepening shadows fall,
Heart of love, enfolding all,
Through the glory and the grace
Of the stars that veil Thy face,
    Our hearts ascend.

When forever from our sight
Pass the stars, the day, the night,
Lord of Angels, on our eyes,
Let eternal morning rise,
    And shadows end.

O MASTER, LET ME WALK WITH THEE

WASHINGTON GLADDEN, 1879

O Master, let me walk with Thee
In lowly paths of service free;
Tell me Thy secret; help me bear
The strain of toil, the fret of care.

Help me the slow of heart to move
By some clear winning word of love,
Teach me the wayward feet to stay,
And guide them in the homeward way.

Teach me Thy patience; still with Thee
In closer, dearer company,
In work that keeps faith sweet and strong,
In trust that triumphs over wrong.

In hope that sends a shining ray
Far down the future's broadening way;
In peace that only Thou canst give,
With Thee, O Master, let me live.

O LOVE, THAT WILT NOT LET ME GO

GEORGE MATHESON, 1882

O Love, that wilt not let me go,
 I rest my weary soul on Thee;
I give Thee back the life I owe,
That in Thine ocean depth its flow
 May richer, fuller be.

O Light, that followest all my way,
 I yield my flickering torch to Thee;
My heart restores its borrowed ray,
That in Thy sunshine's blaze its day
 May brighter, fairer be.

O Joy, that seekest me through pain,
   I cannot close my heart to Thee;
I trace the rainbow through the rain,
And feel the promise is not vain,
    That morn shall tearless be.

O Cross, that liftest up my head,
   I dare not ask to fly from Thee;
I lay in dust life's glory dead,
And from the ground there blossoms red
    Life that shall endless be.

THE NEW HEART

MODERN CHINESE, 1890

Alas, my heart is black,
   By Satan sore deceived,
Far from the upward track
   God's judgment disbelieved,
From Heaven, O Holy Spirit, come!
With Christ's Gospel my heart illume!

Alas, my heart of woe
   With sorrow sick to death!
Fearing Sin's doom to know
   I sigh with wounded breath,
From heaven, O spirit blest, descend!
With Jesus' peace my grief to end.

Alas, my strengthless heart
   Is slow to love God's way,
To hate the wrong, love right,
   While worldly thought bears sway!
From heaven, O spirit, come! complete
My heart, with Christ's perfection sweet!

A DANCE CHANT

IROQUOIS INDIANS

Translated by E. S. Parker

Hail! Hail! Hail!
Listen, O Creator, with an open ear to the words of thy people
    as they ascend to thy dwelling!
Give to the keepers of Thy faith wisdom rightly to do thy com-
    mands.
Give to our warriors and to our mothers strength to perform
    the sacred ceremonies appointed.
We thank Thee that thou hast kept them pure unto this day.
Listen to us still!
We thank Thee that Thou hast spared the lives of so many of
    Thy children to take part in these exercises.
We thank Thee for the increase of the earth
For the rivers and streams,
For the sun and moon,
For the winds that banish disease,
For the herbs and plants that cure the sick,
For all things that minister to good and happiness.
We pray for a prosperous year to come.
Lastly, we give thee thanks, our Creator and Ruler!
In Thee are embodied all things!
We believe that Thou canst do no evil;
We believe that Thou dost all things for our good and for our
    happiness.
Should Thy people disobey Thy commands, deal not harshly with
    them!
Be kind to us, as Thou hast been to our fathers in times long
    gone by,
Hearken to our words as they ascend—
May they be pleasing to Thee, our Creator!
Preserver of all things visible and invisible!

NOT IN DUMB RESIGNATION

John Hay, 1891

Not in dumb resignation,
  We lift our hands on high;
Not like the nerveless fatalist,
  Content to trust and die.
Our faith springs like the eagle,
  Who soars to meet the sun,
And cries exulting unto Thee,
  "O Lord, thy will be done!"

When tyrant feet are trampling
  Upon the common weal,
Thou dost not bid us bend and writhe
  Beneath the iron heel;
In Thy name we assert our right
  By sword or tongue or pen,
And even the headsman's axe may flash
  Thy message unto men.

Thy will,—it strengthens weakness;
  It bids the strong be just:
No lip to fawn, no hand to beg,
  No brow to seek the dust.
Wherever man oppresses man
  Beneath the liberal sun,
O Lord, be there, Thine arm made bare,
  Thy righteous will be done.

THE CHURCH UNIVERSAL

Samuel Longfellow, 1891

One holy church of God appears
  Through every age and race,
Unwasted by the lapse of years,
  Unchanged by changing place.

From oldest time, on farthest shores,
  Beneath the pine or palm,
One unseen presence she adores,
  With silence or with Psalm.

Her priests are all God's faithful sons,
  To serve the world raised up;
The pure in heart her baptized ones,
  Love her communion cup.

The truth is her prophetic gift,
  The soul her sacred page;
And feet on mercy's errands swift
  Do make her pilgrimage.

O living church! Thine errand speed,
  Fulfil Thy task sublime;
With bread of life earth's hunger feed,
  Redeem the evil time!

THY KINGDOM COME

FREDERICK L. HOSMER, 1891

Thy kingdom come—on bended knee
  The passing ages pray;
And faithful souls have yearned to see
  On earth that kingdom's day.

But the slow watches of the night
  Not less to God belong,
And for the everlasting right
  The silent stars are strong.

And lo! already on the hills
  The flags of dawn appear;
Gird up your loins, ye prophet souls,
  Proclaim the day is near:

The day in whose clear shining light
  All wrong shall stand revealed,
When justice shall be clothed with might,
  And every hurt be healed:

When knowledge, hand in hand with peace,
  Shall walk the earth abroad,—
The day of perfect righteousness,
  The promised day of God.

RECESSIONAL

RUDYARD KIPLING, 1897

God of our fathers, known of old,
  Lord of our far-flung battle line,
Beneath whose awful hand we hold
  Dominion over palm and pine:
Lord God of hosts, be with us yet,
Lest we forget, lest we forget.

The tumult and the shouting dies,
  The captains and the kings depart;
Still stands thine ancient sacrifice,
  An humble and a contrite heart:
Lord God of hosts, be with us yet,
Lest we forget, lest we forget.

Far-called our navies melt away,
  On dune and headland sinks the fire;
Lo, all our pomp of yesterday
  Is one with Nineveh and Tyre!
Judge of the Nations, spare us yet,
Lest we forget, lest we forget!

If, drunk with sight of power, we loose
  Wild tongues that have not Thee in awe,
Such boastings as the Gentiles use,
  Or lesser breeds without the law:

Lord God of hosts, be with us yet,
Lest we forget, lest we forget.

For heathen heart that puts her trust
  In reeking tube and iron shard;
All valiant dust that builds on dust,
  And guarding, calls not Thee to guard.
For frantic boast and foolish word,
Thy mercy on thy people, Lord!

g. TWENTIETH CENTURY

AMERICA THE BEAUTIFUL

KATHARINE LEE BATES, 1905

O beautiful for spacious skies,
  For amber waves of grain,
For purple mountain majesties
  Above the fruited plain!
America! America!
  God shed his grace on thee,
And crown thy good with brotherhood
  From sea to shining sea!

O beautiful for pilgrim feet,
  Whose stern, impassioned stress
A thoroughfare for freedom beat
  Across the wilderness!
America! America!
  God mend thine every flaw,
Confirm thy soul in self-control,
  Thy liberty in law!

O beautiful for heroes proved
  In liberating strife,
Who more than self their country loved,
  And mercy more than life!

America! America!
　May God thy gold refine,
Till all success be nobleness,
　And every gain divine!

O beautiful for patriot dream
　That sees beyond the years
Thine alabaster cities gleam
　Undimmed by human tears!
America! America!
　God shed his grace on thee,
And crown thy good with brotherhood
　From sea to shining sea!

THY KINGDOM COME, O LORD

FREDERICK L. HOSMER, 1905

Thy kingdom come, O Lord,
　Wide-circling as the sun;
Fulfil of old thy word
　And make the nations one;—

One in the bond of peace,
　The service glad and free
Of truth and righteousness
　Of love and equity.

Speed, speed the longed-for time
　Foretold by raptured seers—
The prophecy sublime,
　The hope of all the years;—

Till rise at last, to span
　Its firm foundations broad,
The commonwealth of man,
　The city of our God.

THE CITY

FRANK MASON NORTH, 1903

Where cross the crowded ways of life,
    Where sound the cries of race and clan
Above the noise of selfish strife,
    We hear Thy voice, O Son of Man.

In haunts of wretchedness and need,
    On shadowed thresholds dark with fears,
From paths where hide the lures of greed,
    We catch the vision of Thy tears.

From tender childhood's helplessness,
    From woman's grief, man's burdened toil,
From famished souls, from sorrow's stress,
    Thy heart has never known recoil.

The cup of water given for Thee
    Still holds the freshness of Thy grace;
Yet long the multitudes to see
    The sweet compassion of Thy face.

O Master, from the mountain side,
    Make haste to heal these hearts of pain;
Among these restless throngs abide,
    O tread the city's streets again;

Till sons of men shall learn Thy love,
    And follow where Thy feet have trod;
Till glorious from Thy heaven above,
    Shall come the City of our God.

THY KINGDOM, LORD, WE LONG FOR

VIDA SCUDDER, 1905

Thy Kingdom, Lord, we long for,
Where love shall find its own;
And brotherhood triumphant
Our years of pride disown.

Thy captive people languish
In mill and mart and mine;
We lift to Thee their anguish
We wait thy promised sign.

Thy kingdom, Lord, Thy Kingdom!
All secretly it grows;
In faithful hearts forever
His seed the Sower sows.
Yet ere its consummation
Must dawn a mighty doom;
For judgment and salvation
The Son of Man shall come.

If now perchance in tumult
His destined sign appear,—
The rising of the people,—
Dispel our coward fear!
Let comforts that we cherish,
Let old tradition die!
Our wealth, our wisdom perish,
So that He draw but nigh.

In wrath and revolution
The Sign may be displayed
But by thy grace we'll greet it
With spirits unafraid.
The awe-struck heart presages
An advent dread and sure;
Its Master in the poor.

Beyond our fierce confusion,
Our strife of speech and sword,
Our wars of class and nation,
We wait Thy certain Word.
The meek and poor of spirit
Who in Thy promise trust,
Thy Kingdom shall inherit,
The blessing of the just.

THE TROUBADOUR OF GOD

CHARLES WHARTON STORK

I walk the dusty ways of life
But ever my heart beats high,
And my song ascends to the crystal tower
That pierces up through the sky.

For there is my love who holds my heart
Like a bird on silken chain,
Who smote my side with a gladsome wound
And slays me with sweetest pain,
Till the love of the fairest woman on earth
Is a paltry thing and vain.

I trudge at morn right merrily
For oh! my heart is young,
I give good words and a hand at need
To those I walk among,
But I long for the bliss of the bridal hour
When the vesper bell is rung.

Till then I sing as best I may
My love, so kind, so rare,
I mumble not in a monk's dark cell;
Nay, song is braver than prayer.
I go where my brothers may hear my voice
In the glow of the warm bright air.

And though I have never seen my Love
Yet the pulse of my faith is strong,
It fills all the world with loveliness
And it fills my heart with song.

FESTAL SONG

WILLIAM PIERSON MERRILL. 1911

Rise up, O men of God!
  Have done with lesser things,
Give heart, and soul, and mind, and strength
  To serve the King of Kings.

Rise up, O men of God!
  His kingdom tarries long,
Bring in the day of brotherhood
  And end the night of wrong.

Lift high the cross of Christ!
  Tread where His feet have trod·
As brothers of the Son of Man,
  Rise up, O men of God!

THE SUPREME SACRIFICE

John S. Arkwright

O valiant Hearts, who to your glory came
Through dust of conflict and through battle-flame;
Tranquil you lie, your knightly virtue proved,
Your memory hallowed in the Land you loved.

Proudly you gathered, rank on rank to war,
As who had heard God's message from afar;
All you had hoped for, all you had you gave
To save Mankind—yourselves you scorned to save.

Splendid you passed, the great surrender made,
Into the light that nevermore shall fade;
Deep your contentment in that blessed abode,
Who wait the last clear trumpet-call of God.

Long years ago, as earth lay dark and still,
Rose a loud cry upon a lonely hill,
While in the frailty of our human clay
Christ, our redeemer, passed the self-same way.

Still stands his cross from that dread hour to this,
Like some bright star above the dark abyss;
Still, through the veil the Victor's pitying eyes
Look down to bless our lesser calvaries.

These were His servants, in His steps they trod
Following through death the martyr'd Son of God:
Victor He rose; victorious too shall rise
Those who have drunk His Cup of Sacrifice.

O risen Lord, O Shepherd of our Dead,
Whose cross has bought them and whose staff has led—
In glorious hope their proud sorrowing Land
Commits her children to Thy gracious hand.

THE PLOUGHMAN

Karle Wilson Baker

God will not let my field lie fallow.

The ploughshare is sharp, the ˍˍet of his oxen are heavy.
They hurt.

But I cannot stay God from his ploughing,
  I, the lord of the field
  While I stand waiting
His shoulders loom upon me from the mist.
He has gone past me, down the furrow, shouting and singing,
(I had said, it shall rest for a season.
The larks had built in the grass. . . .)

He will not let my field lie fallow.

SUBSTITUTION

Elizabeth Barrett Browning

When some beloved voice that was to you
Both sound and sweetness, faileth suddenly,
And silence against which you dare not cry,
Aches round you like a strong disease and new—
What hope? What help? What music will undo

That silence to your sense? Not friendship's sigh,
Not reason's subtle count; not melody
Of viols, nor of pipes that Faunus blew;
Not songs of poets, nor of nightingales,
Whose hearts leap upward through the cypress trees
To the clear moon; nor yet the spheric laws
Self-chanted, nor the angels' sweet 'All-hails,'
Met in the smile of God: Nay, none of these,
Speak *Thou,* availing Christ!—and fill this pause.

THE WAIL OF PROMETHEUS BOUND

ÆSCHYLUS

Translated by Elizabeth Barrett Browning

O Holy Æther, and swift-wingèd Winds,
And River-wells, and laughter innumerous
Of yon sea-waves! Earth, mother of us all,
And all-viewing cyclic Sun, I cry on you,—
Behold me a god, What I endure from gods!
  Behold, with throe on throe,
  How, wasted by this woe,
I wrestle down the myriad years of time!
  Behold how fast around me
The new King of the happy ones sublime
Has flung the chain he forged, has shamed and bound me!
Woe, woe! today's woe and the coming morrow's
  I cover with one groan, and where is found me
    A limit to these sorrows?
  And yet what word do I say? I have foreknown
Clearly all things that should be; nothing done
Comes sudden to my soul; and I must bear
What is ordained with patience, being aware
Necessity doth front the universe
With an invincible gesture. Yet this curse
Which strikes me now, I find it hard to brave
In silence or in speech. Because I gave
Honor to mortals. I have yoked my soul

To this compelling fate. Because I stole
The secret fount of fire, whose bubbles went
Over the ferule's brim, and manward sent
Art's mighty means and perfect rudiment,
That sin I expiate in this agony,
Hung here in fetters, 'neath the blanching sky.
Ah, ah me! what a sound,
What a fragrance sweeps up, from a pinion unseen
Of a god or a mortal, or nature between,
Sweeping up to this rock where the earth has her bound,
To have sight of my pangs or some guerdon obtain.
Lo, a god in the anguish, a god in the chain!
The god Zeus hateth sore,
And his gods hate again,
As many as tread on his glorified floor,
Because I loved mortals too much evermore.
Alas, me! what a murmur and motion J hear,
As of birds flying near!
And the air undersings
The light stroke of their wings—
And all life that approaches I wait for in fear.

NEARER HOME

Phoebe Cary

One sweetly solemn thought
Comes to me o'er and o'er:
I am nearer home today
Than I ever have been before;

Nearer my Father's house
Where many mansions be;
Nearer the great white throne,
Nearer the crystal sea;

Nearer the bound of life,
Where we lay our burdens down;
Nearer leaving the cross,
Nearer gaining the crown!

But lying darkly between,
  Winding down through the night,
Is the silent unknown stream,
  That leads at last to the light.

Closer and closer my steps
  Come to the dread abysm;
Closer Death to my lips
  Presses the awful chrism.

Oh, if my mortal feet
  Have almost gained the brink;
If it be I am nearer home
  Even today than I think;

Father, perfect my trust;
  Let my spirit feel in death,
That her feet are firmly set
  On the rock of a living Faith.

HIS BANNER OVER ME

Gerald Massey

Surrounded by unnumbered Foes,
Against my soul the battle goes!
Yet though I weary, sore distressed,
I know that I shall reach my Rest:
  I lift my tearful eyes above,—
  His Banner over me is love.

Its Sword my spirit will not yield,
Though flesh may faint upon the field;
He waves before my fading sight
The branch of palm—the crown of light;
  I lift my brightening eyes above,—
  His Banner over me is Love.

My cloud of battle-dust may dim;
His veil of splendor curtain Him!
And in the midnight of my fear
I may not feel Him standing near;
    But as I lift my eyes above,—
    His Banner over me is Love.

GRIEF AND GOD

Stephen Phillips

Unshunnable is grief; we should not fear
The dreadful bath whose cleansing is so clear;
For He who to the Spring such poison gave,
Who rears his roses from the hopeless grave;
Who caused the babe to wail at the first breath,
But with a rapture seals the face of death;
Who circled us with pale aspiring foam,
With exiled Music yearning for her home,
With knockings early and with cryings late,
The moving of deep waters against Fate;
Who starred the skies with yearning with those fires,
That dart through dew their infinite desires;
Or largely silent and so wistful bright
Direct a single look of love all night;
Who gave unto the Moon that hopeless quest,
Condemned the wind to wander without rest;
He, as I think, intends that we shall rise
Only through pain into His Paradise.
Woe! Woe! to those who placidly suspire,
Drowned in security, remote from fire;
Who under the dim sky and whispering trees
By peaceful slopes and passing streams have ease;
Whose merit is their uncommitted sins,
Whose thought is heinous, but they shun the gins
And those o'erflowering pits that take the strong,
The baited sweetness and the honeyed wrong;
Who watched the falling yet who never fell,
Shadows not yet ascended into Hell.

No sacred pang disturbs their secular life,
Eluding splendor and escaping strife;
They die not, for they lived not; under earth
Their bodies urge the meaner flowers to birth:
Unstrung, unfired, untempted was their soul:
Easy extinction is their utmost goal.
To those whom He doth love God hath not sent
Such dread security, such sad content;
Young are they carried to the front of pain,
In coldest anguish dipped again, again;
Or else into His burning are they led,
Desirous of His glory to be dead;
When He descends, like Semele they die,
Proud to be shrivelled in His ecstasy;
Or through the night of life they ebb and flow
Under the cold imperial Moon of woe.
Some of His favourites are too fiercely wrought
To spend upon the sunny earth a thought,
But ever by an inward peril driven,
Neglect the gleaming grass and glimmering heaven.
And some by thorny sweetness are betrayed,
By beauty of those bodies He hath made;
And some o'er wearied, have so tired a head,
They ask like children to be laid in bed.
But He hath branded on such souls His name,
And He will know them by the scars of flame.
As Christ in the dark garden had to drink
The brimming cup from which His soul did shrink;
As Dante had to thread the world of fire,
Ere he approached the Rose of his desire;
So fear not grief, fear not the anguish, thou,
The paining heart, the clasped and prostrate brow;
This is the emblem, and this is the sign
By which God singles thee for fields divine;
From such a height He stoops, from such a bliss,
Small wonder thou dost shudder at His kiss.

THE REFUGE

PSALM XLVI

From Moulton's *Modern Reader's Bible*

God is our refuge and strength,
    A very present help in trouble.
Therefore will we not fear, though the earth do change,
    And though the mountains be moved in the heart of the seas;
Though the waters thereof roar and be troubled,
    Though the mountains shake with the swelling thereof.
        The Lord of Hosts is with us,
        The God of Jacob is our refuge.

There is a river, the streams whereof make glad the city of God,
    The holy place of the tabernacles of the Most High.
God is in the midst of her; she shall not be moved:
    God shall help her at the dawn of morning.
The nations raged, the kingdoms were moved;
    He uttered His voice, the earth melted.
        The Lord of Hosts is with us;
        The God of Jacob is our refuge.

Come, behold the works of the Lord,
    What desolations he hath made in the earth;
He maketh wars to cease unto the end of the earth;
    He breaketh the bow and cutteth the spear in sunder;
He burneth the chariots in the fire.
    Be still and know that I am God:
I will be exalted among the nations,
    I will be exalted in the earth.
        The Lord of Hosts is with us;
        The God of Jacob is our refuge.

THE EVERLASTING ARMS

Psalm XCI

From Moulton's *Modern Reader's Bible*

He that dwelleth in the secret place of the Most High
　Shall abide under the shadow of the Almighty.
I will say of the Lord, 'He is my refuge and my fortress;
　My God, in whom I trust.'
For he shall deliver thee from the snare of the fowler,
　And from the noisome pestilence.
He shall cover thee with his pinions,
And under his wings shalt thou take refuge:
　His truth is a shield and a buckler.
Thou shall not be afraid for the terror by night,
　Nor for the arrow that flieth by day;
Nor for the pestilence that walketh in darkness,
　Nor for the destruction that wasteth at noonday.
A thousand shall fall at thy side,
And ten thousand at thy right hand;
　But it shall not come nigh thee.
Only with thy eyes shalt thou behold,
　And see the reward of the wicked.

For thou, O Lord, art my refuge!
　Thou hast made the Most High thy habitation:
There shall no evil befall thee,
　Neither shall any plague come nigh thy tent.
For he shall give his angels charge over thee,
　To keep thee in all thy ways.
They shall bear thee up in their hands,
　Lest thou dash thy foot against a stone.
Thou shalt tread upon the lion and adder:
　The young lion and the serpent shalt thou trample under feet.
Because he hath set his love upon me, therefore will I deliver
　　him.
　I will set him on high because he hath known my name,
He shall call upon me and I will answer him;

I will be with him in trouble:
I will deliver him and honour him.
With long life will I satisfy him,
    And show him my salvation.

THE PILGRIM'S SONG

Psalm CXXI

From Moulton's *Modern Reader's Bible*

I will lift up mine eyes unto the mountains:
From whence shall my help come?
My help cometh from the Lord,
Which made heaven and earth.

He will not suffer thy foot to be moved,
He that keepeth thee will not slumber.
Behold he that keepeth Israel
Shall neither slumber nor sleep.

The Lord is thy keeper:
The Lord is thy shade upon thy right hand.
The sun shall not smite thee by day,
Nor the moon by night.

The Lord shall keep thee from all evil;
He shall keep thy soul.
The Lord shall keep thy going out and thy coming in,
From this time forth and forever more.

THE LOST CHORD

Adelaide Anne Proctor

Seated one day at the Organ,
    I was weary and ill at ease,
And my fingers wandered idly
    Over the noisy keys.

I know not what I was playing,
  Or what I was dreaming then;
But I struck one chord of music,
  Like the sound of a great Amen.

It flooded the crimson twilight,
  Like the close of an angel's Psalm,
And it lay on my fevered spirit
  With a touch of infinite calm.

It quieted pain and sorrow,
  Like love overcoming strife;
It seemed the harmonious echo
  From our discordant life.

It linked all perplexèd meanings
  Into one perfect peace,
And trembled away into silence
  As if it were loth to cease.

I have sought but I seek it vainly,
  That one lost chord divine,
Which came from the soul of the Organ
  And entered into mine.

It may be that Death's bright angel
  Will speak in that chord again—
It may be that only in Heaven
  I shall hear that great Amen.

b. THE MINISTRY OF PAIN

SORROW

SIR AUBREY DE VERE

Count each affliction, whether light or grave,
  God's messenger sent down to thee; do thou
With courtesy receive him; rise and bow;
And, ere his shadow pass thy threshold, crave

Permission first his heavenly feet to lave;
　　Then lay before him all thou hast; allow
　　No cloud of passion to usurp thy brow,
Or mar thy hospitality; no wave
　　Of mortal tumult to obliterate
　　Thy soul's marmoreal calmness.　Grief should be
Like joy, majestic, equable, sedate,
　　Confirming cleansing, raising, making free;
Strong to consume small troubles; to commend
Great thoughts, grave thoughts, thoughts lasting to the end.

WHO NEVER ATE WITH TEARS HIS BREAD

GOETHE

Translated by Farnsworth Wright

Who never ate with tears his bread,
Who never through the troubled hours
Weeping sat upon his bed,
He knows ye not, ye heavenly powers.

Ye lead us into life amain,
Ye let the poor with guilt be weighted,
And then ye give him o'er to pain,
For guilt must all be compensated.

SORROWS HUMANIZE OUR RACE

JEAN INGELOW

Sorrows humanize our race;
Tears are the showers that fertilize this world:
And memory of things precious keepeth warm
The heart that once did hold them.

　　　　　　　　They are poor
That have lost nothing: they are poorer far
Who. losing, have forgotten: they most poor

Of all, who lose and wish they might forget.
For life is one, and in its warp and woof
There runs a thread of gold that glitters fair,
And sometimes in the pattern shows more sweet
Where there are sombre colors. It is true
That we have wept. But O, this thread of gold,
We would not have it tarnish: let us turn
Oft and look back upon the wondrous web,
And when it shineth sometimes we shall know
That memory is possession.

'TIS SORROW BUILDS THE SHINING LADDER UP

James Russell Lowell

'Tis sorrow builds the shining ladder up,
Whose golden rounds are our calamities,
Whereon our feet planting, nearer God
The spirit climbs and hath its eyes unsealed.

True it is that Death's face seems stern and cold,
When he is sent to summon those we love,
But all God's angels come to us disguised.
Sorrow and sickness, poverty and death,
One after other lift their frowning masks
And we behold the seraph's face beneath,
All radiant with the glory and the calm
Of having looked upon the front of God.
With every anguish of our earthly part
The spirit's path grows clearer; this was meant
When Jesus touched the blind man's lids with clay.
Life is the jailer; Death the angel sent
To draw the unwilling bolts and set us free.

CLEANSING FIRES

Adelaide Anne Proctor

Let thy gold be cast in the furnace,
Thy red gold, precious and bright;
Do not fear the hungry fire,
  With its caverns of burning light;
And thy gold shall return more precious,
  Free from every spot and stain;
For gold must be tried by fire,
  As a heart must be tried by pain!

In the cruel fire of Sorrow
  Cast thy heart, do not faint or wail;
Let thy hand be firm and steady
  Do not let thy spirit quail:
But wait till the trial is over
  And take thy heart again;
For as gold is tried by fire,
  So a heart must be tried by pain!

I shall know by the gleam and the glitter
  Of the golden chain you wear,
By your heart's calm strength in loving,
  Of the fire they have had to bear.
Beat on, true heart, forever!
  Shine bright, strong golden chain!
And bless the cleansing fire,
  And the furnace of living pain!

MY UNINVITED GUEST

May Riley Smith

One day there entered at my chamber door
A presence whose light footfall on the floor
No token gave; and, ere I could withstand,
Within her clasp she drew my trembling hand.

COMFORT IN SORROW

"Intrusive guest," I cried, "my palm I lend
But to the gracious pressure of a friend!
Why comest thou, unbidden and in gloom,
Trailing thy cold gray garments in my room?

"I know thee, Pain! Thou art the sullen foe
Of every sweet enjoyment here below;
Thou art the comrade and ally of Death,
And timid mortals shrink from thy cold breath.

"No fragrant balms grow in thy garden beds,
Nor slumbrous poppies droop their crimson heads;
And well I know thou comest to me now
To bind thy burning chains upon my brow!"

And though my puny will stood straightly up,
From that day forth I drank her pungent cup,
And ate her bitter bread,—with leaves of rue,
Which in her sunless gardens rankly grew.

And now, so long it is, I scarce can tell
When Pain within my chamber came to dwell;
And though she is not fair of mien or face,
She hath attracted to my humble place

A company most gracious and refined,
Whose touches are like balm, whose voices kind:
Sweet Sympathy, with box of ointment rare;
Courage, who sings while she sits weaving there;

Brave Patience, whom my heart esteemeth much,
And who hath wondrous virtue in her touch.
Such is the chaste and sweet society
Which Pain, my faithful foe, hath brought to me.

And now, upon my threshold there she stands,
Reaching to me her rough yet kindly hands
In silent truce. Thus for a time we part,
And a great gladness overflows my heart;

For she is so ungentle in her way
That no host welcomes her or bids her stay;
Yet, though men bolt and bar their house from thee,
To every door, O Pain, thou hast a key!

From THE ORDEAL BY FIRE

EDMUND CLARENCE STEDMAN

Thou, who dost feel Life's vessel strand
Full length upon the shining sand,
And hearest breakers close at hand,

Be strong and wait! nor let the strife,
With which the winds and waves are rife,
Disturb that sacred inner life:

Anon thou shalt regain the shore,
And walk—though naked, maimed, and sore—
A nobler being than before!

No lesser griefs shall work thee ill;
No malice shall have power to kill:
Of woes thy soul hath drunk its fill.

Tempests that beat us to the clay,
Drive many a lowering cloud away,
And bring a clearer, holier day.

The fire, that every hope consumes,
Either the inmost soul entombs,
Or evermore the face illumes!

Roses of asbestos do we wear;
Before the memories we bear,
The flames leap backward everywhere.

THE CELESTIAL SURGEON

Robert Louis Stevenson

If I have faltered more or less
In my great task of happiness;
If I have moved among my race
And shown no glorious morning face;
If beams from happy human eyes
Have moved me not; if morning skies,
Books and my food, and summer rain
Knocked on my sullen heart in vain:—
Lord, Thy most pointed pleasure take
And stab my spirit broad awake!
Or, Lord, if too obdurate I,
Choose Thou, before that spirit die,
A piercing pain, a killing sin
And to my dead heart run them in!

A WANDERER'S LITANY

Arthur Stringer

When my life has enough of love, and my spirit enough of
mirth,
When the ocean no longer beckons me, when the roadway calls
no more,
Oh, on the anvil of Thy wrath, remake me, God, that day!

When the lash of the wave bewilders, and I shrink from the
sting of the rain,
When I hate the gloom of Thy steel-gray wastes, and slink to
the lamp-lit shore.
Oh, purge me in Thy primal fires, and fling me on my way!

When I house me close in a twilit inn, when I brood by a dying
fire,
When I kennel and cringe with fat content, where a pillow and
loaf are sure,
Oh, on the anvil of Thy wrath, remake me, God, that day!

When I quail at the snow on the uplands, when I crawl from
the glare of the sun,
When the trails that are lone invite me not, and the half-way
lamps allure,
Oh, purge me in Thy primal fires, and fling me on my way!

When the wine has all ebbed from an April, when the Autumn
of life forgets,
The call and the lure of the widening West, the wind in the
straining rope,
Oh, on the anvil of Thy wrath, remake me, God, that day!

When I awaken to hear adventures strange throng valiantly
forth by night,
To the sting of the salt-spume dust of the plain, and width of
the western slope,
Oh, purge me in Thy primal fires and fling me on my way!

When swarthy and careless and grim they throng out under my
rose-grown sash,
And I—I bide me there by the coals, and I know not heat nor
hope,
Then, on the anvil of Thy wrath, remake me, God, that day!

IF ALL THE SKIES

Henry van Dyke

If all the skies were sunshine,
Our faces would be fain
To feel once more upon them
The cooling plash of rain.

If all the world were music,
Our hearts would often long
For one sweet strain of silence,
To break the endless song.

If life were always merry,
  Our souls would seek relief,
And rest from weary laughter
  In the quiet arms of grief.

PISGAH

Willard Wattles

By every ebb of the river-side
My heart to God hath daily cried;
By every shining shingle-bar
I found the pathway of a star;
By every dizzy mountain height
He touches me for cleaner sight.
As Moses' face hath shined to see
His intimate divinity;
Through desert sand I stumbling pass
To death's cool plot of friendly grass,
Knowing each painful step I trod
Hath brought me daily home to God.

THE ANGEL OF PATIENCE

John Greenleaf Whittier

To weary hearts, to mourning homes
God's meekest angel gently comes:
No power has he to banish pain,
Or give us back our lost again;
And yet in tenderest love, our dear
And Heavenly Father sends him here.

There's quiet in the angel's glance,
There's rest in his still countenance!
He mocks no grief with idle cheer,
Nor wounds with words the mourner's ear;
But ills and woes he may not cure
He kindly trains us to endure.

c. BRAVERY IS ITS OWN CONSOLATION

THE INEVITABLE

SARAH K. BOLTON

I like the man who faces what he must
With step triumphant and a heart of cheer;
Who fights the daily battle without fear;
Sees his hopes fail, yet keeps unfaltering trust
That God is God,—that somehow, true and just
His plans work out for mortals; not a tear
Is shed when fortune, which the world holds dear,
Falls from his grasp—better, with love, a crust
Than loving in dishonor; envies not,
Nor loses faith in man; but does his best,
Nor ever murmurs at his humbler lot;
But, with a smile and words of hope, gives zest
To every toiler. He alone is great
Who by a life heroic conquers fate.

COURAGE

STOPFORD BROOKE

Oft, as we run the weary way
That leads thro' shadows unto day,
  With trial sore amazed,
We deem our sorrows are unknown,
Our battle joined and fought alone,
  Our victory unpraised.

Faithless and blind! We cannot trace
The witnesses above our race,
  Beyond our senses' ken;
The mighty cloud of all who died
With faithful rapture, humble pride,
  For love of God and man.

And One, the Conqueror of death,
Beginner, finisher of faith,
    Who, for the joy of love,
Endured the cross, despised the shame,
Awakes in us the battle flame,
    And waits for us above.

With patience then we run the race,
With joy and confidence and grace,
    With quiet hope and power;
Cast off the sins that check our speed,
The weights that faith and love impede;
    Withstand the evil hour.

For heaven is round us as we move,
Our days are compassed with its love,
    Its light is on our road:
And when the knell of death is rung,
Sweet hallelujahs shall be sung
    To welcome us to God.

CUI BONO?

Thomas Carlyle

What is hope? A smiling rainbow
    Children follow through the wet;
'Tis not here, still yonder, yonder,
    Never urchin found it yet.

What is life? A thawing iceboard
    On a sea with sunny shore;
Gay we sail; it melts beneath us;
    We are sunk and seen no more.

What is man? A foolish baby,
    Vainly strives and fights and frets;
Demanding all, deserving nothing;
    One small grave is all he gets.

GOD'S PITY

Louise Driscoll

God pity all the brave who go
　The common way, and wear
No ribboned medals on their breasts,
　No laurels in their hair.

God pity all the lonely Folk
　With Griefs they do not tell
Women waking in the night
　And men dissembling well.

In common courage of the street
　The crushed grape is the wine,
Wheat in the mill is daily bread
　And given for a sign.

And who but God shall pity those
　Who go so quietly
And smile upon us when we meet
　And greet so pleasantly.

INVICTUS

William Ernest Henley

Out of the night that covers me,
　Black as the pit from pole to pole,
I thank whatever gods may be,
　For my unconquerable soul.

In the fell clutch of circumstance
　I have not winced nor cried aloud.
Under the bludgeonings of chance
　My head is bloody but unbowed.

Beyond this place of wrath and tears
   Looms but the horror of the shade,
And yet the menace of the years
   Finds and shall find me unafraid.

It matters not how straight the gate
   How charged with punishments the scroll,
I am the master of my fate,
   I am the captain of my soul.

TO THE BRAVE SOUL

WILBUR UNDERWOOD

Strong in a dream of perfect bloom
   The flower strikes its roots in mould,
Not else would pure narcissus cups.
   The April days behold.

And all the scented white of May
   And bird delight that soars and sings,
Transmuted is of strange decay
   Dead leaves and moulderings

O soul elect, lips keen with song,
   O eager heart the gods love well,
Plunge, vision in thine eyes, and let
   Thy feet take hold on hell.

d. VICTORY ON THE SPIRITUAL PLANE

"THEY WENT FORTH TO BATTLE BUT THEY ALWAYS FELL"

SHAEMAS O SHEEL

They went forth to battle but they always fell;
   Their eyes were fixed above the sullen shields;
Nobly they fought and bravely but not well,

And sank, heart-wounded by a subtle spell.
  They knew not fear that to the foeman yields,
  They were not weak, as one who vainly wields
A futile weapon; yet the sad scrolls tell
How on the hard-fought field they always fell.

It was a secret music that they heard,
  A sad sweet plea for pity and for peace;
And that which pierced the heart was but a word,
Though the white breast was red-lipped where the sword
  Pierced a fierce cruel kiss, to put surcease
  On its hot thirst, but drank a hot increase.
Ah, they by some strange troubling doubt were stirred,
And died for hearing what no foeman heard.

They went forth to battle but they always fell:
  Their might was not the might of lifted spears;
Over the battle clamor came a spell
Of troubling music, and they fought not well.
  Their wreaths are willows and their tribute, tears;
  Their names are old sad stories in men's ears;
Yet they will scatter the red hordes of Hell,
Who went forth to battle and always fell.

TEARS

Lizette Woodworth Reese

When I consider life and its few years—
A wisp of fog betwixt us and the sun;
A call to battle and the battle done
Ere the last echo dies within our ears;
A rose choked in the grass; an hour of fears;
The gusts that past a darkening shore do beat;
A burst of music down an unlistening street—
I wonder at the idleness of tears.
Ye, old, old dead, and ye of yesternight,
Chieftains and bards and keepers of the sheep:
By every cup of sorrow that you had,

Loose me from tears, and make me see aright
How each hath back what once he stayed to weep;
Homer his sight, David his little lad!

IO VICTIS

WILLIAM WETMORE STORY

I sing the hymn of the conquered, who fall in the Battle of
 Life,—

The hymn of the wounded, the beaten, who died overwhelmed
 in the strife;

Not the jubilant song of the victors, for whom the resounding
 acclaim

Of nations was lifted in chorus, whose brows wear the chaplet
 of fame,

But the hymn of the low and the humble, the weary, the broken
 in heart,

Who strove and who failed, acting bravely a silent and desper-
 ate part;

Whose youth bore no flower in its branches, whose hopes burned
 in ashes away,

From whose hands slipped the prize they had grasped at, who
 stood at the dying of day

With the wreck of their life all around them, unpitied, unheeded,
 alone,

With Death swooping down o'er their failure, and all but their
 faith overthrown,

While the voice of the world shouts its chorus,—its pæan for
 those who have won;

While the trumpet is sounding triumphant, and high to the
 breeze and the sun

Glad banners are waving, hands clapping, and hurrying feet

Thronging after the laurel crowned victors, I stand on the field
 of defeat,

In the shadow, with those who are fallen, and wounded, and
 dying, and there

Chant a requiem low, place my hand on their pain-knotted
 brows, breathe a prayer,

Hold the hand that is helpless, and whisper, "They only the
    victory win,
Who have fought the good fight, and have vanquished the
    demon that tempts us within;
Who have held to their faith unseduced by the prize that the
    world holds on high;
Who have dared for a high cause to suffer, resist, fight,—if
    need be, to die."
Speak, History! Who are Life's victors? Unroll thy long
    annals and say,
Are they those whom the world called the victors, who won the
    success of a day?
The martyrs, or Nero? The Spartans, who fell at Thermopy-
    læ's tryst,
Or the Persians and Xerxes? His judges or Socrates?
    Pilate or Christ?

FAILURES

Arthur W. Upson

They bear no laurels on their sunless brows,
    Nor aught within their pale hands as they go;
    They look as men accustomed to the slow
And level onward course 'neath drooping boughs.
Who may these be no trumpet doth arouse,
    These of the dark processionals of woe,
    Unpraised, unblamed, but whom sad Acheron's flow
Monotonously lulls to leaden drowse?
These are the Failures. Clutched by Circumstance,
    They were—say not, too weak!—too ready prey
To their own fear whose fixèd Gorgon glance
    Made them as stone for aught of great essay;—
Or else they nodded when their Master-Chance
Wound his one signal, and went on his way.

e. IS THERE NO IMMEDIATE RELIEF?

I. *Heaven Only Can Heal*

COURAGE

PAUL GERHARDT

Translated by John Wesley

Give to the winds thy fears;
 Hope and be undismayed;
God hears thy sighs and counts thy tears,
 God shall lift up thy head.

Through waves and clouds and storms
 He gently clears thy way;
Wait thou His time; so shall this night
 Soon end in joyous day.

Leave to His sovereign sway
 To choose and to command;
So shalt thou wondering own, His way
 How wise, how strong His hand!

Far, far above thy thought
 His counsel shall appear,
When fully He the work hath wrought
 That caused thy needless fear.

Let us in life, in death,
 Thy steadfast truth declare,
And publish with our latest breath,
 The love and guardian care.

THE CHRISTIAN LIFE

SAMUEL LONGFELLOW

I look to Thee in ev'ry need,
    And never look in vain;
I feel Thy strong and tender love,
    And all is well again;
The thought of Thee is mightier far
Than sin and pain and sorrow are.

Discouraged in the work of life,
    Disheartened by its load,
Shamed by its failures or its fears,
    I sink beside the road;
But let me only think of Thee,
And then new heart springs up in me.

Thy calmness bends serene above,
    My restlessness to still,
Around me flows Thy quickening life
    To nerve my faltering will;
Thy presence fills my solitude,
Thy providence turns all to good.

Embosomed deep in Thy great love,
    Held in Thy law, I stand;
Thy hand in all things I behold,
    And all things in Thy hand;
Thou leadest me by unsought ways,
And turn'st my mourning into praise.

IN DARK HOUR

Seumas MacManus

I turn my steps where the Lonely Road
  Winds as far as the eye can see,
And I bend my back for the burden sore
  That God has reached down to me.

I have said farewell to the sun-kissed plains,
  To joy I gave good-bye;
Now the bleak wide wastes of the world are mine,
  And the winds that wail in the sky.

No bright flower blooms, no sweet bird calls,
  Nor hermit ever abode,
Not a green thing lifts one lonely leaf,
  O God, on the Lonely Road!

The thick dank mists come stealing down,
  And press me on every side,
With never a voice to cheer me on
  And never a hand to guide.

I shall cry in my need for a Voice and a Hand,
  And the solace of love-wet eyes—
And an icy clutch will close on my heart,
  When Echo, the mocker, replies.

I know my good soul will fail me not,
  When forms from the dark round me creep,
And whisper 'twere sweet to journey no more,
  But lay down the burden and sleep.

(Look onward and up, O Heart of my Heart,
  Where the road strikes the skies afar!
To cheer you and guide, thro' your darkest hour
  Behold yon beckoning star!)

I set my face to the gray wild wastes,
    I bend my back to the load—
Dear God, be kind with the heart-sick child
    Who steps on the Lonely Road.

COME, YE DISCONSOLATE

THOMAS MOORE

Come, ye disconsolate, where'er you languish,
    Come, at God's altar fervently kneel;
Here bring your wounded hearts, here tell your anguish,—
    Earth has no sorrow that heaven cannot heal.

Joy of the desolate, light of the straying,   .
    Hope when all others die, fadeless and pure,
Here speaks the comforter, in God's name saying,
    "Earth has no sorrow that heaven cannot cure."

Go, ask the infidel what boon he brings us,
    What charm for aching hearts he can reveal,
Sweet as that heavenly promise hope sings us,—
    "Earth has no sorrow that God cannot heal."

SORROW

GEORGE SANTAYANA

Have patience; it is fit that in this wise
The spirit purge away its proper dross.
No endless fever doth thy watches toss,
For by excess of evil, evil dies.
Soon shall the faint world melt before thine eyes,
And, all life's losses cancelled by life's loss,
Thou shalt lay down all burdens on thy cross,
And be that day with God in Paradise.
Have patience; for a long eternity
No summons woke thee from thy happy sleep;

For love of God one vigil thou canst keep
And add thy drop of sorrow to the sea.
Having known grief, all will be well with thee,
Ay, and thy second slumber will be deep.

2. *Love Only Can Heal*

THE HARP OF SORROW

ETHEL CLIFFORD

Sorrow has a harp of seven strings
And plays on it unceasing all the day;
The first string sings of love that is long dead,
The second sings of lost hopes buried;
The third of happiness forgot and fled.
Of vigil kept in vain the fourth cord sings,
And the fifth string of roses dropt away.
The sixth string calls and is unanswered,
The seventh with your name forever rings—
I listen for its singing all the day!

3. *Service Only Can Heal*

SONNET ON HIS BLINDNESS

JOHN MILTON

When I consider how my light is spent
Ere half my days in this dark world and wide,
And that one talent which is death to hide,
Lodged with me useless, though my soul more bent
To serve therewith my Maker, and present
My true account, lest he returning chide;
"Doth God exact day-labor, light denied?"

I fondly ask.　But Patience, to prevent
That murmur, soon replies, "God doth not need
Either man's work or his own gifts; who best
Bear his mild yoke, they serve him best; his state
Is kingly: thousands at his bidding speed,
And post o'er land and ocean without rest;
They also serve who only stand and wait."

4. *Time Only Can Heal*

SORROW

Emily Dickinson

They say that "Time assuages,"—
　　Time never did assuage;
An actual suffering strengthens,
　　As sinews do, with age.

Time is test of trouble
　　But not a remedy.
If such it prove, it proves, too,
　　There was no malady.

EVEN THIS SHALL PASS AWAY

Theodore Tilton

Once in Persia reigned a King
Who upon his signet ring
Graved a maxim true and wise,
Which, if held before the eyes,
Gave him counsel at a glance,
Fit for every change and chance.
Solemn words, and these are they:
"Even this shall pass away."

Trains of camels through the sand
Brought him gems from Samarcand;
Fleets of galleys through the seas
Brought him pearls to match with these.
But he counted not his gain
Treasures of the mine or main;
"What is wealth?" the king would say;
"Even this shall pass away."

In the revels of his court
At the zenith of the sport,
When the palms of all his guests
Burned with clapping at his jests;
He amid his figs and wine,
Cried: "Oh loving friends of mine!
Pleasure comes but not to stay;
Even this shall pass away."

Fighting on a furious field,
Once a javelin pierced his shield;
Soldiers with a loud lament
Bore him bleeding to his tent;
Groaning from his tortured side,
"Pain is hard to bear," he cried,
"But with patience, day by day,—
Even this shall pass away."

Towering in the public square,
Twenty cubits in the air,
Rose his statue, carved in stone,
Then the king, disguised, unknown,
Stood before his sculptured name
Musing meekly, "What is fame?
Fame is but a slow decay—
Even this shall pass away."

Struck with palsy, sere and old,
Waiting at the gates of gold,
Said he with his dying breath:
"Life is done, but what is death?"

Then, in answer to the King,
Fell a sunbeam on his ring,
Showing by a heavenly ray,
"Even this shall pass away."

X. Conduct of Life

    a. PERSONAL
1. *High Aims*
2. *Self-control*
3. *Work*
4. *Humility*
5. *Opportunity*
6. *Loyalty to Your Best Self*
7. *Loyalty to Duty*
8. *Creeds*

    b. SOCIAL (GOD IN ALL GREAT MOVEMENTS)
1. *Social Struggle*
2. *National Affairs*
3. *International Affairs*

ATTAINMENT

MADISON CAWEIN

On the heights of Great Endeavor,—
Where Attainment looms forever,—
Toiling upward, ceasing never,
Climb the fateful Centuries:
Up the difficult dark places,
Joy and anguish in their faces,
On they strive, the living races,
And the dead that no one sees.

Shape by shape with brow uplifted,
One by one where night is rifted,
Pass the victors, many gifted,
Where the heaven opens wide;
While below them, fallen or seated,
Mummy-like, or shadow-sheeted,
Stretch the lines of the defeated,—
Scattered on the mountain side.

And each victor, passing wanly,
Gazes on that Presence lonely,
With moving eyes where only
Grow the dreams for which men die:
Grow the dreams, the far, ethereal,
That on earth assume material
Attributes, and, vast, imperial,
Rear their battlements on high.

Kingdoms, marble-templed, towered,
Where the arts, the many-dowered,—
That for centuries have flowered,
Trampled under War's wild heel,—
Lift immortal heads and golden,
Blossoms of the times called olden,
Soul-alluring, earth-withholden,
Universal in appeal.

As they enter—high and lowly,—
On the hush these words fall slowly:—
Ye who kept your purpose holy,
Never dreamed your cause was vain,
Look!—Behold, through time abating,
How the long, sad days of waiting,
Striving, starving, hoping, hating,
Helped your spirit to attain.

"For to all who dream, aspire,
Marry effort to desire,
On the cosmic heights, in fire
Beaconing, my form appears:—
I am marvel, I am morning!
Beauty in man's heart and warning!—
On my face none looks with scorning,
And no soul attains who fears."

THE CHAMBERED NAUTILUS

Oliver Wendell Holmes

This is the ship of pearl, which, poets feign,
  Sails the unshadowed main,—
  The venturous bark that flings
On the sweet summer wind its purpled wings
In gulfs enchanted, where the Siren sings,
  And coral reefs lie bare,
Where the cold sea-maids rise to sun their streaming hair.

Its webs of living gauze no more unfurl;
  Wrecked is the ship of pearl!
  And every chambered cell,
Where its dim dreaming life was wont to dwell,
As the frail tenant shaped his growing shell,
  Before thee lies revealed,—
Its irised ceiling rent, its sunless crypt unsealed!

Year after year beheld the silent toil
  That spread his lustrous coil;
  Still, as the spiral grew,
He left the past year's dwelling for the new,
Stole with soft step its shining archway through,
  Built up its idle door,
Stretched in his last-found home, and knew the old no more.

Thanks for the heavenly message brought by thee,
  Child of the wandering sea,
  Cast from her lap, forlorn!
From thy dead lips a clearer note is born
Than ever Triton blew from wreathed horn!
  While on mine ear it rings,
Through the deep caves of thought I hear a voice that sings,—

Build thee more stately mansions, O my soul,
  As the swift seasons roll!
  Leave thy low-vaulted past!
Let each new temple, nobler than the last,
Shut thee from heaven with a dome more vast,
  Till thou at length art free,
Leaving thine outgrown shell by life's unresting sea!

EXPECTANS EXPECTAVI

CHARLES HAMILTON SORLEY

From morn till midnight, all day through,
I laugh and play as the others do,
I sing and chatter, just the same
As others with a different name.

And all year long upon the stage,
I dance and tumble and do rage
So vehemently, I scarcely see
The inner and eternal me.

I have a temple I do not
Visit, a heart I have forgot,
A self I have never met,
A secret shrine, and yet, and yet

This sanctuary of my soul
Unwitting I keep white and whole,
Unlatched and lit, if Thou shouldst care
To enter or to tarry there.

With parted lips and outstretched hands
And listening ears Thy servant stands,
Call Thou early, call Thou late,
To Thy great service dedicate.

ATTAINMENT

Ella Wheeler Wilcox

Use all your hidden forces. Do not miss
The purpose of this life, and do not wait
For circumstance to mold or change your fate.
In your own self lies destiny. Let this
Vast truth cast out all fear, all prejudice,
All hesitation. Know that you are great,
Great with divinity. So dominate
Environment, and enter into bliss.—
Love largely and hate nothing. Hold no aim
That does not chord with universal good.

Hear what the voices of the silence say,
All joys are yours if you put forth your claim,
Once let the spiritual laws be understood,
Material things must answer and obey.

2. *Self-Control*

SELF-DEPENDENCE

Matthew Arnold

Weary of myself and sick of asking
What I am and what I ought to be,
At this vessel's prow I stand, which bears me
Forwards, forwards, o'er the starlit sea.

And a look of passionate desire
O'er the sea and to the stars I send:
"Ye who from my childhood up have calmed me,
Calm me, Ah, compose me to the end!

"Ah, once more," I cried, "ye stars, ye waters,
On my heart your mighty charm renew;
Still, still let me, as I gaze upon you,
Feel my soul becoming vast, like you!"

From the intense, clear, star-sown vault of heaven,
Over the lit sea's unquiet way,
In the rustling night air came the answer:
"Wouldst thou *be* as these are: LIVE as they.

"Unaffrighted by the silence round them,
Undistracted by the sights they see,
These demand not that the things without them
Yield them love, amusement, sympathy.

"And with joy the stars perform their shining,
And the sea its long moon-silvered roll;
For self-poised they live, nor pine with noting
All the fever of some differing soul.

"Bounded by themselves, and unregardful
In what state God's other works may be,
In their own tasks all their powers pouring,
These attain the mighty life you see."

Oh, air-born voice! long since, severely clear,
A cry like thine in my own heart I hear:
"Resolve to be thyself; and know that he,
Who finds himself, loses his misery!"

THE STUPID OLD BODY

Edward Carpenter

Do not pay too much attention to the stupid old Body.

When you have trained it, made it healthy, beautiful, and your
willing servant,
Why, then do not reverse the order and become its slave and
attendant.
(The dog must follow the master, not the master the dog.)
Remember that if you walk away from it and leave it behind, it
will have to follow you—it will grow by following, by
continually reaching up to you.
Incredibly beautiful it will become, and suffused by a kind of
intelligence.
But if you turn and wait upon it—and its mouth and its belly
and its sex-wants and all its little ape-tricks—preparing and
dishing up pleasures and satisfactions for these,
Why, then, instead of the body becoming like you, you will
become like the body,
Incredibly stupid and unformed—going back in the path of
evolution—you too with fish-mouth and toad-belly, and im-
prisoned in your own members, as it were an Ariel in a
blundering Caliban.

Therefore quite lightly and decisively at each turning-point in
the path leave your body a little behind—
With its hungers and sleeps, and funny little needs and vanities
—Pay no attention to them;
Slipping out at least a few steps in advance, till it catch you up
again,
Absolutely determined not to be finally bound and weighted
down by it,

Or fossilized into one set form—
Which alone after all is death.

THE WANDERING LUNATIC MIND

Edward Carpenter

Do not pay too much attention to the wandering lunatic Mind.

When you have trained it, informed it, made it clear, decisive,
and your flexible instrument and tool,
Why, then, do not reverse the order and become the mere fatu-
ous attendant and exhibitor of its acrobatic feats (like a
keeper who shows off a monkey).
Remember that if you walk away from it, leaving it as dead,
paying it no attention whatever—it will have to follow you
—it will grow by following, by reaching up to you, from the
known to the unknown, continually;
It will become at last the rainbow-tinted garment and shining
interpreter of Yourself, and incredibly beautiful.
But if you turn and wait always upon it, and its idiotic cares
and anxieties, and endless dream-chains of argument and
imagination—
Feeding them and the microbe-swarms of thoughts continually,
wasting upon them your life-force;
Why, then, instead of your Mind becoming your true companion
and interpreter, it will develop antics and a St. Vitus's
dance of its own, and the form of a wandering lunatic,
Incredibly tangle-haired and diseased and unclean,
In whose features you, in sadness and in vain, will search for
your own image—terrified lest you find it not, and terrified
too lest you find it.

Therefore quite decisively, day by day and at every juncture,
leave your Mind for a time in silence and abeyance;
With its tyrannous thoughts and demands, and funny little fears
and fancies—the long legacy of ages of animal evolution:
Slipping out and going your own way into the Unseen—feeling
with your feet if necessary through the darkness—till some
day it may follow you:

Absolutely determined not to be bound by any of its conclusions;
    or fossilized in any pattern it may invent;
For this were to give up your kingdom, and bow down your
    neck to death.

MY MINDE TO ME A KINGDOM IS

SIR EDWARD DYER

Altered by William Byrd, 1588

My minde to me a kingdom is,
    Such perfect joy therein I finde
As farre exceeds all earthly blisse
    That God or nature hath assignde;
Though much 1 want that most would have,
Yet still my minde forbids to crave.

Content I live; this is my stay,—
    I seek no more than may suffice,
I presse to beare no haughtie sway;
    Look, what I lack my minde supplies.
Loe, thus I triumph like a king,
Content with that my minde doth bring.

I see how plentie surfeits oft,
    And hastie clymbers soonest fall;
I see that such as sit aloft
    Mishap doth threaten most of all.
These get with toile, and keepe with feare;
Such cares my minde could never beare.

No princely pompe nor welthie store,
    No force to win the victorie,
No wylie wit to salve a sore,
    No shape to winne a lover's eye,—
To none of these I yield as thrall;
For why, my minde despiseth all.

Some have too much, yet still they crave,
  I little have, yet seek no more.
They are but poore, though much they have,
  And I am rich with little store.
They poor, I rich; they beg, I give;
They lacke, I leave; they pine, I live.

I laugh not at another's losse,
  I grudge not at another's gaine;
No worldly wave my minde can tosse;
  I brooke that is another's bane.
I feare no foe, nor fawne on friend;
I lothe not life, nor dread mine end.

I joy not in no earthly blisse;
  I weigh not Cresus' wealth a straw;
For care, I care not what it is;
  I feare not fortune's fatal law;
My minde is such as may not move
For beautie bright, or force of love.

I wish but what I have at will;
  I wander not to seeke for more;
I like the plaine, I clime no hill;
  In greatest stormes I sitte on shore,
And laugh at them that toile in vaine
To get what must be lost againe.

I kisse not where I wish to kill;
  I feigne not love where most I hate;
I breake no sleepe to winne my will;
  I wayte not at the mightie's gate.
I scorne no poore, I feare no rich;
I feele no want, nor have too much.

The court ne cart I like ne loath,—
  Extreames are counted worst of all;
The golden meane betwixt them both
  Doth surest sit, and feares no fall;
This is my choyce; for why, I finde
No wealth is like a quiet minde.

My wealth is health and perfect ease;
  My conscience clere my chiefe defence;
I never seeke by bribes to please,
  Nor by desert to give offence.
Thus do I live, thus will I die;
Would all did so as well as I!

THE HAPPY LIFE

SIR HENRY WOTTON

How happy is he born and taught
  That serveth not another's will;
Whose armor is his honest thought,
  And simple truth his utmost skill!

Whose passions not his masters are,
  Whose soul is still prepared for death,
Untied unto the world by care
  Of public fame, or private breath;

Who envies none that chance doth raise,
  Nor vice, who never understood
How deepest wounds are given by praise;
  Nor rules of State, but rules of good;

Who hath his life from rumors freed;
  Whose conscience is his strong retreat;
Whose state can neither flatterers feed,
  Nor ruin make oppressors great;

Who God doth late and early pray,
  More of his grace than gifts to lend;
And entertains the harmless day
  With a well-chosen book or friend!

—This man is freed from servile bands
  Of hope to rise or fear to fall!
Lord of himself, though not of lands;
  And having nothing, yet hath all!

3. *Work*

REALIZATION

Sri Ananda Acharya

I will keep the fire of hope ever burning on the altar of my soul,
I will feed it by day and by night with the fuel of industry and
    the oblation of thought,
Like a spring plant the great purpose is growing in the garden
    of my heart;
I will moisten its roots each morn with the water of new re-
    solve, and with vows of renunciation will I hedge it round;
I will forego all comforts, all pastures, till this plant of my
    purpose bear fruit,
And I will not lose patience if the fruit come not in season,
The Future enters into the Present to weave life's texture after
    the heaven-willed pattern
And the Past is overshadowed and the face of the Present made
    pale.
The map of life is many-coloured, showing many kings' do-
    minions, whose boundaries are the theatres of unremitting
    wars;
I will make this map of one sole colour and Truth shall reign
    the one sole King for all eternity.
All will I sacrifice—Life, Time,—Happiness, nay, the whole
    universe of the gods—
To realize the purpose which Truth proclaims to be the all-
    supreme.

TO THE CHRISTIANS

William Blake

I give you the end of a golden string;
    Only wind it into a ball,—
It will lead you in at Heaven's gate
    Built in Jerusalem's wall.

England! Awake! Awake! Awake!
   Jerusalem thy sister calls!
Why wilt thou sleep the sleep of death,
   And close her from thy ancient walls?

Thy hills and valleys felt her feet
   Gently upon their bosoms move:
Thy gates beheld sweet Zion's ways;
   Then was a time of joy and love.

And now the time returns again:
   Our souls exult, and London's towers
Receive the Lamb of God to dwell
   In England's green and pleasant bowers.

From MILTON

William Blake

And did those feet in ancient time
   Walk upon England's mountains green?
And was the holy Lamb of God
   On England's pleasant pastures seen?

And did the Countenance Divine
   Shine forth upon our clouded hills?
And was Jerusalem builded here
   Among these dark Satanic mills?

Bring me my bow of burning gold!
   Bring me my arrows of desire!
Bring me my spear! O clouds unfold!
   Bring me my chariot of fire!

I will not cease from Mental fight,
   Nor shall my sword sleep in my hand,
Till we have built Jerusalem
   In England's green and pleasant land.

THE SONG OF THE UNSUCCESSFUL

RICHARD BURTON

We are the toilers whom God hath barred
  The gifts that are good to hold,
We meant full well and we tried full hard,
  And our failures were manifold.

And we are the clan of those whose kin
  Were a millstone dragging them down,
Yea, we had to sweat for our brother's sin,
  And lose the victor's crown.

The seeming-able, who all but scored,
  From their teeming tribe we come:
What was there wrong with us, O, Lord,
  That our lives were dark and dumb?

The men, ten-talented, who still
  Strangely, missed the goal,
Of them we are: it seems Thy will
  To harrow some in soul.

We are the sinners, too, whose lust
  Conquered the higher claims,
We sat us prone in the common dust,
  And played at the devil's games.

We are the hard-luck folk, who strove
  Zealously, but in vain;
We lost and lost, while our comrades throve,
  And still we are lost again.

We are the doubles of those whose way
  Was festal with fruits and flowers,
Body and brain we were sound as they,
  But the prizes were not ours

A mighty army our full ranks make,
  We shake the graves as we go;
The sudden stroke and the slow heart-break,
  They both have brought us low.

And while we are laying life's sword aside,
  Spent and dishonored and sad,
Our Epitaph this, when once we have died:
  "The weak lie here, and the bad."

We wonder if this can be really the close,
  Life's fever cooled by death's trance;
And we cry, though it seem to our dearest of foes,
  "God, give us another chance!"

ABOU BEN ADHEM

LEIGH HUNT

Abou Ben Adhem (may his tribe increase!)
Awoke one night from a deep dream of peace,
And saw within the moonlight in his room,
Making it rich and like a lily in bloom,
An angel writing in a book of gold;
Exceeding peace had made Ben Adhem bold,
And to the Presence in the room he said,
"What writest thou?" The vision raised its head,
And with a look made of all sweet accord,
Answered, "The names of those who love the Lord."
"And is mine one?" said Abou. "Nay, not so,"
Replied the angel. Abou spoke more low,
But cheerly still, and said, "I pray thee, then,
Write me as one who loves his fellow-men."
The angel wrote and vanished; the next night
It came again with a great wakening light,
And showed their names whom love of God hath blest,
And lo! Ben Adhem's name led all the rest.

THE SONS OF MARTHA

Rudyard Kipling

The Sons of Mary seldom bother, for they have inherited that
    good part,
But the Sons of Martha favor their mother of the careful soul
    and the troubled heart;
And because she lost her temper once, and because she was
    rude to the Lord, her guest,
Her Sons must wait upon Mary's Sons—world without end
    reprieve or rest.

It is their care in all the ages to take the buffet and cushion
    the shock,
It is their care that the gear engages; it is their care that the
    switches lock:
It is their care that the wheels run truly; it is their care to
    embark and entrain,
Tally, transport and deliver duly the Sons of Mary by land and
    main.

They say to the mountains, "Be ye removed!" They say to the
    lesser floods, "Run dry!"
Under their rods are the rocks reproved—they are not afraid
    of that which is high;
Then do the hilltops shake to the summit, then is the bed of
    the deep laid bare,
That the Sons of Mary may overcome it, pleasantly sleeping
    and unaware.

They finger Death at their glove's end when they piece and
    re-piece the living wires.
He rears against the gates they tend; they feed him hungry
    behind their fires.
Early at dawn ere men see clear they stumble into his terrible
    stall,
And hale him forth like haltered steer and goad and turn
    him till evenfall.

To these from birth is belief forbidden: from these till death
is relief afar—
They are concerned with matters hidden—under the earth-line
their altars are.
The secret fountains to follow up, waters withdrawn to restore
to the mouth,
Yea, and gather the floods as in a cup, and pour them again
at a city's drouth.

They do not preach that their God will rouse them a little
before the nuts work loose;
They do not teach that his pity allows them to leave their
work whenever they choose.
As in the thronged and the lightened ways, so in the dark and
the desert they stand,
Wary and watchful all their days, that their brethren's days
may be long in the land.

Lift ye the stone and cleave the wood, to make a path more
fair or flat.
Lo! it is black already with blood some Son of Martha spilled
for that.
Not as a ladder from earth to heaven, not as an altar to any
creed,
But simple service, simply given to his own kind in their com
mon need.

And the Sons of Mary smile and are blessèd—they know the
angels are on their side,
They know in them is the grace confessèd, and for them are
the mercies multiplied.
They sit at the Feet—they hear the Word—they know how truly
the Promise runs.
They have cast their burden upon the Lord, and—the Lord he
lays it on Martha's Sons.

4. *Humility*

THE SHEPHERD BOY SINGS

John Bunyan

He that is down needs fear no fall,
  He that is low, no pride;
He that is humble ever shall
  Have God to be his guide.

I am content with what I have,
  Little be it or much;
And, Lord, contentment still I crave,
  Because Thou savest such.

Fullness to such a burden is
  That go on pilgrimage:
Here little, and hereafter bliss
  Is best from age to age.

THE HAPPIEST HEART

John Vance Cheney

Who drives the horses of the sun
  Shall lord it but a day;
Better the lowly deed were done,
  And kept the humble way.

The rust will find the sword of fame,
  The dust will hide the crown;
Ay, none shall nail so high his name
  Time will not tear it down.

The happiest heart that ever beat
  Was in some quiet breast
That found the common daylight sweet,
  And left to Heaven the rest.

THE HOUSE BY THE SIDE OF THE ROAD

Sam Walter Foss

There are hermit souls that live withdrawn
   In the place of their self-content;
There are souls like stars, that dwell apart
   In a fellowless firmament.
There are pioneer souls that blaze their paths
   Where the highways never ran—
But let me live by the side of the road
   And be a friend to man.

Let me live in a house by the side of the road,
   Where the race of men go by—
The men who are good and the men who are bad,
   As good and as bad as I.
I would not sit in the scorner's seat,
   Or hurl the cynic's ban—
Let me live in the house by the side of the road
   And be a friend to man.

I see from my house by the side of the road,
   By the side of the highway of life,
The men who press with the ardor of hope,
   The men who faint with strife;
But I turn not away from their smiles nor their tears—
   Both parts of an infinite plan—
Let me live in a house by the side of the road
   And be a friend to man.

I know there are brook-gladdened meadows ahead,
   And mountains of wearisome height;
And the road passes on through the long afternoon,
   And stretches away to the night.
But still I rejoice when the travelers rejoice,
   And weep with the strangers that moan,
Nor live in my house by the side of the road,
   Like a man who dwells alone.

Let me live in my house by the side of the road,
    Where the race of men go by—
They are good, they are bad, they are weak, they are strong,
    Wise, foolish—so am I.
Then why should I sit in the scorner's seat
    Or hurl the cynic's ban?
Let me live in my house by the side of the road,
    And be a friend to man.

O WHY SHOULD THE SPIRIT OF MORTAL BE PROUD?

WILLIAM KNOX

O why should the spirit of mortal be proud?
Like swift-flitting meteor, a fast-flying cloud,
A flash of the lightning, a break of the wave,
He passeth from life to his rest in the grave.

The leaves of the oak and the willow shall fade,
Be scattered around and together be laid;
And the young and the old, and the low and the high,
Shall moulder to dust and together shall lie.

The child that a mother attended and loved,
The mother that infant's affection who proved,
The husband that mother and infant who blessed,
Each, all, are away to their dwellings of rest.

The maid on whose brow, on whose cheek, in whose eye,
Shone beauty and pleasure,—her triumphs are by;
And the memory of those who have loved her and praised,
Are alike from the minds of the living erased.

The hand of the king that the sceptre hath borne,
The brow of the priest that the mitre hath worn,
The eyes of the sage, and the heart of the brave,—
Are hidden and lost in the depths of the grave.

The peasant whose lot was to sow and to reap,
The herdsman who climbed with his goats to the steep,
The beggar who wandered in search of his bread,—
Have faded away like the grass that we tread.

The saint who enjoyed the communion of heaven,
The sinner who dared to remain unforgiven,
The wise and the foolish, the guilty and just,
Have quietly mingled their bones in the dust.

So the multitude goes, like the flower and the weed,
That wither away to let others succeed;
So the multitude comes, like those we behold,
To repeat every tale that hath often been told.

For we are the things our fathers have been;
We see the same sights that our fathers have seen,—
We drink the same stream, we feel the same sun,
And run the same course that our fathers have run.

The thoughts we are thinking our fathers would think;
From the death we are shrinking, they, too, would shrink;
To the life we are clinging, they too would cling;
But it speeds from us all like the bird on the wing.

They loved, but their story we cannot unfold;
They scorned, but the heart of the haughty is cold;
They grieved, but no wail from their slumbers will come;
They joyed, but the voice of their gladness is dumb.

They died,—ay, they died; and we things that are now,
Who walk on the turf that lies over their brow,
Who make in their dwellings a transient abode,
Meet the changes they met on their pilgrimage road.

Yea, hope and despondency, pleasure and pain,
Are mingled together in sunshine and rain;
And the smile and the tear, and the song and the dirge,
Still follow each other like surge upon surge.

'Tis the wink of an eye, 'tis the draught of a breath,
From the blossom of health to the paleness of death,
From the gilded saloon to the bier and the shroud,—
Oh, why should the spirit of mortal be proud?

5. *Opportunity*

TODAY

Thomas Carlyle

So here hath been dawning
    Another blue day:
Think, wilt thou let it
    Slip useless away?

Out of Eternity
    This new day is born;
Into Eternity
    At night will return.

Behold it afore time,
    No eye ever did:
So soon it forever
    From all eyes is hid.

Here hath been dawning
    Another blue day:
Think, wilt thou let it
    Slip useless away?

THE WATER MILL

Sara Doudney

Listen to the water mill,
    Through the live-long day,
How the clanking of its wheels
    Wears the hours away!

Languidly the autumn wind
  Stirs the greenwood leaves;
From the field the reapers sing,
  Binding up the sheaves;
And a proverb haunts my mind,
  As a spell is cast:
"The mill will never grind
With the water that has passed."

Take the lesson to thyself,
  Loving heart and true;
Golden years are fleeting by,
  Youth is passing, too;
Learn to make the most of life,
  Lose no happy day;
Time will never bring thee back
  Chances swept away.
Leave no tender word unsaid,
  Love while life shall last—
"The mill will never grind
With the water that has passed."

Work while the daylight shines,
  Man of strength and will,
Never does the streamlet glide
  Useless by the mill.
Wait not till tomorrow's sun
  Beams upon the way;
All thou canst call thine own
  Lies in thy today.
Power, intellect and health
  May not, cannot last;
"The mill will never grind
With the water that has passed."

Oh, the wasted hours of life
  That have drifted by,
Oh, the good we might have done,
  Lost without a sigh;
Love that we might once have saved

By a single word,
Thoughts conceived but never penned,
Perishing unheard.
Take the proverb to thine heart,
Take! oh, hold it fast!—
"The mill will never grind
With the water that has passed."

IRREVOCABLE

MARY WRIGHT PLUMMER

What thou hast done thou hast done; for the heavenly horses
are swift.
Think not their flight to o'ertake,—they stand at the throne even
now.
Ere thou canst compass the thought, the immortals in just hands
shall lift,
Poise, and weigh surely thy deed, and its weight shall be laid
on thy brow;
For what thou hast done thou hast done.

What thou hast not done remains; and the heavenly horses are
kind.
Till thou hast pondered thy choice, they will patiently wait at
thy door.
Do a brave deed, and behold! they are farther away than the
wind.
Returning, they bring thee a crown, to shine on thy brow ever-
more;
For what thou hast done thou hast done.

OPPORTUNITY

EDWARD ROWLAND SILL

This I beheld, or dreamed it in a dream:—
There spread a cloud of dust along a plain;
And underneath the cloud, or in it, raged

A furious battle, and men yelled, and swords
Shocked upon swords and shields. A prince's banner
Wavered, then staggered backward, hemmed by foes.
A craven hung along the battle's edge,
And thought, "Had I a sword of keener steel—
That blue blade which the king's son bears,—but this
Blunt thing—!" he snapped and flung it from his hand,
And lowering crept away and left the field.
Then came the king's son, wounded, sore bestead,
And weaponless, and saw the broken sword,
Hilt-buried in the dry and trodden sand,
And ran and snatched it, and with battle shout
Lifted afresh he hewed his enemy down,
And saved a great cause that heroic day.

6. *Loyalty to Your Best Self*

HARPS HUNG UP IN BABYLON

ARTHUR COLTON

The harps hung up in Babylon,
Their loosened strings rang on, sang on,
And cast their murmurs forth upon
The roll and the roar of Babylon:
"Forget me, Lord, if I forget
Jerusalem for Babylon:
If I forget the vision set
High as the head of Lebanon
Is lifted over Syria yet,
If I forget and bow me down
To brutish Gods of Babylon."

Two rivers to each other run
In the very midst of Babylon,
And swifter than their current fleets
The restless river of the streets

Of Babylon, of Babylon.
And Babylon's towers smite the sky,
But higher reeks to God most high
The smoke of her iniquity:
"But oh, betwixt the green and blue
To walk the hills that once we knew
When you were pure and I was true."—
So rang the harps of Babylon—
"Or ere along the roads of stone
Had led us captive one by one
The subtle gods of Babylon."

The harps hung up in Babylon
Hung silent till the prophet dawn,
When Judah's feet the highway burned
Back to the holy hills returned,
And shook their dust on Babylon.
In Zion's halls the wild harps rang,
To Zion's walls their smitten clang,
And lo! of Babylon they sang,
They only sang of Babylon:
"Jehovah, round whose throne of awe
The vassal stars their orbits draw
Within the circle of Thy law,
Canst thou make nothing what is done,
Or cause thy servant to be one
That has not been in Babylon,
That has not known the power and pain
Of life poured out like driven rain?
I will go down and find again
My soul that's lost in Babylon."

VIRTUE

George Herbert

Sweet day, so cool, so calm, so bright!
The bridal of the earth and sky:
The dew shall weep thy fall tonight;
  For thou must die.

Sweet rose, whose hue, angry and brave
Bids the rash gazer wipe his eye:
Thy root is ever in the grave,
 And thou must die.

Sweet spring, full of sweet days and roses,
A box where sweets compacted lie;
My music shows ye have your closes,
 And all must die.

Only a sweet and virtuous soul,
Like seasoned timber, never gives;
But though the whole world turn to coal,
 Then chiefly lives.

THE TREE AND THE CHAFF

Psalm I

From Moulton's Modern Reader's Bible

Blessed is the man that walketh not in the counsels of the
 wicked
 Nor standeth in the way of sinners,
Nor sitteth in the seat of the scornful.
But his delight is in the law of the *Lord,*
 And in his law doth he meditate day and night.

And he shall be like a tree planted by the streams of water,
 That bringeth its fruit in its season,
Whose leaf also doth not wither;
 And whatsoever he doeth shall prosper.
The wicked are not so;
 But are like the chaff which the wind driveth away.

Therefore the wicked shall not stand in the judgment,
 Nor sinners in the congregation of the righteous.
For the Lord knoweth the way of the righteous;
 But the way of the wicked shall perish.

THE PILGRIM

RICHARD WIGHTMAN

I am my ancient self,
　　Long paths I've trod,
The living light before,
　　Behind, the rod:
And in the beam and blow
　　The misty God.

I am my ancient self.
　　My flesh is young,
But old, mysterious words
　　Engage my tongue,
And weird, lost songs
　　Old bards have sung.

I have not fared alone.
　　In mount and dell
The one I fain would be
　　Stands by me well,
And bids my man's heart list
　　To the far bell.

Give me nor ease nor goal—
　　Only the Way,
A bit of bread and sleep
　　Where the white waters play,
The pines, the patient stars,
　　And the new day.

THE SERVANTS

RICHARD WIGHTMAN

Singers, sing! The hoary world
Needs reminder of its youth:
Prophet, tell! The darkness lies
On the labyrinths of truth ·

Builder, build! Let rocks uprise
Into cities 'neath thy hand:
Farmer, till! The sun and rain
Hearken for the seed's demand:
Artist, paint! Thy canvases
Patiently convey thy soul:
Writer, write! With pen blood-dipped
Trace no segment, but the whole:
Teacher, teach! Thyself the creed—
Only that a child may know:
Dreamer, dream! Nor hide thy face
Though thy castles crumble low.
Where the toiler turns the sod
Man beholds the living God.

7. *Loyalty to Duty*

RESOLVE

CHARLOTTE PERKINS GILMAN

To keep my health!
To do my work!
  To live!
To see to it I grow and gain and give!
Never to look behind me for an hour!
To wait in weakness and to walk in power.
But always fronting onward toward the light
Always and always facing toward the right,
Robbed, starved, defeated, fallen, wide astray—
On with what strength I have
Back to the way!

THE NAMELESS SAINTS

Edward Everett Hale

I

What was his name? I do not know his name.
I only know he heard God's voice and came,
  Brought all he had across the sea
  To live and work for God and me;
    Felled the ungracious oak;
    Dragged from the soil
    With horrid toil
  The thrice-gnarled roots and stubborn rock;
With plenty piled the haggard mountain-side;
And at the end, without memorial, died.
No blaring trumpets sounded out his fame,
He lived,—he died,—I do not know his name.

II

No form of bronze and no memorial stones
Show me the place where lie his mouldering bones.
  Only a cheerful city stands
  Builded by his hardened hands.
    Only ten thousand homes
      Where every day
      The cheerful play
  Of love and hope and courage comes.
These are his monument, and these alone.
There is no form of bronze and no memorial stone.

III

And I?
Is there some desert or some pathless sea
Where Thou, Good God of angels, wilt send me?
  Some oak for me to rend; some sod,
    Some rock for me to break;
    Some handful of His corn to take

And scatter far afield,
Till it, in turn, shall yield
Its hundredfold
Of grains of gold
To feed the waiting children of my God?
Show me the desert, Father, or the sea.
Is it Thine enterprise? Great God, send me.
And though this body lie where ocean rolls,
Count me among all Faithful Souls.

OBEDIENCE

George MacDonald

I said: "Let me walk in the fields."
  He said: "No, walk in the town."
I said: "There are no flowers there."
  He said: "No flowers, but a crown."

I said: "But the skies are black;
  There is nothing but noise and din."
And He wept as He sent me back—
  "There is more," He said; "there is sin."

I said: "But the air is thick,
  And fogs are veiling the sun."
He answered: "Yet souls are sick,
  And souls in the dark undone!"

I said: "I shall miss the light,
  And friends will miss me, they say."
He answered: "Choose tonight
  If I am to miss you or they."

I pleaded for time to be given.
  He said: "Is it hard to decide?
It will not seem so hard in heaven
  To have followed the steps of your Guide."

I cast one look at the fields,
  Then set my face to the town;
He said, "My child, do you yield?
  Will you leave the flowers for the crown?"

Then into His hand went mine;
  And into my heart came He;
And I walk in a light divine,
  The path I had feared to see.

THE REPLY OF SOCRATES

Edith M. Thomas

This from that soul incorrupt whom Athens had doomed to the death,
When Crito brought promise of freedom: "Vainly thou spendest thy breath!
Dost remember the wild Corybantes? feel they the knife or the rod?
Heed they the fierce summer sun, the frost, or winterly flaws?—
If any entreat them they answer, 'We hear but the flutes of the God!'

"So even am I, O my Crito! Thou pleadest a losing cause!
Thy words are but sound without import—I hear but the voice of the Laws;
And, know thou, the voice of the Laws is to me as the flutes of the God."
Thus spake that soul incorrupt, and wherever, since hemlock was quaffed,
A man has stood forth without fear—has chosen the dark, deep draught!—
Has taken the lone one way, nor the path of dishonour has trod—
Behold! He, too, hears but the voice of the Laws, the flutes of the God!

ODE TO DUTY

WILLIAM WORDSWORTH

Stern Daughter of the Voice of God!
O Duty! if that name thou love,
Who art a light to guide, a rod
To check the erring, and reprove;
Thou, who art victory and law
When empty terrors overawe,
From vain temptations dost set free,
And calm'st the weary strife of frail humanity!

There are who ask not if thine eye
Be on them; who, in love and truth,
Where no misgiving is, rely
Upon the genial sense of youth:
Glad Hearts! without reproach or blot,
Who do Thy work and know it not:
Oh! if through confidence misplaced
They fail, thy saving arms, dread Power! around them cast.

Serene will be our days and bright,
And happy will our nature be,
When love is an unerring light,
And joy its own security.
And they a blissful course may hold
Even now, who, not unwisely bold,
Live in the spirit of this creed;
Yet seek thy firm support according to their need.

I, loving freedom, and untried;
No sport of every random gust,
Yet being to myself a guide,
Too blindly have reposed my trust:
And oft, when in my heart was heard
Thy timely mandate, I deferred
The task, in smoother walks to stray;
But thee I now would serve more strictly, if I may.

Through no disturbance of my soul,
Or strong compunction in me wrought,
I supplicate for thy control;
But in the quietness of thought:
Me this unchartered freedom tires;
I feel the weight of chance desires:
My hopes no more must change their name,
I long for a repose that ever is the same.

Stern Lawgiver! yet thou dost wear
The Godhead's most benignant grace;
Nor know we anything so fair
As is the smile upon thy face:
Flowers laugh before thee upon their beds
And fragrance in thy footing treads;
Thou dost preserve the stars from wrong;
And the most ancient heavens, through thee, are fresh and
    strong.

To humbler functions, awful Power!
I call thee: I myself commend
Unto thy guidance from this hour;
Oh, let my weakness have an end!
Give unto me, made lowly wise,
The spirit of self-sacrifice;
The confidence of reason give;
And in the light of truth thy Bondman let me live!

8. *Creeds*

CREEDS

Karle Wilson Baker

Friend, you are grieved that I should go
Unhoused, unsheltered, gaunt and free,
My cloak for armor—for my tent
The roadside tree:

And I—I know not how you bear
A roof betwixt you and the blue,
Brother, the creed would stifle me
That shelters you.

Yet, that same light that floods at dawn
Your cloistered room, your cryptic stair,
Wakes me too—sleeping by the hedge—
To morning prayer!

MY CREED

ALICE CARY

I hold that Christian grace abounds
    Where charity is seen; that when
We climb to heaven, 'tis on the rounds
    Of love to men.

I hold all else named piety
    A selfish scheme, a vain pretense;
Where center is not—can there be
    Circumference?

This I moreover hold, and dare
    Affirm where'er my rhyme may go,—
Whatever things be sweet and fair,
    Love makes them so.

Whether it be the lullabies
    That charm to rest the nursling bird,
Or the sweet confidence of sighs
    And blushes, made without a word.

Whether the dazzling and the flush
    Of softly sumptuous garden bowers,
Or by some cabin door, a bush
    Of ragged flowers.

'Tis not the wide phylactery,
    Nor stubborn fast, nor stated prayers,
That make us saints: we judge the tree
    By what it bears.

And when a man can live apart
  From works, on theologic trust,
I know the blood about his heart
  Is dry as dust.

MY CREED

Jeanette Gilder

I do not fear to tread the path that those I love long since have
    trod;
I do not fear to pass the gates and stand before the living God.
In this world's fight I've done my part; if God be God He
    knows it well;
He will not turn His back on me and send me down to blackest
    hell
Because I have not prayed aloud and shouted in the market
    place.
'Tis what we do, not what we say, that makes us worthy of His
    grace.

RELIGION AND DOCTRINE

John Hay

He stood before the Sanhedrim;
The scowling rabbis gazed at him.
He recked not of their praise or blame;
There was no fear, there was no shame,
For one upon whose dazzled eyes
The whole world poured its vast surprise.
The open heaven was far too near,
His first day's light too sweet and clear,
To let him waste his new-gained ken
On the hate-clouded face of men.

But still they questioned, Who art thou?
What hast thou been? What art thou now?

Thou art not he who yesterday
Sat here and begged beside the way;
For he was blind.

And I am he;
For I was blind, but now I see.

He told the story o'er and o'er;
It was his full heart's only lore;
A prophet on the Sabbath-day
Had touched his sightless eyes with clay,
And made him see who had been blind.
Their words passed by him like the wind,
Which raves and howls, but cannot shock
The hundred-fathom-rooted rock.

Their threats and fury all went wide;
They could not touch his Hebrew pride.
Their sneers at Jesus and His band,
Nameless and homeless in the land,
Their boasts of Moses and his Lord,
All could not change him by one word.
"I know not what this man may be,
Sinner or saint; but as for me,
One thing I know,—that I am he
Who once was blind, and now I see."

They were all doctors of renown,
The great men of a famous town,
With deep brows, wrinkled, broad, and wise,
Beneath their wide phylacteries;
The wisdom of the east was theirs,
And honor crowned their silver hairs.
The man they jeered and laughed to scorn
Was unlearned, poor, and humbly born;
But he knew better far than they
What came to him that Sabbath-day;
And what the Christ had done to him,
He knew, and not the Sanhedrim.

A CREED

Norman McLeod

I believe in Human Kindness
  Large amid the sons of men,
Nobler far in willing blindness
  Than in censure's keenest ken.
I believe in Self-Denial,
  And its secret throb of joy;
In the love that lives through trial,
  Dying not, though death destroy.

I believe in dreams of Duty,
  Warning us to self-control—
Foregleams of the glorious beauty
  That shall yet transform the soul.
In the godlike wreck of nature
  Sin doth in the sinner leave,
That he may regain the stature
  He hath lost,—I do believe.

I believe in Love renewing
  All that sin hath swept away,
Leaven-like its work pursuing
  Night by night and day by day:
In the power of its remoulding,
  In the grace of its reprieve,
In the glory of beholding
  Its perfection,—I believe.

I believe in Love Eternal,
  Fixed in God's unchanging will,
That beneath the deep infernal
  Hath a depth that's deeper still!
In its patience—its endurance
  To forbear and to retrieve,
In the large and full assurance
  Of its triumph,—I believe.

SOME BLESSEDS

John Oxenham

Blessed are they that have eyes to see.
They shall find God everywhere.
They shall see Him where others see stones.

Blessed are they that have understanding hearts.
To them shall be multiplied kingdoms of delight.

Blessed are they that see visions.
They shall rejoice in the hidden ways of God.

Blessed are the song-ful of soul,
They carry light and joy to shadowed lives.

Blessed are they who know the power of Love.
They dwell in God for God is Love.

Blessed are the dead,
For they are with God.

Blessed are the living,
For they can still serve God.

Blessed are they who rejoice in their children,
To them is revealed the Father-Motherhood of God.

Blessed are the childless, loving children still,
Theirs shall be mightier family,
Even as the stars of heaven.

Blessed are the souls kept virgin for mankind,
Unto them shall be given unbounded kingdom of great joy.

Blessed are the faithful strong,
They are the right hands of God.

Blessed are they that dwell in peace,—
If they forget not God.

Blessed are they that fight for the Right,
They shall save their souls,
For God is with them.

Blessed are they whose memories we cherish,
Our thoughts add jewels to their crowns.

Blessed are they who, through tribulation, have come to perfect trust,
Theirs is the peace which passeth understanding.

Blessed are the burdened of heart to whom the comforter has come.
They foretaste the joy of heaven.

Blessed are the souls all bare before God,
He shall clothe them with His Peace and Love.

Blessed is the people whose heart is set on God,
It shall STAND.

A GENEROUS CREED

ELIZABETH STUART PHELPS

Saying "There is no hope," he stepped
  A little from our side and passed
  To hope eternal. At the last
Crying "There is no rest," he slept.
A sweeter spirit ne'er drew breath;
  Strange grew the chill upon the air,
But as he murmured "This is death,"
  Lo! life itself did meet him there.

He loved the will; he did the deed;
  Such love shall live; such doubt is dust;
He served the truth; he missed the creed.
  Trust him to God. Dear is the trust.

RITUAL NOT RELIGION

TELUGU E. INDIAN, 16th Century A.D.

Will seeing Concan make a dog a lion?
  Or Kasi make a pig as great
As any elephant? How then
  Can they a saintly man create?

Though he should daily read or hear
  The Veds, the sinner still is vile.
Will not its blackness still appear
  Though coal be washed in milk a while.

Thy creed and prayers may both be right,
  But see that truth makes every plan;
Else thou shalt never see the light.
  The truthful is the twice-born man.

The fount of happiness is in
  The heart. The foolish man confides
In man! He's like the stupid swain
  Who seeks the lamb his bosom hides.

b. SOCIAL (GOD IN ALL GREAT MOVEMENTS)

I. *Social Struggle*

From THE PRESENT CRISIS

JAMES RUSSELL LOWELL

Count me o'er earth's chosen heroes,—they were souls that stood
    alone,
While the men they agonized for hurled the contumelious stone,
Stood serene, and down the future saw the golden beam incline

To the side of perfect justice, mastered by their faith divine,
By one man's plain truth to manhood and to God's supreme
design.

By the light of burning heretics Christ's bleeding feet I track,
Toiling up new Calvaries ever with the cross that turns not
back,
And these mounts of anguish number how each generation
learned
One new word of that grand *Credo* which in prophet-hearts
hath burned
Since the first man stood God-conquered with his face to
Heaven upturned.

For Humanity sweeps onward: where to-day the martyr stands,
On the morrow crouches Judas with the silver in his hands;
Far in front the cross stands ready and the crackling fagots
burn,
While the hooting mob of yesterday in the silent awe return
To glean up the scattered ashes into history's golden urn.

THE PRESENT

Adelaide Anne Proctor

Do not crouch to-day and worship
    The old Past whose life is fled,
Hush your voice with tender reverence,
    Crowned he lies, but cold and dead;
For the Present reigns our monarch,
    With an added weight of hours;
Honour her for she is mighty!
    Honour her, for she is ours!

See the shadows of his heroes,
    Girt around her cloudy throne;
Every day the ranks are strengthened
    By great hearts to him unknown;
Noble things the great Past promised,
    Holy dreams both strange and new.

But the Present shall fulfil them,
What he promised, she shall do.

She inherits all his treasures,
She is heir to all his fame;
And the light that lightens round her
Is the lustre of his name.
She is wise with all his wisdom,
Living on his grave she stands;
On her brow she bears his laurels,
And his harvest in her hands.

Coward, can she reign and conquer
If we thus her glory dim?
Let us fight for her as nobly
As our fathers fought for him.
God, who crowns the dying ages,
Bids her rule and us obey;
Bids us cast our lives before her,
Bids us save the great To-day.

2. *National Affairs*

BATTLE HYMN OF THE REPUBLIC

Julia Ward Howe

Mine eyes have seen the glory of the coming of the Lord:
He is trampling out the vintage where the grapes of wrath are
stored;
He hath loosed the fateful lightning of His terrible swift sword:
His truth is marching on.

I have seen Him in the watch-fires of a hundred circling
camps,
They have builded Him an altar in the evening dews and damps;
I can read His righteous sentence by the dim and flaring lamps:
His day is marching on.

I have read a fiery gospel writ in burnished rows of steel:
"As ye deal with my contemners so with you my grace shall
    deal;
Let the Hero, born of woman, crush the serpent with his heel,
  Since God is marching on!"

He has sounded forth the trumpet that shall never call retreat;
He is sifting out the hearts of men before His judgment seat.
Oh, be swift, my soul, to answer Him! be jubilant, my feet!
  Our God is marching on.

In the beauty of the lilies Christ was born across the sea,
With a glory in His bosom that transfigures you and me;
As He died to make men holy, let us die to make men free,
  While God is marching on.

UNMANIFEST DESTINY

Richard Hovey

To what new fates, my country, far
  And unforeseen of foe or friend,
Beneath what unexpected star,
  Compelled to what unchosen end,

Across the sea that knows no beach
  The Admiral of nations guides
Thy blind obedient keels to reach
  The harbor where thy future rides!

The guns that spoke at Lexington
  Knew not that God was planning then
The trumpet words of Jefferson
  To bugle forth the rights of men.

To them that wept and cursed Bull Run,
  What was it but despair and shame?
Who saw behind the cloud the sun?
  Who knew that God was in the flame?

Had not defeat upon defeat,
  Disaster on disaster come,
The slave's emancipated feet
  Had never marched behind the drum.

There is a Hand that bends our deeds
  To mightier issues than we planned;
Each son that triumphs, each that bleeds
  My country, serves Its dark command.

I do not know beneath what sky
  Nor on what seas shall be thy fate;
I only know it shall be high,
  I only know it shall be great.

THE REPUBLIC

Henry Wadsworth Longfellow

Thou, too, sail on, O Ship of State!
Sail on, O Union! strong and great!
Humanity with all its fears,
With all its hopes of future years,
Is hanging breathless on thy fate!
We know what Master laid thy keel,
What Workmen wrought thy ribs of steel,
Who made each mast and sail and rope,
What anvils rang, what hammers beat,
In what a forge, at what a heat
Were shaped the anchors of thy hope!
Fear not each sudden sound and shock,
'Tis of the wave, and not the rock:
'Tis but the flapping of a sail
And not a rent made by the gale!
In spite of rock and tempests' roar,
In spite of false lights on the shore,
Sail on, nor fear to breast the sea!
Our hearts, our hopes, are all with thee,
Our hearts, our hopes, our prayers, our tears,
Our faith, triumphant o'er our fears,
Are all with thee—are all with thee!

From GLOUCESTER MOORS

William Vaughn Moody

This earth is not the steadfast place
We landsmen build upon;
From deep to deep she varies pace,
And while she comes is gone.
Beneath my feet I feel
Her smooth bulk heave and dip;
With velvet plunge and soft upreel
She swings and steadies to her keel
Like a gallant, gallant ship

. . . .

God, dear God! Does she know her port,
Though she goes so far about?
Or blind astray, does she make her sport
To brazen and chance it out?
I watched when her captains passed:
She were better captainless.
Men in the cabin, before the mast
But some were reckless and some aghast,
And some sat gorged at mess.

. . . .

But thou, vast outbound ship of souls,
What harbor town for thee?
What shapes, when thy arriving tolls,
Shall crowd the banks to see?
Shall all the happy shipmates then
Stand singing brotherly?
Or shall a haggard ruthless few
Warp her over and bring her to,
While the many broken souls of men
Fester down in the slaver's pen
And nothing to say or do?

3. *International Affairs*

THE SOUL'S ERRAND

SIR WALTER RALEIGH

Go, soul, the body's guest,
  Upon a thankless errand!
Fear not to touch the best,
  The truth shall be thy warrant:
    Go, since I needs must die,
    And give the world the lie.

Go, tell the court it glows,
  And shines like rotten wood;
Go, tell the church it shows
  What's good and doth no good:
    If church and court reply,
    Then give them both the lie.

Tell potentates they live
  Acting by others' actions;
Not loved unless they give,
  Not strong but by their factions:
    If potentates reply,
    Give potentates the lie.

Tell men of high condition
  That rule affairs of state,
Their purpose is ambition,
  Their practice only hate:
    And if they once reply,
    Then give them all the lie.

Tell those that brave it most,
  They beg for more by spending,
Who in their greatest cost

Seek nothing but commending:
And if they make reply,
Then give them all the lie.

Tell zeal it lacks devotion;
Tell love it is but lust;
Tell time it is but motion;
Tell flesh it is but dust:
And wish them not reply,
For thou must give the lie.

Tell age it daily wasteth;
Tell honor how it alters;
Tell beauty how she blasteth;
Tell favor how she falters:
And as they shall reply,
Give every one the lie.

Tell wit how much it wrangles
In tickle points of niceness;
Tell wisdom she entangles
Herself in overwiseness:
And when they do reply,
Straight give them both the lie.

Tell physic of her boldness;
Tell skill it is pretension;
Tell charity of coldness;
Tell law it is contention:
And as they do reply,
So give them still the lie.

Tell arts they have no soundness,
But vary by esteeming;
Tell schools they want profoundness,
And stand too much on seeming:
If arts and schools reply,
Give arts and schools the lie.

Tell faith it's fled the city;
Tell how the country erreth;

Tell manhood shakes off pity;
Tell virtue least preferreth:
And if they do reply,
Spare not to give the lie.

So when thou hast, as I
Commanded thee, done blabbing;
Although to give the lie
Deserves no less than stabbing:
Yet stab at thee who will,
No stab the Soul can kill!

IN THE DAWN

Odell Shepard

Peace! The perfect word is sounding, like a universal hymn,
Under oceans, over mountains, to the world's remotest rim.

Light! At last the deadly arrows of the Archer find their mark.
Loathsome forms are shuddering backward to the shelter of the
dark.

Hope! The nations stand together on the borders of a dawn
That shall dim the noonday splendor of the ages that are gone.

Peace, and light, and hope of morning! Let the belfries reel
and sway
While the world is swinging swiftly out of darkness into day.

Let the forests of the steeples, blown by one compelling wind,
Swing and sway and clash together one vast peal for all man-
kind,

While we roll up out of darkness, out of death, out of the gloom
Of a blighted planet plunging blindly downward to its doom.

Into light beyond our dreaming, into peace, goodwill toward
men,
Hope beyond the poet's vision, joy beyond the prophet's ken.

While we stand here in the gray dawn, in these early dews of
time,
On this height the toil of ages has but just availed to climb,

Brothers, let us pause a moment. . . . Many a darkling moun-
tain towers
Tall against the stars behind us, only less sublime than ours.

Many a peak of ancient quiet glimmers lonely in the snow
Whence a shout of joy went skyward silent centuries ago.

France, with Europe singing round her in her false dawn fair
and brief;
England, with the vast Armada rocking helpless on the reef;

Rome, when through the Temple of Janus clanged and clashed
each rusty gate;
Athens, hurling Persia homeward headlong like a river in
spate. . . .

All of these have climbed before us to a distant Pisgah-sight
Of a land they never entered. Shall we also lose our light?

Other earlier dawns before this bloomed, and withered. Men
have scaled
Many a peak of dream—and died there. Shall we falter where
they failed?

Shall the nations still, forever, struggle forward one by one?
Or shall we go up together, brother-like, to greet the sun?

We shall falter, strength will fail us, dreams will perish utterly,
Our high hope will be a byword and a scornful memory

If we stand not strong together in this hour, if heart and hand
Be not plighted firm and steadfast, linking alien land to
land . . .

Ah, but see, we stand together, hand in hand and eye to eye!
This, in all the backward ages, has not been beneath the sky.

Other days have had their glory, but these days of triumph are
Kingliest of all that ever dawned upon this ancient star.

And behold! At last our country takes her rightful place with
    men.
Never shall the seas divide her from the world's great need
    again.

That old dream has fled forever, that we dwell, serene and far,
With God's special smile to light us, on some steady separate
    star.

All we are the Old World made us. Where it lost we learned
    to gain.
We have triumphed through its failures, built our joy upon its
    pain.

Greece foretold us, Rome foresaw us, gave us beauty, wisdom,
    law;
France gave vision; England made us strong to win the good we
    saw.

Toiling centuries have struggled upward on a stony way
Just to set the torch of freedom where it flames aloft to-day.

Shall the children of the ages fail them in this mighty trust,
Let their beacon pale and dwindle, quench its beauty in the dust?

Rather, we shall hold it higher, shake its splendor through the
    sky,
Searching out each nook of shadow till the things of darkness
    die.

Where a woman still is vassal, where a child is still a slave,
There shall rise our instant bivouac, there be digged a tyrant's
    grave.

All the old forlorn lost causes, every fair forbidden dream,
And the prophet's hopeless vision and the poet's flitting gleam,

All the hopes of subject peoples, all the dreams of the op-
pressed,
Must be ours, our hopes, our visions. We can never stay or
rest

Till our beacon pales above us, dies into the level ray
Painting every peak and valley with the light of golden day,

Till the rounded earth together, to the last isle of the sea,
All our many-languaged kindred shall be free as we are free.

Praise to all the past that made us in the heat of its desire;
Glory to our elder brothers, those swift runners with the fire

From the dimmest edge of distance, who have perished far
away,
Far beneath the light we stand in, many years before our day.

With the wind their breath is woven, and their holy dust is
whirled
Dizzily along the highways of the swift-forgetting world. . . .

Hearts that dared and brains that labored, hands that toiled to
build our day,
Drifting, drifting through the chambers of dead years, and
blown away!

How their brows were bright with wonder! How their feet
were shod with flame!
Beautiful upon the mountains was the shining way they came.

Freedom wears their names about her as a starry diadem.
In this hour of exultation shall we not remember them?

Buried deep beneath the ages in the dust of old decay.
They have heard our sweet stern bugles blow reveille to the day,

To the golden day they died for, paid for with immortal pains,
And they rise and live within us like great wine along our veins.

They are fragrance in the dawn wind.   They are beauty in th,
  flower. . . .
Let us bow our heads before them humbly now.   This is their
  hour.

———————————

We are standing in the gray dawn of a day they did not know,
On a height they only dreamed of, toiling darkly far below;

But our gaze is toward a summit loftier, fairer, mist-encurled,
Soaring skyward through the twilight from the bases of the
  world.

Other feet than ours may stand there on the mountain's lonely
  crown;
We may faint upon the high trails, fall and lay our burden
  down;

Yet, enough to fill one lifetime is this joy Death cannot
  touch . . .
Peace, and light, and hope of morning!   These are ours, and
  these are much.

Wondrous day to be alive in when, with furious might and
  main,
God is fashioning the future on the anvil-horns of pain!

Every life, however humble, takes a touch of the sublime
From the light that bathes our sun-washed pinnacle of dawning
  time.

Forward, then!   And onward, upward, toward the greater days
  to be,
All the nations singing with us one great song, fraternally.

Up and up, achieving, failing, weak in flesh but strong of
  soul. . . .
We may never live to reach it.   Ah, but we have seen the goal!

THE NEW VICTORY

Margaret Widdemer

Victory comes:
Not hard and laughing as she came of yore,
Her scarlet arms heaped high with spoils of war;
Her slaves, to beating drums,
Low bent and bearing gifts . . .
The black cloud lifts;
And, lifting our long-weary eyes to see,
There dawns upon our sight,
Majestic, crowned with light,
Stern and so quiet—she must keep her strength
To build at weary length
Over again, a scarred and shattered world—
This, then, this is she,
  Our grave Victory!

She follows down the furrows
War-turned across the world,
Where still the spent shell burrows,
Where the black shot was hurled,
And sows the wheat and corn.
The world from anguish born
Again from its old grief,
Looks up athirst,
And hungering,
Daring to dream again
Of flowers unhurt and unstained rain
And Love and Spring:
Knowing that she shall build each place accursed
Into a thing that may some day again
Be our once land of comfort and delight,
Of ease and mockery,
Even forgetfulness:
Even the gift to bless.

Victory paces slowly through the lands:
No lash is in her hands,

She builds herself no triumph arch for cover,
No common marble toy—
She is too great for joy.
She who upbuilds
Each little shattered home
And brings men back to it; and lover gives to lover,
And to the shattered souls its faith again,
And to the world continuance of God—
How should our praise for her
In high crowned buildings stand—oh? how be pent
In built or written thing?
The stable world itself is her great monument.

AN INSPIRATION

ELLA WHEELER WILCOX

However the battle is ended,
    Though proudly the victor comes
With fluttering flags and prancing nags
    And echoing roll of drums,
Still truth proclaims this motto,
    In letters of living light,—
No question is ever settled,
    Until it is settled right.

Though the heel of the strong oppressor
    May grind the weak to dust,
And the voices of fame with one acclaim
    May call him great and just,
Let those who applaud take warning,
    And keep this motto in sight,—
No question is ever settled
    Until it is settled right.

Let those who have failed take courage;
    Tho' the enemy seems to have won,
Tho' his ranks are strong, if he be in the wrong
    The battle is not yet done;

For, as sure as the morning follows
  The darkest hour of the night,
No question is ever settled
  Until it is settled right.

O man bowed down with labor!
  A woman, young, yet old!
O heart oppressed in the toiler's breast
  And crushed by the power of gold!
Keep on with your weary battle
  Against triumphant might;
No question is ever settled
  Until it is settled right.

XI. DEATH AND IMMORTALITY

    a.   PERSONAL IMMORTALITY
    b.   IMPERSONAL IMMORTALITY
    c.   ETERNAL SLEEP

A TRAVELLER

Anonymous

Into the dusk and snow
  One fared yesterday:
No man of us may know
  By what mysterious way.

He had been a comrade long;
  We fain would hold him still;
But, though our will be strong,
  There is a stronger Will.

Beyond the solemn night
  He will find the morning dream,—
The summer's kindling light
  Beyond the chill snow's gleam.

The clear unfaltering eye,
  The inalienable soul,
The calm, high energy,—
  They will not fail the goal!

Large will be our content
  If it be ours to go
One day the path he went,
  Into the dusk and snow!

RESURGAM

ANONYMOUS

"I shall arise." For centuries
    Upon the grey old churchyard stone
These words have stood; no more is said,
    The glorious promise stands alone,
Untouched, while years and seasons roll
    Around it; March winds come and go,
The summer twilights fall and fade,
    And autumn sunsets burn and glow.

"I shall arise"! O wavering heart,
    From this take comfort and be strong!
"I shall arise"; nor always grope
    In darkness, mingling right with wrong;
From tears and pain, from shades of doubt,
    And wants within, that blindly call,
"I shall arise," in God's own light
    Shall see the sum and truth of all.

Like children here we lisp and grope,
    And, till the perfect manhood, wait
At home our time, and only dream
    Of that which lies beyond the gate:
God's full free universe of life,
    No shadowy paradise of bliss,
No realm of unsubstantial souls,
    But life, more real life than this.

O soul! where'er your ward is kept,
    In some still region calmly blest,
By quiet watch-fires till the dawn
    And God's reveille break your rest,
O soul! that left this record here,
    I read, but scarce can read for tears,
I bless you, reach and clasp your hand,
    For all these long two hundred years.

"I shall arise"—O clarion call!
  Time rolling onward to the end
Brings us to life that cannot die,
  The life where faith and knowledge blend.
Each after each, the cycles roll
  In silence, and about us here
The shadow of the great White Throne
  Falls broader, deeper, year by year.

AFTER DEATH IN ARABIA

EDWIN ARNOLD

He who died at Azan sends
This to comfort all his friends:

Faithful friends! It lies, I know
Pale and white and cold as snow;
And ye say, "Abdallah's dead"!
Weeping at the feet and head.
I can see your falling tears,
I can hear your sighs and prayers;
Yet I smile and whisper this:
"I am not the thing you kiss;
Cease your tears and let it lie;
It *was* mine—it is not I."

Sweet Friends! What the women lave
For its last bed in the grave,
Is a tent which I am quitting,
Is a garment no more fitting,
Is a cage, from which at last,
Like a hawk, my soul hath passed.
Love the inmate, not the room—
The wearer, not the garb;—the plume
Of the falcon, not the bars
That kept him from these splendid stars!

Loving friends! be wise, and dry
Straightway every weeping eye.
What ye lift upon the bier
Is not worth a wistful tear.
'Tis an empty sea shell,—one
Out of which the pearl is gone;
The shell is broken, it lies there;
The pearl, the all, the soul, is here.
'Tis an earthen jar, whose lid
Allah sealed, the while it hid
That treasure of his treasury,
A mind that loved him; let it lie!
Let the shard be the earth's once more,
Since the gold shines in his store!

Allah glorious! Allah good!
Now thy world is understood;
Now the long, long wonder ends!
Yet ye weep, my erring friends,
While the man whom ye call dead,
In unspoken bliss, instead,
Lives and loves you; lost, 'tis true,
By such light as shines for you;
But in light you cannot see
Of unfulfilled felicity,—
In enlarging paradise,
Lives a life that never dies.

Farewell, friends, yet not farewell;—
Where I am ye too shall dwell.
I am gone before your face,
A moment's time, a little space.
When ye come where I have stepped,
Ye will wonder why ye wept;
Ye will know by wise love taught,
That here is all and there is naught.
Weep a while, if ye are fain,—
Sunshine still must follow rain;
Only not at death,—for death,
Now I know, is that first breath

Which our souls draw when we enter
Life, which is of all life center.

Be ye certain all seems love,
Viewed from Allah's throne above;
Be ye stout of heart and come,
Bravely onward to your home!
La Allah illa Allah! yea!
Thou love divine, thou love alway!

He who died at Azan gave
This to those who made his grave.

RUGBY CHAPEL

Matthew Arnold

Coldly, sadly descends
The autumn evening. The field
Strewn with its dank yellow drifts
Of withered leaves, and the elms,
Fade into dimness apace,
Silent;—hardly a shout
From a few boys late at their play!
The lights come out in the street,
In the school-room windows;—but cold,
Solemn, unlighted, austere,
Through the gathering darkness, arise
The chapel walls, in whose bound
Thou, my father! art laid.
.   .   .   .   .

O strong soul, by what shore
Tarriest thou now? For that force,
Surely, has not been left vain!
Somewhere, surely, afar,
In the sounding labor-house vast
Of being, is practised that strength,
Zealous, beneficent, firm!

Yes, in some far-shining sphere,
Conscious or not of the past,
Still thou performest the word
Of the Spirit in whom thou dost live—
Prompt, unwearied, as here!
Still thou upraisest with zeal
The humble good from the ground,
Sternly repressest the bad!
Still, like a trumpet, dost rouse
Those who, with half-open eyes
Tread the border-land dim
'Twixt vice and virtue; revivest,
Succorest!—this was thy work,
This was thy life upon earth.

What is the course of the life
Of mortal men on the earth?—
Most men eddy about
Here and there—eat and drink,
Chatter and love and hate,
Gather and squander, are raised
Aloft, are hurled in the dust,
Striving blindly, achieving
Nothing; and then they die—
Perish;—and no one asks
Who or what they have been,
More than he asks what waves,
In the moonlit solitudes mild
Of the midmost ocean, have swelled,
Foam'd for a moment, and gone.

And there are some, whom a thirst
Ardent, unquenchable, fires,
Not with the crowd to be spent,
Not without aim to go round
In an eddy of purposeless dust,
Effort unmeaning and vain.
Ah, yes! some of us strive
Not without action to die
Fruitless, but something to snatch

From dull oblivion, nor all
Glut the devouring grave!
We, we have chosen our path—
Path to a clear-purposed goal,
Path of advance!—but it leads
A long steep journey, through sunk
Gorges, o'er mountains of snow,
Cheerful, with friends, we set forth—
Then, on the height, comes the storm.
Thunder crashes from rock
To rock, the cataracts reply,
Lightnings dazzle our eyes.
Roaring torrents have breached
The track, the stream-bed descends
In the place where the wayfarer once
Planted his footstep—the spray
Boils o'er its borders! aloft
The unseen snow-beds dislodge
Their hanging ruin; alas,
Havoc is made in our train!
Friends who set forth at our side,
Falter, are lost in the storm.

We, we only are left!
With frowning foreheads, with lips
Sternly compressed, we strain on,
On—and at nightfall at last
Come to the end of our way,
To the lonely inn 'mid the rocks;
Where the gaunt and taciturn host
Stands on the threshold, the wind
Shaking his thin white hairs—
Holds his lantern to scan
Our storm-beat figures, and asks;
Whom in our party we bring?
Whom have we left in the snow?

Sadly we answer: we bring
Only ourselves! we lost
Sight of the rest in the storm.

Hardly ourselves we fought through,
Stripped, without friends, as we are.
Friends, companions, and train,
The avalanche swept from our side.

But thou wouldst not *alone*
Be saved, my father! *alone*
Conquer and come to thy goal,
Leaving the rest in the wild.
We were weary, and we
Fearful, and we in our march
Fain to drop down and to die.
Still thou turnedst, and still
Beckonedst the trembler, and still
Gavest the weary thy hand.

.   .   .   .

And through thee I believe
In the noble and great who are gone;
Pure souls honored and blest
By former ages, who else—
Such, so soulless, so poor,
Is the race of men whom I see—
Seem'd but a dream'd of the heart,
Seem'd but a cry of desire.
Yes! I believe that there lived
Others like thee in the past,
Not like the men of the crowd
Who all round me today
Bluster or cringe, and make life
Hideous, and arid, and vile;
But souls tempered with fire,
Fervent, heroic, and good,
Helpers and friends of mankind.

Servants of God!—or sons
Shall I not call you? because
Not as servants ye knew
Your Father's innermost mind,
His, who unwillingly sees
One of his little ones lost—

Yours is the praise, if mankind
Hath not as yet in its march
Fainted, and fallen and died!

See! in the rocks of the world
Marches the host of mankind,
A feeble, wavering line.
Where are they tending?—A God
Marshalled them, gave them their goal.
Ah, but the way is so long!
Years they have been in the wild!
Sore thirst plagues them, the rocks,
Rising all round, overawe;
Factions divide them, their host
Threatens to break, to dissolve.
—Ah, keep, keep them combined!
Else of the myriads who fill
That army, not one shall arrive;
Sole they shall stray; in the rocks
Stagger forever in vain,
Die one by one in the waste.

Then, in such hour of need
Of your fainting, dispirited race,
Ye, like angels, appear,
Radiant with ardor divine!
Beacons of hope, ye appear!
Languor is not in your heart,
Weakness is not in your word,
Weariness not on your brow.
Ye alight in our van! at your voice,
Panic, despair, flee away.
Ye move through the ranks, recall
The stragglers, refresh the outworn,
Praise, re-inspire the brave!
Order, courage, return.
Eyes rekindling, and prayers,
Follow your steps as ye go.
Ye fill up the gaps in our files,

Strengthen the wavering lines,
'Stablish, continue our march,
On, to the bound of the waste,
On, to the city of God.

DEATH

Maltbie Babcock

Why be afraid of death, as though your life were breath?
Death but anoints your eyes with clay. O glad surprise!

Why should you be forlorn? Death only husks the corn.
Why should you fear to meet the thresher of the wheat?

Is sleep a thing to dread? Yet sleeping you are dead
Till you awake and rise, here, or beyond the skies.

Why should it be a wrench to leave your wooden bench?
Why not, with happy shout, run home when school is out?

The dear ones left behind? Oh, foolish one and blind!
A day and you will meet—a night and you will greet.

This is the death of death, to breathe away a breath
And know the end of strife, and taste the deathless life,

And joy without a fear, and smile without a tear;
And work, nor care to rest, and find the last the best.

PROSPICE

Robert Browning

Fear death?—to feel the fog in my throat,
    The mist in my face,
When the snows begin, and the blasts denote
    I am nearing the place,

The power of the night, the press of the storm,
  The post of the foe;
Where he stands, the Arch Fear in a visible form,
  Yet the strong man must go;
For the journey is done and the summit attained,
  And the barriers fall,
Though a battle's to fight ere the guerdon be gained,
  The reward of it all.
I was ever a fighter, so—one fight more,
  The best and the last!
I would hate that death bandaged my eyes, and forebore,
  And bade me creep past.
No! let me taste the whole of it, fare like my peers
  The heroes of old,
Bear the brunt, in a minute pay glad life's arrears
  Of pain, darkness and cold.
For sudden the worst turns the best to the brave,
  The black minute's at end,
And the elements' rage, the fiend-voices that rave,
  Shall dwindle, shall blend,
Shall change, shall become first a peace out of pain.
  Then a light, then thy breast,
O thou soul of my soul! I shall clasp thee again,
  And with God be the rest!

AULD LANG SYNE

JOHN WHITE CHADWICK

It singeth low in every heart,
  We hear it each and all,—
A song of those who answer not,
  However we may call;
They throng the silence of the breast,
  We see them as of yore,—
The kind, the brave, the true, the sweet,
  Who walk with us no more.

'Tis hard to take the burden up,
  When these have laid it down;
They brightened all the joy of life,
  They softened every frown;
But oh, 'tis good to think of them,
  When we are troubled sore!
Thanks be to God that such have been,
  Although they are no more!

More home-like seems the vast unknown,
  Since they have entered there;
To follow them were not so hard,
  Wherever they may fare;
They cannot be where God is not,
  On any sea or shore;
Whate'er betides, Thy love abides,
  Our God, for evermore.

THE CHARIOT

EMILY DICKINSON

Because I could not stop for Death,
He kindly stopped for me;
The carriage held but just ourselves,
And Immortality.

We slowly drove, he knew no haste,
And I had put away
My labor and my leisure, too,
For his civility.

We passed the school where children played,
Their lessons scarcely done;
We passed the fields of gazing grain,
We passed the setting sun.

We paused before a house that seemed
A swelling of the ground;

The roof was scarcely visible,
The cornice but a mound.
Since then, 'tis centuries; but each
Feels shorter than the day
I first surmised the horses' heads
Were toward eternity.

DEATH

EMILY DICKINSON

Death is a dialogue between
The spirit and the dust.
"Dissolve," says Death; the spirit, "Sir,
I have another trust."
Death doubts it, argues from the ground.
The spirit turns away,
Just laying off, for evidence,
An overcoat of clay.

DEATH

EMILY DICKINSON

The bustle in the house
The morning after death
Is solemnest of industries
Enacted upon earth;—

The sweeping up the heart
And putting love away
We shall not want to use again
Until eternity.

RESURGAM

EMILY DICKINSON

At last to be identified!
At last, the lamps upon thy side
The rest of life to see!
Past midnight, past the morning star!
Past sunrise! Ah! what leagues there are
Between our feet and day!

THIRST

EMILY DICKINSON

We thirst at first,—'tis nature's act;
    And, later, when we die
A little water supplicate
    Of fingers going by.

It intimates the finer wants
    Whose adequate supply
Is that great water in the West,
    Termed Immortality.

TWO MYSTERIES

MARY MAPES DODGE

We know not what it is, dear, this sleep so deep and still;
The folded hands, the awful calm, the cheek so pale and chill;
The lids that will not lift again, though we may call and call;
The strange white solitude of peace that settles over all.

We know not what it means, dear, this desolate heart pain;
This dread to take our daily way, and walk in it again;
We know not to what other sphere the loved who leave us go,
Nor why we're left to wonder still, nor why we do not know.

But this we know: our loved and dead, if they should come this
    day,—
Should come and ask us, "What is Life?"—not one of us could
    say.
Life is a mystery, as deep as ever death can be;
Yet, oh, how dear it is to us, this life we live and see!

Then might they say—these vanished ones—and blessed is the
    thought,
"So death is sweet to us, beloved! though we may show you
    naught;
We may not to the quick reveal the mystery of death—
Ye cannot tell us, if ye would, the mystery of breath!"

The child who enters life comes not with knowledge or intent,
So those who enter death must go as little children sent.
Nothing is known. But I believe that God is overhead;
And as life is to the living, so death is to the dead.

THE GOD OF THE LIVING

John Ellerton

God of the living, in whose eyes
Unveiled thy whole creation lies!
All souls are thine; we must not say
That those are dead who pass away;
From this our world of flesh set free;
We know them living unto thee.

Released from earthly toil and strife,
With thee is hidden still their life;
Thine are their thoughts, their words,
    their powers,
All thine, and yet most truly ours:

For well we know, where'er they be,
Our dead are living unto thee.

Not spilt like water on the ground,
Not wrapt in dreamless sleep profound,
Not wandering in unknown despair
Beyond thy voice, thine arm, thy care;
Not left to lie like fallen tree;
Not dead, but living unto thee.

O Breather into man of breath!
O Holder of the keys of death!
O Giver of the Life within!
Save us from death, the death of sin;
That body, soul, and spirit be
Forever living unto thee!

DRYAD SONG

Margaret Fuller

I am immortal! I know it! I feel it!
  Hope floods my heart with delight!
Running on air, mad with life, dizzy, reeling,
Upward I mount,—faith is sight, life is feeling,
  Hope is the day-star of might!

It was thy kiss, Love, that made me immortal,—
  "'Kiss,' Love? Our lips have not met!"
Ah, but I felt thy soul through night's portal
Swoon on my lips at night's sweet, silent portal,
  Wild and sweet as regret.

Come, let us mount on the wings of the morning,
  Flying for joy of the flight,
Wild with all longing, now soaring, now staying,
Mingling like day and dawn, swinging and swaying,
  Hung like a cloud in the light:
I am immortal! I feel it! I feel it!
  Love bears me up, love is might!

Chance cannot touch me! Time cannot hush me!
  Fear, Hope, and Longing, at strife,
Sink as I rise, on, on, upward forever,
Gathering strength, gaining breath,—naught can sever
  Me from the Spirit of Life!

CALL ME NOT DEAD

RICHARD WATSON GILDER

Call me not dead when I, indeed, have gone
Into the company of the ever-living
High and most glorious poets! Let thanksgiving
Rather be made. Say: "He at last hath won
Rest and release, converse supreme and wise,
Music and song and light of immortal faces;
To-day, perhaps, wandering in starry places,
He hath met Keats, and known him by his eyes.
To-morrow (who can say!) Shakespeare may pass,
And our lost friend just catch one syllable
Of that three-centuried wit that kept so well;
Or Milton; or Dante, looking on the grass
Thinking of Beatrice, and listening still
To chanted hymns that sound from the heavenly hill."

LONGING FOR HOME

JEAN INGELOW

A Song of a Boat

There was once a boat on a billow:
Lightly she rocked to her port remote,
And the foam was white in her wake like snow
And her frail mast bowed when the breeze would blow.
  And bent like a wand of willow.

I shaded mine eyes one day when a boat
  Went curtseying over the billow,
I marked her course till,.a dancing mote,
She faded out on the moonlit foam,
And I stayed behind in the dear-loved home;
  And my thoughts all day were about the boat,
  And my dreams upon the pillow.

I pray you hear my song of a boat,
  For it is but short:—
My boat, you shall find none fairer afloat,
  In river or port.
Long I looked out for the lad she bore,
  On the open desolate sea;
And I think he sailed to the heavenly shore,
  For he came not back to me--
        Ah, me!

A Song of a Nest

There was once a nest in a hollow;
Down in the mosses and knot-grass pressed,
Soft and warm and full to the brim;
Vetches leaned over it, purple and dim,
  With buttercup buds to follow.

I pray you hear my song of a nest,
  For it is not long:—
You shall never light, in a summer quest
  The bushes among—
Shall never light on a prouder sitter,
  A fairer nestful, nor ever know
A softer sound than their tender twitter,
  That, wind-like, did come and go.

I had a nestful once of my own—
  Ah, happy, happy I!
Rightly dearly I loved them, but when they were grown
  They spread out their wings to fly.
Oh, one after one they flew away,
  Far up to the heavenly blue.

To the better country, the upper day;
  And—I wish I was going, too.

I pray you what is the nest to me,
  My empty nest?
And what is the shore where I used to see
  My boat sail down to the west?
Can I call that home where I anchor yet,
  Though my good man has sailed?
Can I call that home where my nest was set,
  Now all its hope hath failed?
Nay, but the port where my sailor went,
  And the land where my nestlings be:
There is the home where my thoughts are sent,
  The only home for me—
              Ah, me!

HE DID NOT KNOW

Harry Kemp

He did not know that he was dead;
  He walked along the crowded street,
Smiled, tipped his hat, nodded his head
  To friends he chanced to meet.

And yet they passed him quietly by
  With an unknowing, level stare;
They met him with an abstract eye
  As if he were the air.

"Some sorry thing has come to pass,"
  The dead man thought; he hurried home,
And found his wife before a glass,
  Dallying with a comb.

He found his wife all dressed in black;
  He kissed her mouth, he stroked her head.
"Men act so strange since I've come back
  From over there," he said.

She spoke no word; she only smiled.
But now he heard her say his name,
And saw her study, grief-beguiled,
His picture in a frame.

Then he remembered that black night
And the great shell-burst, wide and **red,**
The sudden plunging into light;
And knew that he was dead.

LYCIDAS

John Milton

Yet once more, O ye laurels, and once more,
Ye myrtles brown, with ivy never sere,
I come to pluck your berries harsh and crude,
And with forced fingers rude
Shatter your leaves before the mellowing year.
Bitter constraint and sad occasion dear
Compels me to disturb your season due;
For Lycidas is dead, dead ere his prime,
Young Lycidas, and hath not left his peer.
Who would not sing for Lycidas? he knew
Himself to sing and build the lofty rhyme.
He must not float upon his watery bier
Unwept, and welter to the parching wind,
Without the meed of some melodious tear.
Begin then, Sisters of the sacred well
That from the seat of Jove doth spring;
Begin, and somewhat loudly sweep the string.
Hence with denial vain and coy excuse;
So may some gentle Muse
With lucky words favor *my* destined urn,
And as he passes turn,
And bid fair peace be to my sable shroud.
For we were nursed upon the self-same hill,
Fed the same flock, by fountain, shade, and rill;
Together both, ere the high lawns appeared

Under the opening eyelids of the morn,
We drove a-field and both together heard
What time the gray-fly winds her sultry horn,
Battening our flocks with the fresh dews of night,
Oft till the star that rose at evening, bright
Toward heaven's descent had sloped his westering wheel.
Meanwhile the rural ditties were not mute,
Tempered to the oaten flute;
Rough Satyrs danced, and Fauns with cloven heel
From the glad sound would not be absent long;
And old Damœtas loved to hear our song.

But oh! the heavy change, now thou art gone,
Now thou art gone, and never must return!
Thee, Shepherd, thee the woods and desert caves,
With wild thyme and the gadding vine o'ergrown,
And all their echoes mourn.
The willows and the hazel copses green
Shall now no more be seen,
Fanning their joyous leaves to thy soft lays.
As killing as the canker to the rose,
Or taint-worm to the weanling herds that graze,
Or frost to flowers, that their gay wardrobe wear,
When first the white-thorn blows;
Such, Lycidas, thy loss to shepherd's ear.

Where were ye, nymphs, when the remorseless deep
Closed o'er the head of your loved Lycidas?
For neither were ye playing on the steep
Where your old bards, the famous Druids, lie,
Nor on the shaggy top of Mona high,
Nor yet where Deva spreads her wisard stream.
Ay, me! I fondly dream
"Had ye been there," . . . for what could that have done?
What could the Muse herself that Orpheus bore,
The Muse herself, for her enchanting son,
Whom universal nature did lament,
When by the rout that made the hideous roar
His gory visage down the stream was sent,
Down the swift Hebrus to the Lesbian shore?

Alas! what boots it with incessant care
To tend the homely, slighted, shepherd's trade,

And strictly meditate the thankless Muse?
Were it not better done, as others use,
To sport with Amaryllis in the shade,
Or with the tangles of Neæra's hair?
Fame is the spur that the clear spirit doth raise
(That last infirmity of noble mind)
To scorn delights and live laborious days;
But the fair guerdon when we hope to find,
And think to burst out into sudden blaze,
Comes the blind Fury with the abhorrèd shears,
And slits the thin-spun life. "But not the praise,"
Phœbus replied, and touched my trembling ears:
"Fame is no plant that grows on mortal soil,
Nor in the glistering foil
Set off to the world, nor in broad rumor lies;
But lives and spreads aloft by those pure eyes
And perfect witness of all-judging Jove;
As he pronounces lastly on each deed,
Of so much fame in heaven expect thy meed."
  O fountain Arethuse, and thou honored flood,
Smooth-sliding Mincius, crowned with vocal reeds,
That strain I heard was of a higher mood:
But now my oat proceeds,
And listens to the herald of the sea,
That came in Neptune's plea.
He asked the waves, and asked the felon winds,
What hard mishap hath doomed this gentle swain?
And questioned every gust of rugged wings
That blows from off each beakèd promontory.
They knew not of his story;
And sage Hippotades their answer brings,
That not a blast was from his dungeon strayed;
The air was calm, and on the level brine
Sleek Panope with all her sisters played.
It was that fatal and perfidious bark,
Built in the eclipse, and rigged with curses dark,
That sunk so low that sacred head of thine.
  Next Camus, reverend sire, went footing slow,
His mantle hairy and his bonnet sedge,
Inwrought with figures dim, and on the edge

Like to that sanguine flower inscribed with woe.
"Ah, who hath reft," quoth he, "my dearest pledge?"
Last came, and last did go,
The pilot of the Galilean lake;
Two massy keys he bore of metals twain
(The golden opes, the iron shuts amain).
He shook his mitred locks, and stern bespake:
"How well could I have spared for thee, young swain,
Anow of such as, for their bellies' sake,
Creep and intrude and climb into the fold!
Of other care they little reckoning make
Than how to scramble at the shearers' feast,
And shove away the worthy bidden guest.
Blind mouths! that scarce themselves know how to hold
A sheep-hook, or have learnt aught else the least
That to the faithful herdsman's art belongs!
What recks it them? What need they? They are sped;
And when they list, their lean and flashy songs
Grate on their scrannel pipes of wretched straw;
The hungry sheep look up and are not fed,
But swoln with wind and the rank mist they draw,
Rot inwardly and foul contagion spread;
Besides what the grim wolf with privy paw
Daily devours apace, and nothing said.
But that two-handed engine at the door
Stands ready to smite once and smite no more."
    Return, Alpheus; the dread voice is past
That shrunk thy streams; return, Sicilian Muse,
And call the vales, and bid them hither cast
Their bells and flowerets of a thousand hues.
Ye valleys low, where the mild whispers use
Of shades and wanton winds and gushing brooks,
On whose fresh lap the swart star sparely looks,
Throw hither all your quaint enamelled eyes,
That on the green turf suck the honeyed showers,
And purple all the ground with vernal flowers.
Bring the rathe primrose that forsaken dies,
The tufted crow-toe, and pale jessamine,
The white pink, and the pansy freaked with jet,
The glowing violet,

The musk-rose and the well-attired woodbine,
With cowslips wan that hang the pensive head,
And every flower that sad embroidery wears;
Bid amaranthus all his beauty shed,
And daffadillies fill their cups with tears,
To strew the laureate hearse where Lycid lies.
For so to interpose a little ease,
Let our frail thoughts dally with false surmise.
Ay me! whilst thee the shores and sounding seas
Wash far away, where'er thy bones are hurled;
Whether beyond the stormy Hebrides,
Where thou perhaps under the whelming tide
Visit'st the bottom of the monstrous world;
Or whether thou, to our moist vows denied,
Sleep'st by the fable of Bellerus old,
Where the great vision of the guarded mount
Looks toward Namancos and Bayona's hold.
Look homeward, Angel, now and melt with ruth;
And, O ye dolphins, waft the hapless youth.

   Weep no more, woeful shepherds, weep no more,
For Lycidas, your sorrow, is not dead,
Sunk though he be beneath the watery floor;
So sinks the day-star in the ocean bed,
And yet anon repairs his drooping head,
And tricks his beams, and with new-spangled ore
Flames in the forehead of the morning sky:
So Lycidas sunk low, but mounted high,
Through the dear might of Him that walked the waves,
Where, other groves and other streams along,
With nectar pure his oozy locks he laves,
And hears the unexpressive nuptial song,
In the blest kingdoms meek of joy and love.
There entertain him all the saints above,
In solemn troops and sweet societies,
That sing, and singing in their glory move,
And wipe the tears forever from his eyes.
Now, Lycidas, the shepherds weep no more;
Henceforth thou art the Genius of the shore,
In thy large recompense, and shalt be good
To all that wander in that perilous flood.

Thus sang the uncouth swain to the oaks and rills,
While the still morn went out with sandals gray;
He touched the tender stops of various quills,
With eager thought warbling his Doric lay:
And now the sun had stretched out all the hills,
And now was dropt into the western bay.
At last he rose, and twitched his mantle blue:
To-morrow to fresh woods and pastures new.

VESPERS

Silas Weir Mitchell

I know the night is near at hand:
The mists lie low on hill and bay,
The Autumn sheaves are dewless, dry;
But I have had the day.

Yes, I have had, dear Lord, the day;
When at thy call I have the night,
Brief be the twilight as I pass
From light to dark, from dark to light.

DEATH

James Oppenheim

This starry world, and I in it . . .
How can I get out of it?

I go to sleep but when I wake I am still here . . .
All night the flame of life burned in my breast and brain as
the stars burn in the breast and brain of the world . . .

And what is Death?
It is a swing-door. I push through, coming out on the other
side.

But the other side is the world, just as this side is the
    world . . .
There is no escape . . .

So I had best do my work now, lest I shall have to do it later
I had best be myself now, lest later I shall have to battle with
    the crusts upon myself,
Lest later I shall have to begin again at the beginning, unlearn-
    ing all my faults. . . .
This was as true a hundred million years ago,
This will be as true a hundred million years from now,
As it is now, at this moment.

FOREVER

John Boyle O'Reilly

Those we love truly never die,
    Though year by year the sad memorial wreath,
    A ring and flowers, types of life and death,
        Are laid upon their graves.

For death the pure life saves,
    And life all pure is love; and love can reach
    From heaven to earth, and nobler lessons teach
        Than those by mortals read.

Well blest is he who has a dear one dead;
    A friend he has whose face will never change—
    A dear communion that will not grow strange;
        The anchor of a love is death.

SEEDS

John Oxenham

What shall we be like when
We cast this earthly body and attain
To Immortality?
What shall we be like then?

Ah, who shall say
What vast expansions shall be ours that day?
What transformations of this house of clay,
To fit the heavenly mansions and the light of day?
Ah, who shall say?

But this we know,—
We drop a seed into the ground,
A tiny, shapeless thing, shrivelled and dry,
And, in the fulness of its time, is seen
A form of peerless beauty, robed and crowned
Beyond the pride of any earthly queen,
Instinct with loveliness, and sweet and rare
The perfect emblem of its Maker's care.

This from a shrivelled seed?—
—Then may man hope indeed!

For man is but the seed of what he shall be,
When, in the fulness of his perfecting,
He drops the husk and cleaves his upward way,
Through earth's retardings and the clinging clay
Into the sunshine of God's perfect day.
No fetters then! No bonds of time or space!
But powers as ample as the boundless grace
That suffered man, and death, and yet, in tenderness,
Set wide the door and passed Himself before—
As He had promised—to prepare a place.

Yea, we may hope!
For we are seeds,
Dropped into earth for heavenly blossoming.
Perchance, when comes the time of harvesting,
His loving care
May find some use for even a humble tare.

We know not what we shall be—only this—
That we shall be made like Him—as He is.

THE CONCLUSION

Sir Walter Raleigh

(Found in his Bible in the Gatehouse at Westminster)

Even such is time, that takes in trust
  Our youth, our joys, are all we have,
And pays us but with earth and dust;
  Who, in the dark and silent grave,
When we have wandered all our ways,
Shuts up the story of our days;
But from this earth, this grave, this dust,
My God shall raise me up, I trust.

AWAY!

James Whitcomb Riley

I cannot say, and I will not say
That he is dead! He is just away!

With a cheery smile, and a wave of the hand,
He has wandered into an unknown land.

And left us dreaming how very fair
It must be, since he lingers there.

And you,—O you, who the wildest yearn
For the old-time step and the glad return,—

Think of him faring on, as dear
In the love of There as the love of Here;

Mild and gentle as he was brave,—
When the sweetest love of his life he gave

To simple things:—where the violets grew
Pure as the eyes they were likened to,

The touches of his hands have strayed
As reverently as his lips have prayed.

Think of him still as the same, I say;
He is not dead—he is just away!

IMMORTALITY

George William Russell (*A. E.*)

We must pass like smoke or live within the spirit's fire;
For we can do no more than smoke unto the flame return;
If our thought has changed to dream, our will unto desire,
  As smoke we vanish though the fire may burn.

Lights of infinite pity star the grey dusk of our days:
Surely here is soul: with it we have eternal breath:
In the fire of love we live, or pass by many ways,
  By unnumbered ways of dream, to death.

MY BIRTH

Minot J. Savage

I had my birth when the stars were born,
  In the dim æons of the past:
My cradle cosmic forces rocked,
  And to my first was linked my last.

Through boundless space the shuttle flew,
  To weave the warp and woof of fate:
In my begetting were conjoined
  The infinitely small and great.

The outmost star on being's rim,
  The tiniest sand-grain of the earth,
The farthest thrill and nearest stir
  Was not indifferent to my birth.

And when at last the earth swung free,
   A little planet by the moon,
For me the continent arose,
   For me the ocean roared its tune;

For me the forests grew; for me
   The electric force ran to and fro;
For me tribes wandered o'er the earth,
   Kingdoms rose, and cities grew.

For me religions waxed and waned;
   For me the ages garnered store;
For me ships traversed every sea;
   For me the wise ones learned their lore;

For me, through fire and blood and tears,
   Man struggled onward up the height,
On which, at last, from heaven falls
   An ever clearer, broader light.

The child of all the ages, I,
   Nursed on the exhaustless breast of time;
By heroes thrilled, by sages taught,
   Sung to by bards of every clime.

Quintessence of the universe,
   Distilled at last from God's own heart,
In me concentered now abides
   Of all that is the subtlest part.

The product of the ages past,
   Heir of the future, then, am I:
So much am I divine that God
   Cannot afford to let me die.

If I should ever cease to be,
   The farthest star its mate would miss,
And, looking after me, would fall
   Down headlong darkening to the abyss.

For, if aught real that is should cease,
   If the All-Father ever nods,
That day across the heavens would fall
   Ragnorok, twilight of the Gods.

From ADONAIS

Percy Bysshe Shelley

He is made one with Nature: there is heard
His voice in all her music, from the moan
   Of thunder, to the song of night's sweet bird;
He is a presence to be felt and known
In darkness and in light, from herb and stone,
Spreading itself where'er that Power may move
Which has withdrawn His being to its own;
   Which wields the world with never-wearied love,
Sustains it from beneath, and kindles it above.

He is a portion of the loveliness
Which once he made more lovely: he doth bear
   His part, while the one Spirit's plastic stress
Sweeps through the dull dense world, compelling there
All new successions to the forms they wear;
Torturing the unwilling dross that checks its flight
To its own likeness, as each mass may bear;
   And bursting in its beauty and its might,
From trees and beasts and men into the Heaven's light.

The splendors of the firmament of time
May be eclipsed but are extinguished not;
   Like stars to their appointed height they climb,
And death is a low mist which cannot blot
The brightness it may veil. When lofty thought
Lifts a young heart above its mortal lair,
And love and life contend for it, for what
   Shall be its earthly doom, the dead live there
And move like winds of light on dark and stormy air.

   .   .   .   .

The One remains, the many change and pass;
Heaven's light forever shines, Earth's shadows fly;
Life, like a dome of many-colored glass,
Stains the white radiance of Eternity,
Until Death tramples it to fragments.—Die,
If thou wouldst be with that which thou dost seek!
Follow where all is fled!—Rome's azure sky,
Flowers, ruins, statues, music, words, are weak
The glory they transfuse with fitting truth to speak.

   .   .   .   .

That Light whose smile kindles the Universe,
That Beauty in which all things work and move,
That Benediction which the eclipsing Curse
Of birth can quench not, that sustaining Love
Which through the web of being blindly wove
By man and beast and earth and air and sea,
Burns bright or dim, as each are mirrors of
The fire for which all thirst; now beams on me,
Consuming the last clouds of cold mortality.

The breath whose might I have invoked in song
Descends on me; my spirit's bark is driven,
Far from the shore, far from the trembling throng
Whose sails were never to the tempest given;
The massy earth and spherèd skies are riven!
I am borne darkly, fearfully, afar;
Whilst, burning through the inmost veil of Heaven
The soul of Adonais, like a star,
Beacons from the abode where the Eternal are.

IMMORTAL

Sara Teasdale

So soon my body will have gone
    Beyond the sight and sound of men,
And tho' it wakes and suffers now
    Its sleep will be unbroken then;

But, oh, my frail immortal soul
  That will not sleep forevermore,
A leaf borne onward by the blast,
  A wave that never finds the shore!

CROSSING THE BAR

Alfred Tennyson

Sunset and evening star,
  And one clear call for me!
And may there be no moaning of the bar,
  When I put out to sea,

But such a tide as moving seems asleep,
  Too full for sound and foam,
When that which drew from out the boundless deep
  Turns again home.

Twilight and evening bell,
  And after that, the dark!
And may there be no sadness of farewell,
  When I embark;

For tho' from out our bourne of Time and Place
  The flood may bear me far,
I hope to see my Pilot face to face
  When I have crossed the bar.

OF ONE SELF-SLAIN

Charles Hanson Towne

When he went blundering back to God,
  His songs half written, his work half done,
Who knows what paths his bruised feet trod,
  What hills of peace or pain he won?

I hope God smiled and took his hand,
    And said, "Poor truant, passionate fool!
Life's book is hard to understand;
    Why could'st thou not remain at school?"

TO NIGHT

Joseph Blanco White

Mysterious night! When our first parent knew
Thee from report divine, and heard thy name,
Did he not tremble for this lovely frame,
This glorious canopy of light and blue?
Yet 'neath the curtain of translucent dew,
Bathed in the rays of the great setting flame,
Hesperus with the host of heaven came,
And lo! Creation widened on man's view.
Who could have thought such darkness lay concealed
Within thy beams, O sun! or who could find
While fly, and leaf, and insect stood revealed,
That to such countless orbs thou mad'st us blind.
Why do we, then, shun Death with anxious strife?—
    If Light can thus deceive, wherefore not Life?

AT LAST

John Greenleaf Whittier

When on my day of life the night is falling,
    And, in the winds from unsunned spaces blown,
I hear far voices out of darkness calling
    My feet to paths unknown,

Thou who hast made my home of life so pleasant,
    Leave not its tenant when its walls decay;
O Love Divine, O Helper ever-present,
    Be Thou my strength and stay!

*B*e near me when all else is from me drifting;
  Earth, sky, home's pictures, days of shade and shine,·
And kindly faces to my own uplifting
  The love which answers mine.

I have but Thee, my Father! let Thy spirit
  Be with me then to comfort and uphold;
No gate of pearl, no branch of palm I merit,
  Nor street of shining gold.

Suffice it if—my good and ill unreckoned,
  And both forgiven through Thy abounding grace—
I find myself by hands familiar beckoned
  Unto my fitting place.

b. IMPERSONAL IMMORTALITY

MISSING

ANONYMOUS

When the anxious hearts say "Where?"
He doth answer "In My care."

"Is it life or is it death?"
"Wait," He whispers. "Child, have faith!"

"Did they need love's tenderness?"
"Is there love like Mine to bless?"

"Were they frightened at the last?"
"No, the sting of death is past."

"Did a thought of 'Home-Love' rise?"
"I looked down thro' Mother-eyes."

"Saviour, tell us, where are they?"
"In My keeping, night and day."

"Tell us, tell us, how it stands."
"None shall pluck them from My Hands."

THE DEAD

Mathilde Blind

The dead abide with us! Though stark and cold
    Earth seems to grip them, they are with us still:
    They have forged our chains of being for good or ill
And their invisible hands these hands yet hold.
Our perishable bodies are the mould
    In which their strong imperishable will—
    Mortality's deep yearning to fulfill—
Hath grown incorporate through dim time untold.
    Vibrations infinite of life in death,
As a star's travelling light survives its star!
So may we hold our lives that, when we are
    The fate of those who then will draw this breath,
They shall not drag us to their judgment bar,
    And curse the heritage that we bequeath.

WHERE RUNS THE RIVER?

Francis William Bourdillon

Where runs the river? Who can say
Who hath not followed all the way
By alders green and selges gray
        And blossoms blue?

Where runs the river? Hill and wood
Curve round to hem the eager flood;
It cannot straightly as it would
        Its path pursue.

Yet this we know: O'er whatso plains
Or rocks or waterfalls it strains,
At last the vast the stream attains;
    And I, and you.

LAST LINES

EMILY BRONTË

No coward soul is mine,
No trembler in the world's storm-troubled sphere;
  I see Heaven's glories shine,
And faith shines equal, arming me from fear.

O God within my breast,
Almighty, ever-present Deity!
  Life—that in me has rest,
As I—undying life—have power in thee!

Vain are the thousand creeds
That move men's hearts: unutterably vain;
  Worthless as withered weeds,
Or idlest froth amid the boundless main.

To waken doubt in one
Holding so fast by thine° infinity;
  So surely anchored on
The steadfast rock of immortality.

With wide-embracing love
Thy Spirit animates eternal years,
  Pervades and broods above,
Changes, sustains, dissolves, creates and rears.

Though earth and man were gone,
And suns and universes ceased to be,
  And Thou were left alone,
Every existence would exist in Thee.

There is not room for Death
Nor atom that his might could render void:
  Thou—THOU art Being and Breath,
And what THOU art may never be destroyed.

THE DEAD

RUPERT BROOKE

Blow out, you bugles, over the rich Dead!
There's none of these so lonely and poor and old
But, dying, has made us rarer gifts than gold.
These laid the world away; poured out the red
Sweet wine of youth; gave up the years to be
Of work and joy, and that unhoped serene
That men call age; and those who would have been,
Their sons, they gave, their immortality.

Blow, bugles, blow! They brought us for our dearth,
Holiness lacked so long, and Love and Pain.
Honor has come back, as a king, to earth,
And paid his subjects with a royal wage;
And Nobleness walks in our ways again;
And we have come into our heritage.

PEACE

RUPERT BROOKE

Now, God be thanked who has matched us with His hour,
  And caught our youth, and wakened us from sleeping,
With hand made sure, clear eye and sharpened power,
  To turn, as swimmers into cleanness leaping,
Glad from a world grown old and cold and weary,
  Leave the sick hearts that honor could not move,
And half-men and their dirty songs and dreary,
  And all the little emptiness of love!
Oh! We who have known shame, we have found release there

Where there's no ill, no grief, but sleep has mending,
Naught broken save this body, lost but breath;
Nothing to shake the laughing heart's long peace there
But only agony, and that has ending;
And the worst friend and enemy is but Death.

THANATOPSIS

WILLIAM CULLEN BRYANT

To him who in the love of Nature holds
Communion with her visible forms, she speaks
A various language; for his gayer hours
She has a voice of gladness, and a smile
And eloquence of beauty, and she glides
Into his darker musings, with a mild
And healing sympathy, that steals away
Their sharpness, ere he is aware. When thoughts
Of the last bitter hour come like a blight
Over thy spirit, and sad images
Of the stern agony, and shroud, and pall,
And breathless darkness, and the narrow house,
Make thee to shudder and grow sick at heart;—
Go forth, under the open sky, and list
To Nature's teachings, while from all around—
Earth and her waters, and the depths of air—
Comes a still voice:—

                Yet a few days, and thee
The all-beholding sun shall see no more
In all his course; nor yet in the cold ground,
Where thy pale form was laid with many tears,
Nor in the embrace of ocean, shall exist
Thy image. Earth, that nourished thee, shall claim
Thy growth, to be resolved to earth again,
And, lost each human trace, surrendering up
Thine individual being, shalt thou go
To mix forever with the elements,
To be a brother to the insensible rock

And to the sluggish clod, which the rude swain
Turns with his share, and treads upon. The oak
Shall send his roots abroad, and pierce thy mould.

Yet not to thine eternal resting-place
Shalt thou retire alone, nor couldst thou wish
Couch more magnificent. Thou shalt lie down
With patriarchs of the infant world—with kings,
The powerful of the earth—the wise, the good,
Fair forms, and hoary seers of ages past,
All in one mighty sepulchre. The hills
Rock-ribbed and ancient as the sun,—the vales
Stretching in pensive quietness between;
The venerable woods—rivers that move
In majesty, and the complaining brooks
That make the meadows green; and, poured round all,
Old Ocean's gray and melancholy waste,—
Are but the solemn decorations all
Of the great tomb of man. The golden sun,
The planets, all the infinite host of heaven,
Are shining on the sad abodes of death
Through the still lapse of ages. All that tread
The globe are but a handful to the tribes
That slumber in its bosom.—Take the wings
Of morning, pierce the Barcan wilderness,
Or lose thyself in the continuous woods
Where rolls the Oregon, and hears no sound,
Save his own dashings—yet the dead are there;
And millions in those solitudes, since first
The flight of years began, have laid them down
In their last sleep—the dead reign there alone.
So shalt thou rest, and what if thou withdraw
In silence from the living, and no friend
Take note of thy departure? All that breathe
Will share thy destiny. The gay will laugh
When thou art gone, the solemn brood of care
Plod on, and each one as before will chase
His favourite phantom; yet all these shall leave
Their mirth and their employments, and shall come
And make their bed with thee. As the long train

Of ages glides away, the sons of men—
The youth in life's fresh spring, and he who goes
In the full strength of years, matron and maid,
The speechless babe, and the gray-headed man—
Shall one by one be gathered to thy side,
By those, who in their turn shall follow them.

So live, that when thy summons comes to join
The innumerable caravan, which moves
To that mysterious realm, where each shall take
His chamber in the silent halls of death,
Thou go not, like the quarry-slave at night,
Scourged to his dungeon, but, sustained and soothed
By an unfaltering trust, approach thy grave
Like one who wraps the drapery of his couch
About him, and lies down to pleasant dreams.

THE IMMORTAL MIND

Lord Byron

When coldness wraps•this suffering clay,
    Ah, whither strays the immortal mind?
It cannot die, it cannot stay,
    But leaves its darkened dust behind.
Then unembodied, doth it trace
    By steps each planet's heavenly way?
Or fill at once the realms of space
    A thing of eyes, that all survey?

Eternal, boundless, undecayed,
    A thought unseen, but seeing all,
All, all, in earth or skies displayed,
    Shall it survey, shall it recall:
Each fainter trace that memory holds
    So darkly of departed years,
In one broad glance the soul beholds,
    And all that was, at once appears.

Before creation peopled earth
  Its eyes shall roll through chaos back;
And where the furthest heaven had birth,
  The spirit trace its rising track.
And where the future mars or makes,
  Its glance dilate o'er all to be,
While sun is quenched or system breaks,
  Fixed in its own eternity.

Above or love, hope, hate or fear,
  It lives all passionless and pure:
An age shall fleet like earthly year;
  Its years as moments shall endure.
Away, away, without a wing,
  O'er all, through all, its thought shall fly;
A nameless and eternal thing
  Forgetting what it was to die.

SAY NOT THE STRUGGLE NAUGHT AVAILETH

Arthur Hugh Clough

Say not the struggle naught availeth,
  The labor and the wounds are vain,
The enemy faints not, nor faileth,
  And as things have been they remain.

If hopes were dupes, fears may be liars;
  It may be, in yon smoke concealed,
Your comrades chase e'en now the fliers,
  And, but for you, possess the field.

For while the tired waves, vainly breaking,
  Seem here no painful inch to gain,
Far back, through creeks and inlets making,
  Comes silent, flooding in, the main.

And not by eastern windows only,
  When daylight comes, comes in the light;

In front, the sun climbs slow, how slowly.
But westward, look, the land is bright!

NOW AND AFTERWARDS

Dinah Muloch Craik

"Two hands upon the breast,
        And labor's done;
Two pale feet crossed in rest,—
        The race is won;
Two eyes with coin-weights shut,
        And all tears cease:
Two lips where grief is mute,
        Anger at peace":
So pray we oftentimes, mourning our lot;
God in his kindness answereth not.

"Two hands to work addressed
        Aye for his praise;
Two feet that never rest,
        Walking his ways;
Two eyes that look above
        Through all their tears;
Two lips still breathing love,
        Not wrath, nor fears":
So pray we afterwards, low on our knees;
Pardon those erring prayers! Father, hear these!

IMMORTALITY

Richard Henry Dana

Oh! Listen, man!
A voice within us speaks that word, startling;
"Man, thou shalt never die!" Celestial voices
Hymn it unto our souls; according harps,
By angel fingers touched, when the mild stars

Of morning sang together, still sound forth
The song of our great immortality.
Thick clustering orbs, and this our fair domain,
The tall, dark mountains, and the deep-toned seas
Join in this solemn, universal song.

Oh, listen, ye, our spirits; drink it in
From all the air. 'Tis in the gentle moonlight;
'Tis floating in day's setting glories; night
Wrapped in her sable robe, with silent step
Comes to our bed and breathes it in our ears:
Night, and the dawn, bright day, and thoughtful eve,
All times, all bounds, the limitless expanse,
As one vast mystic instrument, are touched
By an unseen living Hand, and conscious chords
Quiver with joy in this great jubilee.
The dying hear it; and, as sounds of earth
Grow dull and distant, wake their passing souls
To mingle in this heavenly harmony.

MY HEREAFTER

JUANITA DE LONG

Do not come when I am dead
To sit beside a low green mound,
Or bring the first gay daffodils
Because I love them so,
For I shall not be there.
You cannot find me there.

I will look up at you from the eyes
Of little children;
I will bend to meet you in the swaying boughs
Of bud-thrilled trees,
And caress you with the passionate sweep
Of storm-filled winds;
I will give you strength in your upward tread
Of everlasting hills;

I will cool your tired body in the flow
Of the limpid river;
I will warm your work-glorified hands through the glow
Of the winter fire;
I will soothe you into forgetfulness to the drop, drop
Of the rain on the roof;
I will speak to you out of the rhymes
Of the Masters;
I will dance with you in the lilt
Of the violin,
And make your heart leap with the bursting cadence
Of the organ;
I will flood your soul with the flaming radiance
Of the sunrise,
And bring you peace in the tender rose and gold
Of the after-sunset.

All these have made me happy:
They are a part of me;
I shall become a part of them.

VITÆ SUMMA BREVIS SPEM NOS VETAT
INCOHARE LONGAM

ERNEST DOWSON

They are not long, the weeping and the laughter,
  Love and desire and hate:
I think they have no portion in us after
  We pass the gate.

They are not long, the days of wine and roses:
  Out of a misty dream
Our path emerges for a while, then closes
  Within a dream.

EPITAPH

LOUISE DRISCOLL

Here lies the flesh that tried
   To follow the spirit's leading:
Fallen, at last, it died
   Broken, bruised, and bleeding.
Burned by the high fires
   Of the spirit's desires.

It had no dream to sing
   Of ultimate Liberty
Fashioned for suffering
   To endure transiently,
And conscious that it must
   Return as dust to dust.

It blossomed a weak hour,
   Was rosy, warm and strong;
It went like a wilted flower,
   It ended like a song,
Some one closed a door—
   And it was seen no more.

The grass is very kind
   (It knows so many dead!)
Those whom it covers find
   Their wild hearts comforted;
Their pulses need not meet
   The spirit's need and heat.

Here lies the flesh that held
   The spirit prisoner—
A caged thing that rebelled
   Forced to sub-minister;
Broken it had to be;
   To set its captive free.

It is very glad to rest,
   It calls to roots and rain
Safe in its mother's breast
   Ready to bloom again.
After a day and hour
   'Twill greet the sun—a flower.

OH, MAY I JOIN THE CHOIR INVISIBLE

George Eliot

Oh, may I join the choir invisible
Of those immortal dead who live again
In minds made better by their presence; **live**
In pulses stirred to generosity,
In deeds of daring rectitude, in scorn
Of miserable aims that end with self,
In thoughts sublime that pierce the night like stars,
And with their mild persistence urge men's search
To vaster issues.

       —So to live is heaven:
To make undying music in the world,
Breathing a beauteous order, that controls
With growing sway the growing life of man.
So we inherit that sweet purity
For which we struggled, failed and agonized
With widening retrospect that bred despair.
Rebellious flesh that would not be subdued,
A vicious parent shaming still its child,
Poor anxious penitence, is quick dissolved;
Its discords quenched by meeting harmonies,
Die in the large and charitable air.
And all our rarer, better, truer self,
That sobbed religiously in yearning song,
That watched to ease the burden of the world,
Laboriously tracing what must be,
And what may yet be better,—saw within
A worthier image for the sanctuary,

And shaped it forth before the multitude,
Divinely human, raising worship so
To higher reverence more mixed with love,—
That better self shall live till human Time
Shall fold its eyelids, and the human sky
Be gathered like a scroll within the tomb,
Unread forever.

This is life to come,
Which martyred men have made more glorious
For us, who strive to follow.

May I reach
That purest heaven,—be to other souls
The cup of strength in some great agony,
Enkindle generous ardor, feed pure love,
Beget the smiles that have no cruelty,
Be the sweet presence of a good diffused,
And in diffusion ever more intense!
So shall I join the choir invisible,
Whose music is the gladness of the world.

LIFE'S EVENING

Dudley Foulke

Three score and ten! The tumult of the world
  Grows dull upon my inattentive ear:
The bugle calls are faint, the flags are furled,
  Gone is the rapture, vanished too the fear;
The evening's blessed stillness covers all,
  As o'er the fields she folds her cloak of grey;
Hushed are the winds, the brown leaves slowly fall,
  The russet clouds hang on the fringe of day.
What fairer hour than this? No stir of morn
  With cries of waking life, nor shafts of noon—
Hot tresses from the flaming sun-god born—
  Nor midnight's shivering stars and marble moon;
But softly twilight falls and toil doth cease,
While o'er my soul God spreads his mantle—peace.

MY DEAD

FREDERICK LUCIAN HOSMER

I cannot think of them as dead
  Who walk with me no more:
Along the path of life I tread
  They have but gone before.

The Father's house is mansioned fair
  Beyond my vision dim;
All souls are His, and here or there
  Are living unto Him.

And still their silent ministry
  Within my heart hath place,
As when they on earth walked with me
  And met me face to face.

Their lives are made forever mine;
  What they to me have been,
Hath left henceforth its seal and sign
  Engraven deep within.

Mine are they by an ownership
  Nor time nor death can free;
For God hath given to Love to keep
  Its own eternally.

HABEAS CORPUS

HELEN HUNT JACKSON

(Last Poem)

My body, eh? Friend Death, how now?
  Why all this tedious pomp of writ?
Thou hast reclaimed it sure and slow
  For half a century, bit by bit.

In faith thou knowest more to-day
　　Than I do, where it can be found!
This shriveled lump of suffering clay
　　To which I now am chained and bound,

Has not of kith or kin a trace
　　To the good body once I bore;
Look at this shrunken, ghastly face:
　　Didst ever see that face before?

Ah, well, Friend Death, good friend thou art;
　　Thy only fault thy lagging gait,
Mistaken pity in thy heart
　　For timorous ones that bid thee wait.

Do quickly all thou hast to do,
　　Nor I nor mine will hindrance make;
I shall be free when thou art through;
　　I grudge thee naught that thou must take!

Stay! I have lied: I grudge thee one,
　　Yes, two I grudge thee at this last,—
Two members which have faithful done
　　My will and bidding in the past.

I grudge thee this right hand of mine;
　　I grudge thee this quick-beating heart;
They never gave me coward sign,
　　Nor played me once a traitor's part.

I see now why in olden days
　　Men in barbaric love or hate
Nailed enemy's hands at wild cross-ways,
　　Shrined leaders' hearts in costly state:

The symbol, sign, and instrument
　　Of each soul's purpose, passion, strife,
Of fires, in which are poured and spent
　　Their all of love, their all of life.

O feeble, mighty human hand!
  O fragile, dauntless human heart!
The universe holds nothing planned
  With such sublime, transcendent art!

Yes, Death, I own I grudge thee mine
  Poor little hand, so feeble now;
Its wrinkled palm, its altered line,
  Its veins so pallid and so slow . . .
              (Unfinished here)

·   ·   ·   ·   ·   ·   ·   ·

Ah, well, friend Death, good friend thou art:
  I shall be free when thou art through.
Take all there is,—take hand and heart:
  There must be somewhere work to do.

IMMORTALITY

JOB XIV, 1-12

From Moulton's *Modern Reader's Bible*

Man that is born of woman
Is of few days, and full of trouble;
He cometh forth like a flower, and is cut down,
He fleeth also as shadow and continueth not.

·   ·   ·   ·   ·   ·   ·   ·

For there is hope of a tree if it be cut down,
That it will sprout again,
And that the tender branch thereof will not cease;

    Though the root thereof wax old in the earth,
    And the stock thereof die in the ground,
    Yet through the scent of water it will bud,
    And put forth boughs like a plant.

    But man dieth and wasteth away:
    Yea, man giveth up the ghost, and where is he?
    As the waters fail from the sea,
    And the river decayeth and drieth up.

So man lieth down and riseth not;
Till the heavens be no more they shall not awake,
Nor be roused out of their sleep.

Job XIX, 25-27

For I know that my vindicator liveth,
And that He shall stand up at the last upon the earth;
And after my skin hath been thus destroyed,
Yet without my flesh shall I see God!

Whom I shall see on my side,
And mine eyes shall behold and not another.
—My reins are consumed within me—

(End of speech of Job. He is unable to go on.)

MEN TOLD ME, LORD!

David Starr Jordan

Men told me, Lord, it was a vale of tears
Where thou hadst placed me; wickedness and woe
My twain companions whereso I might go;
That I through ten and three-score weary years
Should stumble on, beset by pains and fears,
Fierce conflict round me, passions hot within,
Enjoyment brief and fatal, but in sin.
When all was ended then I should demand
Full compensation from thine austere hand:
For 'tis thy pleasure, all temptation past,
To be not just but generous at last.

Lord, here am I, my three score years and ten
Are counted to the full; I've fought thy fight,
Crossed thy dark valleys, scaled thy rocks' harsh height,
Borne all the burdens thou dost lay on men
With hand unsparing, three score years and ten.
Before thee now I make my claim, Oh, Lord!
What shall I pray thee as a meet reward?

I ask for nothing! Let the balance fall!
All that I am or know, or may confess
But swells the weight of my indebtedness;
Burdens and sorrows stand transfigured all;
Thy hand's rude buffet turns to a caress,
For Love, with all the rest, thou gavest me here,
And Love is heaven's very atmosphere.
Lo, I have dwelt with thee, Lord! Let me die:
I could no more through all eternity!

From THE RUBAIYAT

OMAR KHAYYAM

Translated by Edward Fitzgerald

Come, fill the Cup, and in the fire of Spring
Your Winter-garment of Repentance fling:
    The Bird of Time has but a little way
To flutter—and the Bird is on the Wing.

Whether at Naishapur or Babylon,
Whether the Cup with sweet or bitter run,
    The Wine of Life keeps oozing, drop by drop,
The Leaves of Life keep falling, one by one.

Each Morn a thousand Roses brings, you say:
Yes, but where leaves the Rose of Yesterday?
    And this first Summer month that brings the Rose
Shall take Jamshyd and Kaikobad away.

Well, let it take them! What have we to do
With Kaikobad the great, or Kaikhosru?
    Let Zal and Rustum bluster as they will,
Or Hastim call to Supper—heed not you.

With me along the strip of herbage strown
That just divides the desert from the sown,
    Where name of Slave and Sultan is forgot—
And peace to Mahmud on his golden throne.

A Book of Verses underneath the Bough,
A Jug of Wine, a Loaf of Bread—and Thou
   Beside me singing in the Wilderness—
Oh, Wilderness were Paradise enow!

Some for the Glories of this World, and some
Sigh for the Prophet's Paradise to come;
   Ah, take the Cash and let the Credit go,
Nor heed the rumble of a distant Drum!

Look to the blowing Rose about us—"Lo,
Laughing," she says, "into the world I blow.
   At once the silken tassels of my Purse
Tear, and its Treasure on the Garden throw."

And those who husbanded the Golden grain,
And those who flung it to the winds Like rain,
   Alike to no such aureate Earth are turned
As, buried once, Men want dug up again.

The Worldly Hope men set their Hearts upon
Turns Ashes—or it prospers; and anon,
   Like Snow upon the Desert's dusty Face,
Lighting a little hour or two—is gone.

Think, in this battered Caravanserai
Whose Portals are alternate Night and Day,
   How Sultan after Sultan in his Pomp
Abode his destined Hour and went his way.

They say the Lion and the Lizard keep
The Courts where Jamshyd gloried and drank deep;
   And Bahram, that great hunter,—the Wild Ass
Stamps o'er his Head but cannot break his Sleep.

I sometimes think that never blows so red
The Rose as where some buried Cæsar bled;
   That every Hyacinth the Garden wears
Dropt in her Lap from some once lovely Head.

And this reviving Herb whose tender Green
Fledges the River-lip on which we lean—
    Ah, lean upon it lightly! for who knows
From what once lovely Lip it springs unseen!

Ah, my Belovèd, fill the Cup that clears
Today of past Regret and future Fears:
    To-morrow!—Why To-morrow I may be
Myself with Yesterday's Seven thousand Years.

For some we loved, the loveliest and the best
That from his Vintage rolling Time hath pressèd,
    Have drunk their Cup a Round or two before,
And one by one crept silently to rest.

And we, that now make merry in the Room
They left, and Summer dresses in new bloom,
    Ourselves must we beneath the Couch of Earth
Descend—ourselves to make a Couch—for whom?

Ah, make the most of what we yet may spend,
Before we, too, into the Dust descend;
    Dust into Dust, and under Dust to lie,
Sans Wine, sans Song, sans Singer, and—sans End!

L'ENVOI

RUDYARD KIPLING

When earth's last picture is painted, and the tubes are twisted
    and dried,
When the oldest colors have faded, and the youngest critic has
    died,
We shall rest, and,—faith, we shall need it,—lie down for an
    æon or two,
Till the Master of all Good Workmen shall set us to work anew!

And those that were good shall be happy: they shall sit in a
    golden chair;
They shall splash at a ten-league canvas with brushes of comets'
    hair;

They shall find real saints to draw from—Magdalen, Peter, and
  Paul;
They shall work for an age at a sitting, and never be tired at all!

And only the Master shall praise us, and only the Master shall
  blame;
And no one shall work for money, and no one shall work for
  fame;
But each for the joy of the working, and each in his separate
  star
Shall draw the Thing as he sees It for the God of the Things
  as They are!

MY OWN HEREAFTER

Eugene Lee-Hamilton

Where angel trumpets hail a brighter sun
  With their superb alarum, and the flash
  Of angel cymbals dazzles as they clash,
Seek not to find me, when my sands are run;
Nor where, in mail of sapphire every one,
  God's sentries man the walls, that light's waves wash
  With an eternal angel—heard faint plash—
But in some book of sonnets, when day's done,
There in the long June twilight, as you read,
  You will encounter my immortal parts,
If any such I have, from earth's clay freed;
Divested of their sins, to be the seed
  Perhaps of some slight good in others' hearts.
That is the only after-life I need.

A CREED

John Masefield

I hold that when a person dies
  His soul returns again to earth;
Arrayed in some new flesh-disguise
  Another mother gives him birth.

With sturdier limbs and mightier brain
The old soul takes the roads again.

Such is my own belief and trust;
   This hand, this hand that holds the pen,
Has many hundred times been dust
   And turned, as dust, to dust again;
These eyes of mine have blinked and shone
In Thebes, in Troy, in Babylon.

All that I rightly think or do,
   Or make, or spoil, or bless, or blast,
Is curse or blessing justly due
   For sloth or effort in the past.
My life's a statement of the sum
Of vice indulged, or overcome.

I know that in my lives to be
   My sorry heart will ache and burn,
And worship unavailingly,
   The woman whom I used to spurn,
And shake to see another have
The love I spurned, the love she gave.

And I shall know, in angry words,
   In gibes, and mocks, and many a tear,
A carrion flock of homing-birds,
   The gibes and scorns I uttered here.
The brave word that I failed to speak
Will brand me dastard on the cheek.

And as I wander on the roads
   I shall be helped and healed and blessed;
Dear words shall cheer and be as goads
   To urge to heights before unguessed.
My road shall be the road I made;
All that I gave shall be repaid.

So shall I fight, so shall I tread,
   In this long war beneath the stars;

So shall a glory wreathe my head,
  So shall I faint and show the scars,
Until this case, this clogging mould,
Be smithied all to kingly gold.

From THE TRAGEDY OF POMPEY THE GREAT

JOHN MASEFIELD

Man is a sacred city built of marvelous earth.
Life was lived nobly here to give such beauty birth.
Beauty was in this brain and in this eager hand:
Death is so blind and dumb, Death does not understand.
Death drifts the brain with dust and soils the young limb's glory.
Death makes women a dream, and men a traveller's story.
Death drives the lovely soul to wander under the sky.
Death opens unknown doors. It is most grand to die.

From THE EVERLASTING MERCY

JOHN MASEFIELD

I opened the window wide and leaned
Out of the pigstye of that fiend
And felt a cool wind go like grace
About the sleeping market-place.
The clock struck three, and sweetly, slowly,
The bells chimed Holy, Holy, Holy;

.   .   .   .   .

And summat made me think of things.
How long those ticking clocks had gone
From church and chapel, on and on,
Ticking the time out, ticking slow
To men and girls who'd come and go,

.   .   .   .   .

And how a change had come. And then
I thought, "you tick the different men."

What with fight and what with drinking
And being alone there thinking,
My mind began to carp and tetter,
"If this life's all, the beasts are better."

O Christ who holds the open gate,
O Christ who drives the furrow straight,
O Christ, the plough, O Christ, the laughter,
Of holy white birds flying after,
Lo, all my heart's field red and torn,
And Thou wilt bring young green corn,
The young green corn divinely springing,
The young green corn forever singing;
And when the field is fresh and fair
Thy blessed feet shall glitter there.
And we will walk the weeded field,
And tell the golden harvest's yield,
The corn that makes the holy bread
By which the soul of man is fed,
The holy bread, the food unpriced,
Thy everlasting mercy, Christ.

TRUTH

John Masefield

Man with his burning soul
Has but an hour of breath
To build a ship of Truth
In which his soul may sail,
Sail on the sea of death.
For death takes toll
Of beauty, courage, youth,
Of all but Truth.

Life's city ways are dark,
Men mutter by; the wells
Of the great waters moan.
O Death, O sea, O tide,

The waters moan like bells.
No light, no mark,
The soul goes out alone
On seas unknown.

Stripped of all purple robes,
Stripped of all golden lies,
I will not be afraid.
Truth will preserve through death;
Perhaps the stars will rise,
The stars like globes.
The ship my striving made
May see night fade.

THE QUESTION WHITHER

George Meredith

When we have thrown off this old suit
  So much in need of mending,
To sink among the naked mute,
  Is that, think you, our ending?
We follow many, more we lead,
  And you who sadly turf us,
Believe not that all living seed
  Must flower above the surface.

Sensation is a gracious gift
  But were it cramped to station,
The prayer to have it cast adrift
  Would spout from all sensation.
Enough if we have winked to sun,
  Have sped the plough a season,
There is a soul for labor done,
  Endureth fixed as reason.

Then let our trust be firm in Good,
  Though we be of the fasting;
Our questions are a mortal brood,
  Our work is everlasting.

We Children of Beneficence
  Are in its being sharers;
And Whither vainer sounds than Whence
  For word with such wayfarers.

A SONG OF DERIVATIONS

Alice Meynell

I come from nothing, but from where
Come the undying thoughts I bear?
  Down, through long links of death and birth,
  From the past poets of earth,
My immortality is there.

I am like the blossom of an hour
But long, long vanished sun and shower
  Awoke my breath i' the young world's air.
  I track the past back everywhere
Through seed and flower and seed and flower.

Or, I am like a stream that flows
Full of the cold springs that arose
  In morning lands, in distant hills;
  And down the plain my channel fills
With melting of forgotten snows.

Voices I have not heard, possessed
My own fresh songs; my thoughts are blessed
  With relics of the far unknown.
  And mixed with memories not my own
The sweet streams throng into my breast.

Before this life began to be,
The happy songs that wake in me
  Woke long ago and far apart.
  Heavily on this little heart
Presses this immortality.

THE FINAL MYSTERY

Sir Henry Newbolt

(A myth of Egyptian origin, which formed part of the instruction given to those initiated in the Orphic mysteries. Written versions of it were buried with the dead.)

Hear now, O Soul, the last command of all—
When thou hast left thine every mortal mark,
And by the road that lies beyond recall
Won through the desert of the Burning Dark,
Thou shalt behold, within a garden bright,
A well, beside a cypress ivory-white.

Still is that well, and in its waters cool
White, white and windless, sleeps that cypress tree:
Who drinks but once from out her shadowy pool
Shall thirst no more to all eternity.
Forgetting all, by all forgotten clean,
His soul shall be with that which hath not been.

But thou, though thou be trembling with thy dread,
And parched with thy desire more fierce than flame,
Think on that stream wherefrom thy life was fed,
And that diviner fountain whence it came.
Turn thee and cry—behold, it is not far—
Unto the hills where living waters are:

"Lord, though I lived on earth, the child of earth,
Yet I was fathered by the starry sky;
Thou knowest I came not of the shadows' birth,
Let me not die the death the shadows die.
Give me to drink of the sweet stream that leaps
From Memory's fount, wherein no cypress sleeps."

Then shalt thou drink, O Soul, and therewith slake
The immortal longing with thy mortal thirst;
So of thy father's life shalt thou partake,
And be forever that thou wert at first.

Lost in remembered loves, yet thou more thou
With them shalt reign in never-ending NOW.

OUR DEAD

ROBERT NICHOLS

They have not gone from us. O no! they are
The inmost essence of each thing that is
Perfect for us; they flame in every star;
The trees are emerald with their presences.
They are not gone from us; they do not roam
The flaw and turmoil of the lower deep,
But have now made the whole wide world their home,
And in its loveliness themselves they steep.

They fail not ever; theirs is a diurn
Splendor of sunny hill and forest grave;
In every rainbow's glittering drop they burn;
They dazzle in the massed clouds' architrave.
They chant on every wind, and they return
In the long roll of any deep blue wave.

c. ETERNAL REST

THE SLEEP

ELIZABETH BARRETT BROWNING

Of all the thoughts of God that are
Borne inward unto souls afar,
Along the Psalmist's music deep,
Now tell me if that any is,
For gift or grace, surpassing this—
    "He giveth His beloved, sleep"?

What would we give to our beloved?
The hero's heart, to be unmoved, ·
The poet's star-tuned harp, to sweep,
The patriot's voice, to teach and rouse,
The monarch's crown, to light the brows?
He giveth His belovèd, sleep.

What do we give to our beloved?
A little faith all undisproved,
A little dust to overweep,
And bitter memories to make
The whole earth blasted for our sake:
He giveth His belovèd, sleep.

"Sleep soft, beloved!" we sometimes say,
But have no tune to charm away
Sad dreams that through the eyelids creep.
But never doleful dream again
Shall break the happy slumber when
He giveth His belovèd, sleep.

O earth, so full of dreary noises!
O men, with wailing in your voices!
O delvèd gold, the wailers heap!
O strife, O curse, that o'er it fall!
God strikes a silence through you all,
And giveth His belovèd, sleep.

His dews drop mutely on the hill,
His cloud above it saileth still,
Though on its slope men sow and reap:
More softly than the dew is shed,
Or cloud is floated overhead,
He giveth His belovèd, sleep.

Aye, men may wonder while they scan
A living, thinking, feeling man
Confirmed in such a rest to keep;
But angels say,—and through the word
I think their happy smile is *heard*—
"He giveth His belovèd, sleep."

For me, my heart that erst did go
Most like a tired child at a show,
That sees through tears the mummers leap,
Would now its wearied vision close,
Would childlike on His love repose
Who giveth His belovèd, sleep!

And, friends, dear friends,—when it shall be
That this low breath is gone from me,
And round my bier ye come to weep,
Let One, most loving of you all,
Say, "Not a tear must o'er her fall!
He giveth His belovèd, sleep."

MARGARITÆ SORORI

WILLIAM ERNEST HENLEY

A late lark twitters from the quiet skies;
And from the west,
Where the sun, his day's work ended,
Lingers as in content,
There falls on the old, grey city
An influence luminous and serene,
A shining peace.

The smoke ascends
In a rosy-and-golden haze. The spires
Shine, and are changed. In the valley
Shadows rise. The lark sings on. The sun,
Closing his benediction,
Sinks, and the darkening air
Thrills with a sense of the triumphing night—
Night with her train of stars
And her great gift of sleep.

So be my passing!
My task accomplished and the long day done,
My wages taken, and in my heart

Some late lark singing,
Let me be gathered to the quiet west,
The sundown splendid and serene,
Death.

THE HILLS OF REST

Albert Bigelow Paine

Beyond the last horizon's rim,
  Beyond adventure's farthest quest,
Somewhere they rise, serene and dim,
  The happy, happy, Hills of Rest.

Upon their sunlit slopes uplift
  The castles we have built in Spain—
While fair amid the summer drift
  Our faded gardens flower again.

Sweet hours we did not live go by
  To soothing note, on scented wing;
In golden-lettered volumes lie
  The songs we tried in vain to sing.

They all are there; the days of dream
  That build the inner lives of men;
The silent, sacred years we deem
  The might be and the might have been.

Some evening when the sky is gold
  I'll follow day into the west;
Nor pause, nor heed, till I behold
  The happy, happy Hills of Rest.

THE PLACE OF REST

George William Russell (*A. E.*)

Unto the deep the deep heart goes,
It lays its sadness nigh the breast:
Only the Mighty Mother knows
The wounds that quiver unconfessed.

It seeks a deeper silence still;
It folds itself around with peace,
Where thoughts alike of good or ill
In quietness unfostered cease.

It feels in the unwounding vast
For comfort of its hopes and fears:
The Mighty Mother bows at last;
She listens to her children's tears.

Where the last anguish deepens—there
The fire of beauty smites through pain:
A glory moves amid despair,
The Mother takes her child again.

THE RENDEZVOUS

ALAN SEEGER

I have a rendezvous with Death
At some disputed barricade,
When Spring comes back with rustling shade
And apple-blossoms fill the air—
I have a rendezvous with Death
When Spring brings back blue days and fair.

It may be he shall take my hand
And lead me into his dark land
And close my eyes and quench my breath—
It may be I shall pass him still.
I have a rendezvous with Death
On some scarred slope of battered hill,
When Spring comes round again this year
And the first meadow-flowers appear.

God knows 'twere better to be deep
Pillowed in silk and scented down,
Where Love throbs out in blissful sleep,
Pulse nigh to pulse. and breath to breath,

Where hushed awakenings are dear....
But I've a rendezvous with Death
At midnight in some flaming town,
When Spring trips north again this year,
And I to my pledged word am true,
I shall not fail that rendezvous.

DREAM FANTASY

WILLIAM SHARP (*Fiona Macleod*)

There is a land of Dream;
I have trodden its golden ways:
I have seen its amber light
From the heart of its sun-swept days;
I have seen its moonshine white
On its silent waters gleam—
Ah, the strange sweet lonely delight
  Of the Valleys of Dream.

Ah, in that Land of Dream,
The mystical moon-white land,
Comes from what unknown sea—
Adream on what unknown strand—
A sound as of feet that flee,
As of multitudes that stream
From the shores of that shadowy sea
  Through the Valleys of Dream.

It is dark in the Land of Dream.
There is silence in all the Land.
Are the dead all gathered there—
In havens, by no breath fanned?
This stir i' the dawn, this chill wan air—
This faint dim yellow of morning gleam—
O, is this sleep, or waking where
  Lie hush'd the Valleys of Dream?

OMNIA EXEUNT IN MYSTERIUM

GEORGE STERLING

The stranger in my gates—lo! that am I,
And what my land of birth I do not know,
Nor yet the hidden land to which I go.
One may be lord of many ere he die,
And tell of many sorrows in one sigh,
But know himself he shall not, nor his woe,
Nor to what sea the tears of wisdom flow;
Nor why one star is taken from the sky.
An urging is upon him evermore,
And though he bide, his soul is wanderer,
Scanning the shadows with a sense of haste—
Where fade the tracks of all who went before:
A dim and solitary traveller
On ways that end in evening and the waste.

REQUIEM

ROBERT LOUIS STEVENSON

Under the wide and starry sky
Dig the grave and let me lie,
Glad did I live and gladly die,
  And I laid me down with a will.

This be the verse you grave for me:
Here he lies where he longed to be;
Home is the sailor, home from the sea,
  And the hunter home from the hill.

EXILE FROM GOD

JOHN HALL WHEELOCK

I do not fear to lay my body down
    In death, to share
The life of the dark earth and lose my own,
    If God is there.

I have so loved all sense of Him, sweet might
    Of color and of sound,—
His tangible loveliness and living light
    That robes me 'round.

If to His heart in the hushed grave and dim
    We sink more near,
It shall be well—living we rest in Him.
    Only I fear

Lest from my God in lonely death I lapse,
    And the dumb clod
Lose Him; for God is life, and death perhaps
    Exile from God.

DEEP SEA SOUNDINGS

SARAH WILLIAMS

Mariner, what of the deep?
                This of the deep:
Twilight is there, and solemn changeless calm;
Beauty is there, and tender, healing balm—
Balm with no root in earth, or air, or sea,
Poised by the finger of God, it floateth free,
And, as it threads the waves, the sound doth rise,—
Hither shall come no further sacrifice;
Never again the anguished clutch at life,
Never again great Love and Death in strife;

He who hath suffered all need fear no more;
Quiet his portion now forevermore.

Mariner, what of the deep?
                    This of the deep:
Solitude dwells not there, though silence reign;
Mighty is the brotherhood of loss and pain;
There is communion past the need of speech,
There is love no words of love can reach;
Heavy the waves that superincumbent press,
But as we labor here with constant stress,
Hand doth hold out to hand not help alone,
But the deep bliss of being fully known.
There are no kindred like the kin of sorrow,
There is no hope like theirs who know no morrow.

Mariner, what of the deep?
                    This of the deep:
Though we have travelled past the line of day,
Glory of night doth light us on our way,
Radiance that comes not how nor whence,
Rainbows without rain, past duller sense,
Music of hidden reefs and waves long past,
Thunderous organ tones from far-off blast,
Harmony, victrix, throned in state sublime,
Couched on the wrecks be-gemmed with pearls of time;
Never a wreck but brings some beauty here;
Down where the waves are stilled the sun shines clear;
Deeper than life, the plan of life doth lie;
He who knows all, fears not. Great Death shall die.

From ODE, INTIMATIONS OF IMMORTALITY

WILLIAM WORDSWORTH

Our birth is but a sleep and a forgetting:
The Soul that rises with us, our life's Star,
    Hath had elsewhere its setting,
        And cometh from afar:

Not in entire forgetfulness,
And not in utter nakedness,
But trailing clouds of glory do we come
From God, who is our home:
Heaven lies about us in our infancy!
Shades of the prison-house begin to close
Upon the growing Boy;
But He beholds the light, and whence it flows,
He sees it in his joy;
The Youth who daily farther from the east
Must travel, still is Nature's Priest,
And by the vision splendid
Is on his way attended;
At length the Man perceives it die away,
And fade into the light of common day.

JERUSALEM, MY HAPPY HOME

ANONYMOUS (From the Latin.)

Jerusalem, my happy home,
  When shall I come to thee?
When shall my sorrows have an end?
  Thy joys when shall I see?
O happy harbor of the saints!
  O sweet and pleasant soil!
In thee no sorrow may be found,
  No grief, no care, no toil.

Thy gardens and thy gallant walks
  Continually are green;
There grow such sweet and pleasant flowers
  As nowhere else are seen;
Quite through the streets with silver sound
  The flood of life doth flow,
Upon whose banks on every side
  The wood of life doth grow.

The saints are crowned with glory great,
  They see God face to face;
They triumph still, they still rejoice;
  Most happy is their case;
For there they live in such delight,
  Such pleasure and such play,
As that to them a thousand years,
  Doth seem as yesterday.

There Magdalene hath left her moan,
  And cheerfully doth sing
With blessed saints, whose harmony
  In every street doth ring.
Ah, my sweet home Jerusalem,
  Would God I were in thee!
Would God my woes were at an end
  Thy joys that I might see!

JERUSALEM, THE GOLDEN

BERNARD OF CLUNY

Jerusalem the Golden,
  With milk and honey blest,
Beneath thy contemplation,
  Sink heart and voice opprest;
I know not, O I know not,
  What social joys are there,
What radiancy of glory,
  What light beyond compare.

They stand, those walls of Zion,
  All jubilant with song,
And bright with many an angel,
  And all the martyr throng:
The Prince is ever in them
  The daylight is serene;
The pastures of the blest
  Are decked in glorious sheen.

There is the throne of David;
  And there from care released,
The song of them that triumph,
  The shout of them that feast;
And they, who with their Leader
  Have conquered in the fight,
Forever and forever
  Are clad in robes of white.

O sweet and blessed country,
   Shall I e'er see thy face?
O sweet and blessed country,
   Shall I e'er win thy grace?
Exult, O dust and ashes!
   The Lord shall be thy part;
His only, his forever,
   Thou shalt be and thou art.

DEATH AND RESURRECTION

George Croly

Earth to earth, and dust to dust!
Here the evil and the just,
Here the youthful and the old,
Here the fearful and the bold,
Here the matron and the maid,
In one silent bed are laid;
Here the vassal and the king
Side by side lie withering;
Here the sword and sceptre rust:
"Earth to earth, and dust to dust!"

Age on age shall roll along,
O'er this pale and mighty throng;
Those that wept them, those that weep,
All shall with these sleepers sleep;
Brothers, sisters of the worm,
Summer's sun, or winter's storm,
Song of peace, or battle's roar,
Ne'er shall break their slumbers more;
Death shall keep his silent trust:
"Earth to earth, and dust to dust!"

But a day is coming fast,
Earth, thy mightiest and thy last;
It shall come in fear and wonder,
Heralded by trump and thunder;

It shall come in strife and spoil;
It shall come in blood and toil;
It shall come in empire's groans,
Burning temples, trampled thrones;
Then, ambition, rule thy lust:
"Earth to earth, and dust to dust!"

Then shall come the judgment sign;—
In the east, the King shall shine,
Flashing from heaven's golden gate,
Thousands, thousands round his state,
Spirits with the crown and plume.
Tremble, then, thou sullen tomb;
Heaven shall open on our sight,
Earth be turned to living light,
Kingdoms of the ransomed just:
"Earth to earth, and dust to dust!"

Then thy Mount, Jerusalem,
Shall be gorgeous as a gem;
Then, shall in the desert rise
Fruits of more than Paradise;
Earth by angel feet be trod,
One great garden of her God;—
Till are dried the martyrs' tears,
Through a thousand glorious years.
Now in hope of him we trust:
"Earth to earth, and dust to dust!"

THE SAINTS IN GLORY

DANTE

From *Paradiso*

Translated by Henry F. Cary

In fashion as a snow-white rose, lay then
Before my view the saintly multitude,
Which in his own blood, Christ espoused. Meanwhile

That other host, that soar aloft to gaze
And celebrate his glory, whom they love,
Hovered around; and, like a troop of bees,
Amid the vernal sweets alighting now,
Now, clustering, where their fragrant labor glows,
Flew downward to the mighty flower, or rose,
From the redundant petals, streaming back
Unto the steadfast dwelling of their joy.
Faces they had of flame, and wings of gold:
The rest was whiter than the driven snow;
And, as they flitted down into the flower,
From range to range, fanning their plumy loins,
Whispered the peace and ardor, which they won
From that soft winnowing. Shadow none, the vast
Interposition of such numerous flight
Cast, from above, upon the flower, or view
Obstructed aught. For, through the universe,
Wherever merited, celestial light
Glides freely and no obstacle prevents.

   All there, who reign in safety and in bliss,
Ages long past or new, on one sole mark
Their love and vision fixed. O trinal beam
Of individual star, that charm'st them thus!
Vouchsafe one glance to gild our storm below.

   If the grim brood, from arctic shores that roamed
(Where Helice forever, as she wheels,
Sparkles a mother's fondness on her son,)
Stood in mute wonder mid the works of Rome,
When to their view the Lateran arose
In greatness more than earthly; I, who then
From human to divine had passed, from time
Unto eternity, and out of Florence
To justice and to truth, how might I choose
But marvel too? 'Twixt gladness and amaze,
I' sooth, no will had I to utter aught,
Or hear. And, as a pilgrim, when he rests
Within the temple of his vow, looks round
In breathless awe, and hopes sometime to tell
Of all its goodly state; e'en so mine eyes
Coursed up and down along the living light,

Now low, and now aloft, and now around,
Visiting every step. Looks I beheld,
Where charity on soft persuasion sat;
Smiles from within, and radiance from above;
And, in each gesture, grace and honor high.
 So roved my ken, and in its general form
All Paradise surveyed.

THE CELESTIAL PILOT

Dante

Translated by Longfellow

And now, behold! as at the approach of the morning,
Through the gross vapors, Mars grows fiery red
Down in the west upon the ocean floor,
Appeared to me,—may I again behold it!—
 A light along the sea, so swiftly coming,
 Its motion by no flight of wing is equalled.
And when therefrom I had withdrawn a little
 Mine eyes, that I might question my conductor,
 Again I saw it brighter grown and larger.
Thereafter, on all sides of it, appeared
 I know not what of white, and underneath,
 Little by little there came forth another.
My master yet had uttered not a word,
 While the first whiteness into wings unfolded;
 But when he clearly recognized the pilot,
He cried aloud: "Quick, quick, and bow the knee!
Behold the Angel of God! fold up thy hands!
 Henceforward shalt thou see such officers!
See, how he scorns all human arguments,
 So that no oar he wants, no other sail
 Than his own wings, between so distant shores!
See, how he holds them pointed straight to heaven,
 Fanning the air with th' eternal pinions,
 That do not moult themselves like mortal hair!"

And then, as nearer and more near us came
 The Bird of Heaven, more glorious he appeared,
  So that the eye could not sustain his presence,
But down I cast it; and he came to shore
 With a small vessel, gliding swift and light,
  So that the water swallowed naught thereof.
Upon the stern stood the Celestial Pilot!
 Beatitude seemed written in his face!
  And more than a hundred spirits sat within.
"In exitu Israel de Egypto"!
 Thus they sang together in one voice
  With whatso in that Psalm is after written.
Then made he sign of holy rood upon them,
 Whereat all cast themselves upon the shore,
  And he departed swiftly as he came.

From VITA NUOVA

Dante

Translated by Gabriel Charles Dante Rossetti

The eyes that weep for pity of the heart
 Have wept so long that their grief languisheth
  And they have no more tears to weep withal:
And now, if I could ease me of a part
 Of what, little by little, leads to death
  It must be done by speech, or not at all.
  And because often, thinking, I recall
How it was pleasant, ere she went afar,
 To talk of her with you, kind damozels,
 I talk with no one else,
But only with such hearts as women's are
 And I will say,—still sobbing as speech fails,—
That she hath gone to Heaven suddenly,
And hath left Love below to mourn with me.

Beatrice is gone up into high Heaven,
 The kingdom where the angels are at peace;
  And lives with them; and to her friends is dead

Not by the frost of winter was she driven
   Away, like others; nor by summer-heats;
      But through a perfect gentleness, instead.
      Far from the lamp of her meek lowly head
Such an exceeding glory went up hence
   That it woke wonder in the eternal sire,
      Until a sweet desire
Entered Him for that lovely excellence,
   So that He bade her to Himself aspire;
Counting this weary and most evil place
Unworthy of a thing so full of grace.

Wonderfully out of the beautiful form
   Soar'd her clear spirit, waxing. glad the while;
      And is in its first home, there where it is
Who speaks thereof and feels not the tears warm
   Upon his face, must have become so vile
      As to be dead to all sweet sympathies.
      Out upon him! an abject wretch like this
May not imagine anything of her,—
   He needs no bitter tears for his relief.
      But sighing comes, and grief
And the desire to find no comforter,
   (Save only Death, who makes all sorrow brief,)
To him who for a while turns in his thought
How she hath been among us, and is not.

With sighs my bosom always laboureth
   In thinking, as I do continually,
      Of her for whom my heart now breaks apace;
And very often when I think of death,
   Such a great inward longing comes to me
      That it will change the colour of my face;
      And, if the idea settles in its place,
All my limbs shake as with an ague-fit;
(Till, starting up in wild bewilderment,
   I do become so spent
That I go forth, lest folks misdoubt of it.
(Afterwards, calling with a sore lament
On Beatrice, I ask, "Canst thou be dead?"
      And calling on her, I am comforted.)

Grief with its tears, and anguish with its sighs,
  Come to me now whene'er I am alone;
    So that I think the sight of me gives pain.
And what my life hath been, that living dies,
  Since for my lady the New Birth's begun,
I have not any language to explain.
  And so, dear ladies, though my heart were fain,
I scarce could tell indeed how I am thus.
  All joy is with my bitter life at war;
    Yea, I am fallen so far
That all men seem to say, "Go out from us,"
  Eyeing my cold white lips how dead they are
But she, though I be bowed unto the dust,
Watches me; and will guerdon me, I trust.

A gentle thought there is will often start,
  Within my secret self, to speech of thee;
    Also of love it speaks so tenderly
That much in me consents and takes its part.
  "And what is this," the soul saith to the heart,
  "That cometh thus to comfort thee and me,
And thence where it would dwell, thus potently
Can drive all other thoughts by its strange art?"
And the heart answers: "Be no more at strife
  'Twixt doubt and doubt: this is Love's messenger,
    And speaketh but his words, from him received;
And all the strength it owns and all the life
  It draweth from the gentle eyes of her
    Who, looking on our grief, hath often grieved."

MY AIN COUNTREE

Mary Lee Demarest

"But now they desire a better country, that is, an heavenly."

I'm far frae my hame, an' I'm weary aftenwhiles,
For the langed-for hame-bringing an' my Father's welcome
    smiles;
I'll ne'er be fu' content, until my een do see
The shining gates o' heaven an' my ain countree.

The earth is flecked wi' flowers, mony-tinted, fresh an' gay,
The birdies warble blithely, for my Father made them sae;
But these sights an' these soun's will as naething be to me,
When I hear the angels singing in my ain countree.

I've his gude word of promise that some gladsome day the King
To his ain royal palace his banished hame will bring:
Wi' een an' wi' hearts runnin' owre we shall see
The King in his beauty in our ain countree.

My sins hae been mony, an' my sorrows hae been sair,
But there they'll never vex me, nor be remembered mair;
His bluid has made me white, his hand shall dry mine ee,
When he brings me hame at last to my ain countree.

Like a bairn to his mither, a wee birdie to its nest,
I wad fain be ganging noo unto my Saviour's breast;
For he gathers in his bosom, witless, worthless lambs like me,
An' he carries them himsel' to his ain countree.

He's faithfu' that hath promised, he'll surely come again;
He'll keep his tryst wi' me, at what hour I dinna ken:
But he bids me still to wait, an' ready aye to be,
To gang at ony moment to my ain countree.

So I'm watchin' aye, an' singin' o' my hame as I wait,
For the soundin' o' his footfa' this side the gowden gate,
God gie his grace to ilka ane wha listens noo to me,
That we may a' gang in gladness to our ain countree.

CHARTLESS

EMILY DICKINSON

I never saw a moor,
  I never saw the sea;
Yet know I how the heather looks,
  And what a wave must be.

I never talked with God,
  Nor visited in heaven;
Yet certain am I of the spot
  As if the chart were given.

THE CHILD'S QUESTION

EMILY DICKINSON

Will there really be a morning?
Is there such a thing as day?
Could I see it from the mountains
If I were as tall as they?

Has it feet like water-lilies?
Has it feathers like a bird?
Does it come from famous countries
Of which I have never heard?

Oh, some scholar, Oh, some sailor,
Oh, some wise man from the skies,
Please to tell a little pilgrim
Where the place called morning lies?

O PARADISE! O PARADISE!

FREDERICK WILLIAM FABER

O Paradise! O Paradise!
  Who doth not crave for rest?
Who would not seek the happy land,
  Where they that loved are blest;
    Where loyal hearts and true,
    Stand ever in the light,
    All rapture through and through,
    In God's most holy sight?

O Paradise! O Paradise!
  The world is growing old;
Who would not be at rest and free
  Where love is never cold;

Where loyal hearts and true
Stand ever in the light,
All rapture through and through,
In God's most holy sight?

O Paradise! O Paradise!
I want to sin no more;
I want to be as pure on earth
As on thy spotless shore;
Where loyal hearts and true,
Stand ever in the light,
All rapture through and through,
In God's most holy sight.

Lord Jesus, Light of Paradise,
Shine on my whole life long,
In all earth's din cause me to hear
Faint fragments of that song,
Where loyal hearts and true,
Stand ever in the light,
All rapture through and through,
In God's most holy sight.

VISION OF THE DAY OF JUDGMENT

Isaiah, Chap. LXIII

From Moulton's *Modern Reader's Bible*

(*Chorus of Watchmen*)

Who is this that cometh from Edom,
With crimsoned garments from Bozrah?
This that is glorious in his apparel,
Marching in the greatness of his strength?

(*He who cometh*)

I that speak in righteousness,
Mighty to save.

(Chorus of Watchmen)

Wherefore art thou red
   In thine apparel,
   And thy garments
Like him that treadeth in the winefat?

(He who cometh)

I have trodden the winepress alone;
And of the peoples there was no man with me:
   Yea, I trod them in mine anger,
   And trampled them in my fury;
   And their lifeblood is sprinkled upon my garments,
   And I have stained all my raiment.
For the day of vengeance was in mine heart,
And the year of my redeemed is come.
And I looked and there was none to help;
And I wondered that there was none to uphold:
Therefore mine own arm brought salvation unto me;
And my fury, it upheld me.
   And I trod down the peoples in mine anger,
   And made them drunk in my fury,
   And I poured their lifeblood on the earth.

GENERAL WILLIAM BOOTH ENTERS HEAVEN

Vachel Lindsay

(Drums)
   Booth led boldly with his big bass drum—
   (Are you washed in the blood of the Lamb?)
   The saints smiled gravely, and they said, "He's come."
   (Are you washed in the blood of the Lamb?)
   Walking lepers followed, rank on rank,
   Lurching bravoes from the ditches dank,
   Drabs from the alley-ways and drug-fiends pale—
   Minds still passion-ridden, soul-powers frail!
   Vermin-eaten saints with mouldy breath

Unwashed legions from the ways of death—
(*Are you washed in the blood of the Lamb?*)

(Banjos)

Every slum had sent its half-a-score
The round world over—Booth had groaned for more.
Every banner that the wide world flies
Bloomed with glory and transcendent dyes.
Big-voiced lassies made their banjos bang!
Tranced, fanatical, they shrieked and sang,
(*Are you washed in the blood of the Lamb?*)

Hallelujah! It was queer to see
Bull-necked convicts with that land make free!
Loons with trumpets blowing blare, blare, blare—
On, on, upward through the golden air!
(*Are you washed in the blood of the Lamb?*)

(Bass drums slower and softer)

Booth died blind, and still by faith he trod,
Eyes still dazzled by the ways of God.
Booth led boldly and he looked the chief:
Eagle countenance in sharp relief,
Beard a-flying, air of high command
Unabated in that Holy Land.
Jesus came out from the Court-House door,
Stretched his hand above the passing poor.

(Flutes)

Booth saw not, but led his queer ones there
Round and round the mighty Court-House square.
Yet in an instant all that blear review
Marched on spotless, clad in raiment new.
The lame were straightened, withered limbs uncurled
And blind eyes opened on a new sweet world.

(Bass drums louder and faster)

Drabs and vixens in a flash made whole!
Gone was the weasel-head, the snout, the jowl;

Sages and sibyls now, and athletes clean,
Rulers of empires, and of forests green!

(Grand chorus of all instruments—Tambourines in the fore-
ground)

The hosts were sandalled and the wings were fire!—
(*Are you washed in the blood of the Lamb?*)
But their noise played havoc with the angel choir.
(*Are you washed in the blood of the Lamb?*)
O, shout Salvation! It was good to see
Kings and princes by the Lamb set free.
The banjos rattled and the tambourines
Jing-jing-jingled in the hands of queens!

(Reverently sung: no instruments)

And when Booth halted by the curb for prayer
He saw his Master through the flag-filled air.
Christ came gently with a robe and crown
For Booth the soldier, while the throng knelt down.
He saw King Jesus—they were face to face,
And he knelt a-weeping in that holy place!
(*Are you washed in the blood of the Lamb?*)

THE LAND O' THE LEAL

Lady Nairne

I'm wearin' awa', John,
Like snaw-wreaths in thaw, John,
I'm wearin' awa'
　　To the land o' the leal.
There's nae sorrow there, John,
There's neither cauld nor care, John,
The day is aye fair
　　In the land o' the leal.

Our bonnie bairn's there, John,
She was baith gude and fair, John;

And oh! we grudged her sair
  To the land o' the leal!
But sorrow's sel' wears past, John,
And joy's a-comin' fast, John,
The joy that's aye to last
  In the land o' the leal.

Sae dear's that joy was bought, John,
Sae free the battle fought, John,
That sinfu' man e'er brought
  To the land o' the leal.
Oh! dry your glistening ee, John,
My saul langs to be free, John,
And angels beckon me
  To the land o' the leal.

Oh! haud ye leal and true, John,
Your day it's wearin' through, John,
And I'll welcome you
  To the land o' the leal.
Now fare-ye-weel, my ain John,
The world's cares are vain, John,
We'll meet and we'll be fain
  In the land o' the leal.

MY PILGRIMAGE

Sir Walter Raleigh

Give me my scallop-shell of quiet,
My staff of faith to walk upon,
My scrip of joy, immortal diet,
My bottle of salvation,
My gown of glory, hope's true gage;
And thus I'll take my pilgrimage!

Blood must be my body's balmer;
No other balm will there be given,
Whilst my soul, like quiet palmer,

Travelleth toward the land of heaven,
Over the silver mountains,
Where spring the nectar fountains.
    There will I kiss
    The bowl of bliss;
And drink mine everlasting fill
Upon every milken hill
My soul will be a-dry before;
But, after, it will thirst no more.

Then by that happy, blissful day,
More peaceful pilgrims I shall see,
That have cast off their rags of clay,
And walk apparelled fresh like me.
    I'll take them first,
    To quench their thirst
And taste of nectar's suckets,
    At those clear wells
    Where sweetness dwells,
Drawn up by saints in crystal buckets.

And when our bottles and all we
Are filled with immortality,
Then the blessèd paths we'll travel,
Strewed with rubies thick as gravel;
Ceilings of diamonds, sapphire floors,
High walls of coral, and pearly bowers.

From thence to heaven's bribeless hall,
Where no corrupted voices brawl;
No conscience molten into gold;
No forged accuser bought or sold;
No cause deferred, no vain-spent journey,
For there Christ is the King's Attorney,
Who pleads for all, without degrees,
And he hath angels but no fees.
And when the grand twelve-million jury
Of our sins, with direful fury,
Against our souls black verdicts give,
Christ pleads his death; and then we live.

Be Thou my speaker, taintless Pleader!
Unblotted Lawyer! true Proceeder!
Thou giv'st salvation, even for alms,
Not with a bribèd lawyer's palms.
And this is mine eternal plea
To Him that made heaven, earth and sea;
That, since my flesh must die so soon,
And want a head to dine next noon,—
Just at the stroke, when my veins start
    and spread,
Set on my soul an everlasting head!
Then I am ready, like a palmer fit,
To tread those blest paths; which before I
    writ.

O death and judgment, heaven and hell,
Who oft doth think, must needs die well.

MARVEL OF MARVELS

Christina Rossetti

Marvel of marvels, if I myself shall behold
With mine own eyes my King in his city of gold;
Where the least of lambs is spotless white in the fold,
Where the least and last of saints in spotless white is stoled,
Where the dimmest head beyond a moon is aureoled.
O saints, my beloved, now moldering to mould in the mould,
Shall I see you lift your heads, see your cerements unrolled,
See with these very eyes? who now in darkness and cold
Tremble for the midnight cry, the rapture, the tale untold,—
"The Bridegroom cometh, cometh, His Bride to enfold."
Cold it is, my beloved, since your funeral bell was tolled:
Cold it is, O my King, how cold alone on the wold.

PARADISE

CHRISTINA ROSSETTI

Once in a dream I saw the flowers
      That bud and bloom in Paradise;
      More fair are they than waking eyes
Have seen in all this world of ours.
And faint the perfume-bearing rose,
      And faint the lily on its stem,
And faint the perfect violet,
      Compared with them.

I heard the songs of paradise;
      Each bird sat singing in its place;
      A tender song so full of grace
It soared like incense to the skies.
Each bird sat singing to its mate
      Soft cooing notes among the trees:
The nightingale herself were cold
      To such as these.

I saw the fourfold River flow,
      And deep it was, with golden sand;
      It flowed between a mossy land
With murmured music grave and low.
It hath refreshment for all thirst,
      For fainting spirits strength and rest:
Earth holds not such a draught as this
      From east to west.

The Tree of Life stood budding there,
      Abundant with its twelvefold fruits;
      Eternal sap sustains its roots,
Its shadowing branches fill the air.
Its leaves are healing for the world,
      Its fruit the hungry world can feed
Sweeter than honey to the taste
      And balm indeed.

I saw the Gate called Beautiful;
　　And looked, but scarce could look within;
　　I saw the golden streets begin,
And outskirts of the glassy pool.
Oh harps, oh crowns of plenteous stars,
　　Oh green palm-branches, many-leaved—
Eye hath not seen, nor ear hath heard,
　　Nor heart conceived.

I hope to see these things again,
　　But not as once in dreams by night;
　　To see them with my very sight,
And touch and handle and attain:
To have all heaven beneath my feet
　　For narrow way that once they trod;
To have my part with all the saints
　　And with my God.

UPHILL

Christina Rossetti

Does the road wind uphill all the way?
　　Yes, to the very end.
Will the day's journey take the whole long day?
　　From morn to night, my friend.

But is there for the night a resting place?
　　A roof for when the slow dark hours begin.
May not the darkness hide it from my face?
　　You cannot miss that inn.

Shall I meet other wayfarers at night?
　　Those who have gone before.
Then must I knock, or call when just in sight?
　　They will not keep you waiting at that door

Shall I find comfort, travel-sore and weak?
　　Of labour you shall find the sum.
Will there be beds for me and all who seek?
　　Yea, beds for all who come.

THE CHERUBIC PILGRIM

JOHANNES SCHEFFLER, "Silesian Poet"

The soul wherein God dwells,—
    What church could holier be?—
Becomes a walking tent
    Of heavenly majesty.

How far from here to Heaven?
    Not very far, my friend,
A single hearty step
    Will all thy journey end.

Though Christ a thousand times
    In Bethlehem be born,
If He's not born in thee,
    Thy soul is still forlorn.

The cross on Golgotha
    Will never save thy soul,
The cross in thine own heart
    Alone can make thee whole.

Hold there! where runnest thou?
    Know Heaven is in thee.
Seek'st thou for God elsewhere,
    His face thou'lt never see.

O, would thy heart but be
    A manger for His birth;
God would once more become
    A child upon the earth.

Go out, God will go in,
    Die thou and let Him live.
Be not—and He will be.
    Wait and He'll all things give.

O shame, a silk worm works
    And spins till it can fly,
And thou, my soul, wilt still
    On thine old earth-clod lie!

THE LIFE ABOVE, THE LIFE ON HIGH

St. Teresa

Translated by Edward Caswall

The life above, the life on high,
Alone is life in verity;
    Nor can we life at all enjoy,
        Till this poor life is o'er;
    Then, O sweet Death! no longer fly
    From me, who e'er my time to die,
        Am dying evermore;
Forevermore I weep and sigh,
Dying, because I do not die.

To him, who deigns in me to live,
What better gift have I to give,
    O my poor earthly life, than thee?
        Too glad of thy decay,
    So but I may the sooner see
    That face of sweetest majesty,
        For which I pine away;
While evermore I weep and sigh,
Dying, because I do not die.

Absent from thee, my Saviour dear,
I call not life this living here,
    But a long dying agony,
        The sharpest I have known;
    And I myself, myself to see
    In such a wrack of misery,
        For very pity moan;
And ever, ever, weep and sigh,
Dying because I do not die.

Ah! Lord, my light and living breath,
Take me, Oh, take me from this death,
   And burst the bars that sever me
      From my true life above!
   Think how I die thy face to see,
   And cannot live away from thee,
      O my eternal Love.
And ever, ever, weep and sigh,
Dying, because I do not die.

I weary of this endless strife;
I weary of this dying life,
   This living death, this heavy chain,
      This torment of delay,
   In which her sins my soul detain.
   Ah! when shall it be mine? Ah! when,
      With my last breath to say,—
No more I weep, no more I sigh;
I'm dying of desire to die.

DIES IRAE

THOMAS OF CELANO

Translated by Wentworth Dillon

That day of wrath, that dreadful day,
Shall the whole world in ashes lay,
As David and the Sibyls say.

What horror will invade the mind,
When the strict Judge, who would be kind,
Shall have few venial faults to find!

The last loud trumpet's wondrous sound
Shall through the rending tombs rebound,
And wake the nations under ground.

Nature and death shall, with surprise,
Behold the pale offender rise,
And view the Judge with conscious eyes.

Then shall, with universal dread,
The sacred mystic book be read,
To try the living and the dead.

The Judge ascends his awful throne;
He makes each secret sin be known,
And all with shame confess their own.

Oh, then, what interest shall I make
To save my last important stake,
When the most just have cause to quake?

Thou mighty, formidable King,
Thou mercy's unexhausted spring,
Some comfortable pity bring!

Forget not what my ransom cost,
Nor let my dear-bought soul be lost
In storms of guilty terror tost.

Thou who for me didst feel such pain,
Whose precious blood the cross did stain,
Let not these agonies be in vain!

Thou whom avenging powers obey,
Cancel my debt, too great to pay,
Before the sad accounting day!

Surrounded with amazing fears,
Whose load my soul with anguish bears,
I sigh, I weep, accept my tears!

Thou who wert moved with Mary's grief,
And by absolving of the thief
Hast given me hope, now give relief!

Reject not my unworthy prayer;
Preserve me from the dangerous snare
Which death and gaping hell prepare.

Give my exalted soul a place
Among thy chosen right-hand race,
The sons of God and heirs of grace.

From that insatiable abyss,
Where flames devour and serpents hiss,
Promote me to thy seat of bliss.

Prostrate my contrite heart I rend,
My God, my Father, and my Friend,
Do not forsake me in my end!

Well may they curse their second breath,
Who rise to a reviving death:
Thou great Creator of mankind,
Let guilty man compassion find!

PEACE

HENRY VAUGHAN

My Soul, there is a Countrie
  Afar beyond the stars,
Where stands a wingèd centrie
  All skilful in the wars.
There, above noise and danger,
  Sweet Peace sits crowned with smiles,
And One born in a manger
  Commands the beauteous files.
He is thy gracious Friend,
  And (O my soul awake!)
Did in pure love descend,
  To die here for thy sake.
If thou canst get but thither,
  There grows the flower of peace,

The Rose that cannot wither,
  Thy fortress, and thy ease.
Leave then thy foolish ranges;
  For none can thee secure
But One who never changes—
  Thy God, thy life, thy cure!

THE WORLD

HENRY VAUGHAN

I saw Eternity the other night,
Like a great ring of pure and endless light,
  All calm as it was bright;
And round beneath it, Time, in hours, days, years,
  Driven by the spheres,
Like a vast shadow moved, in which the world
  And all her train were hurled.
The doting lover, in his quaintest strain,
  Did there complain;
Near him his lute, his fancy, and his flights,
  Wit's sour delights;
With gloves, and knots, the silly snares of pleasure,
  Yet his dear treasure,
All scattered lay, while he his eyes did pour
  Upon a flower.

The darksome statesman, hung with weights and woe,
Like a thick midnight fog, moved there so slow,
  He did not stay nor go;
Condemning thoughts (like sad eclipses) scowl
  Upon his soul,
And clouds of crying witnesses without
  Pursued him with one shout.
Yet digged the mole, and, lest his ways be found,
  Workt under ground,
Where he did clutch his prey; but one did see
  That policy;
Churches and altars fed him; perjuries

Were gnats and flies;
It rained about him blood and tears; but he
    Drank them as free.

The fearful miser, on a heap of rust
Sat pining all his life there, did scarce trust
    His own hands with the dust;
Yet would not place one piece above, but lives
    In fear of thieves.
Thousands there were, as frantic as himself,
    And hugged each one his pelf;
The downright epicure placed heaven in sense,
    And scorned pretense;
While others, slipt into a wide excess,
    Said little less;
The weaker sort, slight, trivial wares enslave,
    Who think them brave;
And poor despised Truth sat counting by
    Their victory.

Yet some, who all this while did weep and sing,
And sing and weep, soared up into the ring;
    But most would use no wing.
"O fools," said I, "thus to prefer dark night
    Before true light!
To live in grots and caves, and hate the day
    Because it shows the way,—
The way which, from this dead and dark abode,
    Leads up to God;
A way where you might tread the sun and be
    More bright than he!"
But, as I did their madness so discuss,
    One whispered thus,
"This ring the Bridegroom did for none provide,
    But for his Bride."

THE WORLD OF LIGHT

HENRY VAUGHAN

They are all gone into the world of light!
　And I alone sit lingering here;
Their very memory is fair and bright,
　And my sad thoughts doth clear;

It glows and glitters in my cloudy breast,
　Like stars upon some gloomy grove,
Or those faint beams in which this hill is drest
　After the sun's remove.

I see them walking in an air of glory,
　Whose light doth trample on my days;
My days which are at best but dull and hoary,
　Mere glimmering and decays.

O holy Hope! And high Humility,
　High as the heavens above!
These are your walks, and you have showed them me,
　To kindle my cold love.

Dear beauteous Death! the jewel of the just,
　Shining nowhere but in the dark!
What mysteries do lie beyond thy dust,
　Could man outlook that mark!

He that hath found some fledged bird's nest may know
　At first sight if the bird be flown;
But what fair grove or dell he sings in now,
　That is to him unknown.

And yet, as angels in some brighter dreams
　Call to the soul, when man doth sleep,
So some strange thoughts transcend our wonted themes,
　And into glory peep.

If a star were confined into a tomb,
  The captive flames must needs burn there;
But when the hand that locked her up, gives room,
  She'll shine through all the sphere.

O Father of eternal life, and all
  Created glories under Thee!
Resume Thy spirit from this world of thrall
  Into true liberty.
Either disperse these mists, which blot and fill
  My perspective still as they pass;
Or else remove me hence unto that hill,
  Where I shall need no glass.

HEAVEN

ISAAC WATTS

There is a land of pure delight,
  Where saints immortal reign;
Infinite day excludes the night,
  And pleasures banish pain.

There everlasting spring abides,
  And never-withering flowers;
Death like a narrow sea divides
  This heavenly land from ours.

Sweet fields beyond the swelling flood
  Stand dressed in living green;
So to the Jews old Canaan stood,
  While Jordan rolled between.

But timorous mortals start and shrink
  To cross this narrow sea,
And linger shivering on the brink,
  And fear to launch away.

Oh! could we make our doubts remove,
  These gloomy thoughts that rise,
And see that Canaan that we love
  With unbeclouded eyes—

Could we but climb where Moses stood,
  And view the landscape o'er,
Not Jordan's stream, nor death's cold flood,
  Could fright us from the shore.

b. THE MODERN CONCEPTION

    I. *There Is a Future Life, but We Do Not Know
    What It Is*

HEAVEN

RUPERT BROOKE

Fish (fly-replete, in depth of June,
Dawdling away their wat'ry noon)
Ponder deep wisdom, dark or clear,
Each secret fishy hope or fear.
Fish say, they have their Stream and Pond;
But is there anything Beyond?
This life cannot be All, they swear,
For how unpleasant, if it were!
One may not doubt that, somehow, Good
Shall come of Water and of Mud;
And, sure, the reverent eye must see
A Purpose in Liquidity.
We darkly know, by Faith we cry,
The future is not Wholly Dry.
Mud unto mud!—Death eddies near—
Not here the appointed End, not here!
But somewhere, beyond Space and Time,
Is wetter water, slimier slime!
And there (they trust) there swimmeth One

Who swam ere rivers were begun,
Immense, of fishy form and mind,
Squamous, omnipotent, and kind;
And under that Almighty Fin,
The littlest fish may enter in.
Oh! never fly conceals a hook,
Fish say, in the Eternal Brook,
But more than mundane weeds are there,
And mud, celestially fair;
Fat caterpillars drift around,
And Paradisal grubs are found;
Unfading moths, immortal flies,
And the worm that never dies.
And in that Heaven of all their wish,
There shall be no more land, say fish.

WHERE LIES THE LAND?

Arthur Hugh Clough

Where lies the land to which the ship would go?
Far, far ahead, is all her seamen know.
And where the land she travels from? Away,
Far, far behind, is all that they can say.

On sunny noons upon the deck's smooth face,
Linked arm in arm, how pleasant here to pace!
Or, o'er the stern reclining, watch below
The foaming wake far widening as we go.

On stormy nights when wild northwesters rave,
How proud a thing to fight with wind and wave!
The dripping sailor on the reeling mast,
Exults to bear and scorns to wish it past.

Where lies the land to which the ship would go?
Far, far ahead, is all her seamen know.
And where the land she travels from? Away,
Far, far behind, is all that they can say.

THE FORTUNATE ISLES

Joaquin Miller

You sail and you seek for the Fortunate Isles,
  The old Greek Isles of the yellow-birds' song?
Then steer straight on through the watery miles,
  Straight on, straight on, and you can't go wrong.
Nay, not to the left, nay, not to the right,
But on, straight on, and the Isles are in sight.
  The Fortunate Isles where the yellow-birds sing,
  And life lies girt with a golden ring.

These Fortunate Isles they are not so far,
  They lie within reach of the lowliest door;
You can see them gleam by the twilight star;
  You can hear them sing by the moon's white shore.
Nay, never look back! Those levelled gravestones,
They were landing steps; they were steps unto thrones
  Of glory for souls that have sailed before,
  And have set white feet on the fortunate shore.

And what are the names of the Fortunate Isles?
  Why! Duty and Love and a large Content.
Lo! these are the Isles of the watery miles,
  That God let down from the firmament.
Lo, Duty and Love, and a true man's Trust;
Your forehead to God, though your feet in the dust;
  Lo, Duty and Love, and a sweet babe's smiles,
  And these, O friend, are the Fortunate Isles.

THE LAND OF THE EVENING MIRAGE

Song of the Sioux Indians

Translated by Dr. A. M. Beede

There's a beautiful island away in the West,
  It's the land of evening mirage;
And the stars and the spirits of dead men have rest
  In the land of the evening mirage.

In the land of the evening mirage,
In the land of the evening mirage,
Where the stars and the spirits of dead men have rest
In the land of the evening mirage.

The big man in the moonlight is peeping for us,
In the land of the evening mirage;
And the grandmother spirits are weeping for us
In the land of the evening mirage.
In the land of the evening mirage,
In the land of the evening mirage,
Where the grandmother spirits are weeping for us
In the land of the evening mirage.

Speed away, speed away to the island so blest,
To the land of the evening mirage,
Where the spirits of dead men forever have rest,
In the land of the evening mirage.
In the land of the evening mirage,
In the land of the evening mirage,
Where the spirits of dead men forever have rest,
In the land of the evening mirage.

THE OTHER WORLD

HARRIET BEECHER STOWE

It lies around us like a cloud,—
The world we do not see;
Yet the sweet closing of an eye
May bring us there to be.

Its gentle breezes fan our cheeks
Amid our worldly cares;
Its gentle voices whisper love,
And mingle with our prayers.

Sweet hearts around us throb and beat,
Sweet helping hands are stirred,
And palpitates the veil between
With breathings almost heard.

The silence—awful, sweet, and calm,—
    They have no power to break;
For mortal words are not for them
    To utter or partake.

So thin, so soft, so sweet they glide,
    So near to press they seem,
They lull us gently to our rest,
    And melt into our dream.

And, in the hush of rest they bring,
    'Tis easy now to see
How lovely and how sweet a pass
    The hour of death may be!

To close the eye and close the ear,
    Wrapped in a trance of bliss,
And, gently drawn in loving arms,
    To swoon to that—from this.

Scarce knowing if we wake or sleep,
    Scarce asking where we are,
To feel all evil sink away,
    All sorrow and all care.

Sweet souls around us! Watch us still,
    Press nearer to our side,
Into our thoughts, into our prayers,
    With gentle helping glide.

Let death between us be as naught,
    A dried and vanished stream;
Your joy be the reality,
    Our suffering life the dream.

DAREST THOU NOW, O SOUL?

WALT WHITMAN

Darest thou now, O Soul,
Walk out with me toward the Unknown Region,
Where neither ground is for the feet, nor any path to follow?

No map, there, nor guide,
Nor voice sounding, nor touch of human hand,
Nor face with blooming flesh, nor lips, nor eyes, are in that
land.

I know it not, O Soul;
Nor dost thou, all is a blank before us,—
All waits, undreamed of, in that region—that inaccessible land.

Till, when the tie is loosened,
All but the ties eternal, Time and Space,
Nor darkness, gravitation, sense, nor any bounds bound us.

Then we burst forth, we float,
In Time and Space, O Soul! prepared for them;
Equal, equipped at last (O joy! O fruit of all!) them to fulfill,
O Soul!

THE IMPRISONED SOUL

WALT WHITMAN

At the last, tenderly
From the walls of the powerful fortressed house,
From the clasp of the knitted locks—from the keep of the well-
closed doors,
Let me be wafted.

Let me glide noiselessly forth;
With the key of softness unlock the locks—with a whisper
Set ope the doors, O soul!

Tenderly! be not impatient!
(Strong is your hold, O mortal flesh!
Strong is your hold, O Love!)

2. *We Are the Builders of the City*

HAIL! THE GLORIOUS GOLDEN CITY

Felix Adler

Hail the glorious Golden City,
 Pictured by the seers of old!
Everlasting light shines o'er it,
 Wondrous tales of it are told:
Only righteous men and women
 Dwell within its gleaming wall;
Wrong is banished from its borders,
 Justice reigns supreme o'er all.

We are builders of that city;
 All our joys and all our groans
Help to rear its shining ramparts;
 All our lives are building stones:
Whether humble or exalted,
 All are called to task divine;
All must aid alike to carry
 Forward one sublime design.

And the work that we have builded,
 Oft with bleeding hands and tears,
And in error and in anguish,
 Will not perish with our years:
It will last and shine transfigured
 In the final reign of Right;
It will merge into the splendors
 Of the City of the Light.

HOME AT LAST

Gilbert K. Chesterton

To an open house in the evening,
Home shall men come,
To an older place than Eden,
And a taller town than Rome.
To the end of the way of the wandering star,
To the things that cannot be and that are,
To the place where God was homeless,
And all men are at home.

BUGLE SONG OF PEACE

Thomas Curtis Clarke

Blow, bugle, blow!
The day has dawned at last,
Blow, blow, blow!
The fearful night is past,
  The prophets realize their dreams,
  Lo! in the east the glory gleams.
Blow, bugle, blow!
The day has dawned at last.

Blow, bugle, blow!
The soul of man is free.
The rod and sword of king and lord
Shall no more honored be;
  For God alone shall govern men,
  And love shall come to earth again.
Blow, bugle, blow!
The soul of man is free.

Blow, bugle, blow!
Though rivers run with blood,
All greed and strife, and lust for life,

Are passing with the flood.
　　The gory beast of war is cowed;
　　The world's great heart with grief is bowed.
Blow, bugle, blow!
The day has dawned at last.

STAINS

Theodosia Garrison

The three ghosts on the lonesome road,
　　Spake each to one another,
"Whence came that stain about your mouth
　　No lifted hand may cover?"
"From eating of forbidden fruit,
　　Brother, my brother."

The three ghosts on the sunless road
　　Spake each to one another,
"Whence came that red burn on your foot
　　No dust or ash may cover?"
"I stamped a neighbor's hearth-flame out,
　　Brother, my brother."

The three ghosts on the windless road
　　Spake each to one another,
"Whence came that blood upon your hand
　　No other hand may cover?"
"From breaking of a woman's heart,
　　Brother, my brother."

"Yet on the earth clean men we walked,
　　Glutton and Thief and Lover;
White flesh and fair it hid our stains
　　That no man might discover."
"Naked the soul goes up to God,
　　Brother, my brother."

THE TRUE HEAVEN

Paul Hamilton Hayne

The bliss for which our spirits pine,
  That bliss we feel shall yet be given,
Somehow in some far realm divine
  Some marvellous state we call a heaven,

Is not the bliss of languorous hours
  A glory of calm measured range,
But life which feeds our noblest powers
  On wonders of eternal change.

A heaven of action, freed from strife,
  With ampler ether for the scope
Of an unmeasurable life
  And an unbaffled boundless hope.

A heaven wherein all discords cease
  Self-torment, doubt, distress, turmoil,
The care of whose majestic peace
  Is god-like power of endless toil.

Toil without tumult, strain or jar,
  With grandest reach of range indeed,
Unchecked by even the farthest star
  That trembles through infinitude;

In which to soar to higher heights
  Through widening ethers stretched abroad,
Till in our onward, upward flights
  We touch at last the feet of God.

Time swallowed in eternity
  No future evermore: no past,
But one unending NOW, to be
  A boundless circle around us cast!

THE CONTINUING CITY

LAURENCE HOUSMAN

God, who made man out of dust,
Willed him to be
Not to known ends, but to trust
His decree.

This is our city, a soul
Walled within clay;
Separate hearts of one whole,
Bound we obey.

All that He meant us to be,
Could we discern,—
Life had no meaning,—or we
Had not to learn.

Thou, beloved, doubt not the truth
Eyesight makes dim!
All life, to age from youth,
Brings us to Him:

Him Whom thou hast not seen,
Canst not yet know:
Human hearts stand between,
His to foreshow.

Couldst thou possess thine own,
That were the key;
He, to Whom hearts are known,
Keeps it from thee.

Thou all·thy days must live,
Thyself the quest;
Plucking the heart to give
From thine own breast.

Till thou, from other eyes,
At kindred calls,
Seest thine own towers arise,
And thine own walls,—

Where, conquering the wide air,
Peopling its waste,
Citadels everywhere
Like stars stand based:

Losing thy soul, thy soul
Again to find;
Rendering toward that goal
Thy separate mind.

THE SPIRES OF OXFORD

WINIFRED M. LETTS

I saw the spires of Oxford
   As I was passing by,
The grey spires of Oxford
   Against a pearl-grey sky;
My heart was with the Oxford men
   Who went abroad to die.

The years go fast in Oxford,
   The golden years and gay,
The hoary colleges look down
   On careless boys at play.
But when the bugles sounded war
   They put their games away.

They left the peaceful river,
   The cricket-field, the Quad,
The shaven lawns of Oxford
   To seek a bloody sod—
They gave their merry youth away
   For country and for God.

God rest you, happy gentlemen,
　Who laid your good lives down,
Who took the khaki and the gun,
　Instead of cap and gown.
God bring you to a fairer place
　Than even Oxford town.

THE DAY IS COMING

William Morris

Come hither lads and hearken, for a tale there is to tell,
Of the wonderful days a'coming, when all shall be better than
　well.

And the tale shall be told of a country, a land in the midst of
　the sea,
And folk shall call it England in the days that are going to be.

There more than one in a thousand in the days that are yet to
　come,
Shall have some hope of the morrow, some joy of the ancient
　home.

For then—laugh not, but listen, to this strange tale of mine,
All folk that are in England shall be better lodged than swine.

Then a man shall work and bethink him, and rejoice in the
　deeds of his hand,
Nor yet come home in the even too faint and weary to stand.

Men in that time a'coming shall work and have no fear
For to-morrow's lack of earning and the hunger-wolf anear.

I tell you this for a wonder, that no man then shall be glad
Of his fellow's fall and mishap to snatch at the work he had.

For that which the worker winneth shall then be his indeed,
Nor shall half be reaped for nothing by him that sowed no seed.

O strange new wonderful justice! But for whom shall we
gather the gain?
For ourselves and for each our fellows, and no hand shall
labour in vain.

Then all *Mine* and all *Thine* shall be *Ours,* and no more shall
any man crave
For riches that serve for nothing but to fetter a friend for a
slave.

And what wealth then shall be left us when none shall gather
gold
To buy his friend in the market, and pinch and pine the sold?

Nay, what save the lovely city, and the little house on the hill,
And the wastes and the woodland beauty, and the happy fields
we till;

And the homes of ancient stories, the tombs of the mighty dead;
And the wise men seeking out marvels, and the poet's teeming
head;

And the painter's hand of wonder; and the marvellous fiddle-
bow,
And the banded choirs of music: all those that do and know.

For all these shall be ours and all men's, nor shall any lack a
share
Of the toil and the gain of living in the days when the world
grows fair.

    .   .   .   .

Come, then, let us cast off fooling, and put by ease and rest,
For the CAUSE alone is worthy till the good days bring the best.

Come, join the only battle wherein no man can fail,
Where whoso fadeth and dieth, yet his deed shall still prevail.

Ah! come, cast off all fooling, for this, at least, we know:
That the Dawn and the Day is coming, and forth the Banners
go.

THE CITY OF GOD

FRANCIS TURNER PALGRAVE

O Thou not made with hands,
Not throned above the skies,
Nor wall'd with shining walls,
Nor framed with stones of price,
　More bright than gold or gem,
　God's own Jerusalem!

Where'er the gentle heart
Finds courage from above;
Where'er the heart forsook
Warms with the breath of love;
　Where faith bids fear depart,
　City of God! thou art.

Thou art where'er the proud
In humbleness melts down;
Where self itself yields up;
Where martyrs win their crown;
　Where faithful souls possess
　Themselves in perfect peace.

Where in life's common ways
With cheerful feet we go;
When in His steps we tread
Who trod the way of woe;
　Where He is in the heart,
　City of God! thou art.

Not throned above the skies,
Nor golden-wall'd afar,
But where Christ's two or three
In His name gather'd are,
　Be in the midst of them,
　God's own Jerusalem!

THE HUMAN OUTLOOK

JOHN ADDINGTON SYMONDS

These things shall be! A loftier race
 Than e'er the world hath known shall rise
With flame of· freedom in their souls,
 And light of knowledge in their eyes.

They shall be gentle, brave and strong,
 To spill no drop of blood, but dare
All that may plant man's lordship firm
 On earth and fire, and sea, and air.

Nation with nation, land with land,
 Unarmed shall live as comrades free;
In every heart and brain shall throb
 The pulse of one fraternity.

New arts shall bloom of loftier mould
 And mightier music thrill the skies,
And every life shall be a song
 When all the earth is paradise.

These things—they are no dreams—shall be
 For happier men when we are gone;
Those golden days for them shall dawn,
 Transcending aught we gaze upon.

THE FAR LAND

JOHN HALL WHEELOCK

We are sighing for you, far land—
 We are praying for you, far land,
All our life long, working, waiting, night and day:
 But as the waves that die to reach the farther shore
 Break our hearts that die to reach you evermore—
 All our hearts are breaking, breaking toward that shore,
O far land, so near and far away!

At the lips of the beloved,
At the breast of the beloved,
Like waves that seek the land, and sink forlorn—
O to reach it we have died, but to that beach
Where the beloved is, love may not reach!
Our children's children even shall not reach
The far land where all of us were born.

Through the terror of the ages
We have sought it, till the ages
Have stamped our lifted faces with our love:
But long though we have wandered, where we are
The far land is not. O that land is far!
Beyond the night, beyond the morning star
The far land grows farther as we move.

In music and in story,
In song and sacred story
We yearned to it, in color and in sound:
But swifter than the soul the secret flies,
The vision pales—beyond, beyond it lies,
Beyond all songs, beyond all harmonies,
The far land that we have never found.

In the sweat of daily labor
In the anguish of our labor
We strove to bind it fast in steel and stone:
But lo—the walls were dust, the work was naught,
And O it was not what the heart had sought!
'Twas something dearer than our blood had bought—
The far land that we have never known.

So we built ourselves a heaven,
Our God we set in heaven,
With prayer and praise we wrought them to our will:
But they could not fill the measure of our love
For the far land—O they were not great enough!
There is nothing, there is nothing great enough!
The far land is something greater still.

We are sighing for you, far land—
We are dying for you, far land,
In the trenches, in the bloody ruck and blind,
We are coming, we are coming, every breath
Is a wave that bears us nearer to you, death
Seals our cry—O might our children find ere death
The far land that we have died to find!

THE END.

INDEX OF TITLES

A

W

Z

INDEX OF AUTHORS

A

INDEX OF FIRST LINES

A

·819

T